T0327248

HELLENIC STUDIES SERIES 78

AGAMEMNON,
THE PATHETIC DESPOT

Recent Titles in the Hellenic Studies Series

Singer of Tales
Third Edition

The Tears of Achilles

Equine Poetics

The Art of Reading
From Homer to Paul Celan

Masterpieces of Metonymy
From the Ancient Greek World to Now

The Aethiopis
Neo-Neoanalysis Reanalyzed

Kinyras
The Divine Lyre

The Theban Epics

Literary History in the Parian Marble

Plato's Four Muses
The Phaedrus and the Poetics of Philosophy

Plato's Wayward Path
Literary Form and the Republic

Dialoguing in Late Antiquity

Between Thucydides and Polybius
The Golden Age of Greek Historiography

Poetry as Initiation
The Center for Hellenic Studies Symposium on the Derveni Papyrus

Divine Yet Human Epics
Reflections of Poetic Rulers from Ancient Greece and India

The Web of Athenaeus

Eusebius of Caesarea
Tradition and Innovations

The Theology of Arithmetic
Number Symbolism in Platonism and Early Christianity

http://chs.harvard.edu/chs/publications

AGAMEMNON, THE PATHETIC DESPOT

READING CHARACTERIZATION IN HOMER

Andrew Porter

Center for Hellenic Studies

Trustees for Harvard University

Washington, D.C.

Distributed by Harvard University Press

Cambridge, Massachusetts, and London, England

2019

Library of Congress Cataloging-in-Publication Data

Names: Porter, Andrew (Classicist), author.
Title: Agamemnon, the pathetic despot : reading characterization in Homer /
 Andrew Porter.
Other titles: Hellenic studies ; 78.
Description: Washington : Center for Hellenic Studies, Trustees for Harvard
 University, 2019. | Series: Hellenic studies ; 78 | Includes
 bibliographical references and index.
Identifiers: LCCN 2019021514 | ISBN 9780674984455
Subjects: LCSH: Agamemnon, King of Mycenae (Mythological character) |
 Homer--Characters.
Classification: LCC PA4037 .P64 2019 | DDC 883/.01--dc23
LC record available at https://lccn.loc.gov/2019021514

Contents

Contents

Acknowledgements

This book began as a doctoral dissertation at the University of Missouri-Columbia, under the direction and shepherding of John Miles Foley†, but has since been expanded and rewritten through the encouragement of numerous colleagues. I am particularly appreciative of the support of Gregory Nagy and Leonard Muellner. Casey Dué proved invaluable for her knowledge and insightful suggestions. I have also profited from suggestions for portions of this work from (known and anonymous) readers and auditors at conferences, through correspondence, and during the review process. I wish to express special gratitude to Joel Christensen, Richard Janko, Susan Langdon, Anatole Mori, Barry Powell, David Schenker, Barbara Wallach, and Ian Worthington; and here at the University of Wisconsin-Milwaukee, to my colleagues who offered feedback, to Elisabetta Cova, Michael Mikoś, Richard Monti, David Mulroy, Kevin Muse, and Jim Shey. Thanks are also due in no small measure to the pleasant and capable editorial staff at CHS, especially to Jill Curry Robbins. A portion of my work also benefitted from a UWM Schwertfeger Family Fund grant, which I acknowledge here with gratefulness.

Finally, I want to thank my parents, Rev. Doug and Ella Porter, for their constant and unreserved love and support that has always been there for our family and gone beyond words; and to my own children, to Steven, Ted and Marissa, and Abigail, who are a source of joy. My wife Nancy, however, as in any good marriage (Proverbs 18.22), deserves praise first and last, and it is to her that I dedicate this work.

1

Introduction

1.1 Characterizing Agamemnon

Homer[1] and his audience knew Agamemnon as the primary leader of well over 1,000 Achaian ships that sailed against Troy.[2] He led an intense ten-year struggle, only to return home and die a miserable death at his wife's hands. His presence in person or name impacts the poetic narratives of the *Iliad* and *Odyssey* in ways exceeded by few other epic personalities, and yet his full character has not been adequately considered. How are we to understand what Agamemnon was like as a character for Homer's audience? More fundamentally, how are we to approach the topic of characterization itself since the discoveries of Parry and Lord and their successors?

The central goal of this book is to explain how characterization works in Homer and to focus on Agamemnon as a test case. To accomplish this goal,

---

[1] I employ "Homer"/"Homeric" throughout to stand for the unknown oral poet (*aoidos*) or poets (*aoidoi*) who sang the *Iliad* and *Odyssey* (cf. Parry 1971:3n2, Martin 1993:227, Edwards 2005:302, and Minchin 2007:3), as well as for these epics as memorialized texts. By "poet" I mean to emphasize a singer's thoughtful artistry through the purposeful use and arrangement of traditional elements that carry inherent meaning for the audience during epic performance. As with the more competent among the *guslari* (South Slavic "epic singers"), such as Salih Ugljanin, Stanko Pižurica, or Avdo Medjedović (see the CD-ROM of archival material in the updated [2000] edition of Lord 1960 edited by Mitchell and Nagy), I assume that the *aoidoi* who sang the *Iliad* and *Odyssey* were accomplished performers (cf. Dué and Ebbott 2010:10, and also Lord's [1960:26] comments about the less competent *guslari*), but that the tradition first gives meaning to what is sung (Foley 1999:56–58, 2002:8–10, and Dué and Ebbott 2010:13, 20–28). As I hope to show throughout the chapters that follow, the Homeric poets were aware of a web of traditional associations and cues and used them to great advantage (cf. the experience of Lord 1960:26). For assumptions and difficulties in defining "Homer," see also Graziosi and Haubold 2005:1–34. My transliteration choices for Greek names are similar to those of *The Homer Encyclopedia* and Powell's recent translation of the *Iliad* and *Odyssey*.

[2] The *Iliad*'s catalogue of ships was later rounded to an even 1,000 ships, preserved for us first in Aeschylus' *Agamemnon* 45. The same count appears in five different Euripidean plays. The more well-known description, however, is derived from Christopher Marlowe, in *Doctor Faustus*, referring to 'Helen of Greece': "Was this the face that launch'd a thousand ships / And burnt the topless towers of Ilium? / Sweet Helen, make me immortal with a kiss."

we will consider the characterization of Agamemnon in the *Iliad* and *Odyssey* from an oral traditional point of view. We turn especially to one branch of oral poetics, "traditional referentiality," to consider the topic of characterization in general and the character of Agamemnon in particular. The goal is to discover and interpret traditional cues within the oral tradition Homer was accessing and creatively employing. We will capture Agamemnon's personality by a careful reading of the epic narratives, where the traits and implications of his personality can be heard against known back stories through the resonance of words, themes, and type scenes, and by considering various other poetic devices.[3]

1.2 Epic Characterization

While Agamemnon as a whole character has proved to be of somewhat less interest to modern scholars than other epic personalities such as Achilles, Helen, and Odysseus,[4] particular aspects of his life or his political position have been considered in some depth.[5] Further, a limited amount of work has been published solely devoted to a consideration of epic characterization itself since the initial findings of Parry and Lord. Most scholars have not attempted to consider what oral traditional research might mean for the study of character.[6] There are a few

---

[3] This involves the venerable task dating back to Aristarchus of explaining Homer from Homer: ἐξηγεῖσθαι τὸν ἄνδρα ἐξ ἑαυτοῦ / *explicare Homerum ex Homero* (Porter 1992).

[4] For a list of some works before the mid-seventies on individual characters, see Heubeck 1974:197. There are, of course, a limitless number of works that touch on a particular character's attributes in some way, without ever defining how characterization is created. My concern here is first with studies of characterization itself undertaken since the foundational work of Parry and Lord, and second, with the study of Agamemnon's entire character in Homer.

[5] Agamemnon can be found as part of larger questions about particular themes in Collins 1988:69–102 (the relation of king and warrior), Taplin 1990 (Agamemnon's status as leading *basileus*), Zanker 1994 (his relation to Achilles), Wöhrle 1999:49–61 (his role as a surrogate father in the "Hierarchie" of father-son type relationships), Haubold 2000 (his role as shepherd), Hammar 2002 (his political role), Wilson 2002 (Agamemnon and compensation), Heiden 2008 (his responsibility for the suffering of the army), Rinon 2008 (his relation to a tragic pattern and lost opportunity), Scodel 2008 (Agamemnon and the theme of saving face), Ammone 2010 (Agamemnon and the *diapeira*), Cairns 2011 (Agamemnon and *atē*), and Holway 2012 (his feud with Achilles). For short portraits of Agamemnon as a character, see Bonnéric 1986:7–11, Auffarth 2002, van Nortwick 2011, and Kanavou 2015:44–48. In terms of Agamemnon's representation in iconographical, lyric, and tragic representation, the *Oresteia* in its narrowest sense has been the central focus (especially events surrounding Agamemnon's death). See especially Prag 1985, Knoepfler 1993, Neschke 1986, Garvie 1986, and Raeburn and Thomas 2011.

[6] There are various more traditional approaches to the study of characterization in the Homeric epics, however, from Griffin 1980:50–81, Collins 1988, Pelling 1990, and Race 1993. Collins reviews a group of scholars who study character through the lens of social institutions, and adopts their structural-functional approach to characterization (following Vernant 1966, Finley 1979, Queller 1981, and Donlan 1982). Griffin's study finds both individuality and depth of presentation for Homeric characters. Pelling considers general psychological tendencies with Homeric

exceptions in general studies of characterization. These include Martin's (1993) foundational discussion of particular points that undergird epic characterization, but also Dué's (2002) detailed study of Briseïs.[7] While not a study of characterization *per se*, Dué shows, though her application of oral poetics, that epic characterization is very much dependent on a character's shared participation in common themes from past stories. It is a point my own study will develop in detail. Further, Minchin (2011a) outlines a convincing theory of how an epic singer organizes, stores, and accesses characterization (for "first-rank heroes"). She uses an appealing model from cognitive science and argues not only for shared, but also individual "themes" (what I call "traits"). She finds that it is the prevalence of "particular themes (that is, individual themes)" that make a character distinctly identifiable and memorable.[8] My own findings parallel hers in certain respects, particularly in her conclusion that "the poet has stored in memory" what is "appropriate" for each character. The present study will outline and then read traditional cues that access this stored knowledge, what I refer to as "tradition."

We might, however, ask why, since the findings of Parry and Lord, there has been such limited research focused on epic characterization in so large a field as Homeric Studies. It may be that many feel that the question of how to approach epic characterization has changed from a literary to a quasi-folktale style inquiry. The question may now be: "How does a character fit a character type or story pattern?" The acceptance of the generally formulaic and oral nature of the Homeric epics can make their narratives appear, at least at first glance, "stereotypical."[9] One could wonder whether the typical portrait of a character

---

characterization. Race's concern is with characters in the *Odyssey*, and his article reveals something of each character's traits. He is not concerned as such with providing a theoretical framework for understanding what characterization is or with the centrality of the background tradition influencing characterization in context. He consequently emphasizes first appearances, rather than considering the local expression of traits against the traditional character already known to Homer's audience. Yet, his article helps demonstrate that many Odyssean characters have a recognizable persona.

[7] Within his discussion, Martin emphasizes epithets, themes, phrases, and narrative focalization. The last point, as we will see, is parallel to my own emphasis throughout on the singer's creative use of tradition and the relation of audience and performer.

[8] Her study, although not meant first as a character study, nevertheless, shows that individual characterization is present in Homer, thanks to the presence of an individual's "themes, goals, and plans."

[9] Minchin (2005:66) rejects the idea that oral poetry is "stereotypical," noting that there is, "on the contrary, a remarkable rich vein of psychological insight in the poet's recreation of everyday behavior patterns in his principal actors." For earlier consideration of the question, see Donlan 1970, 1971, Griffin 1980:70, Martin 1993, and Dué (2002:8), who considers the "syntagmatic," as well as the "paradigmatic," in the Homeric picture of Briseïs. Both particular and typical character elements are found in Homer, as we will consider further in Chapter 2. For discussion of lesser Homeric characters and the question of invention, see Schein 1984:27, Nünlist

leaves any room for individual character depth. Further, to ask what the character of Agamemnon was like for the singer, audience, and even "the tradition," may seem like the wrong question.[10] Yet, it is just this question that I am asking here and in Chapter 2: "Is individuality possible, or must all characters speak and act alike?"[11] It is a question initially raised in many ways by Notopoulos, who had urged that what is needed "is the study of the relationship of the formulaic technique to human characterization ... the extent to which the oral technique can go beyond the typological 'Man' of Geometric vases" (Notopoulos 1964a:65).[12] In short, what does it mean to speak of Homeric characterization? Related to this is the question of how we can "read" character. We must answer these questions before we consider what sort of character Agamemnon himself was for Homer and his audience, in Chapters 3 and 4.

1.3 Reading Characterization Traditionally

The work of one pioneering scholar is of particular interest for our present study. John Foley developed a fuller methodology for reading traditional background for Homeric narrative by showing how tradition affects the way Homeric poetry is heard.[13] Foley's approach of finding meaning through oral "patterning *and* context" (Kelly 2007a:5) was indebted to previous work carried out by a number of scholars.[14] Foley's "traditional referentiality" argues that the narrative instant carries the most meaning when heard against the larger backdrop of the oral traditional register. The title of Foley's 1991 book, *Immanent Art*, encapsulates the argument laid out in greater detail inside and in subsequent work.

---

[10] 2009:240–241, and Kanavou 2015:134–150, although it would be difficult to prove invention in most cases, even for minor characters. Dué's (2002:33–35 *passim*) findings for the multi-forms in the Briseïs tradition suggest the need for caution in making such claims.

[10] Martin (1993) suggests the role of such factors as Russian Formalism (including questions of function) and the "deterministic" view of Homeric poetry that followed upon Parry's initial discoveries, as the reason that many Homerists have avoided exploring the topic of characterization.

[11] This is the question already posed, but left unanswered by Griffin (2011:158), whose principal concern is with character description.

[12] Cf. the call of Martin (1993:227) for a book-length study of "ways of employing the tools of oral-formulaic analysis in the study of characterization."

[13] I had the pleasure of being a graduate student of John's from 2002 to 2007. John was a very generous scholar and took the time to help me consider oral traditional patterns, beginning at the level of language. This made my own research experience quite diverse, since I had come to Missouri upon the completion of a graduate degree in Canada with another leading Homerist from a different school of thought, Prof. Rainer Friedrich of Dalhousie.

[14] This includes, among other scholars after Parry and Lord, Whallon 1969, Muellner 1976, Nagy 1979, Holoka 1983, Lowenstam 1981, Slatkin 1986, 1991, and Sacks 1987.

In short, the meaning that a formula, type scene, or story pattern carried with it was "immanent" when heard. Immanence is attained through "metonymy," which means that a singular instance stands *pars pro toto* (Foley 1991:7–9).[15] As he described it in this and subsequent works, the singer's system of tradition-based expressivity entails the "invoking of a context that is enormously larger and more echoic than the text of the work itself" (Foley 1991:7; cf. 1990:121–157, 1999:18–25, 2002:109–124, and 2005). We must read behind the surface of the immediate text to its connotative meaning by looking to the tradition to which it is referring, starting at the level of traditional diction and continuing up to the level of story pattern (Foley 1990, 1991, 1999:32–34 *passim*).

Foley's central point is that the larger tradition is a very necessary place to look to discern how Homer's audience understood meaning in any passing narrative moment:

> Intone the formulas, instance the typical scenes, and, as long as the audience is reasonably fluent in the register, you accomplish far more than a superficially coherent narrative or metrically acceptable lines. Singular moments are implicitly framed as *familiar situations*.[16]
>
> Foley 1999:33 (italics mine)

Epic narrative moments cannot be fully heard and appreciated without an understanding of the tradition as context ("familiar situations"). Although Wyatt employs a simple analogy, his comments meant to support Foley's general approach are apt: "Modern television is opaque or silly to me because I am not fully aware of the conventions of the genre that the merest child internalizes early on" (Wyatt 2000). To see the bigger picture, so Foley suggests, we must seek to "read behind and between the signs," tapping into "their idiomatic and

---

[15] Foley's work on metonymy (1991:38–36) was especially influenced by Iser (1974). For a consideration of metonym as a linguistic feature, see Barcelona et al. 2011.

[16] Cf. Foley 1991:54–55, on becoming a responsible reader of an oral-derived text.

traditional implications" (Foley 1999:7).[17] When heard in its entirety, Foley's arguments are persuasive and formative.[18]

Foley's methodology has proven influential in a number of recent works.[19] Central to Foley's argument is what he termed the "resonant background" of an active oral tradition (Foley 1999:32), an idea taken up by other scholars.[20] Di Benedetto (1983), in his consideration of Homeric phrases, had presaged and paralleled some of Foley's ideas, especially in his desire to move beyond metrics to read meaning.[21] It is this emphasis on resonant background that forms the

---

[17] Cf. the earlier comments of Anne Amory Parry (1973:7) that this appreciation begins at the level of poetic diction: "Most efforts to define Homeric words start with an etymological hypothesis; ancient scholia abounded with suggestions ranging from the patently ridiculous to the more plausible, and the latter are still accepted. But etymology is still essentially irrelevant to the problem of meaning in a literary context. Whatever the etymology of a word may have been conjectured to be by the early grammarians, or whatever modern scholars may assert that it is, *the meaning of a word for the composer* of the *Iliad* and *Odyssey*, and therefore its proper meaning for us as readers of the poems *can only be determined by its usage in the text of Homer*" (italics mine). This realization does not rule out the sort of connections that form the basis for etymological or comparative studies (such as the Indo-European meaning noted for Diomedes by Benveniste 1969; cf. Schnapp-Gourbeillon 1982:46). It does, however, act as a needed reminder that one must first judge any Homeric meaning by a word's (or idiom's) use in Homer. Further, while traditional meaning begins at the level of words, it continues through theme, type scene, story pattern, and various other poetic devices.

[18] Cairns (2011:113n26) reacts to Foley's methodology in what he reads as extreme claims. He sees "no evidence for the view that *audiences always* activate knowledge of the *totality* of a multiform tradition" (italics mine). His words come as part of a response that questions Wilson's (2002) associations of *poinē* with particular scenes in the *Iliad* (on Wilson's methodological assumptions, see Wilson 2002:185n40). While some of Foley's statements when taken in isolation, could, I suppose, be read in absolute terms as Cairns does, Foley's overall claims for traditional referentiality and audience knowledge as outlined above, should not be. Wyatt (2000) is more measured: "Foley has overdetermined some of the 'words' with which he deals. ... Nonetheless he asks the important question and has gone some way to answering it."

[19] A representative sampling from Homeric Studies includes Ledbetter 1993:485, Bakker 1995:102–103, Dunkle 1997, Danek 1998:13, 509, Danek 2002, Dué 2002, Tsagalis 2004:20, Turkeltaub 2005, Barker and Christensen 2006, Dué 2006, Brown 2006, Kelly (2007a, who includes a referential lexicon), Gaca 2008:159, Sammons 2008:360, Scott 2009:20, Létoublon 2009:37, Dué and Ebbott 2010:13–29 (with a referential commentary for *Iliad* 10), Barker 2011, Porter 2011, Ready 2011, Alden 2012:117, Bierl 2012, Elmer 2013:21–47, Barker and Christensen 2014, Arft 2014, Karanika 2014, Kelly 2014, Porter 2014, and Ready 2015. Foley's ideas have also proven influential in Biblical Studies, Folklore, Linguistics, Old English, South Slavic, and other studies.

[20] Foley's idea of resonant background has been particularly foundational in Dué's (2002:9 *et passim*) study of what she calls "micro" and "macro" narratives that influence audience comprehension of Briseïs, and Graziosi and Haubold's (2005:48–55) consideration of Homeric themes as they relate to the wider epic traditions.

[21] Di Benedetto's earliest work (1983) stressed only resonance within the *Iliad*, while his subsequent research included the *Odyssey*, where he suggested that there can exist not just "formularità esterna (in riferimento alla ripresa di espressioni tradizionali fisse preesistenti)" but also "formularità interna" (1994:ix). He argues that "formularità interna" are essentially recurring formulae that carry meaning, reused (but with replacement, extension, etc., 1994:115–120)

core of the present study. As later readers, we must seek to hear the now written word in Homer's oral register if we wish to understand a narrative description more like the traditional audience would have.

Resonance is especially important, so I am arguing, for a proper understanding of how the poets presented, and how audience members heard and thought of, epic personalities in any given narrative moment. I am consequently extending Foley's ideas to a consideration of Homeric characterization.[22] I am arguing that epic characterization relies upon deep and extensive traditional resonances adhering to each character from his or her participation in past stories.[23] Resonance through traditional referentiality allows the poet to create richer and more suggestive moments of characterization, since words and idioms have taken on tradition-based meaning. Further, resonance from back stories creates audience expectations for the sorts of traits an individual might manifest in a given narrative moment (cf. Minchin 2011a:328–342). Of course, as I will argue in a moment about the *Odyssey*, even the memorialized version of the story we are reading from a written text has been performed before. We cannot, then, simply comprehend characterization in the Homeric text through chronologically linear strategies of character creation. Rather, we must also consider the whole of each epic's language and story as parallel history that can inform any particular moment of character portrayal. As Dué articulates it, we need to consider the "large-scale" and "long distance" associations from within conventions that formed part of the epic song tradition (Dué 2002:19).

The Homeric poet is aware, then, that his audience depends upon tradition-based characterization for a fuller comprehension of a particular narrative moment. After all, as Minchin notes, "the stories themselves (their sequence of action) held this [character] information together" (Minchin 2011a:330). Both

---

by the poet, rather than simply being repeated without meaning (see esp. 1994:122–139). Significantly, Di Benedetto (e.g. 1994:103–121, 1999:210 *et passim*) suggested that one epic idiom was dependent on its other occurrences, albeit not from a strictly oral traditional perspective (his approach includes the neoanalytical, e.g. 1994:104), and without the idea of a larger epic register of a living oral tradition. He envisions not just a singular "risonanza," but also "una serie di risonanze" both within the *Odyssey*, but also from the *Iliad* to the *Odyssey*. My own emphasis stresses a common oral traditional background for both the *Iliad* and *Odyssey* and importantly assumes, and in this I differ with Di Benedetto, the influence of the *Odyssey* tradition upon the *Iliad* for Agamemnon's character traits.

[22] Martin (1993) noted the need for such a study and his article harbingered some of the questions I seek to consider here and in Chapter 2. Dué (2002) has applied Foley's traditional referentiality to her consideration of Briseïs' involvement in particular themes (as captive, prize, girl, daughter, and wife). Scott (2009:20) and Ready (2015:89) have applied Foley's traditional referentiality to the study of the simile.

[23] Cf. the comments of Dué 2002:15–19 and Dué and Ebbott 2010:9. It may even be, as Griffin (1980:73–75) boldly argues, that the character's presence in a narrative drives the plot, rather than merely being subservient to it.

the plot and the character are there in skeletal form in the tradition. To miss the cues found in the register of Homer's traditional language (as we will see in our study of Agamemnon's appeal in the next chapter) or the larger back story is to miss a great deal.[24] Further, at any moment in the story, the poet is able to emphasize certain traditional aspects of character, and context does make a difference in what Homer's audience was hearing during *aoidic* performance. As Kelly remarks, the semantic expressiveness of traditional language involves a "creative dynamic between denotative *and* connotative" [italics mine] meaning (Kelly 2007a:6). It is not a binary. This is true at all levels of Homer's use of traditional elements.

As we will see in Chapters 3 and 4, literary questions and context also have a role to play, even when one accepts the priority of traditional background for "reading" character.[25] Nor would one expect audience members, for example, to have the same view of Agamemnon as a specter in *Odyssey* 11 that they did of him in the thick of the battle for Troy in *Iliad* 11. Yet, the fuller picture of a character from the larger tradition is always somewhat imminent, even if not brought fully "on stage."[26] Consequently, as we will see when we look at *Odyssey* 11, even in Hades the poet assumes our comprehension of what Agamemnon once was, but is no longer. Then again, in *Iliad* 1, when Agamemnon arrogantly refuses to give back Chryseïs, the poet also makes some reference to Agamemnon's own *nostos* and pitiful death.[27]

Yet, what can be said about the composition of the audience, since a referential reading is not always necessary for a limited understanding of the immediate action of a particular scene (Scodel 2002:19).[28] Danek offers a reasonable perspective when he speaks of an "ideally competent audience" (Danek 2002:4,

---

[24] The importance of traditional cues becomes apparent in ironic type-scene inversions of the sort noted by Reece 1993:130–143, Foley 1999:181–183, and Kelly 2012:241–245. Cf. Pantelia's (2002) comments about expectations for the order of mourners in *Iliad* 24. As we will see throughout our present study, the tradition often points beyond the ostensible facts of the immediate moment to larger traditional elements. We will return to consider type scene inversions in Chapter 2, s.v. 2.1.1 Character Consistency.

[25] Janko (1998:10) notes questions of theme as one example. Janko's (1994:xi) comments regarding literary approaches seem sensible.

[26] Scodel (2002:15) argues that sometimes the poet intentionally does not actively "bring on stage" mythic elements known to the audience, because of his intended emphasis at a given narrative moment. Scodel's concern here, through example, includes the thornier issue of how much of the Cyclic Epic material was known to Homer.

[27] We will return to *Odyssey* 11 and *Iliad* 1 in Chapters 3 and 4, respectively.

[28] Scodel does not deny the importance of traditional referentiality to narrative content, but she sees it as a spectrum (Scodel 2002:13): "Traditional referentiality does not mean that everyone knows all the same stories, in the same variants." Cf. 16–17, 24, 173 *et passim*. Cf. Scodel 2005:402.

15, 19). I agree that Homer has a principal audience in mind as he sings.[29] It is not first the uninformed listeners, those members on the periphery of his traditional audience, but those at the core. It is these, for instance, that could really understand the proem of the *Odyssey*, or many other moments in Homer's narrative. This realization does not of course mean that debutants or even strangers to the Homeric stories could not understand much what was sung. The retelling a traditional story, in the very act of its narration, will include much that needs little explanation for a general understanding. Yet, Homeric poetry also reveals that much would be missed without a traditional and informed audience.[30]

We must, moreover, it needs to be emphasized, be cautious here as armchair academics talking about live performance in an oral culture. Field work on the South Slavic epic tradition shows that the performance arena "is more vivid, more arresting, more demanding, more contingent" than we might expect as a reading audience (Foley 2002:84).[31] An eyewitness report from an early (pre-Parry-Lord) researcher in the late 1920's shows that the South Slavic singer often competed with his peers with great drama and enthusiasm, in a performance that could last into the night. The event could leave the audience members on the edge of their seats:

> L'auditoire écoute le chanteur avec le maximum d'attention, d'intérêt et de sympathie pour le héros, et il est parfois extrêmement touché du poème tout entier ou de certains épisodes.[32]
>
> Murko 1928:341

---

[29] Further, Nagy (1979:7, 1990:43, 1996b:38–43) and Dué (2002:2n5, 23–36) suggest the mechanism of Panhellenism (local traditions are de-emphasized) for reducing less recognizable elements for the Homeric audience.

[30] Danek (1998:31) notes Homer's assumption of an informed audience, arguing that from the beginning, the proem "suggeriert daß die Handlung an einem bekannten Punkt innerhalb eines bekannten Rahmens einsetzt." Scodel's (2002:19) views are more cautious about suggesting as much: "Even young children probably knew the names of Achilles and Odysseus. That there was a canon of acts, however, does not define its extent." While it is true that it would be difficult (often impossible; cf. Dué 2002:36) to define the full extent of what is traditional, yet, as I will show, Homer did very often assume for his core audience a certain canon of acts and many other traditional elements.

[31] The memorialized copy of an oral performance cannot fully represent the performance (Powell 2000:107, Foley 2002:82–108, Finnegan 2007:79, Jensen 2011:290, and Ready 2015:47–51; cf. the earlier experience of Notopoulos 1964a:48, with Greek heroic poetry).

[32] Lord (1960:280) praised the work of his predecessor. Further, one can also hear a proudly competitive tone in the response of another singer recorded by Parry, Đemo Zogić, who feels (he claims all the audience was more pleased with his rendition) that he can sing a particular song better than another singer (Suljo Makić, on which see Lord 1960:27). On the importance of competition in early Greek culture, see Nagy 1992:79.

Alternatively, the audience could be full of reproach (Murko 1928:340–342). Upon returning from a performance break, one less capable singer even found "les cordes et l'archet de son instrument [graissés] avec du suif" (Murko 1928:342), which made it impossible for him to continue his song. Apparently the South Slavic singer and his audience took epic performance as intently as Americans take their football, since it was seen as a competition between "warring" sides. Murko describes the intensity of competition:

> En Herzégovine, un jeune homme de dix-neuf ans m'a dit: "Tous autant que nous sommes, ici, nous sommes ennemis les uns des autres. C'est un tourment pour moi quand j'en vois un autre qui en sait plus que moi."
>
> Murko 1928:341

That Homeric epic was once such a living oral tradition implies that it was heard intently and sung by singers that could feel "tourment" and other emotions. The same intensity of performance involvement is pictured for rhapsodic competition, if Plato's (albeit somewhat ironic) portrait of *Ion* is any guide. Ion describes his performance:

> "For whenever I speak anything woeful, my eyes with tears are filled: Whenever [I speak] anything fearful or awesome, my hair stands on end from fear, and my heart leaps!"
>
> ἐγὼ γὰρ ὅταν ἐλεινόν τι λέγω, δακρύων ἐμπίμπλανταί μου οἱ ὀφθαλμοί: ὅταν τε φοβερὸν ἢ δεινόν, ὀρθαὶ αἱ τρίχες ἵστανται ὑπὸ φόβου καὶ ἡ καρδία πηδᾷ.
>
> *Ion* 535c

Not only is the rhapsode emotionally involved, but the audience is described as responding with an equal fervor (τοὺς πολλοὺς ταὐτὰ ταῦτα, 535d) when "struck" (ἐκπλήσσω, 535b) by the power of the performed epic narrative.[33] Every time Ion looks down upon his audience, they are constantly crying (κλάοντας) and grimacing (δεινὸν ἐμβλέποντας), wonder struck (συνθαμβοῦντας) by what they are hearing.[34] While a later rhapsode's recitative performance can be contrasted

---

[33] Cf. the comments of Lada-Richards (2002:413), who notes that Ion was "totally submerged in the roles he incarnates, with the ebb and flow of his emotions entirely congruent with the succession of the passions encoded in the text."

[34] 535e: καθορῶ γὰρ ἑκάστοτε αὐτοὺς ἄνωθεν ἀπὸ τοῦ βήματος κλάοντάς τε καὶ δεινὸν ἐμβλέποντας καὶ συνθαμβοῦντας τοῖς λεγομένοις. Of course, we are receiving this picture, as the dialogue

in kind with the earlier *aoidos'* composition-in-performance, it is clear that Ion undertook his poetic presentation as a living and emotionally charged event.

Homer's "core audience" members, then, were not only the better informed, but also the more personally and passionately involved.[35] They were actively thinking about what the next line might be, attuned to the "moment-to-moment reality of the evolving song" (Foley 2002:84). The proof that Homer's concern was first with core audience members who were quite actively engaged and generally "in the know" should not be missed. There are moments where Homeric poetry (as it stands in our texts) *cannot* be fully understood, even at a surface level, without a metonymic reading of the poet's presentation. Certain epithets and expressions make little sense without a metonymic comprehension of the greater tradition.[36]

Such is the case with Achilles' first Iliadic self-reference to an abbreviated life (1.352): "Mother, since in fact you bore me to be short lived" (μῆτερ ἐπεί μ' ἔτεκές γε μινυνθάδιόν περ ἐόντα). In this case the comment is bewildering to the reader unaware of the larger tradition. Thetis makes a second (but more extensive) reference to Achilles' short-lived life, after she has heard the complaint of her son over the hubristic treatment that he received from Agamemnon:

> Then Thetis answered him, pouring down tears:
> "O my child, why did I raise you, having borne you terribly?
> Would that you, by the ships, without tears and without harm,
> would sit, since now your allotment of life [is] short and not very
>   long;
> But now altogether swift-fated and woeful beyond all men
> you have turned out to be; therefore I bore you with a bad allotment
>   of life in my house.
> But indeed, in order to speak this word to Zeus who delights in
>   thunder,

---

goes on to show, through the rather jaundiced eyes of Plato (cf. *Republic* 10.606e–608b1), on which see Halliwell 1986:1–6, 19–27, 331–336; Murray 1997:14–32; and Rijksbaron 2007:9–14.

[35] If, as I hold as quite likely, the recording of Homeric epic took place by dictation, then the singer may have "imagined" (Jensen 1980:170) his audience, unless the memorialization of the epics took place, as usual, in an aristocrat's residence, with the host and audience members in attendance (though the performance dynamics would have changed, as shown by Ready 2015:1–7, 13–33).

[36] Cf. the presence of allusions noted by Kullmann 1960:13–17. For other examples, see Edwards 1987:52–53. I am not suggesting here, however, that there was a particular written song in the audience's mind, fixed in one exact, static form, since, as Murko (1928:337) noted early on, "Toutes les tentatives faites pour reconstituer un chant dans sa forme originaire sont vaines."

I am going myself to snow-clad Olympos, in case he can be
persuaded.
But you now, sitting by the swift-going ships,
vent your wrath on the Achaians, but stay away from the war
altogether."[37]

τὸν δ' ἠμείβετ' ἔπειτα Θέτις κατὰ δάκρυ χέουσα·
ὦ μοι τέκνον ἐμόν, τί νύ σ' ἔτρεφον αἰνὰ τεκοῦσα;
αἴθ' ὄφελες παρὰ νηυσὶν ἀδάκρυτος καὶ ἀπήμων
ἧσθαι, ἐπεί νύ τοι αἶσα μίνυνθά περ οὔ τι μάλα δήν·
νῦν δ' ἅμα τ' ὠκύμορος καὶ ὀϊζυρὸς περὶ πάντων
ἔπλεο· τώ σε κακῇ αἴσῃ τέκον ἐν μεγάροισι.
τοῦτο δέ τοι ἐρέουσα ἔπος Διὶ τερπικεραύνῳ
εἶμ' αὐτὴ πρὸς Ὄλυμπον ἀγάννιφον αἴ κε πίθηται.
ἀλλὰ σὺ μὲν νῦν νηυσὶ παρήμενος ὠκυπόροισι
μήνι' Ἀχαιοῖσιν, πολέμου δ' ἀποπαύεο πάμπαν·

Iliad 1.413–422

Why the tears? "Therefore I bore you with a bad allotment of life" (τώ σε κακῇ αἴσῃ τέκον)? Why is Achilles' "allotment of life" (αἶσα) short and *mal*?[38] "Cease from the war altogether (πολέμου δ' ἀποπαύεο πάμπαν)!" Why should he wait by the ships and keep himself completely out of the war; and what would happen were he to reenter battle? Thetis just leaves without explaining herself! What does all this portend for the traditionally informed audience member?

A significant traditional cue occurs in line 413. Here, Thetis' sorrowful crying (1.413, κατὰ δάκρυ χέουσα) seems to derive from the register of a funerary lament[39]—"O my child, why did I raise you, having born you terribly" (ὦ μοι τέκνον ἐμόν, τί νύ σ' ἔτρεφον αἰνὰ τεκοῦσα, 414)? This is likely if we compare Thetis' with Hecuba's later lament over her son Hector's corpse (*Iliad* 22.431–32): "Child, I am wretched; Why should I live now, suffering terribly, / since you have died" (τέκον ἐγὼ δειλή· τί νυ βείομαι αἰνὰ παθοῦσα / σεῦ ἀποτεθνηῶτος)?" We observe that both Thetis and Hecuba address their "child" in the first half of

---

[37] All translations from Greek texts throughout are my own. They are meant, in the case of Homer, to retain, as much as possible, the cola of the Greek lines, rather than create a polished English translation. It is nearly impossible, however, as Austin (2009:73) notes, to fully represent Homeric formularity. For a note about the metrical assumptions of this study, see Appendix A.

[38] Chantraine (1968:38, s.v. αἶσα) connects the term αἶσα to an allotment of life by Zeus and close to "destiny," a meaning equivalent to μοῖρα. The common origin of these two nouns from a single verbal form was suggested by Leitzke 1930; Cf. Dietrich 1965:184.

[39] Cf. the tears enveloping the Muses' threnody in *Odyssey* 24.61: οὔ ... ἀδάκρυτον.

the line (1.414 and 22.431). Both ask a rhetorical question brought about by their son's death, or in Achilles' case, portended death.[40] In the case of Thetis, the lament is proleptic, and is, as with other "déplorations anticipées, généralement plus courtes" (Arnould 1990:189).[41] Yet, although brief, it cues the audience to what will eventually transpire—Achilles' death—making the future imminent through the impinging tradition. That Thetis' address is posed as a question proves significant. As Alexiou notes, the opening question of a lament can "emphasize the plight of the mourner" (Alexiou 1974:162). Moreover, a formulaic participle with adverb is common to both laments (Kirk 1985:96): "having born you terribly" (αἰνὰ τεκοῦσα, 1.414) / "suffering terribly" (αἰνὰ παθοῦσα, 22.431).[42] Elements often occurring in a lament, such as distress and anger or an immediate and expressed sorrow (Alexiou 1974:162) are less prolonged in our scene when compared to Hecuba's threnody, but they are there.[43]

Hopefully now the implications are clear. The singer assumes the core audience's knowledge of the looming fate of Achilles when Thetis speaks; and he employs traditional cues that resonate against an oral traditional background for his hearers.[44] Of course the much fuller lamentation by Thetis is found in *Iliad* 18, where it is clear that she thinks of Achilles' death.[45] Yet, Achilles' impending death is already found through metonymy in *Iliad* 1, very early on in the text.

The foregoing exegesis is meant simply to describe what the traditional audience is aware of already. The poet is signaling the death of Achilles, about which the *Iliad* knows much but says little directly. As Schein articulates it: "The most important later event referred to but not told in the *Iliad* is the death of

---

[40] "Since now your allotment of life [will be] short and not very long" (ἐπεί νύ τοι αἶσα μίνυνθά περ οὔ τι μάλα δήν, 416). For a discussion of the meaning of this knowledge for Achilles, see Zanker 1994:77–82.

[41] Kelly (2012) calls such laments "prospective," when outlining their typical elements. Neither Arnould nor Kelly discusses this admittedly highly syncopated example in *Iliad* 1. Tsagalis (2004:139) mentions it in passing. For discussion of the classification of laments, see Tsagalis 2004:27–28n101.

[42] Both are in the *adonean clausula*. For my metrical assumptions, see Appendix A.

[43] They last a mere four lines, cut short by Thetis' resolve to go to Zeus and keep Achilles, at least immediately, from his looming fate. The proleptic lament of Thetis is extended even farther in *Iliad* 18.54–60. Lamentation language (πένθος ἄλαστον; Arnould 1990:147) is also used when Zeus sends for Thetis in *Iliad* 24.105. She is already mourning the future loss of her son. The basis of my textual research throughout is the TLG database (cf. Edwards 1991:55, Di Benedetto 1999:217).

[44] Schadewaldt (1965:264), from a neoanalytical point of view, recognized that the lament of Thetis was also seeing into the future. He argues, however, to my mind the less likely point, that the poet's first reason for including lamentation in *Iliad* 1 was "der täglichen Plage seines Daseins."

[45] On Thetis' lament in *Iliad* 18, see Kakridis 1949:66–68, Schadewaldt 1965:248–251, Tsagalis 2004, Dué 2006:65–66, and Kelly 2012:246–255. There is no antiphonal element in the present prospective lament, however, on which see Tsagalis 2004:48–51.

Achilles" (Schein 1984:25; cf. Whitman 1958:201–203). The entrance of Achilles into the war signifies that "Achilles is virtually dead from the beginning of book 18 on." Further, Schein notes that although Achilles' death is not expressly related in the *Iliad*, nevertheless Homer links his death with that of Hector (Schein 1984:128–167; cf. Dué 2002:14).[46] Dué's remarks concerning lamentation support the centrality not just of Achilles' mortality, but also of his death: "The *Iliad* quotes within its narration of Achilles' *kleos* many songs of lamentation that serve to highlight the mortality of the central hero" (Dué 2006:66). Schadewaldt paints a vivid picture of Achilles' comprehension of his mortality, noting that a large vista opens up for Achilles, but one "unter der Herrschaft des Tods" (Schadewaldt 1965:240). Clearly Homer is not the first singer to weave a tale of Achilles' life and death. The audience is aware of Achilles' fate in a story they have heard in some form many times already. The poet's mental "script" assumes a dependence on a common oral tradition. The actual explication of Achilles' and Thetis' comments is not forthcoming *ostensibly* (without a referential reading of each instant) until *Iliad* 9.410–416, where Achilles, through knowledge given from his mother Thetis, also outlines his choice.[47]

Then there is the matter of certain epithets that clearly contradict the action of the immediate context, something Charles Perrault noted already in the seventeenth century: "Le plus souvent ces épithets vaines et vagues, non seulement ne conviennent point au fait qui est raconté, mais y sont directment opposées."[48] Two instances stand out vividly. I speak of "swift-footed Achilles" (πόδας ὠκὺς Ἀχιλλεύς *Iliad* 1.489)[49] sitting by his ships in anger (*Iliad* 1.488–492; cf. 9.307) and "laughter-loving Aphrodite" (φιλομμειδὴς Ἀφροδίτης *Iliad* 5.375),[50] troubled (382), enfolded in the comforting arms of her mother, complaining before her father Zeus how "arrogant Diomedes" (ὑπέρθυμος Διομήδης 376) has

---

[46] As Nagy (1979:113; cf. Schein 1984:25) has observed, however, the ritual of a real funeral is reserved for Achilles' surrogate, Patroklos.

[47] Willcock (1978:276, followed by Hainsworth 1993:116) suggests that Homer created the choice of Achilles introduced (and only overtly mentioned) here. I reserve decision on this. I hope that I have shown, however, that the actual fate of Achilles is too pervasive and necessary not to have been part of the poet's received tradition. Other references to Achilles' fate (instanced in all but the last of the following examples by some form of ὠκύμορος) include *Iliad* 1.505, 18.95, 18.458, and 21.277. (Less direct allusions to Achilles' fate are made, too, in *Iliad* 11.793–794 and 16.36–37; more direct is Achilles' own words at Patroklos' funeral, *Iliad* 23.144–151.) It is obvious that the poet's core audience has heard this story before.

[48] Perrault (vol. 3, p. 111, from the 1979 reprint of his 1692–1697 work, also cited at length in Shive 1987:6) briefly lists a number of examples, including the first two that I give here.

[49] On the epithet πόδας ὠκὺς Ἀχιλλεύς, see Nagy 1979:326–327.

[50] The possible pun of Hesiod's *Theogony* 200, which connects Aphrodite with μήδεα (on which see Chantraine 1968:677, s.v. μειδιάω), even if accepted, sounds equally out of place in the context of *Iliad* 5. On the importance of not reading the Homeric tradition through the lens of the Hesiodic, see Porter 2014.

stabbed her (336–417). How can such instances make sense without a traditional comprehension of the character's activities?

Parry's theory was that the epithet should be read as a metrically convenient formula, whose usefulness lies in its essential theme. In his 1930 paper he formulated his famous dictum:

> The formula in the Homeric poems may be defined as a *group of words which is regularly employed under the same metrical conditions to express a given essential idea.*[51]
>
> Parry 1971:272 (italics are his; cf. 13; and Lord 1960:49–53)

As subsequent research has pointed out, however, absolute metrical thrift is confined (but even here with exceptions[52]) to epithet formulas. More significantly for our present study, "the idea of thrift has nothing to do with idiomatic meaning" (Foley 1999:211).[53] We must instead read behind the sign to what is being referred to in the tradition. Whallon had earlier shown that epithets can reveal the "essential and unchanging character" of individuals in the epic tradition (Whallon 1969:2)[54]; that an epithet, especially one that is particular

---

[51] I employ the term "formula" and "formulaic" throughout to speak of recurring traditional idioms or patterns of words with one or more important parts recurring as component(s), but with a varying amount of replacement of parts within the traditional idiom (which can also cause variation in length). Cf. Fenik (1968:5), who lists as "typical" any type scene elements that recur two or more times. It is not my intention, however, to limit what is formulaic. Much more work has been done to expand our consideration of what may constitute formulaic elements: Nagler 1967, Hainsworth 1968, Higbie 1990:152–198, Bakker 1997, Clark 1997; cf. the overviews of Russo 1997, 2011 and Edwards 1997. Further, I do not, in contrast to Peabody (1975:97) and Parry (1971:275n1), attempt to limit the minimum length of formulae; nor do I attempt with Sale (1993:101) to define what is a "frequent" or "infrequent formula." I do think that Erbse (1972:180) was unnecessarily hesitant about calling repeated elements formulaic (and so part of the tradition inherited by Homer).

[52] See Shive 1987; on Shive, see Friedrich 2007:30–66, 128–146; see also Visser 1988 and Di Benedetto 1994:122–139.

[53] Cf. the comments of Edwards (1988:27): "Because the epithets are chosen for metrical convenience does not mean that they lack meaning"; and Austin's (2009) arguments about νεφεληγερέτα Ζεύς, extending arguments made by Friedrich 2007. Parry (Parry 1971:46) did show some awareness of this possibility (cf. Martin 1993:225). Particularized epithets, he noted, unlike generic epithets, designated, "a particular feature," but the implications of this idea were not developed (cf. Amory Parry 1973:2–7). Lord (1960:66) thought further about this issue, however, on which see Dué and Ebbott 2010:10.

[54] But see Whallon's larger argument on pages 1–33. While Di Benedetto (1994:123) finds some of Whallon's arguments "troppo generica," I find his central thesis persuasive. See also the comments of Anne Amory Parry 1973:4, 163 *et passim*.

to a character (or even mostly particular as Di Benedetto suggests[55]), instances qualities that stem not first from the immediate moment in the singer's song. They retain their semantic force within the larger tradition.[56] The epithet must be heard against a broader and deeper oral history, or, in Nagy's apposite description: "A distinctive epithet is like a small theme song that conjures up a thought-association with the traditional essence of an epic figure, thing, or concept" (Nagy 1990a:23). The epithet "swift footed" (πόδας ὠκύς) in "swift footed Achilles" (πόδας ὠκὺς Ἀχιλλεύς) was heard as a whole "word."[57] For the ancient audience, it referred to Achilles as a character "using a telltale sign," his swiftness of foot (Foley 1999:210).[58] An epithet, I suggest, brings to the minds of the audience members a character's traditional personality.

The epithet has traditional meaning. It is heard by the singer's audience against the larger tradition, but also within a local narrative context as a singer weaves the tapestry of the traditional story.[59] Di Benedetto's study of Hector's epithets suggests further that the more specialized epithets had even more pronounced local meaning for Homer's audience in cases where a singer had a choice between two metrically equivalent epithets (Di Benedetto

---

[55] Di Benedetto (1994:123; cf. 109): "Il fatto che all'interno del poema un epiteto era riferito *molto frequentemente* a un singolo personaggio era sufficiente per creare negli ascoltatori il senso di un collegamento reale ed inequivocabile tra quell' epiteto e quel personaggio" (italics mine).

[56] Whallon (1969:29–32) answers the question "Would epithets really apply as well to one man as another?" His examples of epithets' appropriateness to particular characters (but inappropriateness to other characters) are telling. The point is made through imaginative, dissonant combinations of particular epithets. Imagine, he says, "Paris staunch in battle" (Ἀλέξανδρος μενεχάρμης), "Telemachos the spear-famed" (Τηλέμαχος δουρικλυτός), or "much devising Achilles" (πολύμητις Ἀχιλλεύς). He is not trying to say that every epithet bears significant qualities, but "only that many of them [do]." Cf. the comments of Vivante 1982:13–14 *passim*; Di Benedetto's (1994:123) observations "di una tendenziale accentuata specializzazione" concerning epithets and his conclusions about Hector's (126) and Agamemnon's (129) epithets; and the arguments of Heath (2001) about Telemachos maturing into his oft-used epithet πεπνυμένος, "the 'final' version of the adult Telemachus who is hinted at with each speech introduction along the way."

[57] On the concept of a phrase as a "word," see Foley 1999:201–237.

[58] Dunkle (1997:228–233) has shown that even Achilles' horses mirror this epithet; and that the traditional noun-epithet combination, "swift footed Achilles," defines Achilles' personality even when he merely supervises the foot and chariot races of *Iliad* 23.

[59] Foley (1999:22) comments that we should discount "neither traditional nor situation-specific meaning." Cf. the comments of Ledbetter (1993:490n20) about the importance of both the horizontal (intra-textual) and vertical (metonymic) readings of Homeric repetition. Anne Amory Parry (1973:2) had complained about her father-in-law's work, that when it came to epithets (especially those deemed contextually inappropriate), "He never considers the possibility that it is the meanings traditionally assigned to such epithets that make them seem inappropriate."

1994:131–139).[60] There may even be irony, then, in such situations as "swift-footed Achilles'" idleness.[61]

The foregoing observations concerning epithets support my approach for considering epic characterization more generally. Like the particular epithet, character is not something first created in a singular occurrence within a narrative moment. Nor can the fuller nature of Homeric characterization be heard in isolation from the larger tradition. Character is something profoundly connected to the tradition the poet has received and is referring to, as it is being heard and understood within a local narrative setting. Although much is lost to us, as later readers we have to try to recreate the web of character traits known to the singer and his core audience.

All that I have said is not intended to deny the poet freedom to employ recognizable tradition in creative ways or for the tradition to change over time and absorb new elements.[62] Indeed, the poet's individual presentation can play dynamically upon the audience's knowledge or expectation (cf. Morrison 1992a, Porter 2014). This is a point that we will return to again and again as we consider particular moments of Homeric characterization. Further, the tradition is itself always developing. The very existence, however, of a recognizable history attached to a particular character frees the poet from the necessity of pure invention, *carte blanche*. A distinct character already invokes a particular *ēthos* for the hearer. As I will note in Chapter 2, significant departures from the inherited picture can be used to the poet's advantage as he unfolds his story.

---

[60] Cf. the earlier discussion of Sacks (1987:105–214). On choice between alternatives and the influence of the local context on the singer's choice, see also Beck 1986, Friedrich 2007, and the important questions raised by Martin 1993:229.

[61] Cf. Aphrodite as discussed earlier by Perrault, and the comments of Graziosi and Haubold 2005:52; cf. Martin's comments about irony in Homer's portrayal of Paris 1993:231–233. We will return to the subject of irony in Chapter 2.

[62] See Finkelberg 2012 on the use of non-formulaic language. On the creative adaptation of *formulae* see Paraskevaides 1984, Richardson 1987:165–184, and Clark 1997:24. Di Benedetto (1994:117) shows that partial modifications of formulae are numerous (cf. 1998, *passim*), and he concludes that (1994:136), "l'atto creativo del poeta non si annulla pur nella utilizzazione di un sistema epitetico già preesistente"; Cf. the salient comments of Scodel 2002:19 and the experience of Murko 1928:337. The poet's creativity is tradition-based, however. Further, John Foley once told me an anecdote of how, when carrying out field research, he witnessed a South Slavic *guslar* turn a grocery list into decasyllabic lines of South Slavic epic on the spur of the moment as he stood there. Cf. the effect of collectors on other epic traditions in Ready 2015:27–33. Yet, variation depends upon the importance of the tradition, rather than on novelty per se, as Dué (2002:1–2, 16–36, following Lord 1960:65) notes.

1.4 The Relation of the *Iliad* and *Odyssey*

Before we consider Homeric characterization further, however, I need to state explicitly an underlying assumption affecting the treatment of the *Iliad* and *Odyssey* in Chapters 2–5. My present consideration allows for the possibility of different poets for the *Iliad* and *Odyssey*, but for a common tradition to which each refers, as, among other things, the underlying traditional vocabulary suggests.[63] Yet the history of the poems from oral performance(s) to written form is obscure. I therefore employ Foley's description of Homeric epic as "oral-derived" (Foley 1990:5–8, 1991:38n42, 2011:603).

"Oral-derived" affirms the inherent oral-traditional essence of the poems. The use and adaptation of formulae, the local overuse of repetitions (clustering), as well as other elements of diction and metrical irregularities, suggest the essential oral nature of the poems.[64] As Di Benedetto concludes: "I poemi omerici presentano una caratteristica formale del tutto peculiare" unconcerned with any written text (Di Benedetto 1994:104).[65] Yet "oral-derived" also accepts and notes by the qualifier "derived" that the Homeric epics come to us through documents with a relatively unknowable textual history from Homer's day to the time of the Alexandrian scholars and the establishment of the Vulgate text. The fact that the poems are written reminds us that they most likely represent an expanded presentation, as Lord observed when making his comparison with South Slavic epic (Lord 1956, 1960:124–128). Lord reminds us that our *Iliad* and *Odyssey* cannot ever be entirely identical with the sung text in the normal performance arena. The study of *enjambement* and other poetic elements may

---

[63] Beyond the shared traditional vocabulary (note the sensible comments of Bowra 1962:62–64), the changes in epic diction over time are mapped by Janko (1982:47), whose findings support the close dates of memorialization for the *Iliad* and *Odyssey*. I find Janko's findings convincing for each of the (longer) epic traditions. For critical responses to Janko's glottochronologic approach, see Fowler 1983, Jones 2010, Olson 2012:10–15, and Vergados 2013:142–145. On the similarity of the gods' activities in the *Iliad* and *Odyssey*, see Reinhardt 1948:86–88 and Allan 2006. Di Benedetto (1999:217) sees the role of the deities in the *Odyssey* as "semplificato," except that Athena's role is greatly expanded. He suggests that the difference between epics is one of emphasis, through expansion or contraction. For further similarities and differences between the *Iliad* and *Odyssey*, see Van Duzer 1996:313–318.

[64] On the use and adaptation of *formulae*, see Hainsworth 1968 and Di Benedetto 1994:103–121, 177–231; on clustering, see Di Benedetto 1994:108–115 and Beye 2006:82; on metrical irregularities and other indications of the oral nature of the Homeric epics, see Janko 1990 and 1998: esp. 7–9. For other observations suggesting the oral nature of Homeric poetry, see Austin 2009:70–73. For the possibilities of influence by the scribe and collector in dictation and editing, see Ready 2015:13–45.

[65] Cf. the earlier comments of Nagy (1979:42): "when we are dealing with the traditional poetry of the Homeric (and Hesiodic) compositions, it is not justifiable to claim that a passage in any text can refer to a passage in another text." Cf. n. 21 in this chapter.

also suggest as much (Dukat 1991, Friedrich 2007).[66] The dictated manuscript will be longer and provide opportunity for the "exceptional singer" to expand traditional themes and story length and to "build his lines somewhat differently" (Lord 1960:128, 127, respectively).[67] The process of dictation itself could also have a negative effect on verse formation, something that Parry had earlier noted; but really, the variables in the details of the process of dictation are themselves uncertain and manifold, as Ready's survey of the issue demonstrates.[68] The *Iliad* and *Odyssey* are representatives of songs built in a somewhat artificial environment. We cannot know exactly what the first, dictated texts looked like. Nor did the performance tradition suddenly stop with these memorializations, but continued to live on (cf. Dué 2001 and Scodel 2002:58).

Further, as I argue in greater detail in Chapter 2, the *Odyssey* poem and the character of Odysseus as we have it in the *Iliad* shows that our written version of the *Iliad* in fact postdates some oral version of the *Odyssey*. There must have been an oral story similar to our *Odyssey*, known to the *Iliad* poet composing his song. The question of the relation of the *Iliad* to the *Odyssey* and therefore of the relationship of individuals who appear in each epic is an important one. It affects how we should understand the character of Agamemnon in each epic. My findings suggest a different emphasis from that of Heubeck, who writes, "What is certain is that the figure of Odysseus as it appears in the *Odyssey* is shaped by what the poet found in the *Iliad* and took from there" (Heubeck 1988:19–20). I agree that the *Iliad*'s story does play a significant role in shaping the action of the *Odyssey* (including, as Heubeck notes, Odysseus' movement from an Iliadic hero to a hero who experiences the loss of glory and humiliation).[69] Yet, while this

---

[66] For a critique of Friedrich's reaction to M. Parry, see Austin 2009:88–96; on the challenges and salient questions posed by the process of dictation itself, see Ready 2015:13–20.

[67] Cf. the comments of Powell 2000:107 and Jensen 2011:290.

[68] Parry 1971:450–451. On dictation, see M. Parry in A. Parry 1971:451, Janko 1990, 1998, Powell 1997, Haslam 1997:80–84, and Kelly 2007a:10–11. Ready (2015) reviews the variables in the process of dictation by comparing other oral and oral-derived epics and reminds us that neither Homer nor his patron possessed electronic recording equipment. His emphasis is therefore on pre-Parry collectors. Ready presents some intriguing possibilities for the dictation process and suggests a possible range of variables (and outcomes) for the undoubtedly changed performance and recording dynamics (speed, pause, input, and influence by scribe or collector, etc.). Nagy (1990b:52–81; 1996:69–77, 2002, 2004:36; cf. Bakker 2005) suggests that fixation took place through the performance tradition and occurred at the feast of the Panathenaia. Ready's (2015:60–63 *passim*) recent work supports this as a possibility and reminds us of the importance of the term "oral-derived." While I think it is less likely that the poets who gave us the Homeric epics were themselves especially literate, Foley's work (2002:22–57), outlining the diversity of worldwide oral poets, has made me more agnostic on the issue, although the contrast made by Austin (2009:92–96) between Homeric and Virgilian lines must still be reckoned with.

[69] Heubeck (1988:3–23), while accepting an oral background for the Homeric epics, privileges writing. Cf. Friedrich 2007:140–144. For suggestions of the *Odyssey*'s allusions to the *Iliad*, see

is true, the opposite is also accurate. The Odysseus of the *Iliad* is referred to in ways that presume the audience's knowledge of the sort of story one finds in the *Odyssey*, a point suggested earlier by Nagy: "The *Iliad* is recording the fact that Odysseus already has an *Odyssey* tradition about him" (Nagy 1979:2).[70] Each epic story had been told before in some *similar* fashion. Performed versions of the *Odyssey* predate our present written version of the *Iliad*.[71] The *Iliad* itself alludes to such traditions, however obliquely, when Homer narrates, at a moment of uncertainty in the war, the danger of a *nostos* for the Achaians beyond what was fated.[72] Their return stories had already been told.

Nor is it likely in the general illiteracy of late-eighth-century Greek society that earlier written versions would have served much of a practical purpose. So the influence took place orally, through *aoidic* performance.[73] As Lord observed through his study of the South Slavic comparison, even reading a song from a songbook to an illiterate *guslar* did not determine how the singer would render his own uniquely crafted performance (Lord 1960:79). This realization does not deny that writing and the process of textual transmission have influenced the form of our present manuscripts of the Homeric epics (e.g. see Bolling 1925 and

---

Rinon's (2006:209–211) discussion of "mise en abyme" and the first song of Demodokos in *Odyssey* 8. For the history of "mise en abyme," see Van Duzer 1996:45n110.

[70] Cf. similar conclusions by Olson 1990:5, Danek 1998:2, cf. 12, Dué 2002:12–17 *passim*, Scodel 2002:21, Lentini 2006:13–14, and Barker 2009:59; but also the neoanalyst view that some oral version of Cyclic epics predated the oral version of the Homeric epics (Burgess 2001:33). For an extended discussion of "cycle," see Fantuzzi and Tsagalis 2015:1–7; see 28–34, on the creation of the term "epic cycle." On the difficulty of arriving at definitive conclusions about the "Epic Cycle," see Burgess 2015a.

[71] Lord, as Dué (2000:21n2) points out, preferred to speak of Homeric tradition as being "multiform," rather than containing "variants."

[72] ὑπέρμορα νόστος ἐτύχθη, *Iliad* 2.155. The *Iliad*, unsurprisingly, ostensibly foregrounds little of the post-Trojan War events. Much of the audience, however, would have been aware of "what happened later" all the same. This lack of foregrounding is necessary, nevertheless, since the plot of the *Iliad* itself is set before the actual return of Agamemnon. Consequently, when, through his embassy, Agamemnon offers Achilles a home in Pylos (*Iliad* 9.291–295), he is acting as anyone would who was not yet aware that he would fall into the snare of his unfaithful wife upon his arrival home. There is a fiction that is kept up here. After all, the *Iliad aoidos*, unlike the *aoidos* of the *Odyssey*, is not singing a *nostos* tale. There may be oblique references to the *Odyssey* story, however, in such instances as Priam's reply to Helen in the *Teichoskopia*, where Odysseus is likened to a ram (cf. *Iliad* 3.197 and *Odyssey* 9.432, etc.). Cf. the observations of Maronitis 2004:133–146. We will consider other potential references in Chapters 3–5.

[73] Nagy (1979:42): "it is not justifiable to claim that a passage in any text can refer to another passage in another text"; Di Benedetto (1994:103): "È certo che il destinatario dell' Iliade era un pubblico che il poeta raggiungeva esclusivamente attraverso una comunicazione orale"; cf. Scodel 2012:27, Barker and Christensen 2014:250, Kelly 2012, and Martin 2013. On the question of literacy, see Enos 2002 and Wilson 2009.

Apthorp 1980).[74] Rather, it acknowledges the essential oral traditional nature of our poems.

The idea that the *Iliad* poet knew and had in mind an oral story *similar* to our *Odyssey* when composing his poem will be a point we will consider further. We will see in the course of this book that Homer may have had in mind not only the return of Odysseus, but also the *kakos nostos* ("dismal return") of Agamemnon, as he characterized Agamemnon in the *Iliad*. This tenet forms the impetus for the way I structure Chapters 3 and 4, where we will examine the evidence from Homer, looking first at the *Odyssey* and then at the *Iliad*.[75]

Even the history of the *Odyssey* as a written poem continues to intrigue. It challenges any simple limitations we might put on its use and presentation in actual performance, for instance, within the genre of fifth-century drama. For example, in one speech from Euripides' *Trojan Women* (lines 425–45), Cassandra presents the events of Odysseus' wanderings out of order when considered against the sequence we have narrated at any point in our *Odyssey*. Are Euripides and his Classical Greek *theatai* more concerned with the homecoming events themselves than with their chronological sequence?[76] Are the events thought of as separate episodes from within the post-war period of Odysseus' return?[77] The case of Euripides' *Trojan Women* offers evidence of the freedom for variation in the fifth century, even after the creation of written versions of Homer

---

[74] For a consideration of editing by the collector or scribe involved in the dictation process itself, see Ready 2015.

[75] We need not be concerned that the language of our present copies of the two epics, as Janko (1982, 2012) has argued, makes the *Iliad* a bit earlier than the *Odyssey*. His findings are not meant to address oral Ur-forms. Further, his findings suggest relative memorialization in writing, rather than the actual date that the *Iliad* was recorded in printed form. Cf. n. 63 in this chapter.

[76] Cf. the variable order of Palnadu and Sirat Bani Hilal epics, which only kept a strict chronological order when versions were artificially induced (Jensen 2011:37–41); and also Dué's (2002:32–36) findings for multi-forms of the Briseïs tradition in the iconographical tradition.

[77] Cf. Malkin (1998:52), who also suggests that "episodes *from Homer* were sung separately" in the fifth century. He notes as evidence Herodotus 1.116, Thucydides 1.110, and Plato *Ion* 539b. What exactly is meant by Plato's later comments about Hipparchus demanding that the rhapsodes "run through" Homer's poetry "alternately in order" (*Hipparchus* 228b–c: καὶ ἠνάγκασε τοὺς ῥαψῳδοὺς Παναθηναίοις ἐξ ὑπολήψεως ἐφεξῆς αὐτὰ διιέναι, ὥσπερ νῦν ἔτι οἴδε ποιοῦσιν) is not clear. In any case, it is really quite impossible to know whether Plato reflects earlier or just contemporary conventions when he makes his temporal comparison ὥσπερ νῦν ἔτι οἴδε ποιοῦσιν. Martin (2015:21) suggests "on-demand" performance of epic episodes; and Burgess (2012:286; cf. 2001:111) sees evidence in early Polyphemos iconography that "episodes from the *Odyssey* may have circulated independently." On the existence of various travel narratives in the *Odyssey*, see Burgess 2012.

for didactic purposes.[78] The freedom for chronological variation in Euripides is an analogue, I suggest, for the performative background of the *Odyssey* as epic, which, I am arguing, needs to be read not just *after*, but also *alongside*, the *Iliad*.[79]

---

[78] See Beck (1964:72–146), who suggests that Homer became a standard "school" text. On early schools, see Herodotus 6.27, Thucydides 7.29, Aristophanes *Clouds* 961–983, Aristotle fr. 233 *PCG*, Plutarch *Life of Alcibiades* 7.1.

[79] In this regard, the *Odyssey* itself begins near the end of events, with the devastation that has inflicted Odysseus' house during his absence (books 1–2), and moves back into events of the past through various retrospective narratives of the Trojan War (books 3 and 4, pre-*nostos* tales), such as those told by Nestor and Menelaos to Telemachos, and by Odysseus himself of his own absence during his *nostos* (books 9–12). On types of retrospective narrative (*prolepsis* and *analepsis*), see Genette 1980:48–85; cf. De Jong 2007a:3–8. On epic time, see also De Jong 2007b:17–37. Cf. Foley (1995:115–142) on the chronology of Odysseus' account to Penelope in *Odyssey* 23.310–341.

2

Characterization in Homer and Agamemnon's Appeal in *Iliad* 4

2.1 Traditional Characterization

Our discussion in the last chapter argued that Homeric characterization is tradition-based. Epic characters, at least the major ones, are already known in some detail to Homer and his core audience by distinguishable character traits. The existence of recognizable characterization attached to a particular figure frees the poet from the necessity of pure invention, *carte blanche*. A distinct character already invokes a particular *ēthos* for the hearer. We will consider theory in action in a moment, by reviewing the lineup of Homeric characters in a central moment from *Iliad* 4. The choice of this text is appropriate for a preliminary consideration of the methodology used throughout this book, since this Homeric narrative moment involves Agamemnon and a number of other leading heroes (cf. Minchin's [2011a:331] rationale for choosing *Iliad* 23.). We will see there that Homer already has an idea of what each of his main characters is like from his tradition.

Considering each individual as he is presented will not only provide examples of reading characterization in Homer, but also introduce nicely the object of our query in the ensuing chapters, Agamemnon himself. Before we turn to *Iliad* 4, however, we need to affirm several other factors supporting Homer's tradition-based characterization that complement our discussion in Chapter 1. First, Homeric tradition included some consistency of character; second, an individual character had a recognizable and distinct history; and third, characterization was principally created through word and deed, rather than by abstraction. We will also consider, in the midst of our discussion of Homeric epic, evidence from other oral and oral-derived traditions.

2.1.1 Character Consistency

Homeric characterization is tradition-dependent. Parry and Lord's studies of the South Slavic *guslari* can be seen to support this conclusion, since learning the tradition was part of each singer's rise to a place of proficiency in his craft (Lord 1960:13–29).[1] The conservative nature of the Homeric tradition tends to keep alive character traits that have been established and maintained by singers within the song tradition over time (cf. Minchin 2011a:341–342). A character calls forth in any particular moment of his or her appearance character traits present in other instances inherent within the tradition. This axiom holds true both for action "within character" and conversely action "out of character." The singer can be inventive and a character is never fully static, yet the consistent nature of the character a singer knows from the tradition in which he works will form the basis for much that he invents.[2] To apply Lord's description of the singer's narrative to characterization, there is a "stable skeleton" of character known to singer and audience (Lord 1960:99).

Character is more than either an original creation on the one hand or a generic type on the other. As Dué (2002:1–20) remarks, there was a universal ("paradigmatic") aspect of a character's existence in the tradition that was of importance to the poet working with his tradition. Shared common themes join the stories of various characters for the poet working through his tradition. Yet, there was also depth to particular characters (what Dué calls the "syntagmatic") known to Homer and his core audiences of both the *Iliad* and *Odyssey* (cf. Griffin 1980:50–80 and Minchin 2011a:328–342), although we, as later readers, "have only a narrow window into the larger tradition" (Dué 2002:36).[3] There are further, characters with greater and lesser traditional material adhering to them, what Minchin contrasts as "first-rank heroes" versus those with less significant activity in the poems (Minchin 2011a:330).[4] For the Homeric epics,

---

[1] I observe from Lord's description that three things were common to South Slavic epic singers: illiteracy, a desire to become proficient in singing, and training in the tradition over a long period of time. Training for the singer began at youth and carried on until he could compose his own song from the tradition. Development began young and had three stages. The first stage involved a youth sitting, listening to others sing, and deciding he also wanted to sing. The second stage involved the youth learning to sing, with and without musical accompaniment. When he practiced, his work was increasingly channeled within the framework of traditional rhythmic and word patterns. The second stage ended and the third stage began when a singer was competent enough to compose a song and sing it all the way through before a critical, traditional audience. Lord's description of the education of the singer is in agreement with that of Murko (1928:332–333), which predates his own research.

[2] Cf. the arguments of Lang (1983) and Edmunds (1997) about consistency in story details.

[3] See Dué 2002 on the loss of many syntagmatic versions of the Briseïs story, but the importance of the paradigmatic themes to the poetic tradition; and cf. the story of Dolon in Dué and Ebbott 2010:106–119.

[4] Character creation in Homer, at least in the case of minor characters, is possible, but not really demonstrable, since we cannot recapture the full performance tradition (cf. Scodel 2002:30–33). Homer is not creating most of the traditions he uses, which are much older than his performance

the surest measuring stick we have of a character's importance within the tradition is the quantitative (and qualitative) analysis of that character's appearances in the Homeric epics themselves.[5]

We are made openly aware of the traditional nature of particular (or "syntagmatic") characterization and character consistency in the case of Achilles, who refuses to show much mercy to the *Presbeia*. His refusal to help his *philoi* (*Iliad* 9.228–251) or to be moved to action by their pleas for help (and Agamemnon's offer of reparations) stands in stark contrast to earlier tradition we have of him embedded within the *Iliad*.[6] Achilles' *philoi*, the internal audience, are necessarily distraught at his rejection of their supplications. Homer's external audience is too, though for even greater, metonymic reasons. Homer's core audience would not only hear the sadness of the *philoi* at Achilles' rejection, but also be cognizant of the ominous events it harbingers: the death of Patroklos, but also that of Achilles himself.[7] They are aware that Achilles' momentary and resolute departure from pity (a part of the larger *mēnis* theme) is replete with portentous consequences understood neither by himself nor by the visiting Achaian embassy. It exemplifies a case of "metonymic irony."[8] Achilles' character seems temporarily lopsided. He was held to be a hero who could show pity, at least before Hector killed his closest friend.[9]

---

context. This is likewise the case with other performed epic traditions such as the South Slavic and Armenian, which we will be considering in a moment.

[5] Cf. Turkeltaub (2007a), who follows this methodological approach to show that there is a hierarchy of perception of Homeric divinities, by different Homeric characters. Turkeltaub means to disambiguate the normal, but insufficient division between gods and humans.

[6] C.f. *Iliad* 6.414–428, 11.104–106, 21.100–113; 24.748–759; and Goldhill 1990a:75 (but contrast the view of Griffin 1980:53–56). Collins (1988:16n12, from a neoanalyst perspective) notes that the inclination of Achilles to show pity is also extant in the *Cypria* and *Aethiopis*.

[7] See our discussion of Achilles' self-reference to an abbreviated life in Chapter 1. Dué and Ebbott (2011:100) suggest a similar impact on the external audience through their knowledge of the Rhesos tradition.

[8] On "metonymic irony," see Porter 2011:512–513 (and the bibliography listed there); cf. the "metapoetic" discussion of Kelly (2012:229–245) for prospective lamentation. We will revisit *Iliad* 9 in Chapter 4.

[9] For Achilles' own statement on the matter, see *Iliad* 21.100–105 and his pitiless reply to Priam's son Lykaon. Zanker (1994) argues that Achilles' return to battle after Patroklos' death is not rationally but emotively based; not for honor (he had rejected the embassy in *Iliad* 9), but for revenge that was emotionally driven. The affectively driven actions of Achilles (present in his refusal to aid his comrades) and his grief-fed *aristeia*, return, Zanker argues, both in his brutal treatment of the corpse of Hector and in his responsive acceptance of the supplicating Priam. Kim (2000:151) stresses Achilles' reaffirmation of pity and the necessary corollary (in her emphasis on the active meaning of pity) of saving his *philoi*, but suggests that Achilles' conception of just who his *philoi* are now includes not only Achaians, "but all humans." Ledbetter (1993) sees Patroklos' character as representing Achilles' more compassionate side.

This change in character is a cue to the audience that something is happening. This sort of cue, by a change from what is expected or usual, is not only found in the case of Homeric characters. It is also present within Homeric type scenes, as we first noted in Chapter 1. Type scene elements exhibit the capacity for purposeful manipulation or inversion to signal something of note in the narrative. Ironic inversions are present in a number of scenes in the *Odyssey*. They include the ambivalence of the Phaiacians (instead of a normal guest welcome), Polyphemos' eating of his guests (rather than providing a meal), and the suitors use of food as weapons (in place of provisions offered by host to guest).[10] In these cases, the unexpected occurs against the background of the expected. Morrison has aptly summarized the situation: "If a sequence of certain elements typically leads to an outcome, the conventionality of such a sequence will generate expectations of that outcome" (Morrison 1992a:42).[11] When the unexpected occurs, Homer's core audience would notice. This parallels Homer's presentation of character, where change or inconsistency suggests something for singer and audience members aware of the tradition.

When a particular articulation of character or character trait is inverted in some way, the poet may be signaling something momentous within his story. We have suggested that such is the case with Achilles, but one can also see that the poet uses changed character at a central moment in the *Iliad*'s narrative involving Idomeneus.[12] A notable departure from Idomeneus' normally stalwart and resolute character occurs just before the Trojans drive the Achaians to their ships. It helps signal not only the dire situation the Achaians face after Patroklos' death (including the onslaught and *aristeia* of a Hector newly protected by Achilles' armor), but also the impending presence of something and someone greater in the plot—the return of Achilles himself. Yet, even here Homer constructs the divergence from what is normal gracefully. To show the oddity of his retreat, the poet prefaces Idomeneus' decision with his attendant

---

[10] See Reece 1993:167–168, but also 10–11, 53–54, 56, 82–84, 93, 132; and cf. changes in the traditional order of mourners in Pantelia 2002. For a similar consideration of inversions for "prospective" lamentation in Homer, see Kelly 2012:244.

[11] Foundational works on type scene elements include Arend 1933 and Fenik 1968, 1974.

[12] Idomeneus' retreat: *Iliad* 17.605–625. This is one of only two moments of Idomeneus not acting as he usually would. One other, smaller regression occurs in *Iliad* 8.78. There it acts as a traditional cue pointing to the necessity of an embassy to Achilles. The poet chooses to give much greater emphasis to the episode we deal with from *Iliad* 17, where he slows the narrative down and adds more emphasis via speeches (a narrative effect noted by Austin 1966:306). One incidence of a harsh rejoinder comes too from Poseidon *déguisé* (*Iliad* 13.206–239) but does not suggest cowardice on Idomeneus' part. The stalwart and fearless nature of Idomeneus is clearly indicated in his manifold appearances in the *Iliad*: 1.145, 2.645–652, 3.230–233, 4.252–272, 5.43–47, 7.162–165, 8.263, 11.510–515, 13.240–521, 16.345–350, 17.258–259, 19.309–313, 23.450–498; and he and his crew also enjoy a successful *nostos*: *Odyssey* 3.191–192.

Meriones' advice that the situation is hopeless not only for him, but for all the Achaians (*Iliad* 17.622–623). The poet has Meriones, who has just seen their spare driver Koiranos killed in their chariot, plead with Idomeneus: "But even you yourself know that the Achaians' strength is no longer!" (γιγνώσκεις δὲ καὶ αὐτὸς ὅ τ' οὐκέτι κάρτος 'Αχαιῶν, 17.623).

The choice of "strength" (κάρτος/κράτος) defines the central moment in the narrative's focus, as it does elsewhere in Homer. The word carries connotations that show its importance as more than just a description of physical prowess. A few examples should suffice to underscore its referential power. In *Iliad* 1.509, "strength" (κράτος) is made key to the Trojans gaining hegemony over the Achaians; in *Iliad* 2.118, it is the basis for Zeus bringing about the downfall of cities; in *Iliad* 6.387, when the Trojans are losing, the Achaians' rise is measured in terms of an increase in "strength" (κράτος). In *Iliad* 9.254, "strength" (κάρτος) is the divine gift centrally desired by Achilles, and, in *Iliad* 17.562, by Menelaos, to hold the Trojans away from Patroklos' corpse. In the *Odyssey*, it is the quality that is required for Menelaos to capture the shape-shifting Proteus (4.415), but it also forms the foundation for Alkinoös' rule over the Phaiacians (6.197). It is the key to success in martial combat and in civilian life, as its use in Homer suggests, and it is here said, notably, to be absent from the Achaians.[13] What can even an Idomeneus do in such a situation but leave the battlefield? We hear the poet next commenting for his own audience that Ajax notices how Zeus has suddenly shifted the tide of war.[14] Idomeneus' retreat, consequently, by its very abnormality, helps signal the momentous nature of what is taking place within the larger story as the poet unfolds it for his listening audience.

Examples from other oral or oral-derived stories also suggest the traditional nature of characterization and the significance of moments when someone acts "out of character." For any comparison, the question of genre is paramount (Foley 1991:15), even though all epic traditions are not equal.[15] Yet, we compare only epic traditions, since there can be an even greater qualitative difference

---

[13] Κράτος/κάρτος shows up thirty three times in Homer. See further: *Iliad* 9.25, 39, 11.192, 207, 319, 753, 12.214, 13.484, 743, 15.216, 16.524, 17.206, 613, 623, 18.308, 20.121, 24.293, 311; *Odyssey* 1.70, 359, 3.370, 4.415, 5.4, 9.393, 11.353, 21.280, and 21.353.

[14] *Iliad* 17.626–627: Οὐδ' ἔλαθ' Αἴαντα μεγαλήτορα καὶ Μενέλαον / Ζεύς, ὅτε δὴ Τρώεσσι δίδου ἑτεραλκέα νίκην.

[15] The present inclusion of non-Greek traditions for comparison is not meant to imply that characterization occurs at the same depth in all literature of every culture. Overall, the impression of many other traditions, including the South Slavic, is that of somewhat less depth in the complexity of the expression of characterization. Cf. the comments of Kelly (2014:51), who compares the foes of Ancient Near Eastern battle scenes with those of the *Iliad* and finds the latter much more individuated; and cf. also the conclusions of Karahashi and Lopez-Ruiz (2006:100), in their comparison of Euripides' *Hippolytus* and the *Epic of Gilgamesh*, about the importance of noting transformations that result from, among other things, "different sites of

in depth of characterization between epic characters and characters found in other genres, such as Aesop's fables, or shorter mythical stories, such as those of the aboriginal tribes of Australia.[16] Character consistency is illustrated by the South Slavic epic trickster figure, Tale of Orašac. While Tale's character history is more comparable to Odysseus than Idomeneus, he suggests some presence of character depth in South Slavic epic poetry comparable to Homer's. An inimitable and irascible character, he appears in diverse performances of epic tales of weddings and battles, including that sung by Avdo Medjedović, *The Wedding of Smailagić Meho*, and *The Wedding of Mustajbeg's Son Bećirbeg*, performed by Halil Bajgorić. In both of these stories, the character of Tale "the fool" is made more colorful with a mount that is really an "anti-horse," the sort of horse no hero would ever ride.[17] Yet, it well suits Tale's unusual persona.[18] A short excerpt from each epic performance will catch something of the flavor of this hero's mounted appearance:

> And this is how he had decked his mouse-gray horse. The reins were reeds from the riverbank. There was neither proper saddle nor pack-carrier on the mouse-gray horse, but only the blanket from the smelly goat. Over the blanket hung a broken-down saddle of sorts... There were no stirrups on the saddle but only two slings of reeds ... Tale's legs hung free. ...[19]

> Lord 1974:199

> What sort of Turkish Disaster is this,
> Who rides a stout dun-colored horse,
> Both legs hanging over the one side
> And on the other side a nail-studded walking stick?

> Foley 2004:67, vs. 690–693

---

cultural production." Further, as Ready's (2015) findings suggest, there is a place for the use of a variety of oral-derived epic traditions, which will be the case here.

[16] On the latter, see Berndt and Berndt (1994). However, even in Australian aboriginal tales, one sees tribal groups and representative characters in some metonymic depth within the tradition (though less specifically than in Homer, where strict metrical constraints encourage long-time conservative retention of traditional information). See, for instance, the figure of the Wirindji in two tales of the "same" story, one told by men and the other by women (167–175). While the story pattern seems quite varied between the two tellings, the character of the Wirindji is generally consistent.

[17] Nb. the comments of Foley 1995:36n14.

[18] Contrast, for example, the preparation of a "properly" prepared horse for Smail's son, Meho, in Lord 1974:105–106.

[19] This descriptive passage is paralleled in *The Wedding of Mustajbeg's Son Bećirbeg* (Foley 2004:61, vs. 450–454).

This anti-hero, "fool Tale," or "great fool Tale," as he is often called, has a traditional consistency discernible in multiple performances. Foley characterizes him as: "garrulous, choleric, counter-heroic, even slapstick ... [yet] essential to any mission's success" (Foley 2004:40).[20] He will be part of the effort to bring the Turkish bride Zlata to her awaiting Turkish groom Bećirbeg, after the first attempt of the Turkish Wedding party had been foiled by the Christian adversaries led by Baturić Ban. Tale will also keep the nefarious Christian enemy Baturić Ban from swindling the Turks of gold in the guise of a beggar.[21] Without him the wedding will not go forward. His characterization lives as a consistent persona in the tradition that the poets of South Slavic epic sang to their audiences.

In Armenian epic tradition we find a consistency similar to Idomeneus and other Homeric characters in the hero Sanasar.[22] Sanasar is an epic hero with a number of traditional stories and items adhering to, demarcating, and giving substance to his character. These include his talking and high-jumping horse, Kourkig Jelaly, his Lightning Sword, and his particular kin relations and heroic achievements (see e.g. Shalian 1964:44–46, 60–61, 79, 82, 85, and 87). The better part of his exploits also involve his younger twin-brother, Baghdasar, the lesser

---

[20] The tradition requires his presence for an undertaking (Foley 1995:33): "The central paradox of his epic existence is that, no matter how egregiously unheroic his actions, dress, or retinue, the Moslem force assembled for either of the great group efforts in this storytelling tradition—a battle or a wedding—simply is not considered complete, or even viable, without Tale's participation."

[21] Tale is rather miserly and foils the plan of the enemy leader, Baturić Ban, by offering him his cane instead. See Foley 2004:66–68, vs. 636–714.

[22] Our main text here is the 1964 English translation of Shalian, which is based upon an Armenian composite edition (Russell 2004:xvi). For an overview of the textual history of one of only two translations of a composite text drawn from "village story" versions, see Hacikyan 2000:969. For a review of Shalian that favors his translation as "obviously more scholarly" (than Surmelian's 1964 edition), see Jansen 1967; cf. the comments of Gulbekian (1984:105). The epic is often referred to as *The Daredevils of Sassoun*. "Daredevils" makes reference to the four epic "cycles" with their leading heroes first recorded by Bishop Garegin Srvandzteants in 1874, the first transcription of an otherwise completely oral epic (on the history of the Armenian epic, see Hacikyan 2000:963–989). Central conflicts within the epic tradition go back to 850–852 AD and an Armenian resistance to an Arab Caliphate. For a consideration of cross-cultural elements in Armenian epic, see Haroutynian 1997. The Shalian text is removed from the original oral performance (to borrow from the observations of Ready 2015) by being based upon dictation (13–33), and second, by being an edited version (cf. 34–45). The Homeric epics, as oral-derived texts, may also be products of at least some of the same transcriptional and editing practices (cf. my comments in Chapter 1, *passim*, but including n. 68), although it is unlikely that the Homeric epics were stories selected as small slices of rather larger transcriptions as is the case with the English versions of the Armenian epics (on which see Hacikyan 2000:965–966).

hero in the pair, who is consistently presented as a more hotheaded and foolish brother.[23]

In Armenian epic, Sanasar is consistently portrayed as the leader, and lead he does, almost without exception, showing himself the better hero, quicker to act and more intelligent than Baghdasar. For example, the maiden Deghtzoum Dzam chooses Sanasar over Baghdasar (Shalian 1964:65, 68, 71); Sanasar has much greater strength and skill as displayed by a duel with maces (Shalian 1964:72–75); and Sanasar passes the milk-drinking heroic test seven times more quickly than Baghdasar (Shalian 1964:78, 89). Here the emphasis lies in the disparity between the brothers' prowess, since Baghdasar not only takes seven times as long to drink the milk, but does so despite taking the test on an empty stomach! Sanasar kills twice as many pahlevans as Baghdasar and has the more powerful hurl of a large millstone at a dragon (Shalian 1964:89 and 96, respectively); and Sanasar even decides what to do with the millstone (Shalian 1964:96). Baghdasar, however, is more hotheaded and foolish, as the epithet, "foolish Baghdasar" confirms (Shalian 1964:67, 70, 71; and 71, where it is used as a predicate descriptive). The Danish folklorist Axel Olrik long ago pointed out that an uneven differentiation in power is a traditional, or we might suggest, "typical" element of *Sage* when twins, which he allows in the broad sense of "two people who appear together in the same role," are involved as major (rather than minor) characters (Olrik 1909:136).[24]

Consequently, one moment in the Armenian epic narrative comes as a surprise to readers of the text not conversant with the traditional stories, though it was most likely full of irony for an informed Armenian audience. It is an instance where a character's action is changed, as we saw with Diomedes, to signal something greater in the plot. The moment is one of the last extant scenes in the recorded Armenian epic about Sanasar and Baghdasar. The two heroes are shown traveling home toward Sassoun for the wedding of Sanasar to the newly rescued "golden braids." Suddenly a "blue horseman" yelling objections about their having the maiden comes charging at them. As is traditionally the case, Sanasar takes the initiative, saying he will go and see what the challenger is saying. Baghdasar's response, which first echoes the normal filial relationship,

---

[23] On Baghdasar as the younger brother, see Shalian 1964:75; on his being hotheaded and foolish, see Shalian 1964:36.

[24] Cf. Antinoos over Eurymachos in the *Odyssey* (1.384–387, 400–405; Fenik 1974:198, 207), but also the hegemony of Gilgamesh over Enkidu in the Gilgamesh epic (2.96–115) and Jacob over Esau in Genesis (25.21–34, 27.40, 33.12–17), on which see also Lord 1990. For other possible twins in Homer, see Clark 2007 and Frame 2009:105–130; on Vedic twins, 59–102, 238n139. On the ultimate origin of the Armenian twins as divine twins, see Haroutyunian 1997:87. For consideration of other "twins" in other ancient literature, see Uther (2004:386) tale type 711, The Beautiful and the Ugly Twin Sisters, and Clark 2007.

nevertheless suddenly challenges Sanasar's conventional hegemony: "You always take up the challenge; I am taking it up this time" (Shalian 1964:106). The natural leader, Sanasar, quickly allows his brother Baghdasar to assume the lead, a cue that one must assume resonated with meaning for the traditional audience who would know that "something was amiss." Indeed, the ensuing scene witnesses Baghdasar riding out at full pace and tackling "him," only to discover in the tussle that he has in reality thrown to the ground a "her," a maiden come not to fight but to marry him. Moreover, the unknown assailant turns out to be the sister of "golden braids"! The traditional audience would be alerted by the sudden change in character roles that something is about to happen. Baghdasar is about to get his girl, too. The change in what one might have expected of Sanasar is necessitated by the story pattern and carries important implications for the audience—now both heroes enter Sassoun ready to wed.[25]

In the cases of Achilles, Idomeneus, Tale, and Sanasar, the larger story pattern affects the presentation and reception of character at particular narrative moments. Yet, a character's presence brings certain expectations. The storyteller plays on the audience's knowledge of a particular character's conventional role and past history in the tradition. Variation from the norm carries implications for poet and audience. As with type scenes components, traditional character traits connected with actual events in the character's recognizable history form expectations in the audience's mind. Anomalies can signal something of significance in the plot. For leading heroes of Greek epic, the traditional nature of characterization is assumed by poet (and audience), an assumption supported, rather than negated, by moments when an individual acts "out of character." As Minchin notes for Homeric characterization, "the predictability of each hero's temperament is essential to the success of the episode" (Minchin 2011a:331). However much the picture we have of an individual is conditioned by the typical elements common to a given character type (or story pattern), Homer's tradition includes particular individuals with pronounced character traits.

2.1.2 Character Traits and History

Stressing the importance of a character's history does not deny the importance of character type or story pattern in shaping and preserving a particular character, something also influential in the history of a particular story.[26] There is

---

[25] Armenian weddings, even into the mid-20th century, still involved a mock capturing of the wife (Surmellian 1964:75n4).

[26] See Bakker (2013:13–35) for the typology of the *nostos* as a quest; and Foley (1999:115–167) for a detailed analysis of the traditional nature and implications of the Return Song pattern (see pp. 169–199 and Appendix I). Homeric studies, moreover, have learned much from comparative

no doubt that Nestor, for instance, is the acme of *exempla* for a wise old hero, or that Idomeneus is built up as a typically resolute and eager warrior.[27] Rather, I mean to affirm that actual characters with particular histories live within Homer's tradition as real persons with distinct stories and personalities, the way literary characters also have the potential to live within a successive book series. Further, to employ Malkin's maxim, "type cannot freely replace content" (Malkin 1998:49). Within a given storytelling tradition, particular characters have their own individualized stories and personalities that make them who they are: Agamemnon was the paramount *basileus* over the forces at Troy and was killed upon returning home; Odysseus outwitted the Cyclops and went home to a faithful wife; Nestor gave excellent advice and was a warrior from the former generation; Tale bested his army's adversary, Baturić Ban, in the guise of a beggar; and Sanasar won "golden braids." Nor are the suitors of the *Odyssey*, as much as they share common faults in their foolishness, all the same.[28] Not only a typical pattern, then (such as the "return song" or heroic lifecycles), but also the particular character histories are traditional. Homer has particular characterization in mind when he weaves his story. Put another way, it would be strange to see Agamemnon in a story pattern for a *nostos* involving a faithful wife, to see Odysseus die an early death at Troy or Thebes, for Tale to play anything but the indispensable fool, or to be presented with a Sanasar who

---

work, which has proven that local stories are influenced by imported story patterns (such as those of the Near East). On this, see especially Nagy 1990a:7–17, Burkert 1992, Bernabé 1995, West 1997:334–437, Ready 2012, and Rollinger 2015.

[27] The motif of aged sagaciousness (youthful thoughtlessness) is first seen clearly articulated in the words of Menelaos when arranging for the cutting of oaths between the Trojans and Achaians before his duel with Alexandros in *Iliad* 3.105–110. More will be said about Nestor's wisdom in Chapter 4, s.v. 4.2.1 Agamemnon's Dishonoring and Hubristic Actions: 1.6–344. For further consideration of the theme of youthful impetuousness (Antilochos'), see Collins 1988:81–82 and Minchin 2011a:334–335.

[28] Fenik (1974:198–205) outlines the consistent characterization of Antinoos and Eurymachos in the *Odyssey*, who are quite different individuals. Unlike Antinoos, "the heedless criminal impatient of warning or delay," Eurymachos (see *Odyssey* 21.249–255), is a "guileful dissembler," fearful of what people will say of him. Race (1993:84–88) adds the suitors Leokritos, Amphinomos, Ktesippos, Agelaos, and Leodes to the clearly individualized characterization of suitors. Friedrich (1991), against earlier views, argues for a consistent characterization of Zeus in the *Odyssey*. Aristotle recognized the importance of tradition in the telling of stories (*Poetics* 1453b22–26): τοὺς μὲν οὖν παρειλημμένους μύθους λύειν οὐκ ἔστιν, λέγω δὲ οἷον τὴν Κλυταιμήστραν ἀποθανοῦσαν ὑπὸ τοῦ Ὀρέστου καὶ τὴν Ἐριφύλην ὑπὸ τοῦ Ἀλκμέωνος· αὐτὸν δὲ εὑρίσκειν δεῖ καὶ τοῖς παραδεδομένοις χρῆσθαι καλῶς. To dissolve what traditionally went together would not be effective or bring about the desired affective response in the audience who would likely be jarred by a complete change in the tradition. By Aristotle's time, however, rhetoric had also made character something other than it was in the early epic tradition. The *Poetics* and *Rhetoric* embody this change. May (1988:9) notes that Aristotle's *ethos* is not based upon "previous reputation, but the impression he [the speaker] makes during a speech." On deception in Attic oratory, see Kremmydas 2013.

did not marry "golden braids."[29] To illustrate using a situation that will arise in Chapter 4, the constantly recurring rumblings of Agamemnon to head home and abandon the Achaian assault on Troy, while never a real option, do call into question Agamemnon's leadership qualities and give us a glimpse of his traditional personality for singer and audience.

Character traits arise in the minds of Homer's audience members as he tells a particular story. Character is reformed in a given, local instance of epic song performance, and it involves not only the singer's words, but also the core audience's knowledge of a shared tradition. Therefore, character development within a particular tale's telling will not be exactly what we might expect, for instance, from character presentation within a single novel.[30] Instead, epic characterization occurs against the backdrop of the known tradition, even when the poet chooses to stress some range of experiences or portray character development within his song.[31] For, while the poet can create new action and even expand a character's presentation and enhance his or her story, the poet already has in mind traditional traits for whatever scene is being built.[32] Since neither the *Iliad* nor the *Odyssey* could have been performed in one sitting, they of

---

[29] Cf. the argument of Whallon and the discussion of particular epithets in Chapter 1.

[30] Cf. Burgess (2015b:42): "Nor is much effort spent on character development." The novel, however, is itself an example of a genre that allows for the creation of a tremendous amount of newness and surprise. On the differences between oral and written authorship, see especially the important observations of Austin 2009:92–96. Of the incessant differences between Homer and Virgil, for instance, Austin (94) appropriately comments: "The Homeric hexameter is a wave that unfurls as it reaches the shore, not the boisterous wave driven under a high wind, but the gentler, quieter roll of the surf, with one wavelet after another breaking on the shore, until the final wave, cresting, breaks and completes the line. Virgil does not create waves in the Homeric fashion ... his hexameter is the product of a writing culture; it could never be mistaken for the product of a pre-literate age."

[31] On character development, Friedrich (1991) argues that Odysseus displays some qualitative difference in temperament within the plot of the *Odyssey*, between the unrestrained and vaunting hero who blinds the Cyclops and the chastened hero who restores order on Ithaca; Heath (2001:31) argues that the epithet πεπνυμένος "belongs to the Telemachus of the tradition," who Homer is able to show how he got where he is; and cf. the findings of Hinckley (1986) for the consistent characterization of Telamonian Ajax. To my mind, these scholars' observations can be seen to affirm that the poet still had a range of character development to play with precisely because he already had the character's fuller personality in mind as his *telos* when he composed his traditional rendition.

[32] We can never from our vantage point, however, circumscribe or demarcate the "full" story of any epic figure. The extent of an oral traditional story cannot be as easily defined as literary stories not derived from oral tradition. Further, later representations in other literary genres show that there is an evolution of particular characters over time. Stanford's *Ulysses Theme* (1963) remains an excellent text for considering the evolution of Odysseus' character from epic to drama and later literature. Blondell (2013) likewise traces Helen's ambiguous nature from Homer to Isocrates.

necessity demonstrate, by their very existence, that the characters represented there were not being created anew in each performance.

Many characters have lengthy traditional stories attached to them that affect their presentation *in situ*. Such is the case with Odysseus. As we noted briefly in Chapter 1, he is referenced in the *Iliad* by epithets, many of them principally used for him, which make more sense in the *Odyssey*. To continue this thought in greater detail, even early on in the *Iliad* (following our written text chronologically), Odysseus is named "Odysseus of many strategies" (πολύμητις Ὀδυσσεύς),[33] "Zeus-born Odysseus of many devices" (διογενὲς Λαερτιάδη πολυμήχαν'), "much-enduring divine Odysseus" (πολύτλας δῖος Ὀδυσσεύς), and "enduring Odysseus" (τλήμων Ὀδυσσεύς): he is presented as a man full of cunning, stratagems, and endurance for no apparent reason.[34] These epithets carry meaning from the longer traditional story from which they came, meaning that lies beyond the temporal moment where they occur in a particular memorialized text. The lesson Odysseus' appearances teach us is that a major character cannot leave behind his or her words and deeds in the larger story tradition when involved in a particular narrative instant. Further, the traditional external audience is expected to have a greater awareness of a character than characters within the story itself, the internal audience.

2.1.3 Characterization Through Word and Deed

Another point that needs emphasizing is one that has been implicit all along, namely, that action in "word" and "deed" defines character in the ancient mind, that "parola e azione" receive "lo stesso rango nel poema" (Dentice Di Accadia 2012:187; cf. Barck 1976:91 and Griffin 1980:75). This truism will form the basis for our studies of character in this and subsequent chapters. The concept is central in Phoinix's emotional appeal to Achilles in *Iliad* 9, where he reminds the recalcitrant hero that he was sent by Achilles' father to teach him "of words, a speaker to be, and a doer of deeds" (μύθων τε ῥητῆρ' ἔμεναι πρηκτῆρά τε ἔργων, 443). It is a sentiment, in one form or another, heard quite often in Homer.[35]

---

[33] The formula is found in position C1 to line end, but the formula's flexibility and tenacity is shown by its appearance as Ὀδυσεὺς πολύμητις, as part of a bridged first hemistich.

[34] There is no need to list the many instances of these epithets' occurrences, but the earliest textual references are: πολυμήτις Ὀδυσσεύς: *Iliad* 1.311; διογενὲς Λαερτιάδη πολυμήχαν' Ὀδυσσεῦ: *Iliad* 2.173; πολύτλας δῖος Ὀδυσσεύς: *Iliad* 8.97 (τλήμων Ὀδυσσεύς, *Iliad* 10.231, 498, is unique in this form in Homer). We will revisit πολυμήτις Ὀδυσσεύς later in this chapter.

[35] Cf. *Iliad* 9.443; cf. 1.395, 505, 5.879. The traditional formula that predominates for male "work" in the *Iliad* is that of war, πολεμήϊα ἔργα, a formula that occupies the adonean clausula in *Iliad* 2.338, 5.428, 7.336, 11.719, 13.727, 730, except for its singular occurrence in the last hemistich of *Odyssey* 12.116. For a study of unspoken thought, beyond word and deed, as an important factor in characterization (particularly in the *Odyssey*), see de Jong 1997. For a discussion of the

Abstraction is less important in epic; rather, concrete stories come to mind when the *aoidos* sings to his audience. Abstraction of recognizable qualities (including ideas present in particularized epithets) is the result of recurring action in the real life of the character from traditional story performances, whether told in direct or reported speech. Put another way, it is the objective words and deeds rather than the subjective (or abstracted) "internal qualities of self" that matter (Collins 1988:18n18; cf. Roochnik 1990, and Burgess 2015b:42–43).[36]

We turn now to a case study of traditional characterization to see theory in practice. In Agamemnon's appeal in *Iliad* 4, both in the appeal itself and in the narrative surrounding it, I suggest that its central characters are best interpreted against the whole background tradition of the *Iliad* (and *Odyssey*).

2.2 Typical and Specific Appeals

In *Iliad* 4, the truce established for the duel between Paris and Menelaos has been broken. Agamemnon has just witnessed his brother barely evade death and has sent his herald Talthybios to fetch Machaon (193–197), who provides medical assistance (217–219). Meanwhile, so we are told, Agamemnon "ranged through the ranks of his fighters" (ἐπεπωλεῖτο στίχας ἀνδρῶν, 231) exhorting and appealing to the leading *basileis* to fight against the Trojans.[37] Before the specific addresses to individual *basileis* (and their respective troops) and heroic pairs (251–400), however, we are given two possible "typical" appeals in *oratio recta* with the general sentiment of what would be said in each case (234–239, 243–249). In these appeals, we see Agamemnon's classification of two types of warriors. The first group of warriors is that which Agamemnon finds eagerly

---

importance of being a good speaker, see Schofield 1986:6–31. Yet, as Dentice Di Accadia (2012:56) rightly notes, the formulaic "parola e azione" is also found within a narrative setting, something that is important to remember (cf. Chapter 1, where I emphasized that traditional language cues were heard in a local narrative context).

36 This is not to deny that Homer was capable of some level of psychological depth in his characters. Griffin (1980:50–80) suggests there is, although Griffin's emphasis lies in poetic creativity, rather than poetic creativity through tradition, my principal emphasis here.

37 In ancient commentary the whole scene is referred to as the "'Revue' [of the troops]" (*epipōlēsis*). Chantraine (1968:877, s.v. πέλομαι) offers "approcher" for ἐπιπέλομαι. For a general introduction to the "catalogue-type sequence" see Kirk 1985:353–354; on the scene's oratory, see Dentice Di Accadia 2012:145–154; on the typical preparations and exhortation to battle, the last section of a battle anticipatory sequence, see Schadewaldt 1966:29–40. Morrison (1992a:42, 132), who follows Schadewaldt with some variation, sees nine elements in a prelude to the battle anticipatory sequence: 1. Divine incitement to battle; 2. Mortal decision to fight; 3. Sacrifice; 4. Meal; 5. Gathering of the army; 6. Arming (the whole army or an individual); 7. Marching to battle; 8. Review of troops; and 9. Exhortation. Morrison 1992a:132n18: "The category of exhortation includes advice, criticism, or warning (cf. *Iliad* 2.381–393, 4.223–421, 19.408–417)." Cf. the two Aiantes *neikos* toward the troops, in *Iliad* 12.265–268.

fighting, whom he exhorts all the more: "And so those he would see eager of the Danaans with the swift-horses, / these, standing nearby, he kept constantly exhorting with speech" (καί ῥ' οὓς μὲν σπεύδοντας ἴδοι Δαναῶν ταχυπώλων, τοὺς μάλα θαρσύνεσκε παριστάμενος ἐπέεσσιν, 232–233). We learn that part of Agamemnon's first type of exhortation is founded upon the assurance that Zeus will punish the oath-breaking Trojans who will become carrion; part is the traditional promise of future war prizes for the victorious warriors who will lead away women and children as booty, if they act now (238–239).[38]

A second group of warriors is described next—those Agamemnon sees as hanging back: "But those he should see slacking off from hated war, / these he would greatly chastise with angry speech" (Οὕς τινας αὖ μεθιέντας ἴδοι στυγεροῦ πολέμοιο, / τοὺς μάλα νεικείεσκε χολωτοῖσιν ἐπέεσσιν, 4.240). Part of his exhortation to this second group is a call to consider the way they are acting before their peers, since many appear to him to be unmoved by shame.[39] These Agamemnon keeps chastising (νεικείεσκε) as inactively gazing, like some young fawns, worn out while playing in the fields (242–246). As is the case for those eagerly fighting, so here also, the exhortation is partially based, albeit negatively, upon the question of Zeus' activity. They are holding back, Agamemnon insinuates in his interrogation, until they see whether the hand of the son of Kronos will prove effective.[40] In this way, the eager warriors fight, stirred on by promises based upon Zeus' help, while the hesitant warriors are chastised for not believing that such help will be forthcoming. This is Agamemnon's approach as the singer describes it.

After an overview of Agamemnon's typical appeals, the poet provides Agamemnon's specific appeals to particular troops (4.251–400). This move from the general to the particular is a part of the singer's traditional structuring of his oral delivery.[41] At this moment in the singer's story, when the poet moves

---

[38] For the motif of promised future booty in other martial exhortations, cf. *Iliad* 1.127–129, 2.323–332, 350–356, 8.286–291, and 9.277–282.

[39] Ἀργεῖοι ἰόμωροι ἐλεγχέες οὔ νυ σέβεσθε; (4.242).

[40] ὄφρα ἴδῃτ' αἴ κ' ὕμμιν ὑπέρσχῃ χεῖρα Κρονίων; (4.249).

[41] It mirrors somewhat the structure of *Iliad* 2. There, Odysseus takes the scepter from Agamemnon and is first described in general terms. He strikes any man who is shouting and not obeying orders (2.198–199). To such a person, the poet relates, a speech was given, and the poet then furnishes the general import of what he said (200–206). Not long after in the same book (although the situation is now the *agorē*), we find an extended and specific account of Odysseus' carrying out this action. Yet, now the harangue is directed toward a specific individual, Thersites, who is crying aloud against Agamemnon (225–242). Odysseus then addresses the specific situation (246–264) in detail. The structural logic of this method of presentation by the poet, moving from the general to the specific, may be compared to other oral devices. For instance, the poet's logic in argumentation often presents us first with a general statement before he fills in the details of the premises with proof or analogy (e.g. *Iliad* 14.313–340); or in a character's use of stories

us towards the instances of specific appeals, Agamemnon's words will be directed principally toward the *basileis* leading their troops. In particular, the speeches focus on five leading individual hegemons or heroic pairs: Idomeneus, Aiantes, Nestor, Menestheus and Odysseus, and Diomedes and Sthenelos.[42] Agamemnon's address, when heard against a traditional background as it was by the poet's external audience, helps us to perceive and evaluate better the tenor of Agamemnon's appeal as it relates to individual heroes. This will become important for drawing conclusions from the words Agamemnon chooses and the types of appeals he employs. Equally important for our reading of characterization will be the way the poet himself references each hero descriptively in the narrative in which the *oratio recta* is embedded.[43]

2.2.1 Agamemnon's Appeal To Idomeneus: 4.251–272

Idomeneus is characterized by a traditional formula in the fourth colon. He is "like a boar in strength" (συΐ εἴκελος ἀλκήν, 4.253; cf. *Iliad* 13.471), a traditional heroic description otherwise applied in this form only to the greater Ajax (*Iliad* 17.281), but more widely in other formulaic phrases to heroes such as Diomedes (*Iliad* 5.783). It is indicative of excellent and resolute warrior valor. The tenor of Agamemnon's appeal to Idomeneus is further described as "honeyed" (προσηύδα μειλιχίοισιν), a pleasing formulaic phrase also used in Odysseus' conciliatory *rapprochement* of Ajax in the underworld (*Odyssey* 11.552). When considering Agamemnon's address within the warrior types found in the typical appeals,[44] it is clear that Idomeneus and his warriors represent the first group for Agamemnon. He sees them as eager for battle. Within this specific appeal, Agamemnon reminds Idomeneus of the "honor" (τιμή) in which he has been held in the past. His honor has been publicly recognized and validated within the warrior community by his being given a premier place by Agamemnon "both in war and in other work, / and in feasts" (ἠμὲν ἐνὶ πτολέμῳ ἠδ' ἀλλοίῳ ἐπὶ ἔργῳ / ἠδ' ἐν δαίθ', *Iliad* 4.258–259). At feasts, he is now reminded, if ever the

---

(parable or digression), where the poet first has an individual make a general point, before connecting the story to a concrete situation (e.g. *Iliad* 9.508–523).

[42] The very listing of leading *basileis* in battle scenes is itself common within the tradition. Cf. *Iliad* 7.164–167, 8.253–265, where our five individuals and pairs play a prominent role.

[43] Cf. Clay (1983:21–25) on the distinction between the narrator's speech inspired by the muse and the speech of his characters; and Taplin (1990:64) also appropriately distinguishes between a character's and an audience's view.

[44] Idomeneus is often mentioned (also counting by pairs where indexed in this way) among the first warriors: *Iliad* 1.46: second; 2.406: second; 6.436: second; 7.165: fourth; 8.78: first; 8.263: third; 17.258: second; 19.311: fourth.

Achaians drink their portion, still "your cup always stands full" (σὸν δὲ πλεῖον δέπας αἰεὶ ἕστηχ', 262–263). He can drink as his appetite urges.[45]

The excellent warrior valor of Idomeneus is portrayed equally in other parts of the *Iliad*. In *Iliad* 13.206–333, Poseidon recognizes this traditional character trait in him during his battle against Aineias. Idomeneus is described as a warrior who will take up his armor and encourage martial spirit in his fellow fighters. When Poseidon (in the likeness of Thoas) sees him, Idomeneus has just finished giving instructions to help a fallen comrade and is stopping by his own tent for armor. As the god observes our hero, the narrator characterizes Idomeneus as "yet eager to face battle" (ἔτι γὰρ πολέμοιο μενοίνα / ἀντιάαν, *Iliad* 13.214–215). Immediately after an exchange with Poseidon (*déguisé*), Idomeneus encounters his attendant Meriones, to whom he says that he doesn't "crave" sitting among the tents, but fighting.[46] Idomeneus faces no small task, considering his opponent. Yet, he stands his ground against Trojan Aineias, "as when some boar in the mountains, trusting in his own courage" (ὡς ὅτε τις σῦς οὔρεσιν ἀλκὶ πεποιθώς, *Iliad* 13.471)—so the simile begins. The simile, as Ready appropriately notes, centers upon Idomeneus and is less concerned with extending its metaphor directly to Idomeneus' opponent.[47] Further, I note that "trusting in his own courage" (ἀλκὶ πεποιθώς) is a traditional idiom used five times in Homer. It is employed in similes involving lions' or boars' great and resolute daring as a mirror for a hero's persona. It is used of Aineias (*Iliad* 5.299) as a lion, standing over the body of a fellow Trojan; of Menelaos (17.61) as a lion, during his *aristeia*; and of the Aiantes (17.728), when they turn on the Trojans as a wild boar against hunting dogs. "Trusting in his own courage" (ἀλκὶ πεποιθώς) is used of Hector (*Iliad* 18.158), who, as if a lion, keeps snatching at Patroklos' corpse; and of Odysseus (*Odyssey* 6.130), who emerges from the bushes as a lion, confident in his strength. The great and resolute daring of Idomeneus is unquestionable in the poet's mind. Further, the poet's choice of this traditional idiom and boar simile takes on greater emphasis in the local arrangement of his song lyrics. He has chosen to juxtapose a traditional language cue and simile with

---

[45] This motif too is a traditional element in exhortation to greater action by a leading commander. Cf. Menelaos' exhortation in *Iliad* 17.248–251.

[46] οὐδέ τοι αὐτὸς / ἧσθαι ἐνὶ κλισίῃσι λιλαίομαι, ἀλλὰ μάχεσθαι, *Iliad* 13.252–253.

[47] Ready (2011:246) further cautions against reading the hunters and dogs (*Iliad* 13.475) in this simile as referring to Aineias, since, unlike in other similes where such an emphasis is intended, Homer uses the plural. I am not so sure about this point, since often a singular animal can be used to replace a plural group of heroes in the main comparison, as in *Iliad* 17.728, *supra*.

yet another simile, where Idomeneus is further characterized by negation.[48] He is not full of fear "as some boy just come to manhood" (τηλύγετον ὥς, 13.470) would be.[49]

Idomeneus' appearance here and at every point in the *Iliad* indicates that he is a warrior who gets quickly to the task at hand and does not give in under the pressure of battle. Only in two cases, as we noted earlier, does Idomeneus retreat. These departures from his normal response form part of the poet's intentional plan within the larger story pattern that will see Achilles return to the field.[50] Idomeneus, then, is known to be a man of action and great valor. The poet describes Agamemnon's response to Idomeneus with a traditional formula, "glad in heart" (γηθόσυνος κῆρ, 4.272), in the adonean clausula, which marks approval in the observer.[51] This formulaic phrase occurs not only in military scenes (so with Nestor, in *Iliad* 4.326), but also in peacetime activities, where proactive rural viticultural work elicits from the poet the same formulaic depiction of the affirming royal response (*Iliad* 18.557).[52] The image we have of Idomeneus as a character in *Iliad* 4, then, is consonant with the picture of this stalwart warrior in his wider portrayal throughout the *Iliad* poet's song. Both Agamemnon and the poet-narrator assume and make reference to Idomeneus' traditional character.

---

[48] Cf. the comments of Scott 2009:141. Lord (1953:132–133) and Ready (2015:4) suggest that the piling up of similes is a likely result of the slowed process of dictation of the Homeric poems.

[49] The sense of being at the cusp of adulthood is seen most clearly in *Odyssey* 16.19, with reference to Odysseus. But compare Helen's remorse in *Iliad* 3.173–175 over leaving her daughter at the very moment she was coming of age. The use in Homer seems to be this (and perhaps connected with τέλος) rather than referring to an "only" child, since in *Iliad* 5.153, Phainops has two such sons. The A scholiast (Erbse 1969–1988:3.494) suggests that τηλύγετος ὁ τηλοῦ τῆς ἡλικίας γεγονὼς τοῖς γονεῦσι, μεθ' ὃν οὐκ ἄν τις γένοιτο. See the discussion in *LfgrE* 22:467–469, s.v. τηλύγετος (Nordheider).

[50] Cf. n. 9 in this chapter.

[51] Alternatively, γήθησεν ἰδών occurs three times in the *Iliad* (4.283, 4.311, 10.190) and twice in the *Odyssey* (13.226, 22.207), and provides an apposite equivalent form to cover the second to third cola (A2–C1). Further, that this formulaic phrase is part of a larger formulaic system, often involving a participle and κῆρ (in our phrase, the adjective "glad" [γηθόσυνος] fills the place usually held by a participle), is clear from *Iliad* 1.44 "angered in heart" (χωόμενος κῆρ), 7.428 "grieving in heart" (ἀχνύμενοι κῆρ), and 15.10 "foolish in heart" (κῆρ ἀπινύσσων). See also *Iliad* 7.431, 9.555, 19.57, 23.37, 165, 284, 443, 24.773; *Odyssey* 10.67, 12.153, 250, 270, 373, 22.188, 24.420; other expressions provide a description of an emotional state in the adonean clausula when a finite verb is needed (e.g. *Iliad* 11.274, 400: ἤχθετο γὰρ κῆρ).

[52] *Iliad* 18.555–558: τρεῖς δ' ἄρ' ἀμαλλοδετῆρες ἐφέστασαν· αὐτὰρ ὄπισθε / παῖδες δραγμεύοντες ἐν ἀγκαλίδεσσι φέροντες / ἀσπερχὲς πάρεχον· βασιλεὺς δ' ἐν τοῖσι σιωπῇ / σκῆπτρον ἔχων ἑστήκει ἐπ' ὄγμου γηθόσυνος κῆρ.

2.2.2 Aiantes: 4.273–292

The next appeal of Agamemnon is directed toward the two Aiantes, the greater and the lesser. They are addressed, as is often the case in the *Iliad*, as a pair.[53] The two are armed and have a throng of foot soldiers eager for battle following them. The troops are "bristling with spears and shields" (σάκεσίν τε καὶ ἔγχεσι πεφρικυῖαι, 4.282). Agamemnon says that he would urge them on, except that it is not appropriate for him to do so (οὔ τι κελεύω, *Iliad* 4.286). Agamemnon states that if a desire for war like theirs came into the hearts of all the Achaians, Troy would fall and be sacked (291). The assumption would then be that war prizes would be distributed to the victorious.[54] As with Idomeneus, Agamemnon's pleasure at the Aiantes' eagerness is indicated by a formula of joy at what he has seen: "having seen, he was glad" (γήθησεν ἰδών, 283). The traditional idiom suggests that Agamemnon thinks that the Aiantes are supporting "his authority and safety" (Kelly 2007a:270). The emphasis in this scene is on the completely martial character of these foremost heroes.[55]

There are a couple of moments (as with Idomeneus) in Homer's tradition as we have it, however, when these heroes act somewhat less heroically. The first instance occurs when there is need within the poet's story rendition for retreat to provide a causal reason for the sending of an embassy to Achilles (*Iliad* 8.78–79); and again to furnish an impetus for Achilles to send in Patroklos to assist the weary and wounded Achaians (*Iliad* 16.122–129). In all other instances of the Aiantes' appearances in the *Iliad*, they are completely and unquestionably eager and ready fighters whenever their talent is needed. This truism applies to instances of the heroes as individual warriors or together. The eventual help of the lesser Ajax (*Iliad* 17.730–734), expected in the tradition surrounding this pair, will, for example, help stave off the Trojans from Patroklos at the last moment. Yet, it will be Telemonian Ajax, as the greater member of the heroic pair (*Iliad* 2.527–529; 12.349–350, 378)[56] and second only to Achilles in martial

---

[53] For the warriors together, see *Iliad* 5.519–527, 6.435–439, 7.161–169, 8.253–262, 10.227–228, 12.333–412, 13.43–80, 126, 197–205, 701–708, 16.555–561, etc. For Telamonian Ajax, see *Iliad* 1.141–145, 2.768–769, 3.225–229, 4.473–489, 5.610–625, 7.169–322, 8.220–226, 329–334, 10.172–176, 11.5–9, 11.464–594, 14.409–420, 17.102–124, 166–168, 304–365, etc. The lesser Ajax is not usually referenced alone. See Polinskaya (2011) for a balanced summary of his place in Homer. Further, Ebbott (2003:41–43) suggests that Homer may have retained an older meaning for the second member of this dual, in the person of Teucer as a *nothos* to the greater Ajax.

[54] Cf. n. 38 on the motif of promised future booty.

[55] Traill (1990) sees heroes like Ajax (but also Agamemnon and Diomedes) as foremost heroes, but suggests that Homer, because of his "nationalism," does not permit such a picture of Hector.

[56] Cf. my earlier comments (s.v. 2.1.1 Character Consistency) about heroic pairs, but also Ebbott's (2003:39–40) argument for the theme of "dominant" versus "recessive" brothers in relation to the Ajax's shield.

strength (*Iliad* 2.768-769; cf. Nagy 1979:32), who will make possible the return of the body of the fallen Patroklos (*Iliad* 17.125-734). By this act he is characterized as superior to both Idomeneus and Diomedes. The epithet "huge" (μέγας) is often attached to this "big and burly" hero to fill out the second hemistich of the line,[57] and is seldom seen with other figures (Camps 1980:23). Even more exclusive to the greater Ajax is the epithet "bastion of the Achaians" (ἕρκος Ἀχαιῶν, *Iliad* 3.229, 6.5, and 7.211). Further, a traditional (and identically recurring) block of material conjoins Achilles and Ajax as warriors of foremost prowess.[58]

While Agamemnon's address to the Aiantes in *Iliad* 4 is short, it nevertheless conforms to the character of this pair in the tradition we find in the rest of the *Iliad* singer's song. The very brevity of the exchange between Agamemnon and Ajax itself assumes the tradition of the greater Ajax as more a man of deeds than many words. It will be the authoritative nod of the generally curt Ajax, after all, that will provide the impetus to begin the speeches of the embassy to Achilles (*Iliad* 9.223).[59] In the speeches of the embassy, when through ring composition the poet returns us third to Ajax after the speeches of Odysseus (9.225-306) and Phoinix (9.434-605), we are given only a characteristically short and brief supplication.[60] It is tacked onto a warrior's honest estimation of the hopelessness of the present effort to persuade Achilles to return to aid his comrades (9.624-642). This is most appropriate for a man whose martial prowess is matched by a corresponding terseness of speech.

2.2.3 Nestor: 4.293-326

Following his brief address to the Aiantes, Agamemnon comes next upon Nestor. The poet provides an elaborate description of Nestor's activities immediately before Agamemnon addresses him. In the poetic presentation, a number of traditional referents serve to characterize Nestor in ways consonant with

---

[57] *Iliad* 5.610, 12.364, 13.321, 14.409, 15.471, 560, 17.628, 715, 23.708, 722, 811, and 842.

[58] *Iliad* 8.222-26=11.5-9: στῆ δ' ἐπ' Ὀδυσσῆος μεγακήτεϊ νηῒ μελαίνῃ, / ἥ ῥ' ἐν μεσσάτῳ ἔσκε γεγωνέμεν ἀμφοτέρωσε, / ἠμὲν ἐπ' Αἴαντος κλισίας Τελαμωνιάδαο / ἠδ' ἐπ' Ἀχιλλῆος, τοί ῥ' ἔσχατα νῆας ἐΐσας / εἴρυσαν, ἠνορέῃ πίσυνοι καὶ κάρτεϊ χειρῶν·

[59] This does not deny the rhetorical power of what Ajax does eventually say (albeit to Odysseus and his other colleagues, but in earshot of Achilles), a point made by Rees 2002:24-25 and Dentice Di Accadia 2012:199.

[60] I use ring (or chiastic) composition throughout to refer both of the structure and the content (i.e. themes) of passages. In the present example we see the poetic chiasm in Ajax's (A) nod to Phoinix (B), then Phoinix's to Oydsseus (C), in *Iliad* 9.223; and there follows by three speeches in reverse order: (C) Odysseus' (225-305), (B) Phoenix's (434-605), and, lastly, (A) Ajax's (624-642). On defining ring structure, see Whitman 1958:87, Lohmann 1970:12-13, Lowenstam 1983:12, Stanley 1993:6-26, 307n21, and Dunkle 1997:233; for a comparative approach, see especially Douglas 2007; for other approaches to ring structure (differing or more restrictive than my use of the term here), see Minchin 2011b.

his representation in the rest of the tradition available to us, both synchronically and diachronically. Nestor's characterization both in the fifty-two days of the *Iliad* poet's immediate timeline, but also in his multigenerational actions presented through retrospective story, provides us with a richly cohesive portrait.

In the present scene, Nestor is first described by an epithet that serves well to establish his traditional trait as the "clear-voiced speaker of the Pylians" (λιγὺν Πυλίων ἀγορητήν, 1.248), an epithet spoken, notably, by the poet as narrator (Dentice Di Accadia 2012:17).[61] Indeed, his many appearances in Homer show that he is "un abile oratore" and is so without exception (Dentice Di Accadia 2012:17).[62] While Plato may be right to make Odysseus the stronger speaker,[63] Lardinois's finding, that Nestor "embodies the most esteemed manner of speaking in the epic," hits the right note (Lardinois 2000:648).[64] Nestor stands to speak sensible counsel after Achilles throws the scepter to the ground (*Iliad* 1.245–284); appropriately, a council is held by his ship (*Iliad* 2.53–54); Nestor exhorts Agamemnon to accept advice and is praised for it (*Iliad* 2.336–394); and Nestor scolds the *basileis* and instills a need for action (*Iliad* 7.23–160). Even in the lying dream sent to Agamemnon, Nestor's character is the guise chosen by the *Oneiros*, whose advice, false though it is (*Iliad* 2.16–34), is received and believed by Agamemnon. It appears as though the tradition holds Nestor in great admiration, so much so that not only is the prayer given him by the poet in *Iliad* 15 received favorably by Zeus (70–373)—something not always the case by any means in Homer—but his call to battle is characterized positively, including a description of divine approbation for his martial exhortation (659–670).[65]

Nestor's actions show him to be an exemplary character. An extended description (*Iliad* 4.294–310; cf. *Iliad* 2.360–368) by the poet-narrator draws the

---

[61] The epithet is traditional, and it no doubt represents a long-used formula kept close to Nestor for obvious reasons (cf. the argument for character-appropriate epithets that we considered in Chapter 1).

[62] Dentice Di Accadia (2012:204–216) further argues against scholarly nay-sayers, for the "successo oratorio" of "un abile oratore." Minchin (1991:273) notes that the *Iliad* shows awareness of Nestor's skill in words in three ways: through testimony of the poet or Nestor's peers; the reaction and response of his companions to his advice; and the gifts he has been offered in recognition of his services as counselor and strategist. Martin (1989:23–24) calls Nestor "the veteran performer and orator."

[63] Plato (*Phaedrus* 261c.) even has Nestor collaborating with Odysseus to produce a treatise on rhetoric. The oratorical skills of the pair became proverbial (e.g. Cicero *Brutus* 40; Quintilian *Institutio* 12.10.64), however Nestor is described as less powerful in his eloquence.

[64] Lardinois also finds in his study that, in contrast to some other Iliadic characters (like Achilles), most of Nestor's *gnomai* are second-person sayings, which, he argues, creates a more authoritative style of speaking.

[65] Reyes (2002:25) suggests that Nestor's appeals are made on the basis of honor, central to Homeric society.

listeners' attention to the sagacious and balanced preparation that informs Nestor's leadership style. Nestor is portrayed as a wise strategist here and throughout the tradition. Barker notes his ability to "manage dissent" (Barker 2009:63), a trait almost missing in Agamemnon, as we will see in Chapter 4. After the poet has outlined the superlative martial ability of Menestheus (2.546–554), the Catalogue of Ships stipulates that no one could challenge him in his strategic ability except "Nestor alone" (Νέστωρ οἶος, 2.555). Nestor was older (προγενέστερος ἦεν, 2.555) and wiser. Nestor's organizational ability is demonstrated by the thoughtful arrangement of his troops (4.297–300). He places "horses at the front with horsemen and chariots" (ἱππῆας μὲν πρῶτα σὺν ἵπποισιν καὶ ὄχεσφι), behind these the infantry "many and noble" (πολέας τε καὶ ἐσθλούς), and finally "in the midst, he drove the cowardly" (κακοὺς δ' ἐς μέσσον ἔλασσεν). They must each fight, even if unwilling to do so (καὶ οὐκ ἐθέλων τις). Nestor gives advice to the charioteers to keep control of their horses and not get caught in the thick of the foot soldiers (4.301–302). He suggests a *via media* between overly zealous and overly cautious individualism (μηδέ ... οἶος, 303–304), extremes that weaken the common effort (ἀλαπαδνότεροι γὰρ ἔσεσθαι, 4.305). His advice affirms the observations of Roisman that Nestor's central task was "to foster and preserve the solidarity of the community" (Roisman 2005:36).[66]

In his advice to charioteers on just how to fight, we find expansion through "historical" vignette, doubtless from Nestor's own experience in bygone days: "Just so did earlier warriors sack cities and strongholds, / such a purpose and spirit did they hold in their hearts" (ὧδε καὶ οἱ πρότεροι πόλεας καὶ τείχε' ἐπόρθεον / τόνδε νόον καὶ θυμὸν ἐνὶ στήθεσσιν ἔχοντες, 4.308–309). It is appropriate in the foregoing passage that the poet has "clear-voiced" Nestor's last words return through ring composition to his own introduction to the passage, by the use of "holding" (ἔχοντες), which aurally recalls "to hold" (ἐχέμεν, 302). More significantly for our purposes, however, is the realization that the whole vignette, invoking the earlier "glory days," echoes the depth of the traditional character of Nestor.

Next, the narrator joins in affirming Nestor's ability, describing him as "knowing well wars of old" (πάλαι πολέμων εὖ εἰδώς, 4.310). Agamemnon acknowledges, however, that age has weakened Nestor's knees, though he would wish for him a physical strength to match his spirit (313). The comments of

---

[66] Roisman mediates between the poet's high regard for Nestor and some modern scholars' reservations about his military ability (Kirk 1985:360–361, Postlethwaite 2000:82) by arguing that Nestor's sagaciousness and balance are found in his sustaining the values of the community, rather than in the actual tactics he employs. One has to be careful, however, to remember that the *aoidoi* and their tradition may not have been experts in military matters. To the *Iliad* poet and his audience, he and his abilities appear to be held in high regard.

Agamemnon trigger a passionate reflection from the aged hero. We hear about Ereuthalion, killed by a younger Nestor in a past generation. Nestor is relating his individual heroic history, a habit typical of older heroes.[67] His story is also embedded with specific details of Nestor's life experiences within the diachrony of the singer's tradition. Yet, we are given fewer specifics here than we might wish, at least as a non-traditional audience. Homer is assuming background knowledge in his core audience of the sort described in Chapter 1. It is not until later in the *Iliad* (7.136–160) that the circumstances of Nestor's battle with his opponent are described in greater detail. Nestor will say that he was given cause for a victor's boast after "I killed the strongest man" (κάρτιστον κτάναν ἄνδρα, 7.155). In both *Iliad* 4 and 7, a wish to return to a state of youthfulness signals the invocation of the *exemplum* that follows.[68] The reference to Nestor's *aristeia* affirms the close connection between characterization and action in oral-derived literature that we considered earlier. This dependence of characterization upon narrated heroic feat further supports the central importance of tradition in keeping alive each character's history for future audiences.

After his illustration of former prowess in book 4, Nestor assures the son of Atreus that he will continue in the present time to fulfill the role his age and experience demand, and so he commands the charioteers with counsel and "authoritative orders" (μύθοισι, 4.323).[69] We see, then, that the exchange between Nestor and Agamemnon and the description of the poet-narrator refer to a well-respected and well-represented sagacious hero with adhering heroic feats from a former generation. The actions of Nestor and his men invoke a double use of the formulaic pleasure of Agamemnon (γήθησεν ἰδών, 311; γηθόσυνος κῆρ, 326).[70] The scene is replete with tradition-dependent characterization for the singer and his core audience.

2.2.4 Menestheus and Odysseus: 4.327–364

In the brief exchange we find here, little can be said about Menestheus son of Peteos and leader of the Athenians, since we do not find great depth for his

---

[67] Cf. Phoinix in *Iliad* 9.447–484 and Laertes in *Odyssey* 24.376–382. Nestor has lived through three generations, according to the poet in *Iliad* 1.250–252 (see Frazer 1971, for the translation of time in this verse).

[68] 4.321: εἰ τότε κοῦρος ἔα; 7.132–133: αἶ … ἡβῷμ', with ring closure at 7.157, εἴθ' ὡς ἡβώοιμι.

[69] On the use of μῦθος in Homer as an authoritative speech act, see Martin 1989:22–26. Martin (22) notes in his contrast between *muthos* and *epos* that "*muthos* implies authority" in the *Iliad* that "is largely about situations in which power is in dispute, up for grabs." Martin's argument uses comparisons with disputes of Cretan mountain villagers (studied by Herzfeld 1985a, 1985b).

[70] See the earlier discussion of these traditional formulae in this chapter, s.v. 2.2.1 Agamemnon's Appeal to Idomeneus: 4.251–272.

character in Homer's present song. Instead, the spotlight is conspicuously (but not exclusively) on the superior Odysseus.[71] Odysseus himself is immediately named by the poet-narrator using the familiar and virtually exclusive epithet "of many strategies" (πολύμητις, 4.329) and his attachment to the Kephallenian force.[72] Both heroes are unmistakably treated by Agamemnon as part of those hanging back and deserving of chastisement. Odysseus is addressed second by Agamemnon. Yet, so traditional is his connection with "ruse" (δόλος) that he is not even invoked by name when Agamemnon scurrilously intones: "And you [sg., i.e., Odysseus], excelling in evil ruses, with a heart set on gain, / why do you [pl., i.e., Odysseus and Menestheus], cowering, stand aloof, and await others?" (καὶ σὺ κακοῖσι δόλοισι κεκασμένε κερδαλεόφρον / τίπτε καταπτώσσοντες ἀφέστατε, μίμνετε δ' ἄλλους, *Iliad* 4.339–340). Agamemnon, interestingly, chooses the singular nameless address for Odysseus alone before moving to the plural (to include Menestheus). There is no question but that he is glaring at him. In not naming Odysseus, Homer may be mimicking one theme in the story pattern of the *Odyssey*.[73] This instance of temporary namelessness would assume audience knowledge of Odysseus' nearly nameless existence during the narrative of his *nostos*.[74] Further, what are we to make of Agamemnon's degrading tone and negative portrayal of Odysseus' character qualities? More to the point, what does the tradition make of it?

The "ruse" (δόλος) of Odysseus is especially well known from the *Odyssey* poet's presentation, so we will begin there first. Nestor proffers his positive

---

[71] The tradition we have in Homer is consistent in making Menestheus a lesser heroic character. Cf. *Iliad* 12.330–334.

[72] πολύμητις ᾽Οδυσσεύς (occurring in the adonean clausula): *Iliad* 1.131, 440, 3.200, 4.349, 10.148, 382, 400, 423, 488, 554, 14.82, 19.154, 215; *Odyssey* 2.173, 5.214, 7.207, 240, 7.302, 8.152, 165, 412, 463, 474, 486, 9.1, 11.354, 377, 13.311, 416, 14.191, 390, 439, 15.380, 16.201, 17.16, 192, 353, 453, 18.14, 51, 124, 312, 337, 365, 19.41, 70, 106, 164, 220, 261, 335, 382, 499, 554, 582, 20.36, 168, 183, 226, 21.274, 21.404, 22.1, 22.34, 60, 105, 170, 320, 371, 390, 430, 490, 23.129, 247, 263, 24.302, 330, 356, 406. A variant of this epithet, ᾽Οδυσεὺς πολύμητις, occurs in the first hemistich in *Iliad* 3.268, 23.709, and 755. A singular occurrence of πολύμητις in the genitive with Hephaistos (*Iliad* 21.355) is anomalous. For other epithets, see n. 34.

[73] If one assumes resonance between the *Odyssey* and *Iliad* as suggested in Chapter 1.

[74] Cf. Danek (1998:33), who suggests that the *Odyssey* poet tells Homer's audience "eine bekannte Geschichte," one, as I have argued in Chapter 1, known to the audience of the *Iliad*. On Odysseus' namelessness in the *Odyssey*, see further Fenik 1974:5–60 (who begins with Nausikaa's query), Clay 1983:27–30, and Peradotto 1994:94–119. Austin's (1972:15) comments amount essentially to the referential significance of Odysseus' namelessness, since he suggests that it carries "an irony larger than the immediate moment" that is "echoing through the poem." Odysseus' namelessness has been taken as concealing trickery (see Segal 1983:28) or "subversive" (Van Nortwick 2010:45–64). While Odysseus was certainly capable of trickery and a trickster figure in Homer's tradition, as I argue above, the *Odyssey* (like the *Iliad*) is generally not negative about Odysseus' relation to "ruse" (δόλος).

reflections of Odysseus to Telemachos as one far superior to others "in all ruses" (παντοίοισι δόλοισι, *Odyssey* 3.122). To the Phaiacians, Odysseus reveals himself by proclaiming: "I am Odysseus, son of Laertes, who, because of my ruses / am a concern to all people" (εἴμ' Ὀδυσεὺς Λαερτιάδης, ὃς πᾶσι δόλοισιν / ἀνθρώποισι μέλω, 9.19). Back on Ithaca, Athena offers an admiring summary, which is intentionally enclosed in an ironic future less vivid construction. We as the audience know what has not been overtly revealed, that in fact Odysseus is trying to fool a divinity. Athena admiringly comments: "Shrewd he would be and wily, who would leave you behind / in all [your] ruses, even if a god should encounter you" (κερδαλέος κ' εἴη καὶ ἐπίκλοπος, ὅς σε παρέλθοι / ἐν πάντεσσι δόλοισι, καὶ εἰ θεὸς ἀντιάσειε, *Odyssey* 13.291–292). Beyond the fore-going examples, Odysseus' connection with "ruse" (δόλος) is clear from other scenes in the *Odyssey*, including Odysseus' actions in helping to take Troy as described by Nestor (3.118–123). The wooden horse is described as a "ruse" (δόλος) that Odysseus leads (8.492–520).[75] "Ruse" (δόλος) is further used to characterize Odysseus, who, with a cunning strategy in mind, replies to the mean-hearted proposal of Antinoos (18.36–57); and also of Odysseus' thoughts when he is attempting to acquire the bow from the suitors (21.273–284) for the purpose of restoring his *oikos* to an ordered state. In all, Odysseus' "ruse" (δόλος) is generally communitarian and preserving in its focus and inspires "admira-tion" (Marquart 1992:252n15).[76] Penelope, Odysseus' wife, is positively associ-ated with "ruse" (δόλος), too, as de Jong and Zerba have shown.[77]

As we would expect, the "ruse" (δόλος) tradition is also connected with Odysseus in the *Iliad*. Again, however, it is employed in a more complimen-tary way by others than it is by Agamemnon. Helen uses the word to describe Odysseus in the *Teichoskopia* (3.200–204), and her description meets with affir-mation by Priam (nor is there anything derogatory in anyone's tone). The word is also invoked by the poet-narrator of Odysseus in the funeral games for Patroklos (23.725–737). As he displays his wrestling ability, the spectators look

---

[75] See Danek 1998:161–162, on possible background stories.

[76] Marquardt (1992:252n15) contrasts the δόλος of Odysseus in the *Odyssey* with that of Aigisthos: "Both Odysseus and Aigisthos are undeniably clever, but πολύμητις Odysseus (e.g. 13.311, 5.214) is held up for our admiration because he is cunning to maintain his marriage bond and his loyal household, while δολόμητις Aigisthos (1.300, 3.198) is presented as a villain for his successful assault on the sanctity of a marriage bond and the stability of an οἶκος." We will consider the tradition-based implications of δολόμητις in Chapter 3. See also Gasti (1992), who contrasts the communitarian values of Odysseus against those of Ajax. Thus, while Homer doubtless has "trickster" traditions in mind (Russo 1992:68–70), the trickster Odysseus acts for the benefit of the community. Such, too, was the case with Tale in the South Slavic example we considered earlier.

[77] See for example de Jong (2001:50–51) and Zerba (2009:305–306) on *Odyssey* 2.89–110, 19.137–140, and 24.125–129, and the δόλος of the loom.

on in "wonder." There are no examples of a negative association of this word root in the *Odyssey* or *Iliad* with Odysseus, outside of this disparaging remark by Agamemnon.[78]

In contrast, Agamemnon's unflattering use of "ruse" (δόλος, *Iliad* 4.339) for Odysseus, may suggest the less than adroit nature of Agamemnon's rebuke (of which I will say more). Yet, as insulting as it is, Agamemnon's address—"you [i.e., Odysseus], excelling in evil ruses, with a heart set on gain" (σὺ κακοῖσι δόλοισι κεκασμένε κερδαλεόφρον, *Iliad* 4.339)—contains several of the same significant descriptive elements that Athena uses in the *Odyssey*. These include not only ability in the employment of "ruses" (δόλοι), but also (for anyone wanting to best Odysseus) an exceptionally "shrewd" (κερδαλέος) disposition,[79] a character trait that Agamemnon uniquely turns for the worst against Odysseus, as we have seen. It is important to note that while the epithet "with a heart set on gain" (κερδαλεόφρων) could be used in the offensive manner Agamemnon induces (cf. *Iliad* 1.149 and the retort by Achilles against Agamemnon), more often "gain" (κέρδος) is in reality something that warriors seek to possess to achieve the best advantage in a particular situation. In *Iliad* 10.44, Agamemnon says that he and Menelaos have need of gainful [counsel] (κερδαλέη [βουλή]); in *Iliad* 10.224–225, Diomedes suggests that two warriors working together can better recognize "gain" (κέρδος); in *Iliad* 13.458, Deïphobos considers "what is more gainful" (κέρδιον) and decides to fetch Aineias; and in *Iliad* 14.23, Nestor considers "what is more gainful" (κέρδιον) and decides to search for Agamemnon. These instances are representative of the far more numerous examples of the many positive associations for this word in Homer.

---

[78] Stanford (1968:13) outlines the descent of Odysseus in later literature and correctly, I think, notes that this picture is not what we see in Homer. Stanford's view of Homer's Odysseus is substantiated by the picture of Odysseus' character traits outlined by De Jong 2001:134. We must resist a simple caricature of Odysseus based on later, baser portraits of this well-spoken hero, created after the advent of formal rhetoric. Odysseus became a vehicle for caricature, especially of seductively unethical and amoral *logoi* (cf. Odysseus as a figure in later philosophy, in Montiglio 2011). Of course, this is not to deny that the Homeric Odysseus could represent a more civically minded Odysseus than might have been the case in the past before the performance tradition of our *Iliad* and *Odyssey* (Clay 1983:70). Danek (1998:161) seems to imply as much, by suggesting "anderer (früherer, alternativer) Versionen der Geschichte." I am hesitant to use his strong tone for an oral culture, however, or to agree that somehow Homer is correcting (korrigieren) and replacing (ersetzen) other versions (cf. the discussion of "variant" versus "multiformity" in Dué 2002:21, and her reference to Lord 1960:120, Lord 1995:23, and Nagy 1996a). Danek's emphasis on the competitive nature of the Homeric performance arena, however, is important (cf. our consideration of Murko and Plato's *Ion* in Chapter 1).

[79] Used positively, this would highlight Odysseus' ability in the same area. Related to Odysseus' δόλος is his ability to endure (πολύτλας δῖος Ὀδυσσεύς / ὁ τλήμων Ὀδυσσεύς) with others for the sake of a mission, on which see Dué and Ebott (2010:289, 75–76) and the *lochos* theme.

Odysseus replies to Agamemnon's scornful valuation and rebuke in an unhappy tone, "looking at him darkly" (τὸν δ' ἄρ' ὑπόδρα ἰδών, *Iliad* 4.349), a formula that Holoka has shown highlights a significant breach in social conventions.[80] I note, moreover, beyond Holoka's findings, that this formula (consistently appearing in the first hemistich) is always followed by a formulaic phrase of address in the second hemistich and a rebuke soon after.[81] In the present case, Odysseus asks Agamemnon the traditional question, "What sort of word has fled the barrier of your teeth?" (ποῖόν σε ἔπος φύγεν ἕρκος ὀδόντων, *Iliad* 4.350). This added traditional idiom occurs eight times in total in Homer and carries recognizable meaning.[82] Certainly, as Erasmus noted, the phrase suggests that *loquendi temeritas* should be avoided (Wolfe 2015:66). Further, this formula means more than the sum of its parts in what it implicates. As Foley has shown, in every case the formula acts as a "rhetorical fulcrum" employed "by an older or more experienced figure chiding a younger or less experienced speaker for the rashness of his or her remarks" (Foley 1999:226–227). He suggests the idiomatic English equivalent: "You should know better!" Foley's choice of expression is a dynamic equivalent in translational terms, idiom for idiom, not word for word, since, if taken apart, the English saying becomes illogical and loses its sense. A young person really should *not* know better. The idiom, however, is employed in circumstances that mean, to suggest another English expression: "I expected better things from you!" Indeed, Agamemnon should have known better, and both Odysseus and the troops expected better things from their paramount *basileus*.

Further, in the ensuing remonstration, Odysseus invokes his own son within a vivid and emotional challenge to Agamemnon's misrepresentation of his character:

> You will see,[83] if you wish, and if these matters are a concern to you,
> The dear father of Telemachos mixing with the foremost fighters
> of the horse-taming Trojans. You, however, babble uselessly!

---

[80] Holoka (1983:4, 7) further suggests its utility as part of a response to encourage propriety. Holoka (3n6) mentions instances of the formula's appearance beyond Homer and finds its usage consistent with its epic appearances.

[81] *Iliad* 1.148, 2.245, 4.349, 4.411, 5.251, 5.888, 10.446, 12.230, 14.82, 15.13, 17.141, 17.169, 18.284, 20.428, 22.260, 22.344, 24.559; *Odyssey* 8.165, 17.459, 18.14, 18.337, 18.388, 19.70, 22.34, 22.60, and 22.320.

[82] Cf. *Iliad* 4.350, 14.83, *Odyssey* 1.64, 3.230, 5.22, 19.492, 21.168, and 23.70.

[83] The vividness of Odysseus' challenge is achieved through a future indicative in the apodosis. Monro (1893:298) denies the use of the future in the apodosis to suggest any imperatival sense, yet a light imperatival emphasis is clearly intended here. Goodwin (1897:165) observes that a future can act "as an emphatic form," something "especially common when the condition contains a strong appeal to the feelings"; and Wilmott (2007:87) observes that the future indicative can have a "deontic" force.

ὄψεαι αἴ κ' ἐθέλησθα καὶ αἴ κέν τοι τὰ μεμήλῃ
Τηλεμάχοιο φίλον πατέρα προμάχοισι μιγέντα
Τρώων ἱπποδάμων· σὺ δὲ ταῦτ' ἀνεμώλια βάζεις.

Iliad 4.353–355

The reference to Telemachos is a metonymic "tag" for the singer and audience as they navigate the web of tradition that adheres to Odysseus.[84] In this instance, the metonym may bring to mind Odysseus' *nostos* to Ithaca, including both his struggle to return and the consequent action to restore order (told in some form by epic singers before our present version of the *Odyssey*, as we noted in Chapter 1). After all, when Odysseus left Ithaca, Telemachos was but a child. It is unlikely that this metonym was meant for a child, one who had not yet experienced the stuff of adult life and whose central part in myth only begins with the sorts of events we find described in the *Telemachy*. Nor are children a central narrative concern for ancient writers (Heath 2001:132 and Golden 2003).

Other metonyms, such as the patronymic "son of Laertes" (Λαερτιάδης) and the epithet "of many devices" (πολυμήχανος), play a similar role in the tradition. These are irrevocably attached to Odysseus' *nostos* and Ithaca. These two epithets are often found together as they are in the ensuing words of Agamemnon when he addresses Odysseus for a second time (*Iliad* 4.358) as "Zeus-born son of Laertes, Odysseus of many devices" (διογενὲς Λαερτιάδη πολυμήχαν' Ὀδυσσεῦ). The adjective "of many devices" (πολυμήχανος) is in fact almost always part of a vocative construction that references Odysseus as Laertes' son.[85] The singular exception occurs when Athena encourages Telemachos by suggesting Odysseus' present thoughts, even though he is yet absent: "Consider how he will arrive, since he is much-devising" (φράσσεται ὥς κε νέηται, ἐπεὶ πολυμήχανός ἐστιν, *Odyssey* 1.205).[86] This singular occurrence of the epithet "of many devices"

---

[84] There is a lack of evidence in Homer to state categorically whether or not Τηλεμάχοιο φίλον πατέρα is a traditional epithet, although the bridged A colon and the logical necessity of taking φίλον πατέρα together lend weight to the suggestion. Further, προμάχοισι μιγέντα does occur again in *Odyssey* 18.379, modifying an accusative. The finite equivalent for a nominative subject, προμάχοισιν ἐμίχθη, is also well represented (*Iliad* 5.134, 8.99, 13.642, and 15.457) in the same metrical position, which suggests at any rate the need to divide the cola at C1. For my assumptions about Homeric colometrics, see Appendix A.

[85] In all the occurrences of these epithets, I observe the following axiom: while the patronymic is found without the epithet πολυμήχανος, the epithet πολυμήχανος is never found without this patronymic. Odysseus is named in Homer with his patronymic in *Iliad* 2.173, 3.200, 4.358, 8.93, 9.308, 9.624, 10.144, 19.185, 23.723; *Odyssey* 5.203, 9.19, 10.401, 10.456, 10.488, 10.504, 11.60, 11.92, 11.405, 11.473, 11.617, 13.375, 14.486, 16.167, 16.455, 17.361, 22.164, and 24.542.

[86] The epithet is used only once of another character (and in its feminine form predicatively), by Odysseus of Kirke in *Odyssey* 23.321. In this way, it is like πολύμητις, which is only used otherwise of Hephaistos by the poet, as we noted earlier (n. 72).

(πολυμήχανος) as a predicate adjective indicates the strength of its attachment to Odysseus. It suggests a traditional character quality, one well apprehensible to both singer and audience.[87] It also suggests, as we reviewed in Chapter 1, that such epithets were heard by Homer's audience in a local narrative context.

The resolute nature of Odysseus as a loyal leader is shown in the action of *Iliad* 11, when key leaders, wounded, have been forced to leave the field, "but spear-famed Odysseus was left alone" (οἰώθη δ' Ὀδυσεὺς δουρὶ κλυτός, 11.401). He is inspired by a wish to use his faculties to assist his companions and to avoid being a coward. Odysseus stands his ground after self-debate with his *thumos*, since he does not wish to be counted among the cowards (n.b. the κακοί of *Iliad* 11.408). In Sullivan's explanation of the meaning of this scene in relation to the *thumos*, Odysseus is "recalling the way in which brave men act," but "he already knows that a brave man must stand" (Sullivan 1984:84). Further, Odysseus' character at this point is described by an opponent, Sokos, as "much praised" (πολύαινε, *Iliad* 11.430), precisely *because* of his "ruse" (δόλος) and "toil" (πόνος). Even Odysseus' enemy saw his characteristic δόλος ("ruse") in terms that suggested positive, rather than malevolent, martial qualities. The poet has put into Sokos' mouth descriptions that make him, although Odysseus' opponent, a spokesperson of the greater epic tradition. Of course, we realize that this is the poet at work through his character's voice. Homer is making this reference to the greater tradition that is Odysseus, for his external audience.

We have seen, then, that we cannot divorce Agamemnon's comments or Odysseus' response in *Iliad* 4 from the adventures of the *nostos* hero of the *Odyssey*. As I have suggested, Odysseus' character and Agamemnon's comments about his character (along with Odysseus' response) must be heard against the larger epic tradition. Homer expected as much from his audience. When heard in this way, there exists an obvious disconnect between Agamemnon's evaluation and the tradition's characterization of this intelligent hero. Agamemnon's misapprehension and caustic vilification of Odysseus would have struck Homer's audience as unfair, to say the least.[88] As we will see throughout this study, Agamemnon is, nevertheless, being true to his own character, and his words usually come back to haunt him (as they do here, despite his unsuccessful attempt to mitigate their impact in 4.358–363). It is true, as Dentice Di Accadia argues, that Agamemnon can "adeguare alla nuova circostanza" (Dentice Di Accadia 2012:149), but surely

---

[87] This is especially so here since it is used alone, proleptically, preparing for Odysseus' name a couple of lines later in *Odyssey* 1.207.

[88] My findings differ markedly from Lowenstam's (1993:81), who comments: "Agamemnon himself demonstrates how a man of authority should regulate the warriors subordinate to him." As we see here (and will observe throughout the *Iliad* in Chapter 4), it is Agamemnon's qualities as a leader, rather than Odysseus', that are in doubt.

these are circumstances that he has created.[89] Agamemnon's incompetence as a leader is a central concern of the poet and his tradition, as we are seeing.

2.2.5 Diomedes and Sthenelos: 4.365–418

Next Agamemnon comes upon Diomedes standing among the chariots with Sthenelos beside him. It becomes immediately clear that Agamemnon will also address this pair as members of the second group in the "typical" appeals. He will chastise them as among those hanging back and gazing:

> Ah me, son of battle-wise horse-taming Tydeus,
> why do you cower,[90] and why do you stare at the embankments of
> war['s soldiery]?[91]
> It was not dear to Tydeus thus to cringe,
> but far before his dear companions to fight against the enemy,

> ὤ μοι Τυδέος υἱὲ δαΐφρονος ἱπποδάμοιο
> τί πτώσσεις, τί δ' ὀπιπεύεις πολέμοιο γεφύρας;
> οὐ μὲν Τυδέϊ γ' ὧδε φίλον πτωσκαζέμεν ἦεν,
> ἀλλὰ πολὺ πρὸ φίλων ἑτάρων δηΐοισι μάχεσθαι,

> *Iliad* 4.370–373

Agamemnon's appeal to Diomedes is tradition-laden since it is effected through his father Tydeus, whose history is related in order to shame Diomedes into action.[92] Note the emphasis in Agamemnon's charge that Diomedes is shrinking away (τί πτώσσεις, 371), achieved through local recurrence of the idea of shrinking away found in the wording of Agamemnon's *exemplum* of Tydeus, who never did (οὐ ... πτωσκαζέμεν ἦεν, 372). This emphasis is intended to make the inactivity of Diomedes appear to be of the worst sort. The caustic charge of continually hanging back provides the contrast that initiates the ensuing

---

[89] Dentice Di Accadia (202:149) is overly generous with Agamemnon when he concludes, "Il re, nel mitigare le critiche espresse in precedenza [*Iliad* 4.358–363], mostra di non essere uno sprovveduto quanta ad abilita oratoria."

[90] Chantraine (1968:948–949, s.v. πτήσσω) suggests modern equivalents such as "chercher refuge," "esquiver," and "se cacher." The ensuing infinitive form πτωσκαζέμεν (4.372) comes from a variant root of πτώσσεις (4.371).

[91] Here γέφυρα is clearly metaphorical.

[92] The poet-narrator earlier described Diomedes first through his patronymic: εὗρε δὲ Τυδέος υἱὸν ὑπέρθυμον Διομήδεα, 4.365. The appeal to Diomedes through his father also occurs in *Iliad* 5.125 (cf. *Iliad* 1.115, where Diomedes' prayer is framed around this metonym) and 10.283–295 (cf. Schnapp-Gourbeillon 1982:56).

retrospective narrative. The narrative frames the character of Diomedes' father through exploit, with an added emphasis on his fearlessness (οὐδε … τάρβει, 387–388) in athletic competition among strangers, where he won "easily" (ῥαϊδίως, 390). Both descriptions are made more emphatic through necessary *enjambement*. Further, Tydeus did so despite his being completely and ridiculously outnumbered by an ambush set with fifty Kadmeian men and their two "godlike" leaders. This retrospective narrative is told by Agamemnon to enhance a disparaging conclusion: Tydeus' present progeny is only good at talking. Tydeus "begat a son / worse than him in a fight, but better in an assembly" (τὸν υἱὸν / γείνατο εἶο χέρεια μάχη, ἀγορῇ δέ τ᾽ ἀμείνω, 399–400).

The address of Agamemnon meets with a respectful silence by Diomedes: "Thus he spoke, but him in no way did strong Diomedes address, / revering the reproach of the revered *basileus* (ὣς φάτο, τὸν δ᾽ οὔ τι προσέφη κρατερὸς Διομήδης / αἰδεσθεὶς βασιλῆος ἐνιπὴν αἰδοίοιο, 4.401–402). The poet's use of silence as a response for Diomedes is quite apposite. In Diomedes' appearances in the *Iliad*, he is consistently shown as the younger warrior (*Iliad* 14.112) well able to take orders from his superiors and say what is acceptable.[93] It is not an indication of Diomedes' cowardice;[94] nor is Diomedes doubting himself, but, as in other scenes, showing his "self-assured" nature.[95] Sthenelos, however, who is included as a target of Agamemnon's rebuke, is not content to accept these castigating comments, and so he attempts to correct the "lie" used to foster shame. He replies with their former martial actions at Thebes to suggest that he and Diomedes, the poet's chief interest here, actually excel their fathers (4.405). Diomedes tells Sthenelos to be quiet, however, with the formulaic phrase "looking at him darkly" (τὸν δ᾽ ἄρ᾽ ὑπόδρα ἰδών, 411), underscoring the cultural inappropriateness of his response to Agamemnon as a socially inferior warrior.

It is interesting to note that in both *Iliad* 2.225–242 (where Thersites speaks) and in 4.405–409 (where Sthenelos speaks), a lower-class figure addresses Agamemnon with a true and fair representation of reality. In the first case, Achilles had said much the same thing as Thersites;[96] in the second, Sthenelos is saying what we might expect Diomedes to say (were he as responsive as

---

[93] Here we detect a traditional trait and a character type—a paramount *basileus* speaking to a younger warrior—as partial cause of Diomedes' immediate acquiescence (*Iliad* 4.401–402, 413).

[94] In this conclusion, I differ from Dentice Di Accadia (2012:150).

[95] Cf. the conclusions of de Jong (2005:17) on Diomedes' meeting with Glaukos in *Iliad* 6.123–129.

[96] Cf. the similar observations of Schadewaldt 1966:152, Whitman 1958:161, Kirk 1985:142, Rose 1988:19, McGlew 1989:290–292, Patzek 1992:132, Lowenstam:1993:78, Barker 2009:60 (cf. 56–61 for a close consideration of Thersites and the management of dissent), and Elmer 2013:93. Seibel (1995:386) suggests that Odysseus "tritt in Thersites seinem alter ego gegenüber." Dentice Di Accadia (2012:121–139) gives a thorough overview of approaches to the figure of Thersites in this episode, albeit his principal concern is with rhetoric.

Odysseus). Yet each suffers a rebuke by a superior in rank (Odysseus/Diomedes) who acts to maintain the social gradation (cf. Ruzé 1997:52 and Stuurman 2004:173).[97] The remarks themselves, one notes, are not corrected. The man, not the argument, was rejected. The poet, however, affirms the social mores of his constituency, where aristocratic values would not sanction the outburst of an importunate underling. It is such scenes that put into serious question Dalby's conclusions about Homer's principal performance arena as non-aristocratic (Dalby 1995:279).[98] Consequently, the response of Sthenelos is ill-received by Diomedes, and he is quickly urged to silence by his overlord, an injunction that again reinforces Diomedes' own acquiescence in the face of authority:

> *Tetta*,[99] in silence sit, and be persuaded by my authoritative
>   command,
> For I am not vexed at Agamemnon shepherd of the people,
> who is urging on the well-greaved Achaians to fight.

> τέττα, σιωπῇ ἧσο, ἐμῷ δ' ἐπιπείθεο μύθῳ·
> οὐ γὰρ ἐγὼ νεμεσῶ Ἀγαμέμνονι ποιμένι λαῶν
> ὀτρύνοντι μάχεσθαι ἐϋκνήμιδας Ἀχαιούς·

Iliad 4.412–414

It is evidently not in character for Diomedes suddenly to speak like an Odysseus. He is controlled by respect for Agamemnon's office.[100] He will, however, store up this insult and later reveal Agamemnon's inequitable gaff in dire circumstances, during a critical assembly in book 9. The character of Diomedes is housed within the tradition that Homer and his core audience are accessing.

---

[97] The address that begins the rebuke of Sthenelos is more familial than that received by Thersites, however. Dentice Di Accadia (2012:138) feels that Thersites, although speaking "la verità" represents "antieroico" speech that is contrary to the spirit and ethics of the poem itself.

[98] I will return to this issue in Chapter 4, s.v. 4.2.6 Grievances against Agamemnon—Revisiting His Past Wrongs: Book 9.

[99] Of τέττα, Chantraine (1968:1096, s.v. τατᾰ) notes that it is a "terme amical et familier" and parallel to τατᾰ, and has continued on through Latin in such familial terms as the French *la tante*. I leave it untranslated here, however, since it is not possible with its singular occurrence in Homer to know the range of possible nuances.

[100] Respect is emphasized by the poet's use of a *figura etymologica* in 4.402: αἰδεσθεὶς βασιλῆος ἐνιπὴν αἰδοίοιο.

2.3 Impetuous Agamemnon

We have seen that most of the individuals whom Agamemnon reviewed had a particular history and character embedded within Homer's song tradition. Further, we have also become aware that the appeal of Agamemnon is illustrative of the character of the *anax andrōn* himself. There are clear signs of Agamemnon's traditional characterization in the tenor of the appeals.[101] Most immediately in his address to Odysseus and Diomedes, we observe a thoughtless and impetuous leader, given to sudden anger and uneven castigation. In Odysseus' case, Agamemnon's rash and insulting remarks are soon retracted and replaced with a placating reply:

> Zeus-born son of Laertes Odysseus of many devices
> I am neither chastising you excessively nor giving you orders;
> For I know that your heart in your chest
> knows gentle thoughts; For you think the same things as I in point of
>   fact.
> But come, we will make good these things afterward, if any evil now
> has been uttered, but all these things may the gods make of no effect.

> διογενὲς Λαερτιάδη πολυμήχαν' Ὀδυσσεῦ
> οὔτέ σε νεικείω περιώσιον οὔτε κελεύω·
> οἶδα γὰρ ὥς τοι θυμὸς ἐνὶ στήθεσσι φίλοισιν
> ἤπια δήνεα οἶδε· τὰ γὰρ φρονέεις ἅ τ' ἐγώ περ.
> ἀλλ' ἴθι ταῦτα δ' ὄπισθεν ἀρεσσόμεθ' εἴ τι κακὸν νῦν
> εἴρηται, τὰ δὲ πάντα θεοὶ μεταμώνια θεῖεν.

Iliad 4.358–363

Here we observe a softening of the initial blow with the adverb "excessively" (περιώσιον) and the positive listing of Odysseus' "gentle thoughts" (ἤπια δήνεα). Then follows Agamemnon's affirmation that Odysseus thinks as he himself does, with a promise to make amends in the future for any present "evil" (κακόν) on his part. Agamemnon ends with a wish that the gods make all things "of no effect" (μεταμώνια), a wish that, as we will see in Chapter 4, Agamemnon is not granted. This error will return as one of many grievances to haunt him.

---

[101] Appeals to the troops are traditional and can include some level of rebuke (cf. *Iliad* 12.265–277, 408–413, 13.117–125, 15.502–514, 15.659–666), but the tenor of Agamemnon's appeal is highly problematic, as I suggest here and in Chapter 4.

Agamemnon's conciliatory words are especially needed after his insulting remarks. His characterization of Odysseus resonates discordantly against the tradition known to both singer and audience. No clear apology ever comes to Diomedes, however, which causes residual rancor in the future. Nor is there a need to suggest that we should make much of the participle "standing" (ἑσταότ', 4.366), as though it necessarily implies loafing of some sort.[102] The poet uses the same participle later on in an anthropopathic portrayal to show that all the Trojans, even the horses, are waiting for dawn to engage the Achaians (*Iliad* 8.565). One can stand and wait actively, so the Trojan horses may suggest, without meaning to avoid duty. In fact, much the same remark used against Diomedes was employed against Odysseus and his men (*Iliad* 4.328–329). For them, however, a clearer context is given for evaluating the damning charge Agamemnon brings. Specifically, the poet-narrator remarks, in a contrariety not to be missed (but contrast Agamemnon's scurrilous charge in 4.347–348), that Odysseus' men had not yet heard the battle shout (οὐ γάρ πώ σφιν ἀκούετο λαὸς ἀϋτῆς, 4.331). The external audience listening to Homer knows that something is wrong with Agamemnon's insinuation. As we will see, this is too often the case with the Achaians' imperious leader. While the poet makes it clear that Odysseus was not aware of the recommencement of battle (in contrast with Agamemnon's convicting comments), in the case of Diomedes, we do not hear anything immediately about whether or not his inactivity is culpable. Instead, the poet suspends emphasizing Agamemnon's present impropriety until a critical moment in his story, in book 9. There, the poet will give Diomedes an extended complaint.

Agamemnon alleges that Diomedes has been inactively and fearfully peering at the battle ranks: "Why do you shrink away, and why do you gaze at the embankments of war['s soldiery]?" (τί πτώσσεις, τί δ' ὀπιπεύεις πολέμοιο γεφύρας, 4.371). The use of the verb "gaze" (ὀπιπεύω) perspicuously displays Agamemnon's state of mind. As Snell pointed out some time ago (although he did not mention "gaze," [ὀπιπεύω]), verbs of seeing in Homer (many of which were dropped from use in later literature) have particular meanings (Snell 1953:1–4).[103] The verb *opipeuō* ("gaze") carries with it a sense of active and intense gazing or peering in its use in Homer, always in some sense surreptitiously. Beyond the verb's present use in *Iliad* 4.371, in *Iliad* 7.243 Hector employs

---

[102] Kirk's (1985:367–368) confusion over the use of this term would be resolved if he took Agamemnon's misrepresentation of Diomedes' intent into account. Further, Leaf (1902:180) had earlier noted Diomedes' active waiting, when he suggested he was waiting in his chariot, since "ἵπποισι, here as often = chariot, and goes with ἅρμασι by hendiadys."

[103] As I suggest beginning in Chapter 1 (see especially n. 17 and "Reading Characterization Traditionally"), however, any claim for lexical meaning in Homer must be based upon a consideration of Homer's traditional lexicon.

it in his retort to Ajax. There it is connected to a sly gazing by stealth (perhaps of the cowardly sort).[104] It is also used once in the *Odyssey* (19.67), where Melantho mistakenly sees Odysseus as a covert *voyeur*.[105] Chantraine's suggestions— "lorgner" ("ogle"), "guetter" ("view intently"), and "épier" ("spy on")—support my reading of this verb's meaning in Homer, and in particular, Agamemnon's use of the verb *opipeuō* ("gaze") here.[106]

But what of Diomedes' character in Homer's tradition? Certainly Diomedes is well known for his bravery. His reaction to Nestor in *Iliad* 8 is especially indicative of this attribute. The field is being cleared of Achaians who are fleeing back to the ships under pressure from the Trojan advance. All except Diomedes. Homer pictures his capability, almost single-handedly, to pen the Trojans back up in their city. This truly epic portrayal of heroism at its apex so irritated Leaf (1900:341) that he felt it should be cut out.[107] Zeus' portent indicates that the tables have turned for the worse against the Achaians (133–136, 169–171). This situation is necessitated by the demands of the larger plot, to bring the Achaians to see their need to send an embassy to Achilles. Yet, what can be done with the relentless Diomedes who will not leave the field? The poet has Nestor address Diomedes and quell his fears. Diomedes' fear is not of death, but of any possibility whatsoever of dishonor. He dreads that someday Hector will boast he fled in fear to the ships (146–150). Nestor, however, aware of Diomedes' character, reassures him:

> O my battle-wise son of Tydeus, what have you said?
> For if in fact Hector is going to say you are evil and cowardly,
> nevertheless the Trojans and Dardanians will not be persuaded
> nor the wives of the great-hearted, shield-bearing Trojans,
> for whom you cast in the dust [their] husbands in [their] vigor.

> ὤ μοι Τυδέος υἱὲ δαΐφρονος, οἷον ἔειπες.
> εἴ περ γάρ σ' Ἕκτωρ γε κακὸν καὶ ἀνάλκιδα φήσει,

---

[104] *Iliad* 7.242–243: ἀλλ' οὐ γάρ σ' ἐθέλω βαλέειν τοιοῦτον ἐόντα / λάθρη ὀπιπεύσας, ἀλλ' ἀμφαδόν, αἴ κε τύχωμι.

[105] *Odyssey* 19.66–67: ξεῖν', ἔτι καὶ νῦν ἐνθάδ' ἀνιήσεις διὰ νύκτα / δινεύων κατὰ οἶκον, ὀπιπεύσεις δὲ γυναῖκας;

[106] Chantraine 1968:808, s.v. ὀπιπεύω, and cf. *LfgrE* 17.731, s.v. ὀπιπεύω (R. Führer), who has "ausspähen." The verb is likely derived from a hypothetical appellative ὀπιπή according to Chantraine (cf. Beekes 2010:1091, s.v. ὀπιπεύω).

[107] Leaf (1900:341) argues that it must be an interpolation because "there is no indication of any general rally on the Greek side, and the idea that Diomedes could unaided have caused a general rout of the enemy seems to be a mere outbidding of his exploits."

ἀλλ' οὐ πείσονται Τρῶες καὶ Δαρδανίωνες
καὶ Τρώων ἄλοχοι μεγαθύμων ἀσπιστάων,
τάων ἐν κονίῃσι βάλες θαλεροὺς παρακοίτας.

Iliad 8.153–156

As Nestor remarks to Diomedes, even the Trojans and Dardanians appear to know that he is nothing short of fearless, no matter what their own foremost hero Hector should boast. Yet, the poet is intent on further displaying Diomedes' inexorable courage and personal ethic to avoid community shame at all costs. Even with Nestor's sagacious verbal reassurance, the hero is minded to turn again and face Hector and so still hesitates to leave the field: "Three times he pondered anxiously in his mind and spirit" (τρὶς μὲν μερμήριξε κατὰ φρένα καὶ κατὰ θυμόν, 8.169). The emphatic nature of the intensifier "three times" (τρίς) and the traditional idiom "in his mind and spirit" (κατὰ φρένα καὶ κατὰ θυμόν) should not be missed.[108] The formula "in his mind and spirit" occurs after verbs of pondering (μερμηρίζω, φράζομαι, ὅρμαινω) with reference to a great number of heroes facing central moments of decision: of Achilles as he ponders whether or not to use the sword he is drawing from his scabbard (*Iliad* 1.193); of Odysseus' considering whether or not to go after Sarpedon (5.671); and of Tydeus, perplexed about whether to stay and fight Hector or return to the ships (8.169). Even Poseidon must decide "in his mind and spirit" whether or not to stand and face Zeus (15.163), who has sent Iris to tell him to get out of the war. Telemachos' problems require serious consideration, too, when he must consider just how he will kill the suitors (*Odyssey* 1.294), as he is prodded along by Athena (*déguisée*); and Odysseus faces the decision of what to do as he heads dangerously toward the rocky coast of Scheria that seems impenetrable (5.365, 424), and then again (with attendant irony for Homer's audience), when he is pensively pondering what the residents of the island are like (6.118).[109] The

---

[108] For the intensifying nature of τρίς, see: *Iliad* 1.213, 5.136, 436, 437, 6.435, 8.169, 170, 11.462, 463, 13.20, 16.702, 703, 784, 785, 18.155, 157, 228, 229, 20.445, 446, 21.80, 176, 177, 22.165, 251, 23.13, 817, 24.16, 273; *Odyssey* 3.245, 4.86, 4.277, 5.306, 6.154, 155, 8.340, 9.65, 361, 11.206, 207, 12.105, 21.125, 126. The traditional formula is κατὰ φρένα καὶ κατὰ θυμόν. Kelly (2007a:198–199) also notes an element of portending aggression in the Iliadic examples of the κατὰ φρένα καὶ κατὰ θυμόν formula, an element implicated too, in most of the moments of pondering in the *Odyssey*.

[109] Larger formulaic systems that include κατὰ φρένα καὶ κατὰ θυμόν allow for the interchange of various verbs and other elements, according to local metrical necessities and grammar. Other examples of pondering (μερμηρίζω, φράζομαι, ὅρμαινω) with this formula in the *Iliad* include Odysseus, alone in the battlefield after saving Diomedes, pondering whether to stand his ground or retreat (11.411); Menelaos, likewise pondering whether to stay or retreat from guarding the corpse of Patroklos (17.106); but also Achilles, questioning with heavy heart whether Patroklos has died, just before a messenger arrives to confirm his worst fear (18.15). In the *Odyssey*, the formulaic "pondering in his mind and spirit" is used to describe Menelaos considering whether

formula also occurs with a verb of knowing (οἶδα), and the emphatic nature of the idiom is no less apparent in these cases.[110] The existence, moreover, of the singular formulaic integers from the larger equation (either "in his mind," κατὰ φρένα, or "in his spirit," κατὰ θυμόν) employed with the same or similar verbs suggests that the poet wanted, through the use of "in his mind and spirit," to create extra emphasis and delay a bit longer over this narrative moment in *Iliad* 4. Further, the mental anxiety that such a decision stirs up in Diomedes is made all the more prominent by the recurrence of "he pondered anxiously" (μερμήριξε[ν]) in a virtual anadiplosis (167, 169).[111] The poet's choice to cluster together these two traditional formulae within three lines further accentuates the moment (cf. Kelly 2007:198). Yet, Zeus is immediate and imminent with his warning signs to Diomedes, which, like Diomedes' pondering, are also given thrice (170–171).

Even, however, if we were to allow that Odysseus' men are in some way culpable for not hearing that the clamor of war had already begun, which seems quite unreasonable, and that Diomedes is in this instance uncharacteristically avoiding engagement in battle (although the comments of Agamemnon would make each character's [in]activity more sinister than this), the reaction of Agamemnon seems impetuous at best and despotic at worst. In Elmer's overly restrained (yet accurate) description of the scene, Agamemnon's attitude "is at odds with the normative structures of Achaian life"; and he "provokes," rather than "prevents" disorder (Elmer 2013:90).[112] The immediate response of Odysseus (and the future response of Diomedes) appears to call into question the approach Agamemnon takes in his appeal to these leading *basileis*. In Diomedes' case, by *Iliad* 9, Agamemnon's unsupportable accusation will be openly rejected by all (see *Iliad* 9.34–36, 14.126, and Chapter 4).

In this chapter, we have considered how the Homeric poet and his audience depended upon tradition-based characterization for a fuller comprehension of

---

to ask Telemachos, as yet unknown to him, to declare who his father is (4.117, 120); and of Odysseus, as he considers whether and when to investigate Kirke's island (10.151), whether and when to kill the traitorous serving women (20.10), and how quickly he should (finally) reveal himself to Laertes (24.235). In *Odyssey* 4.813, the poet makes the nature of Penelope's pondering clear, by introducing the formula using ἐρέθω.

[110] The object of what is known in one's mind and spirit includes the reality that "sacred Ilion" will fall (Agamemnon in *Iliad* 4.163 and Hector in 6.447), or Achilles not knowing whether Aineias' spear will pierce his shield (20.264), or Peisistratus knowing that Nestor will be angry for him not returning with Telemachos (his *xeinos*) who is, should he stay, in danger of delaying, just as Odysseus was throughout his *nostos* (*Odyssey* 15.211).

[111] διάνδιχα μερμήρικεν is itself formulaic (cf. *Iliad* 1.189, 13.455).

[112] Elmer's remark does not deny the Homeric proclivity of allowing disorder to have a free hand before the poet reimposes order and regularity, as he notes (Elmer 2013:86).

a particular instant of character portrayal in the narrative moment. In other words, how the audience, especially one that did not rely upon literacy for the communication of cultural history, would listen to a traditional story. They considered traditional characters with a great wealth of background information that influenced how they interpreted an action or character trait. Homeric characterization of an individual, such as each of those addressed by Agamemnon in his appeal to the troops, is built, then, not "in an instant," but rather, "at the instant within a tradition." Further, we have seen that there existed for the poet and his core audience consistency of characterization within the oral tradition being accessed.

Significant for our upcoming consideration of Agamemnon as a character (Chapters 3 through 5) is the fact that there are hints of his pathetic nature within the tradition surrounding *Iliad* 4. Agamemnon's character becomes apparent at particular moments in his address to his leading *basileis*. In particular, in our survey of Agamemnon's address to Odysseus and Diomedes, we observed his thoughtless, impetuousness, and despotic leadership style, one given to sudden anger and abrasive speech. In Odysseus' case, I remarked that we could not divorce Agamemnon's comments or Odysseus' response in *Iliad* 4 from the adventures of the *nostos* hero of the *Odyssey*. Odysseus' character and Agamemnon's comments about his character (along with Odysseus' response), when read in light of the larger Homeric tradition, demonstrate that there was a disconnect between Agamemnon's and others' evaluation of this intelligent hero who was known to use his trickster talents towards good ends. There was nothing sinister about Odysseus' character combining *dolos* and *kerdos*, "ruse" and "gain"; and there are no examples, outside of the instance with Agamemnon, of a negative association of these two words with Odysseus in the *Iliad* or *Odyssey*. We noted, too, that it was rather ironic that even Odysseus' enemy saw his characteristic *dolos* in terms that suggested useful martial qualities.

In Odysseus' case, Agamemnon's initial impetuous and insulting remarks were soon retracted and replaced with a placating reply. No clear apology, however, ever came to the hero Diomedes in book 2, a fact that causes residual rancor for the future. We observed that Agamemnon felt Diomedes had been gazing at the battle but had decided to stay out of the fray. Yet, we do not know that this was the case at all, since Agamemnon thought the same thing about Odysseus, which we know was certainly not true. Agamemnon's use of the verb "gaze" (ὀπιπεύω) to describe how Diomedes was looking, I suggested, perspicuously displays Agamemnon's state of mind (and inept leadership traits), since this sort of intense gazing or peering in Homer suggests a certain amount of surreptitiousness. Yet, as we also saw in our detailed survey of Diomedes in word and deed, Agamemnon's estimation is completely out of step with the poet's tradition and his presentation of this hero in the rest of the *Iliad*. The poet shows us a Diomedes whose traditional, inexorable courage is instanced by language cues within a local narrative context. In *Iliad* 8, he ponders and finally agrees, although hardly convinced, to leave the field. The Trojans and Dardanians, we realize, could never doubt his character. Agamemnon's error in *Iliad* 4, we noted, will form the basis for Diomedes' grievance against him in the near future. In the ensuing chapters we will consider the characterization of Agamemnon in greater detail, beginning with his appearances in the *Odyssey*.

3

The Characterization of Agamemnon
in the *Odyssey*

3.1 Introduction

Agamemnon is in Hades by the time the action of the *Odyssey* opens. This necessitates that his personal appearances be incorporeal and only in the underworld (*Odyssey* 11 and 24). Agamemnon as a traditional character is with us in greater and lesser ways beyond his apparitions as a specter, however. He appears metonymically, through retrospective narrative by others in various episodes.[1] Agamemnon is invoked in ways that connect him intimately with the Trojan War and its immediate aftermath, the *nostoi*, and later still the *Oresteia*; there also exist possible allusions to the House of Atreus Saga of past blood guilt.[2] Our task here is to elucidate the most significant of Agamemnon's appearances as a basis for more general comments in this and subsequent chapters. It will become evident that certain features of Agamemnon's story persistently adhere to his character.

Our consideration of Agamemnon will follow the chronology of the *Odyssey*, but we must keep in mind what I have suggested in many ways already in the preceding chapters. For the traditional audience (whom we must seek to emulate), the story of the *Odyssey* was not new; rather, it was already known

---

[1] *Odyssey* 1.30–39, 299–300, 3.136–156, 162–164, 193–198, 232–235, 247–275, 305–308, 4.90–92, 512–537, 548, 8.77–79, 9.263–266, 11.168–169, 380–466, 13.383–385, 14.70–71, 117, 497, 19.183, 24.20–97, 101–124, 186, and 191–204.

[2] By Oresteia I mean the events surrounding the revenge taken by Orestes. Of course, this is in reality a continuation and consequence of the *kakos nostos* and an extension of the story of the House of Atreus. For an overview of the House of Atreus myth, see especially Gantz 1993:489, 540, and 544–556. For a consideration of the overall *nostos* theme (Homeric and extra-Homeric), see Bonifazi (2009), who argues that the root meaning of *nostos* for Homer is escaping death and saving oneself. I think, however, that Odysseus' (like Agamemnon's) main goal is getting home safely. While I agree with Bonifazi that there is "multidirectionality" (506) in Homer, the primary goal for the Homeric *nostos* is unidirectional.

in some form to Homer's core audience.[3] The details from different events in Agamemnon's life that appear scattered throughout the epic were tightly interwoven and interdependent for Homer and his listeners. While the chronological ordering of events within the *Odyssey* could doubtless change as we noted in Chapter 1, the traditional depth of individual characters nevertheless provided a shared connection between the singer and his core audience. Only careful consideration of Agamemnon's manifold appearances in the *Odyssey* will allow us to hear what sort of character the poet and his tradition had in mind. Further, as noted in Chapter 2, characterization for the ancient audience was not abstracted and separated from events, but rather, attached inextricably to "word and deed." Consequently, both of these aspects, language and action, will be considered in close detail in what follows. The format of this chapter on the *Odyssey* (and the ensuing chapter on the *Iliad*) will of necessity be a commentary on Agamemnon's appearances. Within the *Odyssey*, we will see emerge a part of the traditional portrait of Agamemnon known to Homer, through his personal voice from Hades or as a character within recited tales.

3.2 Commentary

3.2.1 Agamemnon's *Nostos* and the *Oresteia*: 1.30–43

The first reference to Agamemnon occurs at the very opening of the *Odyssey*'s tale, in the divine assembly scene. In this scene we hear of Agamemnon indirectly through the patronymic "son of Agamemnon" (Ἀγαμεμνονίδης, 30, a hapax) attached to his son Orestes, the hero of the *Oresteia*, here remembered by Zeus as the killer of Aigisthos. Orestes' revenge and the whole *Oresteia* is of course only possible following the death of Agamemnon, killed "upon his return" (νοστήσαντα, 36) from the Trojan War. The purpose of the *Oresteia* story for the poet of the *Odyssey* is to show that humans like Aigisthos are responsible for their actions, and that Aigisthos' fate prefigures the fate of the suitors. It is "ein zentrales Thema der Apologoi" (Danek 1998:35).[4] Moreover, Agamemnon's death at his wife's hands, as we will see, is employed to warn Odysseus to be more thoughtful.

---

[3] Of course, we cannot hear the epic exactly as the ancient audience, since much of the story content and many of the performance dynamics are lost to us (see Chapter 1, notes 31, 35, and 68). We can, however, recover something of the original impact of idioms, patterns, and rhetorical devices that appear in the text.

[4] Cf. West in Heubeck, West, and Hainsworth 1988:77, Louden 1999:19, and Saïd 2011:122.

3.2.2 Agamemnon Taken By A "Ruse Strategist": 1.299–300

Athena disguised as Mentes converses with Telemachos as they sit near the haughty suitors who are inflicting themselves on the absent Odysseus' *oikos*. In the course of their conversation she references the example of Orestes: "Or have you not heard of the sort of fame that divine Orestes took hold of / among all people?" (ἢ οὐκ ἀΐεις οἷον κλέος ἔλλαβε δῖος Ὀρέστης / πάντας ἐπ' ἀνθρώπους, 1.298–299). She urges Telemachos to consider how he could kill the suitors, and encourages him to grow up. Athena intimates that there will be future *kleos* if he should act like Orestes.[5] Within one premise of Athena's persuasive argument (a statement contained within a question), we find our second reference to Agamemnon. Athena asks with some incredulity whether Telemachos has not yet heard of the sort of *kleos* Orestes gained (299), "since he killed a father-murderer, / Aigisthos the ruse strategist, because he killed his noble father" (ἐπεὶ ἔκτανε πατροφονῆα, / Αἴγισθον δολόμητιν, ὅ οἱ πατέρα κλυτὸν ἔκτα). Athena's comment that Orestes' father was killed by a "ruse strategist" (δολόμητις) is of special interest. This particularized epithet is employed almost exclusively of Aigisthos in Homer, except, interestingly enough, once, where it occurs as an epithet with Clytemnestra (and once by Hera of Zeus).[6] The nearly exclusive sharing of this epithet with Clytemnestra (who was also involved in the killing of Agamemnon),[7] suggests that it assumes the depth of the tradition related to the murder but also the connection between epithets and characterization, traditional backstories, and metonymy (see Chapter 1). The epithet is overwhelmingly negative, something not always the case with the individual verbal integers that make up this traditional expression, as we saw already with "ruse" (δόλος) in Chapter 2.[8]

We must, then, distinguish carefully the inherent meaning of the epithet "ruse strategist" (δολόμητις) as a traditional "word" from the individual occurrences of the separate words, "ruse" (δόλος) and "strategy" (μῆτις), from which it is formed. This conclusion is supported by a reading of these three distinct words within Homer. The "ruse strategist" (δολόμητις) epithet has adhering to it when used, consistently negative associations such as parricide. By contrast, "ruse" (δόλος) or "strategy" (μῆτις), individually, often have positive associations related to trickery and cunning, which in themselves can serve either good or bad ends. Such positive denotations for the latter words are evinced in *Odyssey* 9.422, where both words are found in close proximity to one another

---

[5] For the motif of promised future booty, see Chapter 2, n. 38.

[6] *Odyssey* 1.300, 3.198, 250, 308, 4.525; 11.422 of Clytemnestra; *Iliad* 1.540 of Zeus.

[7] More will be said on Clytemnestra's involvement in the killing of her husband.

[8] See Chapter 2, s.v. 2.2.4 Menestheus and Odysseus: 4.327–364.

in a description of Odysseus. In that scene Odysseus is using "ruse" (δόλος) and "strategy" (μῆτις) to save his companions. Reading the meaning of δόλος ("ruse") or μῆτις ("strategy") requires that we not assume that either word is inherently "bad," morally speaking, in the eyes of Homer or his audience. This is not to deny that these individual words are sometimes connected with negative acts, rather, just to note that, unlike in the case of the epithet δολόμητις, they need not be. In this second reference to Agamemnon, then, we learn that he was the object of a strategic ruse orchestrated by a "ruse strategist" (δολόμητις), his wife's lover, Aigisthos. Consequently, so we are told, Aigisthos paid for his actions with his life.

3.2.3 Nestor's Stories of Quarrel, *Nostoi*, and *Oresteia*: 3.136–310

Telemachos is visiting Nestor after leaving Ithaca by stealth. He wants to ascertain whether his father is alive or dead (*Odyssey* 1.287–292). In Pylos he follows Athena's earlier counsel and questions Nestor, who outlines in his characteristically plenary response information that relates a quarrel, various *nostoi*, and the *Oresteia*.[9] Each story adds to our understanding of events centrally connected with Agamemnon's history as a character. Nestor's narrative begins with a quarrel between the two sons of Atreus (3.136–146) that will effectively result in two separate departures and Agamemnon's arrival home alone (West in Heubeck, West, Hainsworth 1988:168).[10] Agamemnon is named several times in this narrative by means of the traditional patronymic, "son of Atreus" ('Ατρεΐδην).[11] Nestor's retrospective suggests that Agamemnon's stance in what appears to be a quarrel with his brother—Agamemnon wishes first to appease Athena's wrath and then to leave—is the plan of a "thoughtless child" (νήπιος), "for he did not know that she [Athena] was not about to yield" (οὐδὲ τὸ ἤδη, ὃ οὐ πείσεσθαι ἔμελλεν, 3.146).

The many instances of the vocative of νήπιος used of adults suggest "thoughtlessness" as part of the traditional meaning of this word in both the *Iliad* and *Odyssey*.[12] The term is generally unfavorable and often foreboding. Instances

---

[9]   On Nestor's loquacious nature, see Chapter 2, s.v. 2.2.3 Nestor: 4.293–326.

[10] Barker (2009:77 and 114n88) adds that Athena's hostility in spurring on this quarrel is a result of Ajax's earlier crimes.

[11] See *Odyssey* 3.156, 164, 193, 248, 268, and 305, but once in the plural inclusive of Menelaos in 3.136.

[12] These representative samples taken chronologically from the appearances of νήπιος in the *Iliad* and *Odyssey* suggest the possible connotations of this oft-used term. The use of νήπιος other than as a vocative to A1 (it is not used elsewhere in this form; for metrical terms, see Appendix A), as when it is employed as a description of a character within a narrative, does allow for less pejorative and even neutral implications (e.g. *Odyssey* 2.313, 4.818, 11.449), but calumnious

of its use in the *Iliad* include: Aphrodite of Diomedes on his thoughtless rampage (*Iliad* 5.406); Hector of the thoughtless fortifications of the Achaians (8.177); and the poet-narrator of Asios, who is the only Trojan who does not heed Polydamas and leave his chariot behind and so suffers as a consequence (12.113; cf. 127). Hera employs the term to describe the thoughtlessness of working against Zeus (15.104). It is used by the poet-narrator of Patroklos, who is entreating Achilles to return to battle (but, the poet adds, he was entreating his own "evil death" [θανάτον τε κακόν, 16.46]); and again of Patroklos, who lets go of the injunction of Achilles to avoid chasing the Trojans back to Troy (16.87–96), so the poet tells us, in his state of *atē* (16.686). Menelaos uses it in his speech to the Trojan Euphorbos in an *exemplum* meant to deter his opponent from facing him, a warning that goes tragically unheeded (17.32).

The instances of the vocative forms of *nēpios* in the *Odyssey* equally suggest thoughtlessness. Some examples include the especially telling and ominous comment of the poet-narrator speaking in apostrophe of Odysseus' men who ate the cattle of Helios: "Fools, who gobbled down the cattle of Hyperion Helios; Yet he took away their homecoming day!" (νήπιοι, οἳ κατὰ βοῦς Ὑπερίονος Ἠελίοιο / ἤσθιον· αὐτὰρ ὁ τοῖσιν ἀφείλετο νόστιμον ἦμαρ, 1.8). We find it voiced by Nestor of Agamemnon who, in his dispute with Menelaos, had no idea that Athena wasn't to be persuaded (3.146).[13] Menelaos, too, is asked if he should be addressed as νήπιος by the sea nymph Eidothea. She is shocked to watch him allowing his men to experience such hopelessness (4.371). The reason she thinks the term suits Menelaus is his negative state of inaction.[14] We get the point, when in the same line Menelaos is also asked if he is "senseless" (χαλίφρων), with the added force of "so very much" (λίην τόσον) stuck in for good measure.[15]

A contrast can be made between the address "thoughtless child" (νήπιος) and the metrically equivalent address, "[O] child" ([ὦ] τέκος), used always with

---

castigation can attend this usage as well (e.g. *Odyssey* 9.44, 273). For similar findings in the *Iliad*, see Kelly 2007a:205–208. For a consideration of the associated impaired mental activity in adults suggested by *nēpios* (and a consideration of *nēpios* and its derivative *nēputios*), see the detailed study of Edmunds 1990:60–97.

[13] Menelaos also uses it to describe Eteoneus (so, as a predicate nominative rather than a vocative), who failed miserably to show proper hospitality to Telemachos and Peisistratos (*Odyssey* 4.31–32).

[14] As Kelly (2007a:205) has shown for the *Iliad* and I find also applies to the *Odyssey*, these judgments also cue the audience to the "disjuncture between the intention or understanding of the character so labelled and the actuality of any situation."

[15] The weight of this intensifying adverbial addition, while grammatically modifying the first hemistich with νήπιος, by its position in the second hemistich, can also be understood to intensify the second hemistich's χαλίφρων. The junction between the first and second hemistich, after all, is the most likely moment where the *aoidos* took a breath, as Nagy (2000:14) notes.

favorable associations.[16] Some typical examples suffice to make the point. It is used affectionately by Nestor (*Iliad* 23.626) when he addresses Achilles during the funeral games for Patroklos. Priam (*Iliad* 24.423) employs it to address his unexpected but welcome helper Hermes. Hermes had come in the guise of a youthful attendant of Achilles and offered timely and efficacious information about Hector's body. In this last example, a formulaic hemistich preceding a favorable address by Priam—"Thus he [Hermes] spoke and he [Agamemnon] rejoiced" (ὣς φάτο, γήθησεν δέ, 424)—further affirms the traditionally positive tenor of "O child" ([ὦ] τέκος) as an address, if we consider its other occurrences in Homer.[17] "[O] child" ([ὦ] τέκος) is also used by Alkinoos who addresses his daughter (*Odyssey* 6.68) with all the paternal love one might expect of such a scene. Odysseus addresses Athena using this appellation (*Odyssey* 7.22) when she comes disguised as a "little maiden" (παρθενική, 7.20).[18] Suffice it to say, in summation, that the idiom "O child" ([ὦ] τέκος) is at odds in its traditional implications with the metrically equivalent "thoughtless child" (νήπιος) employed in the passage under consideration to characterize Agamemnon. It seems, then, that the very propensity of Agamemnon to act thoughtlessly is itself a traditional trait, highlighted here through an unfavorable and foreboding traditional idiom.[19]

---

[16] It should be noted that both formulaic forms of address can be used in the first colon (to A1), and so the presence or absence of an initial consonant (to precede ν or ὦ) does not affect the poet's vocabulary choice. The vocative τέκος appears with or without ὦ, depending on the poet's metrical needs. See also the findings of Edmunds 1990:3.

[17] The half-line formula "Thus x spoke and y rejoiced" (ὣς φάτο, γήθησεν δέ) occurs with a great many characters in its present position (to B2, or with an elided δ' to B1). It describes Diomedes' happy state after he realized his inherited *xenia* relationship with Glaukos (*Iliad* 6.212). It characterizes Athena who is ranging among the Danaans after she has heard Menelaos' willingness to defend Patroklos' body, if only he had her aid (*Iliad* 17.567). Odysseus is depicted by this formula too, after he has heard from Alkinoos of his suitability as a model son-in-law and been given assurance of his conveyance home to Ithaca (*Odyssey* 7.329). Further examples of this favorable idiom include *Odyssey* 8.199, 385, 13.250, and 18.281.

[18] [ὦ] τέκος (cf. also 24.425, 732, 18.170), ἐμὸν τέκος (*Iliad* 21.331, 22.56), and μοι τέκος (*Iliad* 18.95) may act as syncopated or alternative forms of the much more common and always affectionate or respectful vocative φίλον τέκος, when for metrical reasons, φίλον is not possible: *Iliad* 3.162, 192, 5.373, 8.39, 9.437, 444, 14.190, 18.63, 21.509, 22.38, 183, 24.373, *Odyssey* 4.611, 16.25, 19.474, 23.5. The use of τέκος within larger epithets, however, such as αἰγιόχοιο Διὸς τέκος Ἀτρυτώνη and preceded by the formulaic ὦ πόποι, is not always used as a positive address (cf. ὦ πόποι ἀργυρότοξε Διὸς τέκος [*Iliad* 21.230] used by Skamandros in disgust to address Apollo). The use of the vocative even here, however, is not intended to deny a positive relationship between Zeus and Athena, when used by Hera in disgust (*Iliad* 2.157, 5.714, 8.352, 427, 21.420). It is, however, a different idiom than the formula φίλον τέκος.

[19] We will meet this same descriptive term characterizing Agamemnon again in Chapter 4, where, in considering his conduct in *Iliad* 2.38, I will suggest that he seems to misapprehend what the best course of action should be.

When we consider Nestor's comment in *Odyssey* 3.146 (νήπιος, οὐδὲ τὸ ᾔδη, ὃ οὐ πείθεσθαι ἔμελλεν) against the backdrop of the synchronic instances of "thoughtless child" (νήπιος) just outlined, it is not easy to excuse Agamemnon's thoughtlessness merely on the grounds that he did not know what the gods were up to.[20] The limited perspective of Agamemnon is not the sole reason for Nestor's use of this adjective; rather, it also insinuates the element of thoughtless miscalculation, often, as can be seen in the foregoing examples, by a character involved in a foolhardy action. There is, moreover, a certain amount of ironic disdain directed toward the person it references and his choice in a particular situation. Nestor, by using this word, becomes the poet's spokesman for the tradition as a whole. Nestor's speech tells of Agamemnon and Menelaos parting company in "strife" (ἔρις, *Odyssey* 3.136) at the beginning of the *nostoi*. Certain of these returns, such as Nestor's, end in a happy *telos*. Others terminate in misfortune, including Agamemnon's, the paradigmatic example of a *kakos nostos*. Nestor's story unfolds some of the events of Agamemnon's *nostos*, including: "how he came and how Aigisthos devised lamentable destruction" (ὥς τ᾽ ἦλθ᾽ ὥς τ᾽ Αἴγισθος ἐμήσατο λυγρὸν ὄλεθρον, 3.194). From this point the moral is intended most directly for Telemachos, who, Nestor notes, must act as stoutly as Orestes. It is an exhortation that spurs on Telemachos to opine about the suitors' oppression and to verbalize his strong wish for a *tisis*, although his concluding comments display pessimism about whether the gods will ever bring this to pass (3.208–209). Nestor's remarks encourage hope, including a wish for Athena's help. Any optimism is once again rejected by Telemachos, however, who insists, ironically, that such an outcome could never come to pass (3.225–228).[21]

The ironic conversation between Nestor and Telemachos is broken by the rhetorical question and admonition of none other than Athena herself in the guise of Mentor, who touches on several elements of Agamemnon's sad *nostos*. Her speech is meant to connect the traditional audience to the suffering Odysseus. She says that she would rather suffer yet get home (as the traditional audience knows will be the case with Odysseus) than (*Odyssey* 3.234–235), "reaching home be destroyed at the hearth, as Agamemnon / was destroyed by the ruse of Aigisthos and his own wife" (ἐλθὼν ἀπολέσθαι ἐφέστιος, ὡς Ἀγαμέμνων / ὤλεθ᾽ ὑπ᾽ Αἰγίσθοιο δόλῳ καὶ ἧς ἀλόχοιο). Through Athena's remarks, we learn

---

[20] We note a reference to contrary divine activity, a regular feature that reminds us of the dual nature of causality in Homer (brought out explicitly by Nestor in this instance). We will return to the question of Homeric causality in greater detail in Chapter 4, s.v. 4.2.10 Agamemnon and *Atē*: 19.76–144.

[21] Irony exists here because of the external audience's "superior position and knowledge" (Porter 2011:513; see also the extensive bibliography listed there) that in fact Odysseus will return. On irony, see also Chapter 2.

that Agamemnon was killed "at the hearth" (ἐφέστιος), and that he was killed by the "ruse" (δόλος) of both Aigisthos and "his own wife." These are important elements not overtly mentioned in *Odyssey* 1.299–300, which we examined earlier in this chapter. The hearth was a place where one was supposed to be under the protection of the gods and where "sanctity was inherent in the place."[22] The etymology of "at the hearth" (ἐφέστιος) includes "hearth" (ἑστία), a term employed, as Chantraine notes, "également pour désigner une divinité du foyer," of Hestia.[23] The metonymy would not have been missed by Homer's auditors. To be killed at anyone's hearth was something miasmatic to the Greek mind, whether at one's own *oikos* or at the *oikos* of another as a guest (under the watchful eye of Zeus *xenios*).[24] This is further illustrated from somewhat later Greek literature. The attachment of "pollution" (variously called ἄγος, λῦμα, μίασμα, or μύσος) to the hearth is assumed by Aeschylus (see *Choephoroe* 965–971 and *Eumenides* 169–172). The expiation ceremony for Jason and Medea's murder of Apsyrtos is likewise connected to the hearth in Apollonius (*Argonautica* 4.693–717). The hearth, central in issues of pollution and purification (aspects of the sacred), was of first importance to the *polis* and its colonies (Malkin 2011:211, Tsakirgis 2007:225–226). The conception of the hearth as a sacred place is early, since Hestia is already a personified goddess in Hesiod's *Theogony*.[25] Further, the name of public officials in Classical Athens, *Peristiarchoi*, the "Around the Hearth" officials, affirms the central importance of the hearth for the *oikos* (Parker 1983:21); yet, more broadly, the hearth symbolizes the political life of Greek communities (Kajava 2004). We can see, then, that Agamemnon's death at the hearth of a "royal" relative carries miasmic meaning in the minds of both Homer and his core audience, both for the *oikos* and for the nascent Greek *polis*.

The question of whose hearth Homer is talking about is a problem for some scholars, however, who immediately assume the dramatic tradition that Agamemnon was killed in his own home. They see the reference "at the hearth" (ἐφέστιος) here as a rather "loose" use, since Agamemnon was not killed at "his own" hearth. They somehow feel that Homer should have made this clearer.[26]

---

[22] See Parker (1983:51 *et passim*) on issues of pollution and purification; see Nilsson (1940:76–77) and *LfgrE* 13:1250, s.v. ἰστίη (H. W. Nordheider), on Zeus *xenios*.

[23] Chantraine 1968–1980:379, s.v. ἑστία.

[24] Cf. *Odyssey* 9.266–271 and Dowden 2006:79.

[25] *Theogony* 454 (ἱστίην). Kajava 2004:2: "In any case, the cult of Hestia as a goddess in her own right obviously goes back to those remote times when fire and hearth, as essential constituents of society, were regarded as divine and magic elements. The consequence of all this was that, besides the current Greek word for 'hearth,' *Hestia* was the name of its tutelary goddess, being, moreover, sometimes used to refer to 'altar,' and thus more equivalent to βομός or ἐσχάρα."

[26] See West in Heubeck, West, and Hainsworth (1988:174): "'at home,' used a little loosely, since Agamemnon is said to have been killed in Aegisthus' house (iv. 524ff., xi 409ff.)."

Yet, as we noted, to be killed at anyone's hearth was something that would have been miasmatic to the Greek mind and there exists really nothing untraditional or idiosyncratic about Homer's use of "hearth" here to reference the hearth of another. In all of its occurrences (*Iliad* 2.125, *Odyssey* 3.234, 7.248, 23.55) it stands without identifiers. There is no Homeric instance of its being used with a possessive or reflexive pronoun.[27] In fact "at the hearth" (ἐφέστιος) can be used when one person relates his presence at the hearth of another (*Odyssey* 7.248), again without grammatical cue. In short, in this passage there is no "loose use." We who are not members of the traditional audience first learn at this moment in the written text that Agamemnon was killed at a hearth. That is all we know. The context within which Homer's core audience hears "hearth" at this point, by contrast, is the larger tradition. They know already that Agamemnon was killed at the hearth of another, his cousin Aigisthos. Although this element is known to them through other renditions of this traditional story, it is not yet known to us as readers of a unique, written, and monumental text. We must glean information as we work our way through the pages of a text. It is a "fact" that we must wait to read until book 4.[28] For now, we as a later reading audience know only that Agamemnon was destroyed by his wife and her lover when he returned to his kingdom, and that the murder took place at a hearth.

The conversation with Nestor is turned by Telemachos to the circumstances surrounding Agamemnon's "death and baleful fate" (θάνατον καὶ κῆρα μέλαιναν, 3.242), a formula that allows the poet to dwell on a narrative moment and make the event more terrible by hendiadys.[29] This exact hendiadys is only employed in the *Odyssey*, where it harbingers: the portending fate of the suitors (2.283, 24.127); Odysseus' presumed death by the work of the gods, ironically, as the disheartened Telemachos speaks to Athena in the guise of Mentor (3.242); and the near fate of the prophet Theoklymenos, who fled Argos after killing a man (15.275). It is also used by the poet as narrator (*Odyssey* 22.14) to describe the impending doom of Antinoos as he reaches for his goblet, but instead finds death from Odysseus' arrow. The *Iliad* employs an analogous expression, but fitting a different metrical shape: "slaughter and baleful fate" (φόνον καὶ κῆρα μέλαιναν), heard in the threats of Sarpedon to Tlepolemos (5.652) and Odysseus to Sokos (11.443), which each soon carried out. It is heard too, in the initial thought of Priam's son Lykaon (21.66). He seeks first to flee from Achilles' wrath,

---

[27] The first overt reference within Greek literature to whose house the hearth is actually in where one comes, is found (and for emphasis only) in Aeschylus *Eumenides*. There we find Orestes a suppliant at the hearth of Apollo's house (ἱκέτης ὅδ' ἀνὴρ καὶ δόμων ἐφέστιος/ ἐμῶν, 577).

[28] This is another example of the traditional core audience's (ad)vantage(d) point of reference, a point we first considered in Chapters 1 and 2.

[29] In other places, the poet uses only a singular noun, with or without an epithet.

but is unsuccessful, and next, to supplicate him—"But you respect me and take pity on me" (σὺ δέ μ᾽ αἴδεο καί μ᾽ ἐλέησον, 21.74)—without success. Although Achilles had captured him and accepted ransom for his release just twelve days earlier (21.80–81), Lykaon now meets an Achilles with implacable fury, fed by Patroklos' recent death (21.99–135).

Further, in *Odyssey* 3, Telemachos asks "How did wide-ruling Agamemnon die?" (πῶς ἔθαν᾽ Ἀτρεΐδης εὐρὺ κρείων Ἀγαμέμνων; 248). The epithet, "wide-ruling" (εὐρὺ κρείων) is used only of Poseidon (*Iliad* 11.751) beyond Agamemnon. It clearly marks the son of Atreus as a paramount *basileus* and leader of a Pan-Hellenic force at Troy. Although the epithet is used only here in the *Odyssey*, it is widely employed in the *Iliad*.[30] Moreover, Telemachos inquires of Nestor where Menelaos was when Agamemnon died, and what death the "ruse strategist" (δολόμητις) Aigisthos devised in his absence (249–251).

Nestor's characteristically garrulous reply (253–328) outlines the background to Clytemnestra's affair with Aigisthos, including the delay of Menelaos in Egypt. All the pre-*nostos* and *nostos* events work to create the right conditions for the homicide. While Menelaos is delayed, Aigisthos is described as charming Agamemnon's wife with words and devising lamentable things in Mycenae (303). To characterize Aigisthos' *entreprise amoureuse*, Homer employs the iterative "he continually charmed" (θέλγεσκε, 264), to fit his metrical needs.[31] The iterative form of this verb occurs only here of all extant Greek literature, supporting its identity as a unique creation *in situ* by the poet for his narrative needs. The metrically unusable imperfect for which the iterative is substituted and the narrative itself suggest the passing of time.[32] This makes the iterative form an appropriate fit for the poet keen to recall the continual wooing of Clytemnestra by Aigisthos; but also other events, such as disposing of the supervising singer, a move that helped lead to Clytemnestra's seduction.[33] Hernández (2002:322)

---

[30] *Iliad* 1.203, 355, 411, 3.178, 7.107, 322, 11.107, 238, 751, 13.112, 16.273, and 23.887.

[31] The poet completes the adonean clausula with ἔπεσσιν: πόλλ᾽ Ἀγαμεμνονέην ἄλοχον θέλγεσκεν ἔπεσσιν, 264.

[32] [ἔ]θελγε[ν]: *Iliad* 12.255, 15.594, 21.276, 604, 24.343, *Odyssey* 1.57, 5.47, 12.40, 44, 14.387, 16.195, 17.514, 521, 18.282, 24.3.

[33] On the supervising singer led off by Aigisthos to a desert island, see *Odyssey* 3.263–275; on the determination of Aigisthos, despite divine warning, see *Odyssey* 1.35–43. Olson (1990:66) argues that that the audience would be thinking of Penelope when hearing of Clytemnestra: "Perhaps Penelope's resistance to the suitor [like Clytemnestra's to Aigisthos] will collapse as well, now that Telemachos [like the singer who guarded Clytemnestra] is absent from the household." Tsitsibakou-Vasalos (2009:198) sees a parallel in Homer's mind and language between the adultery of Aigisthos-Clytemnestra and Ares-Aphrodite (*Odyssey* 8.266–236). See Danek (1998:92–93), however, for caution against more speculative neoanalytical readings. He agrees instead with Olson (1995:24–42) by suggesting that Homer had variants in mind (but "daß bestimmte Elemente hervorgehoben, andere unterdrückt werden").

comments that "Agamemnon is a dismal failure in his attempt to have a poet tend the queen on his behalf, and he seems at least indirectly responsible for the poet's unfortunate end." Further, the consequence for Aigisthos' killing of Agamemnon is narrated by the poet. It is the revenge of Orestes, described with the traditional idiom "he killed his father-murderer" (ἔκτανε πατροφονῆα, 307; cf. *Odyssey* 1.299). Orestes' killing of Clytemnestra is not directly related, but it is insinuated in the description of the burial mound "for his hateful mother and cowardly Aigisthos" (μήτρος τε στυγερῆς καὶ ἀνάλκιδος Αἰγίσθοιο, 310).[34] Yet, this moves us beyond the scope of Agamemnon.

In Nestor's narrative, then, we have learned that a quarrel between the sons of Atreus effectively resulted in two separate departures and Agamemnon's arrival home alone. Significantly, as we saw, the language of Nestor's retrospective implied that Agamemnon's stance in this quarrel with his brother was the plan of a "thoughtless child" (νήπιος), "for he did not know what he was about to suffer" (οὐδὲ τὸ ἤδη, ὃ οὐ πείσθαι ἔμελλεν). The many appearances of the vocative νήπιος, a term we have already considered, emphasized the "thoughtlessness" of Agamemnon. By using this word, Nestor became the spokesman for the tradition as a whole, and the implications for Agamemnon were portentous. It would be a lack of forethought that would bring about his death. Further, in the conversation between Nestor and Telemachos, we heard about the pitiful circumstances surrounding Agamemnon's "death and baleful fate," and the sorry tale of "wide-ruling" (εὐρὺ κρείων) Agamemnon as paramount *basileus*, killed upon his return home. In our overview of *Odyssey* 3, then, we see the same sort of portrait of Agamemnon continue to emerge that we began to see in Chapter 2. Agamemnon is a pathetic victim, in part thanks to his own thoughtlessness on a number of occasions.

3.2.4 Menelaos' Delay and Agamemnon's Death: 4.90–92

Telemachos has just entered the palace of Menelaos, an abode resplendent with treasures from its owner's exotic wanderings during his delayed *nostos* (4.81–85). In reply to Telemachos' admiration over his home's apparent affinity to that of Olympian Zeus, Menelaos replies that his absence from Argos came at a cost (4.90–92):

> While I, about these parts, gathering much substance
> was wandering, meanwhile another man killed my brother
> by stealth, unexpectedly, by the ruse of his destructive wife.

---

[34] This is the only reference to the matricide in Homer that I am aware of.

εἷος ἐγὼ περὶ κεῖνα πολὺν βίοτον ξυναγείρων
ἠλώμην, τεῖός μοι ἀδελφεὸν ἄλλος ἔπεφνε
λάθρῃ, ἀνωϊστί, δόλῳ οὐλομένης ἀλόχοιο.

Menelaos' story emphasizes that the death of Agamemnon involved "another man" (ἄλλος) who goes unnamed but who is clearly assumed to be known to the audience, while the "ruse" (δόλος) is made possible through Agamemnon's "destructive wife" (οὐλομένη ἄλοχος). Agamemnon is killed "by stealth" (λάθρῃ), in circumstances where he was not personally expecting—"unexpectedly" (ἀνωϊστί)—what came. Reading this traditional word is difficult. Its only other occurrence is in *Iliad* 21.39. There the poet tells us that Achilles comes upon Lykaon, a young son of Priam and Laothöe, whom we considered earlier in relation to the formula "slaughter and baleful fate" (θάνατόν τε κακὸν καὶ κῆρα μέλαιναν). As we saw, Achilles had ransomed Lykaon the last time he caught him (but twelve days earlier), after Achilles had captured him on a night foray. The poet even provides details of that prior event. Achilles had surprised Lykaon as he was cutting fig branches for chariot rails from his father's orchard (35–38). He captured the unwary youth and then sold him into oppressive slavery from which he had only recently escaped. At the base of the rare descriptive word "unexpectedly" (ἀνωϊστί) is "expect" (οἴομαι), a verb that stresses a rather more personal note of reflection or thoughtfulness, which, in both Lykaon's and Agamemnon's cases, was clearly absent.[35] Agamemnon "did not expect, feel, or personally think"[36] that such a situation would arise. This adds one more example, however passing, to the many other instances of Agamemnon's thoughtlessness. Further, while Lykaon was given a short respite from his fate, on his second meeting, as we noted, Achilles did not hesitate to take his life. Agamemnon was not even this lucky, and lost his life through a lack of caution the first time around.

3.2.5 Proteus' Account of Agamemnon's Death: 4.512–537

Telemachos questions Menelaos about his father, and in his response we discover more about Agamemnon's history as a character in Homer's tradition. Menelaos' speech includes a retrospective narrative about his time in Egypt during his delayed *nostos*. He was not experiencing favorable winds to speed his journey from Pharos back to Argos, yet received divine assistance through the advice of the nymph Eidothea who took pity on him (4.364). Menelaos followed the

---

[35] Chantraine 1968:785, s.v. οἴομαι, contrasts νομίζω (unused by Homer) and ἡγέομαι.

[36] Chantraine 1968:785, s.v. οἴομαι suggests for οἴομαι *avoir l'impression /sentiment /croire personelle-ment (que)*.

sea nymph's advice. He trapped Proteus and received information that proves advantageous in our current quest for the characterization of Agamemnon in the *Odyssey*.

In the text under immediate consideration, Proteus first relates to Menelaos that: "somehow your brother fled from the baneful Fates and escaped in hollow ships" (σὸς δέ που ἔκφυγε κῆρας ἀδελφεὸς ἠδ᾽ ὑπάλυξεν / ἐν νηυσὶ γλαφυρῇσι, *Odyssey* 4.512–513). Some critics have regarded the subsequent narrative (514–520) as an interpolation. As Stephanie West notes, "If Agamemnon was making for the Argolid, we should not expect him to be near C. Malea, the southernmost tip of the Peloponnese" (in Heubeck, West, and Hainsworth 1988:224).[37] This proposition, when used to rearrange the text, fixes some immediate geographical difficulties, but misses other possible traditional allusions. Is there an argument, other than interpolation (which has no textual support)? I suggest that the poet (and his tradition), although less intent on geographical accuracy in the real world sense, is concerned with making connections with other traditional *nostoi* stories and certain ominous events that are imminent for Agamemnon as he returns home.[38] The "interpolation" is really an important part of the singer's inherited tale, which becomes clear when we consider the traditional language cues the poet includes.

In *Odyssey* 4.514, Agamemnon is described as almost reaching the "sheer mountain" (ὄρος αἰπύ) of Malea. Malea's geographical position is, like the island of Pharos, problematic (West in Heubeck, West, and Hainsworth 1988:224–225). Of course, a traditional poet's knowledge of the areas he speaks of need not be firsthand, since he is working as a poet in a tradition. Many elements in Homer seem concerned with real world accuracy, while others are more likely blended ideas, kept as traditional components from past performances of the same or related stories (cf. the judgment of Talbert 1985:8). Certainly this is the case with other epic traditions. Honko reports that, in his team's venture to explore the physical geography of Siri epic, he took the singer Gopala Naika to locations he had sung about but never visited. Honko comments:

> What was shocking indeed was the discovery that our singer had not seen the places we now went to examine together with him. Yet they were within walking distance. ... It was only our foreign type of (dis)believing

---

[37] It is traditionally the place where ships are blown off course, as Danek (1998:118) notes. We will return to consider this point in greater detail.

[38] In this way, my emphasis is on the meaning of Homer's traditional language, rather than with the singer's concern with multiple versions of Agamemnon's return, on which see Danek 1998:117–120, 237.

which the singer sensed and which made him suggest that we should go and see the places in question.[39]

Honko 1998:323

The singer of Siri epic was not fully aware of the topography of his song lyrics. Yet, as Danek (1998:117) notes, simply appealing to Homer's lack of geography should "nur ein letzter Ausweg sein," at least as the major motivating factor. The appeal to geographical inaccuracy, in fact, misses the point. Rather, more central for our consideration of the Homeric singer's mental topography is the meaning of the formulaic element "sheer mountain" (ὄρος αἰπύ) to the poet and his audience. An analysis of this noun-epithet combination shows that it is a traditional element in Homer's repertoire, occurring in both the *Iliad* and *Odyssey*. It is a traditional way "mountain" (ὄρος) is indexed as a formulaic part of the last hemistich of a line with a preceding genitive of the mountain's name.[40]

The concern over geographical obfuscation in *Odyssey* 4.514–515 may be partly met if we consider that perhaps the early audience heard this component of Menelaos' narrative not simply as a set of nautical directions, but rather as making reference to something traditional within the songs they were hearing. In particular, this is the place where a *nostos* can experience difficulty. For the same toponym and formulaic epithet that we have heard attached to Agamemnon, "'sheer mountain' of Malea" (Μαλείων ὄρος αἰπύ, B2 to line end, 3.287), conjoin to provide the central moment of departure also for Menelaos who is driven to Egypt, as Powell (1970:430) notes.[41] Menelaos then misses his opportunity to thwart the homicide of his brother (3.303). The same spot consequently connects the two events within the larger *nostoi*, but also intertwines two component stories related to the events at the beginning of the *Oresteia*: Agamemnon's homicide and Menelaos' absence. Odysseus also experiences problems at this spot (*Odyssey* 9.80–81), which positions him to begin his adventures with the inhuman Polyphemos. The "'sheer mountain' of Malea"

---

[39] As a contrast to Honko, we might take the example of the byliny collector, Marjanović (in Čolaković 2007:338, quoted in Ready 2015:31), who corrected topographical or historical confusion by byliny singers, a practice that consequently resulted in a "lack of mythic poems in his collection."

[40] The formulaic element, found twice in the *Iliad* (2.603, 2.829) and twice in the *Odyssey* (3.287, 4.514), forms part of a larger formula beginning at either B1 or B2. The sole exception to the use of this epithet is really present *metri causa* in *Iliad* 2.868: the epithet ἀκριτόφυλλον is used instead, when the singer had in his mind a place that would end at C1: οἳ Μίλητον ἔχον / B1 Φθιρῶν / C1 τ' ὄρος ἀκριτόφυλλον.

[41] Powell observes a correspondence in the story patterns of Menelaos and Odysseus within their *nostoi* and remarks that "both Odysseus and Menelaos lost their way home here." My findings are much in agreement with his, and his earlier suggestions are supported by my analysis of the traditional language.

(Μαλείων ὄρος αἰπύ), then, is a place of portending difficulty for a *nostos*, and the *Odyssey* poet invokes its implications here as he develops his tale.

Furthermore, what is perhaps equally noteworthy in our attempt to apprehend metonymic elements in Homer's portrayal of Agamemnon is where Agamemnon ends up. He is blown closer to the abode of Aigisthos (4.514–518):

> But when indeed quickly he was about to reach the sheer mountain
> of Malea,
> then indeed a storm wind, having snatched him up,
> bore him upon the fishy sea, deeply groaning,
> to the outskirts of the land, where Thyestes lived in his abode,
> before, but then Aigisthos son of Thyestes lived [there].

> ἀλλ' ὅτε δὴ τάχ' ἔμελλε Μαλειάων ὄρος αἰπὺ
> ἵξεσθαι, τότε δή μιν ἀναρπάξασα θύελλα
> πόντον ἐπ' ἰχθυόεντα φέρεν βαρέα στενάχοντα,
> ἀγροῦ ἐπ' ἐσχατιήν, ὅθι δώματα ναῖε Θυέστης
> τὸ πρίν, ἀτὰρ τότ' ἔναιε Θυεστιάδης Αἴγισθος.

Although the order, textual history, and geographical particularities of these verses are problematic, they nevertheless contain a very important narrative element. For it seems that Homer wishes us to see Aigisthos as living near Agamemnon within the kingdom of the son of Atreus and in his father's palace. This appears to be the case, no matter if "near" is still, in real world terms, fairly far away by land. It was near enough, thanks to the gale (θύελλα, 515).

The ensuing verses (4.519–520, in particular) are difficult to interpret, at least from a stringently logical point of view of the sort a ship's navigator might employ. What is Agamemnon doing at such a southerly point near Cape Malea in the first place if he is heading toward the Argolid from the Troad? Is there part of Agamemnon's *nostos* we are not privy to, but that is here hinted at? Or does the geographical location also suggest the influence of the historical double kingship of Sparta and Argos (so between Menelaos and Agamemnon)?[42] There is no indication of precisely when this constitutional polity actually began. It was clearly in place by the Archaic period and likely also well established in the Late Geometric period, which may be the period shaping our poet's understanding and narrative in his descriptive *mélange*.[43] This "collegiate kingship"

---

[42]   Cf. West in Heubeck, West, and Hainsworth 1988:224. Danek (1998:117) rejects this idea.

[43]   The system of dual kingship, however, could have originated much earlier, during the Dorian influx after 1100 BC, since it might have represented an ameliorating response between two ethnic groups. The first mention of dual kingship (other than this possible reference in Homer) occurs in Herodotus (6.52), where two characteristically opposed explanations (mythological

could represent an earlier performance component rather than a later contextualization by the poet. The traditional story of the potentially historical reign of Agis and Eurypon—Dorian and Argive, respectively—could have provided the model that allowed for a united view of Argolis and Laconia (Cartledge 2003:90) and consequently made a more southerly destination for Agamemnon possible. The singer's description of mythical events, then, may have been influenced in a general way by historical stories and political realities.

What, moreover, can we make of the direction taken after Cape Malea? It was obviously a northeasterly wind that got Agamemnon home from the Troad, and yet a regularly prevailing wind would have continued to carry him south to Cythera, not north along the Peloponnesus.[44] In order to keep the text as it stands, we would, I suggest, have to interpret this change in wind direction (now from the south) as another traditional language cue. It is a potentially destructive storm wind in what it portends and represents an example of malevolent divine activity of the sort that kept Odysseus and his men on Thrinakia—an unyielding wind also from the south (ἄλληκτος ἄη νότος, *Odyssey* 12.325). It was this sort of incessant wind that brought Agamemnon back to "Argos" and Thyestes' abode.[45] The scene then has an ominous aura attached to it, as implicated by the adversative statement, "but backwards the gods turned the wind [southerlies replacing northerlies], and they arrived home" (ἂψ δὲ θεοὶ οὖρον στρέψαν, καὶ οἴκαδ' ἵκοντο, *Iliad* 4.520). The same somber tone is set here as in the Thrinakian corollary, where the southerly wind keeps Odysseus and his men in a dangerous situation.[46]

Alternatively, Bothe's rearrangement (placing verses 517–518 immediately after 520), which forms the basis of Lattimore's translation, offers another possible solution, but one not without difficulties.[47] Bothe's rearrangement of

---

versus historical) are offered. Although there is no secure date for the inception of dual kingship, yet as noted by Ian Worthington in private correspondence, "it must have taken place during the Dark Ages, and is probably related to whatever it was that brought monarchy in Greece as a whole to an end and replaced it with eupatrid rule." Herodotus defines the separate roles of the two founding families (6.56–60). On the whole question, see Fraser 1898:312, Murray 1973:161–162, and Cartledge 2002:55–67; 2003:90–91.

[44] See Thomas and Stubbing 1962; and West in Heubeck, West, and Hainsworth 1988:224. Cf. the route of Odysseus in *Odyssey* 9.80–81.

[45] On the larger meaning of Argos, see Wace and Stubbings 1962:289–290.

[46] This, it seems to me, is a missing component to the otherwise excellent observations of Bill 1930:112–113.

[47] See West in Heubeck, West, and Hainsworth 1988:224–225 for disputes over the exact extent of territory and the implications of toponyms related to the kingdoms of the Atreidai in the Peloponnesus. Janko, in private response to my query over this passage, noted that Bothe's rearrangement raises another problem: "It's unparalleled in the textual transmission of either Homeric epic for a couplet to have been displaced in the entire paradosis, which is what Bothe's

lines, while a possible solution, has no textual support. Interpolation without textual support should remain an explanation of last resort. I am arguing instead that in the text as we have it, the poet wants us to consider Agamemnon, not just in relation to Aigisthos, but also in relation to Thyestes. What can be affirmed for *Odyssey* 4.514–518 as it stands is that the ensuing narrative of 519–537 wants us to see Aigisthos as living close enough to take the action he did. In this reading, certain formulaic components from the inherited tradition gain greater importance than real-life geography in the poet's mythic landscape. One key to making sense of this difficult passage, at least in the poet's presentation (geographical difficulties notwithstanding), may lie in what the traditional language is portending, in this case, impending danger. It is a danger already comprehended by the informed audience and further cued by formulae related to geographical locations and adverse winds. Agamemnon is facing a dilemma, and the language supports the intensity of what follows, his demise.

We turn now to consider lines 517–518 in their context, without textual rearrangement. In these two verses, we are suddenly brought face to face with an imminent peril from a story in Agamemnon's past—the House of Atreus: "At the outskirts of the land, where Thyestes lived in his abode / before, but then Aigisthos son of Thyestes lived [there]" (ἀγροῦ ἐπ᾽ ἐσχατιήν, ὅθι δώματα ναῖε Θυέστης / τὸ πρίν, ἀτὰρ τότ᾽ ἔναιε Θυεστιάδης Αἴγισθος). We experience here an early form of *correctio*. The poet is relating the story to his audience and says that Agamemnon arrived "at the outskirts of the country,"[48] where Thyestes was living, but then he notes: "Before, but then Aigisthos son of Thyestes lived [there]" (τὸ πρίν, ἀτὰρ τότ᾽ ἔναιε Θυεστιάδης Αἴγισθος). Other examples of *correctio* exist in Homer. I find three other related instances whose language parallels 518 in having "Before, but then" (τὸ πρίν, ἀτάρ) followed by an ensuing contrast created by a second temporal marker (such as "then," τότε or "now," νῦν) and the specifics of the *correctio* (*Iliad* 6.125, 16.573 and *Odyssey* 4.32). Similar poetic *correctio* is also known to us from the catalogue of ships in the

---

otherwise attractive transposition requires, so I would discount that." Powell's translation of the *Odyssey* also rejects Bothe's rearrangement of the text.

48 Stanford (1958:220) suggested "the part beyond the cultivated area," but this will not quite do. The phrase ἀγροῦ ἐπ᾽ ἐσχατιήν means "at the outskirts of the land" (although Redfield [1975:189–199] may be correct in suggesting the mediatory meaning of this phrase between nature and culture). Its other three occurrences in Homer are all in the *Odyssey*: Odysseus is compared to a burning log in an ash heap that someone buries "at the outskirts of the land" as he buries himself on the seashore of Phaiacia (5.489); Eurymachos offers Odysseus work "at the outskirts of the land" where he makes stone fences and grows trees (18.358); and "at the outskirts of the land" is where the swineherd lives (24.150). The idiom minimally suggests that Thyestes, and Aigisthos before him, lived out of view of the public eye.

case of Philoctetes (*Iliad* 2.716–725) and Achilles (2.768–779).[49] Taken together, these instances suggest a rhetorical device for Homer with possible significance in our present passage.

It appears that the poet, through rhetorical *correctio* in *Odyssey* 4.518, is acknowledging the dismal story of the House of Atreus well known in the Classical period. After Homer, we are assured, this tale included Thyestes' bedding of Atreus' wife, Aerope, and Atreus' retributive and repulsive feeding of Thyestes' children to their father. The domestic drama continues when Aigisthos is born through Thyestes' incestuous relations with his surviving daughter, Pelopia. It is she who gives birth to the future avenger, Aigisthos. The bloody past of the House of Atreus is, however, not presented to us in any clear detail until Aeschylus' *Agamemnon* (1217–1244, 1583–1611).[50] This does not mean that authors after Homer are simply inventing the stories clustering around this tale, since here we have indication that the poet may have had some knowledge of it. I am suggesting that this allusion by the singer added suspense and increased the hearer's sense of foreboding at what was known to be imminent—Aigisthos' long-awaited revenge through killing Agamemnon. The allusion to Thyestes may be the poet's way of acknowledging this portentous back story that increases tension for the audience of the *Odyssey*, but which the poet chose not to retell in any detail.[51] While it is impossible to say exactly what elements from the House of Atreus story were known in the Late Geometric and early Archaic period (i.e., the putative time of the memorialization of the *Iliad* and

---

[49] I am indebted to Richard Janko, in private communication, for noting these last two examples of *correctio*. In these cases I note the use of the formula ἀλλ' ὅ μέν to introduce the *correctio*. Cf. also *Iliad* 7.229, *Odyssey* 3.410.

[50] Securing details from early poets like Stesichorus is difficult because of the fragmentary and secondary nature of the material (Davies 1969 is of little help; see Neshke 1986, on the *fragmenta*). Pindar (*Pythian* 11) mentions the killing of Iphigeneia and the presence of Cassandra, but clearly Pindar did not invent his illustrations. It is within Aeschylus (see Garvie 1986:ix–xli) that clear evidence of story details of the House of Atreus (including the *Oresteia*) is found. For a detailed collection of the iconographic evidence, see Prag 1986 and Knopfler 1993. For an outline of the myth, see Gantz 1993:540, 544–556, 587.

[51] Did Atreus' cooking up of his children prove a little too grisly or physical (likewise Homer avoids details about eating, sex, or other bodily functions), or was it just the case that the story was not part of the poet's intended ὄιμη? (The story of Thyestes then is only background information, while the story of Aigisthos' dastardly actions is centrally noted in the *Odyssey*.) Doubtless Homer chose song components that matched his audience's tastes and his own narrative emphasis at any particular moment. Nor should we assume that the performance of the *Iliad* and *Odyssey* necessarily called for the same sort of rendition by the poet (regardless of whether or not the *Iliad* and *Odyssey* were sung by the same poet). After all, the tenor of each poem is different (Bowra 1962:61–72 and Saïd 2011:258–259; cf. our discussion in Chapter 1, n. 63).

Odyssey in writing),[52] such hints within the text are suggestive of some level of knowledge. The question of the singer's and audience's knowledge of this story will resurface again in Chapter 4 when we discuss another potential reference to Thyestes in the *Iliad*.

In our passage from the *Odyssey* under immediate consideration, Proteus continues his story. In doing so, he includes details of Aigisthos' ambush (εἶσε λόχον, 4.531), before commenting (534-535): "This one [Agamemnon] then, not recognizing the destruction, he [Aigisthos] led and killed, / having fed [Agamemnon] dinner, as someone kills an ox at a trough" (τὸν δ᾽ οὐκ εἰδότ᾽ ὄλεθρον ἀνήγαγε καὶ κατέπεφνε / δειπνίσσας, ὥς τίς τε κατέκτανε βοῦν ἐπὶ φάτνῃ). Agamemnon's ignorance of the trap set for him is emphasized—a lack of awareness that led to the success of the plot to take his life. Agamemnon's death is here represented by a traditional simile from Proteus' mouth. He was killed in a miserable manner, like an ox slaughtered at feeding time. This is a descriptive line that we will hear again later in Agamemnon's own story when it will be housed in a first person narrative.[53] In *Odyssey* 4, a final reference to Agamemnon occurs after Menelaos recounts Proteus' tale near the end of his speech (4.584). Menelaos reports that he made a cenotaph for Agamemnon in Egypt to render his *kleos* "unquenchable" (ἄσεβεστος). Menelaos acts as any good brother would when faced with the news of Agamemnon's death in a most unheroic manner.

3.2.6 Agamemnon's Joy: 8.75–82

In the Phaiacian palace of King Alkinoos and Queen Arete, Odysseus is being entertained as a newly arrived suppliant. After he arrives, the singer Demodokos is stirred by the Muse to find a poetic "pathway" (οἴμη) for his song.[54] In this

---

[52] Janko (1982; cf. 2012) establishes the likely chronological order of Homer's works. Janko's principal contribution is not meant to suggest absolute dating, but rather, relative chronology, which places the *Iliad*, at most, a few decades before the *Odyssey*. Martin West's (1995) arguments for a very late date for the *Iliad* are only partially convincing. The actual evidence he presents suggests that we need not place the memorialization of Homer's *Iliad* any later than 700 BC. (Cf. Fowler 2004b:225n22). Yet, the question is not easily answered, since the process of textualization is itself a vexed one. See the discussion of "oral-derived," in Chapter 1.

[53] In *Odyssey* 11.411, which we will consider shortly.

[54] The term οἴμη is found in the *Odyssey* (8.74, 471; 22.347) with this meaning. On the possible derivation of οἴμη, including οἶμος (note the reading, attested in some manuscripts, of οἶμος ἀοιδῆς in *Homeric Hymn to Hermes* 451), see Chantraine (1968:783, s.v. οἴμη) who proffers "chemin." Edwards (1987:19) comments on the sparse use of the motif of the Muse's invocation in the *Iliad* (only four times), a motif even less overtly induced in the *Odyssey*.

case, Demodokos is being directed to a "quarrel" (νεῖκος) between Odysseus and Achilles, who strove with vehement words (8.76–78):

> Thus once they contended at the gods' abundant feast
> with vehement words, but the ruler of men Agamemnon
> was rejoicing in his mind, because the best of the Achaians were
>   contending.

> ὥς ποτε δηρίσαντο θεῶν ἐν δαιτὶ θαλείῃ
> ἐκπάγλοισ᾽ ἐπέεσσιν, ἄναξ δ᾽ ἀνδρῶν Ἀγαμέμνων
> χαῖρε νόῳ, ὅ τ᾽ ἄριστοι Ἀχαιῶν δηριόωντο.

Little can be substantiated about this struggle between Odysseus and Achilles outside of this short narrative by the poet, a narrative tied together by ring structure: "contended/were contending" (δηρίσαντο/δηριόωντο). Nagy (1979:42–58) has gone some way in suggesting that the story, rather than being an ad-hoc invention meant to mimic *Iliad* 1,[55] contains traditional themes discernable in a number of places in Homer.[56] In other words, it is a traditional story since it is built with traditional components. One scholiast's conjecture proves less convincing, since he holds that the story is meant as a pointed contrast between Odysseus' "intelligence" (σύνεσις) and Achilles' "courage" (ἀνδρεία). The heroes are pictured as drinking together (παρὰ πότον), with Agamemnon in attendance, when a veritable symposium turns ugly. A "disagreement" (διαφορά) broke out, based upon what each hero thought would be the best way to take Troy. The imaginative scholiast has Achilles advising that they "act with brute force" (βιάζεσθαι) and Odysseus, that they "aim at guile" (δόλῳ μετελθεῖν).[57] Yet, of greater concern in our search for Agamemnon's character

---

[55] Marg (1956) and Rüter (1969:247–254) had earlier suggested a connection with the quarrel between Agamemnon and Achilles in the *Iliad* 1; so also now Rinon (2006:210–211). The difficulty with this view poses, however, is that the wrath of Achilles would then be based, not upon dissention between Achilles and Agamemnon (as in the *Iliad* we know), but between Achilles and Odysseus (cf. the comments of Broeniam 1996:5). Further, as Notopoulos (1964:32–33) comments: "to maintain that the wrath of other heroes is a pale copy of the wrath of Achilles would only point to an unimaginative bookish mentality," and so miss "a common theme in oral epics." On the possible link of this dispute and the one related in the *Cypria*, see Proclus 34, Strabo 1.2.4, and Kullmann 2015:121.

[56] Nagy suggests, for example, a convergence in themes between this story in the *Odyssey* and the embassy in *Iliad* 9. Broeniman (1996), building on Nagy's argument of shared themes, views the episode as an aberrant representation of the *Iliad*, quite appropriate for the odd Phaiacians. Finkelberg (1987:128–132) sees it as Homer's creation of a doublet anticipating the upcoming Trojan horse song to place greater emphasis on Odysseus.

[57] Σ *Odyssey* 8.75 (Dindorf 1855:361–362). The scholiast's placing of the event "after the death of Hector" (μετὰ τὴν Ἕκτορος ἀναίρεσιν), however, seems too late.

in Homer is Agamemnon's affective reaction to these heroes' contention. As is clear from the foregoing passage, the poet portrays Agamemnon elated at the turn of events. Agamemnon "was rejoicing in his mind" (χαῖρε νόῳ). But just why did Agamemnon react in this way? The poet next has Demodokos sing (8.79-83):

> For thus to him giving an oracular response, declared Phoibos Apollo
> in sacred Pytho, when he had stepped over the stone threshold
> to make consultation. For then next the start of the harm was rolling
>   along,
> for both Trojans and Danaans, by the plans of great Zeus.

> ὣς γάρ οἱ χρείων μυθήσατο Φοῖβος Ἀπόλλων
> Πυθοῖ ἐν ἠγαθέῃ, ὅθ᾽ ὑπέρβη λάϊνον οὐδὸν
> χρησόμενος. τότε γάρ ῥα κυλίνδετο πήματος ἀρχὴ
> Τρωσί τε καὶ Δαναοῖσι Διὸς μεγάλου διὰ βουλάς.

The context makes reference to an oracle of Apollo and the plans of Zeus, but it all remains difficult to interpret. Homer's core audience was perhaps better informed, either through knowledge of traditional themes or another full epic story. Yet, we are given the reason for Agamemnon's rejoicing in mind. It is the oracle of Apollo, a cause signaled by the particle "for" (γάρ, 79). This particle is most easily taken in the normal parataxis of story development as causative;[58] a usage Denniston confirms when he notes that "for" (γάρ) is

> commoner in writers whose mode of thought is simple than in those whose logical faculties are more developed. The former tend to state a fact before investigating its reason, while the latter more frequently follow the logical order, cause and effect, whether they employ subordination or co-ordination of clauses.[59]

> Denniston 1950:58

The reason for Agamemnon's joy, then, is not the quarrel between Achilles and Odysseus, itself, a point made some time ago by Snell: "Agamemnon's

---

[58] On Homer's paratactic rather than periodic style, see Edwards 1987:55-60.
[59] Although overly simplistic, Denniston's findings may suggest one difference between oral and some literary composition. The particle γάρ suggests that explanation or expansion, so premises, follow the conclusion. It is a question of arrangement. This phenomenon is common in Homer's mode of oral composition. See for instance *Iliad* 1.9, 55, 63, 78, 113, 120, etc.

delight does not spring from the altercation of the two most valiant heroes ... but from his recollection of Apollo's prophecy that Troy would fall when the best heroes contended with one another" (Snell 1953:12). Agamemnon had formerly consulted Delphi, here given in its usual Homeric locative form of "in Pytho" (Πυθοῖ; cf. *Iliad* 9.405).[60] Agamemnon was looking to the fall of Troy as his source of joy (although the heroes were reveling in their own competition to be the best). Odysseus breaks into tears as he hears the singer's rendition of these events, and yet even Odysseus' weeping (8.86) is best seen as related to the struggle at Troy, rather than simply his contention with Achilles. In fact, the same description of Odysseus' crying occurs much later in the same book as Arnould (1990:102) notes. There the poet further includes a simile that likens Odysseus' tears to that of a women lying over the body of her husband (523–524). She had just witnessed atrocities. Not only has she see him fight "for the city and children trying to beat off the pitiless day" (ἄστεϊ καὶ τεκέεσσιν ἀμύνων νηλεὲς ἦμαρ, 525) but she had been nearby "and caught sight of him dying and gasping for breath" (ἡ μὲν τὸν θνῄσκοντα καὶ ἀσπαίροντα ἰδοῦσα (526). The emphasis, then, if we read the moment with traditional resonance in mind, is first the tragedy of war for Odysseus. We will return to this point, since Agamemnon's joy may be seen as jarring when contrasted with Odysseus' tears.

Is there anything more about Agamemnon's disposition that we can learn from these verses? At first glance, there seems to be an element of mindful "calculation" in the phrase "he was rejoicing in his mind" (χαῖρε νόῳ), of the sort that Snell (1953:8–22) first articulated, where "*noos*=understanding." Snell contrasted *noos* with "*thumos*=emotion." A closer consideration, however, shows in fact that the collocation "he was rejoicing in his mind" (χαῖρε νόῳ) was more likely chosen by the singer over the much more prevalent "but he was rejoicing in his *thumos*" (χαῖρε δὲ θυμῷ) to suit his metrical needs.[61] The singer who has the formula "but he was rejoicing in his *thumos*" (χαῖρε δὲ θυμῷ) in his traditional lexicon, creates—at the level of unconscious fluency of course—a synonymous formulaic hapax "he was rejoicing in his mind" (χαῖρε νόῳ) through analogy. So no difference in meaning is intended here by the poet.

---

[60] The institution of an oracle at Pytho cannot be securely dated earlier than the eighth century (Fontenrose 1978:4). The other common place of oracular consultation (but filling different metrical positions) is Piraean Dodona: *Iliad* 16.233–234, *Odyssey* 14.327, and 19.296.

[61] χαῖρε δὲ θυμῷ: *Iliad* 14.156, 21.423, 22.224, *Odyssey* 8.483, 14.113, 24.145. Both phrases likely mean the same thing. The substitution of "in mind" (νόῳ, 8.78, to A2) in the run-over line is an instance of necessary *enjambement*. It occurs because the singer is one syllable shy of the space needed for "but in spirit" (δὲ θυμῷ) when placed before the upcoming formulaic phrase "because the best of the Achaians" (ὅ τ' ἄριστοι Ἀχαιῶν, A2–C2). This phrase is itself a variation of the more oft used singular ὅ τ' ἄριστος Ἀχαιῶν (*Iliad* 1.222, 412, 2.82, 5.103, 414, etc.), on which see Nagy 1979.

What we conclude from this episode is that Agamemnon rejoiced at what he believed to be the commencement of an oracle's fulfillment, rather than merely a *neikos* between two heroes. Yet the poet juxtaposes Agamemnon's immediate rejoicing with the realities of what actually followed: "the start of the pain was rolling along" (κυλίνδετο πήματος ἀρχή, 8.81). This is a consequence, the poet observes, which affected Achaians as well as Trojans. It is what we saw caused Odysseus great *goos*. It moved the poet himself to set Odysseus' tears through simile against the tragic reality of war, where women lost their husbands, and, seeking to guard their corpses, are hit with spear butts and dragged away into slavery (827–829). The story of the Trojan War and its aftermath is not a tale of immediate victory. Rather, it was a ten-year-long, drawn-out war that brought ensuing hardship, including doom for many on their voyage home and especially for Agamemnon. He had been away a long time as we noted earlier in this chapter, which to Homer and his tradition is part of the cause of his wife's unfaithfulness.[62] What seemed a boon turned to grief and misery for all, as the poet himself tells us (83).

Agamemnon's rejoicing is set immediately against such backstories. It suggests to Homer's core audience an Agamemnon who is both naive and thoughtless in his comprehension, and impetuous in his reaction to the quarrel. His response seems callously arrogant when heard within the local context through Odysseus' tears. Nor is it likely that Agamemnon's rejoicing was in any way a rational, calculated response, free of the normal sort of emotively fed feelings sprung from the *thumos*. After all, the hapax phrase, "he was rejoicing in his mind" (χαῖρε νόῳ), acts as an equivalent expression for "he was rejoicing in his *thumos*" (χαῖρε δὲ θυμῷ). Agamemnon's is a gut reaction, one that lacks the thoughtful and measured response one might expect from so central an Achaian leader.

3.2.7 The People of Agamemnon of the Greatest Fame: 9.263–266

In Odysseus' introduction to the pitiless Cyclops we find our next reference to Agamemnon. Odysseus and a dozen of his handpicked *hetairoi* have entered the cave of Polyphemos and helped themselves to his food.[63] Polyphemos' arrival and menacing insinuations strike immediate fear into Odysseus and his crew

---

[62] See Nestor's Stories of Quarrel, *Nostoi*, and *Oresteia*: 3.136–310, and Homer's use of θέλγεσκε in *Odyssey* 3.264, which highlighted the passage of time.

[63] Reece (1993:131) observes that this is the only Homeric hospitality scene in which the host is not at home when the guests arrive; Cf. Schein 2016:37. This is quite in keeping with the other type scene inversions found in the Polyphemos episode, as Reece (130–143) notes.

(9.256–257). Odysseus is able to respond all the same, and while doing so, affirms that they were part of Agamemnon's force at Troy (263–266):

> But the people of Atreus' son Agamemnon we boast ourselves to be,
> of whom indeed now greatest under heaven is his fame;
> For so great a city he sacked and destroyed a people
> [so] numerous.

> λαοὶ δ' Ἀτρεΐδεω Ἀγαμέμνονος εὐχόμεθ' εἶναι,
> τοῦ δὴ νῦν γε μέγιστον ὑπουράνιον κλέος ἐστί·
> τόσσην γὰρ διέπερσε πόλιν καὶ ἀπώλεσε λαοὺς
> πολλούς.

Agamemnon is here associated with the fall of Troy, including the sacking of the city. The sacking of the city is made emphatic through a final colon of synonymous parallelism, "and destroyed a people" (καὶ ἀπώλεσε λαούς, 265), followed in the next line by the enjambed adjective "[so] numerous" (πολλούς). The emphasis harkens back to the heroic efforts needed to fight against and capture Troy, and not surprisingly, the description of Agamemnon's reward for such an effort, "under heaven is his fame" (ὑπουράνιον κλέος ἐστί), finds a parallel in the *Iliad*. In the *Doloneia* we find a similar formulaic collocation of words for (promised) future fame (so, naturally εἴη, not ἐστί) for anyone who will respond to the call for action.[64] In the Iliadic example, the call to action is taken up unsurprisingly by Diomedes, who is the first to respond to Nestor's challenge delivered to the flagging troops.[65]

The metonym "under heaven is his fame" (ὑπουράνιον κλέος ἐστί), then, is known from a heroic context in the Trojan War story. Its use in the *Odyssey* by Odysseus is meant as "Droh- und Prahlgebärde" (Danek 1998:181) against Polyphemos, as it makes reference to the heroic world of the Trojan War and Agamemnon as the paramount leader of that military expedition.[66] The local context, however, seems full of irony. Odysseus speaks this traditionally suggestive language to an ogre who, as we have already heard from Odysseus in his retrospective narrative, is "wild, and neither recognizes justice well nor

---

[64] *Iliad* 10.212–213: μέγα κέν οἱ ὑπουράνιον κλέος εἴη / πάντας ἐπ' ἀνθρώπους, καί οἱ δόσις ἔσσεται ἐσθλή.

[65] See Chapter 2, s.v. 2.2.5 Diomedes and Sthenelos: 4.365–418.

[66] Danek follows Friedrich (1987) in seeing this as an indication that Odysseus is still in the world of the κλέος-driven Heroic epic, rather than the newer world of Odyssean virtues.

customs" (ἄγριον, οὔτε δίκας εὖ εἰδότα οὔτε θέμιστας, 9.215).[67] His consequent actions bear this characterization out most immediately (287–295). Homer, his external audience, and Odysseus as retrospective narrator (unlike Odysseus as a character in his own story) know that making reference to Agamemnon will have no effect on the monster. This tension takes away from the character of Agamemnon as a hero. The boast seems hollow.

What was the audience thinking about as it heard this story and the comment about Agamemnon's fame, "greatest under heaven" (μέγιστον ὑπουράνιον)? Olson (1990:68) is right to ascribe to the scene we are considering "a grimly ironic quality" in light of Odysseus' reference to the *kleos* of Agamemnon and Agamemnon's *nostos*. Homer's audience had constantly in mind what we have already heard overtly sung, the paradigmatic *kakos nostos* of Agamemnon.[68] So while the language of the passage elicits thoughts of Agamemnon as a paramount *basileus* and his eventual triumph in the Trojan War, there is also something ominous in the meaning of this traditional phrase in its present context. This is another example of the need always to gauge one aspect of Agamemnon's characterization by the whole range of stories attached to him and known to singer and audience.[69] Set within the events of *Odyssey* 9 and Odysseus' rude reception by the ogre Polyphemos (a tale whose dismal outcome is recognized proleptically by the audience), and against the backdrop of the *kakos nostos* of Agamemnon, Odysseus' declaration seems portentous. The presentation of the *kleos* of Agamemnon carries an ambiguous and sardonic quality that Homer's audience would not have missed. A similar ambiguity over Agamemnon's heroic prowess will be noted in Chapter 4. There we will consider the placement and abruptness of Agamemnon's *aristeia* and ask why the leader of all the Achaian forces at Troy is given such short shrift in what should be a high moment of personal heroic glory.

3.2.8 The *Nekuia*: 11.380–466

The first reference to Agamemnon in Odysseus' underworld visit comes early on from the mouth of Odysseus himself. He tells his mother Antikleia that he followed Agamemnon to Troy (11.168–169). The poet next brings on stage moments from

---

[67] Heubeck in Heubeck and Hoekstra (1989:28) comments that here "Odysseus is still unaware that he is outside the heroic milieu, and confronted by a being as unimpressed by the deeds and status of heroes as by the moral order of the heroic world."

[68] This is unsurprising if we consider that "the contrast between the homecoming of Odysseus and Agamemnon ... seems to preoccupy the poet of the Odyssey from beginning to end," as Tsagalis (2008a:41n38) reminds us. He notes the proclivity in *Odyssey* 1.32–34, 298–300, 3.194–198, 4.519–537, 11.385–461, 13.383–385. See also Klinger 1964:75–79, and Hölscher 1967.

[69] Cf. my earlier remarks in 3.2.6 Agamemnon's Joy: *Odyssey* 8.75–82.

Agamemnon's life and death beginning with Odysseus' comments to Alkinoos during the intermezzo in Odysseus' *apologos*. In his reply to the Phaiacian king, Odysseus begins with general comments that seem to anticipate the story of Agamemnon, as de Jong (2001:286.) observes.[70] For here Odysseus speaks, as she notes, in a way that ostensibly refers to his "companions" (ἑταῖροι, *Odyssey* 11.412), but actually applies only to Agamemnon's *nostos*. He notes the "cares" (κήδεα, 382) of his companions, who "on their *nostos* perished by the will of an evil woman" (ἐν νόστῳ δ' ἀπόλοντο κακῆς ἰότητι γυναικός, 384).

The *Nekuia* then immediately resumes via Odysseus' narrating his encounter with Agamemnon. The *psyche* of Agamemnon arrives, "grieving" (ἀχνυμένη, 11.388), in the company of those who "in the house of Aigisthos death and fate encountered" (οἴκῳ ἐν Αἰγίσθοιο θάνον καὶ πότμον ἐπέσπον, 389).[71] A teary meeting follows, stirred in its heightened intensity by an Agamemnon who is but a dim shadow of his former self, without force or vigor (393–394). Odysseus addresses Agamemnon using a traditional epithet, one suggestive of Atreus' son's full rank as paramount *basileus* at Troy: "Atreus' son renowned, ruler of men Agamemnon!" (Ἀτρεΐδη κύδιστε, ἄναξ ἀνδρῶν Ἀγάμεμνον, 397).[72] Indeed, there are other less weighty ways of addressing Agamemnon in direct address that the poet could have chosen.[73] For a short form of address, the appellation "Atreus' son" (Ἀτρεΐδη), contained within the larger formula above, is often employed.[74] The singer chose an epithet of greater scope and meaning. The poet's choice, however, placed as it is in Odysseus' address to the former paramount *basileus* at Troy now in the underworld, rings rather hollow. Moreover, the string of interrogatives that ensue, employing the rhetorical device of the "erroneous question" (de Jong 2001:287), would have struck the audience, who knew how Agamemnon died, with the full force of metonymic irony (11.398–403):

---

[70]   For the *Nekuia* more generally, see Eisenberger 1973:160–191, Crane 1988:96–100, Olson 1990, Danek 1998:214–250, and Saïd 2011:174–177.

[71]   *Odyssey* 11.387–389=24.20–24, except for a minor variation in 11.387 and 24.20.

[72]   This full address to Agamemnon is also used in *Iliad* 2.434, 9.96, 9.163, 677, 697, 10.103, 19.146, 199, *Odyssey* 11.397, and 24.121.

[73]   This, however, is the traditional way the poet uses to address "Agamemnon" (Ἀγάμεμνον) by name, since "Agamemnon" (Ἀγάμεμνον) does not exist *en seul* as a vocative in the singer's lexicon of expressions. Ἀγαμέμνων is employed without an epithet in the nominative and all oblique cases, however. Yet, other fuller expressions are available, as Friedrich has shown. I think that Friedrich's (2007:48) listing of Ἀτρεΐδη κύδιστε, ἄναξ ἀνδρῶν Ἀγάμεμνον with such metrically equivalent expressions as Ἀτρεΐδη κύδιστε φιλοκτεανώτατε πάντων (*Iliad* 1.122), demonstrates not the post oral nature of the epithet system of oral poetics, but rather, that the epithet could actually be heard in its local as well as traditional context as suggested in Chapter 1 (see s.v. 1.3 Reading Characterization Traditionally).

[74]   For example, *Iliad* 1.59, 222, 232, 282, 2.242, 254, 284, 344, 434, 3.182, etc.

What bane now has subdued you of abasing death?
Or you with the ships, did Poseidon subdue,
having stirred up for grievous winds a miserable blowing?
Or you did hostile men injure on dry land,
cutting out cattle and beautiful flocks of sheep
or for [some] city fighting and for [its] wives?

τίς νύ σε κὴρ ἐδάμασσε τανηλεγέος θανάτοιο;
ἠέ σέ γ᾽ ἐν νήεσσι Ποσειδάων ἐδάμασσεν
ὄρσας ἀργαλέων ἀνέμων ἀμέγαρτον ἀϋτμήν;
ἦέ σ᾽ ἀνάρσιοι ἄνδρες ἐδηλήσαντ᾽ ἐπὶ χέρσου
βοῦς περιταμνόμενον ἠδ᾽ οἰῶν πώεα καλὰ
ἠὲ περὶ πτόλιος μαχεούμενον ἠδὲ γυναικῶν;

There may be in this extended rhetorical question, with its mention of "wives" (γυναικῶν), a thought bridge for the poet in his composition, as I will suggest shortly. The lines are also subtly suggestive in another way. They enumerate the traditional manner in which heroic men die (nor is piracy a dishonorable venture when it involves pillaging the enemy).[75] Moreover, Agamemnon's response by priamel denies each of the possibilities in order (11.405–408):

Zeus-born son of Laertes Odysseus of many devices,
not me in the ships did Poseidon subdue
having stirred up for grievous winds a miserable blowing,
nor me did hostile men injure on dry land,

διογενὲς Λαερτιάδη, πολυμήχαν᾽ Ὀδυσσεῦ,
οὔτ᾽ ἐμέ γ᾽ ἐν νήεσσι Ποσειδάων ἐδάμασσεν
ὄρσας ἀργαλέων ἀνέμων ἀμέγαρτον ἀϋτμήν,
οὔτε μ᾽ ἀνάρσιοι ἄνδρες ἐδηλήσαντ᾽ ἐπὶ χέρσου,

The apparent intent of this pedantic, line-by-line negation by Agamemnon is to draw out through the parallelism of the neighboring narratives the momentous import of the miasmatic event he next describes—his own death. It is notable that the same erroneous question asked here of Agamemnon by Odysseus is employed by Agamemnon in his address to Amphimedon in *Odyssey* 24 (as we will see). There, dissimilar to Agamemnon, Amphimedon does not reply in a priamel, but instead simply narrates the events surrounding the killing of

---

[75] Cf. Thucydides 1.5.2 and 6.5.4, whose comments may be influenced by Homer. Cf. Strabo 1.3.2. On piracy and heroes, see Souza 1999:20–23.

the suitors. Evidently a more rhetorical emphasis is intended by the poet in the present context of his song. Agamemnon's line-by-line response builds and looks toward what is to come, the cardinal point,[76] when Agamemnon suddenly breaks away from his responsion to recite the real cause of his demise, the ultimate point of interest (11.409–411):

> Rather for me, Aigisthos, having contrived death and doom,
> killed [me] with [the help of my] destructive wife, having called me
>   toward the *oikos*,
> having fed [me] a meal, as someone kills an ox at a trough.

> ἀλλά μοι Αἴγισθος τεύξας θάνατόν τε μόρον τε
> ἔκτα σὺν οὐλομένῃ ἀλόχῳ οἶκόνδε καλέσσας,
> δειπνίσσας, ὥς τίς τε κατέκτανε βοῦν ἐπὶ φάτνῃ.

There is close parallelism of words, events, and themes between the erroneous question and the response. Further, the cardinal point and the lines immediately following, although not completely parallel in wording, do in fact continue the cognitive response working within the singer's mind. In response to the erroneous question that had Agamemnon cutting out the flocks of the enemy (402), we hear instead that Agamemnon and his men died like slaughtered animals (411, 413). Moreover, women act passively as an object of the men's piratical and heroic raiding in the erroneous question (403), but in the reply (411), a female is the active co-perpetrator of the crime, helping to subdue the returning hero and his *hetairoi*. The rhetorical descent is clear: from the chance for a male to find heroic honor, to the reality of shameful acts and being unspeakably dishonored. From women as object of passive plunder to a woman who destroys with active aggression. The chiastic contrast between question and response is stark and the rhetorical device most effective in picturing the pathetic demise of the Achaians' foremost leader. And to think, this all happened in a domestic setting, rather than in battle!

The foregoing portentous correspondences in theme, as the poet first implicates and then explicates actual events, help increase audience tension as Agamemnon speaks. The observations of Beye (2006:151) about the *Oresteia* are apt here: "there are tensions in the plot which make even the practiced listener of this story speculate and fantasize." This tension in the plot may also, through irony, suggest something for our comprehension of Agamemnon's character: his utter thoughtlessness in regard to the potential danger for himself and his men who experience complete surprise at the bloody turn of events. The animal

---

[76] On the cardinal point, see Race 1982:14–15.

metaphor "an ox at a trough" (βοῦν ἐπὶ φάτνῃ) may do more than just suggest victimization (though it does this too); it may hint at a lack of reflective human forethought.

The narrative of Agamemnon continues with the pathetic events of the *kakos nostos*: the feast, the slaughter of his men, and the killing of Cassandra by Clytemnestra (11.412–423). We already hear early on in this story that Aigisthos had Clytemnestra's assistance in the killing.[77] As yet, however, we have not been told overtly (as readers of the text) that she actually helped in the *physical* act of the murder itself, something we will not learn about until much later in our written texts (*Odyssey* 24.97). Yet, the theme of the scheming "ruse strategist" (δολόμητις) Clytemnestra is already front and center throughout the exchange between Agamemnon and Odysseus (11.422, 428–430, 437).

Agamemnon's reply to Odysseus also includes an element that we can see, by comparison with its use later on, is of the sort to arouse pity. Specifically, I refer to the formula of 11.412 that records Agamemnon's description of his death. He says that he died "by a most pitiable death" (οἰκτίστῳ θανάτῳ).[78] Agamemnon makes this traditional idiom more emphatic by a summary priamel,[79] which (following a foil in 416–418) ends with the climax: "but these things especially, upon viewing, you would have lamented in [your] spirit" (ἀλλά κε κεῖνα μάλιστα ἰδὼν ὀλοφύραο θυμῷ, 418). The theme of pity for Agamemnon is extended to his men and Cassandra by the poet's choice of words and the image he presents (421–426). In line 421, we hear the "most pitiable ... voice" (οἰκτροτάτην ... ὄπα) of Cassandra as she is killed over Agamemnon. Agamemnon lay dying, but when dead, "Clytemnestra ruse strategist" (κλυταιμνήστρη δολόμητις 422), "dog-faced" (κυνῶπις, 424) turned away (νοσφίσατ', made emphatic by necessary *enjambement*), unwilling even to fulfill the customary act of shutting his eyes and mouth.[80]

In the foregoing narration by the *Odyssey* poet we have the first fairly full and overt exposition of the events surrounding Agamemnon's death. De Jong (2001:288) argues that: "Agamemnon presents Clytemnestra, who had

---

77 "Aigisthos ... killed [me] with [my] destructive wife" (Αἴγισθος ... ἔκτα σὺν οὐλομένῃ ἀλόχῳ, 409–410).

78 νῦν δ' ἄρα σ' οἰκτίστῳ θανάτῳ ἁλῶναι. This formula is likewise found in *Odyssey* 24.34, where it acts as a description of Agamemnon's death told to him to him by Achilles in conversation between these two shades in the underworld.

79 On the summary priamel, see Race 1982:31.

80 We will consider the connotations of κυνῶπις in greater detail in Chapter 4 (s.v. 4.2.1 Agamemnon's Dishonoring and Hubristic Actions: 1.6–344), where we see it applied to Agamemnon himself. The conflict caused by the homecoming hero (with concubine in tow) will also be considered in more detail there. I will simply note here, as Danek (1998:234) persuasively argues, that this tension is already present for Homer within his tradition, where Agamemnon is remembered as thoughtlessly naive.

maintained a 'low profile' in previous versions of the 'Oresteia' story, as its main culprit." The traditional audience, however, remembering not only one moment but the experiences of many epic performances was likely well aware of Clytemnestra's role. We will revisit the active part played by Clytemnestra in Agamemnon's death in greater detail when we consider one traditional phrase in *Odyssey* 24. Suffice it to say here that the momentary presentation of one element in the greater story pattern can provide emphasis, but not to the complete exclusion of other known elements. While we as linear, textual readers only become aware at this point of certain facts, by contrast, the traditional audience, through metonymy, was already more cognizant of them even where the singer is less direct (cf. Olson 1995:39). A point made in Chapter 2 bears reemphasizing here: that the singer enjoys retelling the story he presents, which is quite different from saying that the story was generally foreign or unknown to his core audience. Why and when the singer chooses to engage more fully certain aspects of his traditional story through expansion is a question of the singer's style. When he wishes, he creates emphasis by more intently focusing our gaze on a particular scene. In the present scene, Agamemnon's experience of Clytemnestra is being used by the poet as a warning to Odysseus himself (cf. de Jong 2001:288–289).[81] This poetic purpose becomes particularly evident in the words of Agamemnon directly following Odysseus' commiserative comments (11.436–439). The poet has Agamemnon reply by admonishing Odysseus not to be gentle with his wife or to reveal everything he knows, but rather to reveal part of his account while keeping part hidden (441–443).

Through knowledge gained in retrospect (see 11.524–529) and with a fear of women candidly avowed, Agamemnon also advises Odysseus not to bring his ship home "openly" (ἀναφανδά, 455). The stress here appears to be on Odysseus taking Agamemnon as an example to avoid, and to do this by careful forethought. The traditional idiom used by Agamemnon to introduce a second piece of advice for Odysseus—"But this other matter to you I speak, but you cast [this] in your heart" (ἄλλο δέ τοι ἐρέω, σὺ δ' ἐνὶ φρεσὶ βάλλεο σῇσιν, 454)—is a formula that occurs fourteen times in Homer. A consideration of all its occurrences yields its implications in the present context. The formula is used by a character to suggest the presence of extremely fervent emotion and personal

---

[81] Foley (1999:140) shows the background of the story pattern and the necessary ambiguity attached to this scene for an audience aware that "the wrong fork in the narrative road" was taken by Agamemnon who advises caution. This would add to the suspense of the scene, though the audience was aware that Penelope would be faithful and secure for Odysseus a safe *nostos*. In Foley's words (in private correspondence), we are dealing with "the difference between two complementary frames of reference, the Return Song [pattern] and *this* Return Song." For Penelope's part in the Return Song morphology, see Foley 1999:142–157.

participation in the information being shared.[82] Several examples will suffice to show its traditional tenor. It is used by Achilles to Agamemnon (*Iliad* 1.297), not long after Achilles has dashed the scepter to the ground in anger and disgust, just before the assembly is dissolved; by Zeus to Hera (4.39), after the poet has noted Zeus' own state as "greatly vexed" (μέγ' ὀχθήσας, 30), itself a traditional idiom stressing an emotional pitch;[83] by Diomedes to Sthenelos (5.259), who has advocated for retreat, only to receive a sharp rebuke; by Achilles to Phoinix (9.611), who tells his foster father to beware taking the side of his enemy; and by Hera to Zeus (16.444), to warn him not to save Sarpedon.[84]

In *Odyssey* 11, the strong emotion of Agamemnon and injunction to Odysseus for prudent action in the future seem apt. Suspense is created too, as Odysseus, limited in his perspective of cosmic actions and divine plan, does not know just how (or if!) things will work out. Yet, Agamemnon's dismal fate, couched in emotionally charged words of warning by Agamemnon himself, acts as a caution for Odysseus that things could end badly if he is not more careful. The whole conversation is brought to a close through ring composition: "we stood, grieving, thick tears flowing down" (ἕσταμεν ἀχνύμενοι, θαλερὸν κατὰ δάκρυ χέοντες, 466; cf. 391). Through the idiomatic cue of an emotional warning, we see the poet's portrayal of Agamemnon as an example to be avoided by planning. Odysseus should act less naively and more thoughtfully than Agamemnon.

---

[82] The formula is usually followed by a very strong warning or plea as suggested here by ἄλλο. The use of the first part of this well attested idiom also occurs in three other places beyond those I note here (*Iliad* 15.212, 23.82, and *Odyssey* 24.248), each with different concluding hemistiches, and may be instances of formulae by analogy.

[83] μέγ' ὀχθήσας is used a total of thirteen times in Homer, always preceded by τὴν δέ or τὸν δέ, to complete the first hemistich to B1. It is used of Zeus, greatly vexed because of Thetis' request for him temporarily to assist the Trojans and so pit himself against Hera (*Iliad* 1.517); again of Zeus, in a confrontation with Hera (4.30) and in his reaction to Poseidon's strong speech against the Achaian wall (7.454); of Poseidon in his reaction to Hera's proposal to fight against Zeus (8.208); again of Poseidon, in his reaction to Zeus' authoritarian orders (15.184); of Achilles in his emotional reaction to Patroklos' request for his armor (16.48); of Menelaos, guarding the corpse of Patroklos against a glory-seeking Panthoös (17.18); of Achilles, speaking of his own and Patroklos' death (18.97); of Achilles, vexed by his horse Xanthos given voice to prophesy his death (19.419), and again of Achilles who is troubled by the deception of Apollos (22.14). In the *Odyssey*, it is first used of Menelaos, vexed by the lack of hospitality shown by his servant to Telemachos and Peisistratos (4.30); again of Menelaos, agitated by Telemachos' report of the rapacious suitors (4.332); and of Eumaios, utterly concerned for the disguised Odysseus' safety (15.325).

[84] The other instances of its use include: Patroklos to Hector (*Iliad* 16.851); Lykaon to Achilles (21.94); Odysseus to Telemachos (*Odyssey* 16.281, 299); Penelope to Eumaios (17.548); Odysseus to Penelope (19.236); and Penelope to Odysseus (19:570).

3.2.9 Avoiding Agamemnon's *Nostos*: 13.383–385

Odysseus has returned to Ithaca. He has just been met by Athena in the form of a herdsman (13.222), who subsequently reveals her identity.[85] The two sit and, employing what Athena describes as innate skills common to both of them (296–299, 372–373), devise the destruction of the suitors. During the course of her first speech in their planning session (375–386), Athena reveals the particulars of what has been portending for Odysseus for some time, an encounter with the hubristic and troublesome suitors.[86] Odysseus' reaction is one of great surprise and appreciation, as he hears a few more details describing the state of his *oikos*. His astonishment is made emphatic by a great deal of hyperbaton, and the Greek word order is nearly impossible to effect in English prose. Odysseus exclaims (13.383–385):

> O my my really now![87] By Agamemnon Atreus' son's
> evil fate I was expecting[88] to perish in the palace,
> if to me, you, each of these things, goddess, had not spoken in due
>   measure.

> ὦ πόποι, ἦ μάλα δὴ Ἀγαμέμνονος Ἀτρεΐδαο
> φθείσεσθαι κακὸν οἶτον ἐνὶ μεγάροισιν ἔμελλον,
> εἰ μή μοι σὺ ἕκαστα, θεά, κατὰ μοῖραν ἔειπες.

Odysseus' reply is emphatic. He was expecting to perish and even earlier than he would have thought possible, had not Athena warned him.[89] His reply emphatically makes reference to Agamemnon through his patronymic "Atreus' son," and includes reference to Agamemnon's "evil fate." Yet, there has been no lead-up for Odysseus making such a reference—certainly nothing in the recorded words of Athena. By this point, what the poet means to do is to reestablish for

---

[85] On the centrality of Athena in Homer's version of the *Odyssey*, see Schwinge 1993.

[86] Cf. the prophecies of the Cyclops (*Odyssey* 9.526–536) and Teiresias (*Odyssey* 11.110–120).

[87] The first hemistich—ὦ πόποι, ἦ μάλα δή—found ten times in Homer, must clearly be kept together in any English translation that wishes to retain the original idiom intact (although the first part of the lager idiom, ὦ πόποι, admits of many possible variations, depending upon what is coming at the end of the line). Chantraine (1968–1980:928) notes its onomatopoeic nature. As part of other expressions or alone, ὦ πόποι occurs fifty times in Homer.

[88] Hoekstra in Heubeck and Hoekstra (1989:187; cf. Stanford [1958:213]) notes that the verb μέλλω in Homer indicates less futurity than likelihood. The use of the future infinitive, however, does suggest futurity (Chantraine 1963:307) and also immediacy (Monro 1891:203; Chantraine 1963:308) in the expected outcome.

[89] Chantraine's (1963:308) summary makes clear the type of futurity intended by the infinitive after μέλλω in Odysseus' words: "l'accent et mis sur l'énonciation d'un événement à venir plutôt que sur la volonté."

the hearer in his present rendition of Odysseus' *nostos* the close companionship of Odysseus and Athena (temporarily absent during most of the *Nostoi* tales).[90] Homer's core audience know, however, as listeners informed by the larger tradition, that Odysseus is not about to walk uninformed into a trap that would turn him into a sorry hero of a *kakos nostos*.[91] Odysseus' retort, then, is not random. It seeks instead to recall in our minds Agamemnon as a paradigm that portends the possibility of imminent danger to be avoided at all costs by planning. Suspense is at a high pitch. This is because the other adverse outcome for Odysseus, that he could experience a *kakos nostos*, exists *in potentia*.[92] Tension is created despite the traditional audience's knowledge of Odysseus as a capable character and his sure participation within a known story that has him achieve a successful homecoming.[93] The sudden and unexpected reference to Agamemnon and the connotations of his pathetic *nostos* act as an effective foil for Odysseus' own journey home.

The whole scene surrounding this reference to Agamemnon (13.383), including the collaborative plans of Odysseus and Athena, and even Odysseus' consequent disguise (429–439), acts to emphasize the common effort that will retake the Ithacan *polis*. Through this united effort, Ithaca's *basileus* and his family will be restored to hegemony, surely portrayed by the *Odyssey* poet as a good thing that will reinstate social order. Athena rejoins Odysseus first, to be followed by Odysseus' faithful servants and family members, one by one. In this way, Agamemnon's fate will not be Odysseus' fate, thanks to the well-considered scheme of Odysseus (and his patron deity). The miserable homecoming of Agamemnon is avoided by careful forethought, something not a part of Agamemnon's story or traditional character traits, so it seems.

---

[90] See Odysseus' complaint (13:316–323) and Athena's response (339–343). Clay (1983:54–68) connects this absence with the theme of Athena's wrath. I also see it as part of an overall emphasis in the *Odyssey* on human motivation and self-responsibility—an increasing humanism (an emphasis one may legitimately contrast with that of the *Iliad*). Cf. the connection of human motivation and justice in Deneen 2003:63–66.

[91] See my comments in Chapter 2 (s.v. 2.1.2 Character Traits and History).

[92] The first words of Telemachos to the disguised Odysseus (*Odyssey* 16.73–77) concern the potentially ambivalent plans of Penelope and so increase the tension within the poet's traditional rendition. On the possibility of variable *nostoi* even for Odysseus (e.g. to Thesprotia) and the appropriation of Odysseus by particular communities over time, see Malkin 1998:126–134.

[93] As Foley (1999:138) expresses it: "From this perspective the trek homeward is foreordained from the initial book of the *Odyssey*: there is no question that the hero will inevitably reach Ithaka after requisite trials and tribulations. But what he finds there must always to some degree hang in the balance. Even if the names of Odysseus and Penelope themselves forecast a successful reunion of long-suffering hero and his equally long-suffering faithful wife, the expressive force of the Return *sēma* introduces a palpable tension."

3.2.10 Agamemnon As Paramount *Basileus*: 14.70–71, 117, 497

The embedded references to Agamemnon in *Odyssey* 14 occur during a conversation between the swineherd Eumaios and Odysseus disguised as a beggar. The first two occurrences of Agamemnon in this book refer to Odysseus having left for Ilion or supposedly perishing there, "for the sake of Agamemnon's honor" (Ἀγαμέμνος εἵνεκα τιμῆς, 14.70–71), words spoken by Eumaios and repeated in Odysseus' retort (117). The "honor" (τιμή) in each case is that attached to Agamemnon's office as paramount *basileus*.

The third reference to Agamemnon is housed within a lying tale told by a disguised Odysseus as yet unrecognized by his servant-host, Eumaios.[94] Odysseus tells a story in order to test Eumaios' hospitality. In his fictive rendition, he makes himself a nameless soldier who is treated kindly by Odysseus during a night foray. In the tale, he describes how Odysseus has another servant return at night "to Atreus' son Agamemnon, shepherd of the people" (Ἀτρεΐδη Ἀγαμέμνονι, ποιμένι λαῶν, 14.497) so that he, cold and in danger of freezing to death, could have his mantle (486–502). The adonean epithet "to the shepherd of the people" (ποιμένι λαῶν), here attached to the formulaic "to Atreus' son Agamemnon" (Ἀτρεΐδη Ἀγαμέμνονι, used three times in Homer) recalls, among other things, the role of Agamemnon as the paramount leader of the Achaian host. Since "to Atreus' son Agamemnon" (Ἀτρεΐδη Ἀγαμέμνονι) already exists in the dative, as does the even shorter "to Atreus' son" (Ἀτρεΐδη), it may be that the poet's choice of the fuller noun-epithet formula, "to Atreus' son Agamemnon, shepherd of the people" (Ἀτρεΐδη Ἀγαμέμνονι, ποιμένι λαῶν), reflects a conscious wish to emphasize the office of Agamemnon as well as his person.

Further, for the core audience, aware not only of the stories contained in the *Iliad*, but likely many more related to Agamemnon as paramount *basileus*, no doubt the epithet "to the shepherd of the people" (ποιμένι λαῶν) conjured up apposite parallel tales to which we are no longer privy.[95] It is important to note that the epithet itself does not signify whether or not Agamemnon is in fact a "good shepherd." Its use in the Homeric tradition, according to Haubold (2000:20), may even imply something negative about the actual character of Agamemnon, the likelihood of failure: "Failure of the shepherd is the rule, not the exception." Haubold's contribution is intended to correct what he sees as the prevalent view (influenced, he says, by the more positive picture of the

---

94 The "lying" tale that Odysseus recounted doubtless had parallels in other contemporary "true" tales involving night raids that were actually part of the Trojan War stories. The *Doloneia*, which we will consider in the next chapter, may represent such a tale.

95 The epithet is used fifty-six times in Homer, all in the dative and accusative cases, to describe various characters. For lists of its occurrence in Homer, Hesiod, and other early epic traditions, see Haubold 2000:197.

shepherd in the Judeo-Christian tradition). That said, it is important to note that the epithet can be used in Homer to describe a shepherd who is not a failure, as Haubold also mentions. In other words, even with this title, Agamemnon *could have been* a good shepherd. He just wasn't, however, as we are discovering. We will revisit this theme again in greater detail in Chapter 5.

3.2.11 *Nekuia Deutera: Odyssey* 24.19–97

The poet takes us to the underworld for a second time, and again we meet and hear the *psyche* of Agamemnon.[96] As I noted earlier in this chapter, virtually the same lines introduce both appearances of Agamemnon in the underworld in *Odyssey* 11 and 24.[97] In *Odyssey* 24, Agamemnon comes grieving, surrounded by those who also met their fate in the house of Aigisthos. In this compressed scene, Agamemnon and his men will meet up with Achilles (and the newly arrived suitors) for the first time. The meeting of Achilles and Agamemnon does not occur when we might expect it to in a purely chronological account, but such a consideration is unnecessarily reductionist.[98] This dexterously woven poetic presentation reminds us that while the tradition preserves particular character traits and events, the poet in fact has extensive opportunity in his choice of presentation for *variatio*. What he achieves by his conflation of time frames is the occasion to verbalize a number of themes and events that form a part of Agamemnon's history.

Achilles is the first to address Agamemnon, and it is clear that he is aware how Agamemnon died (although we are not told how he knows). The reality of what Agamemnon's appearance in Hades means is unfolded as Achilles speaks. Homer is playing up the narrative moment. The scene is presented as the first meeting of Achilles and Agamemnon since their deaths. Achilles sounds shocked, even as he speaks, since all the Greeks considered Agamemnon dear to Zeus. After all, he had ruled over many noble men in Troy (24.26). Achilles continues (28–29): "Yet in fact for you [Agamemnon] early on, bent on approaching, was / a destructive

---

[96] The sudden switch to the underworld has been seen as a problem for some time (Σ *Odyssey* 23.296 [Dindorf 1855:722]): Ἀριστοφάνης δὲ καὶ Ἀρίσταρχος πέρας τῆς Ὀδυσσείας τοῦτο ποιοῦνται. This is argued on stylistic and linguistic grounds (Merkelbach 1951:142–155, Erbse 1972:166–244), although many scholars feel it is authentic and important for the overall story (Moulton 1974:127n23, Heubeck 1974:128–130, Danek 1998:463, Saïd 2011:218, and Marks 2008:62–81), which is my own position. For an outline of the debate, see especially Wender 1978:19–38 and Marks 2008:62–81; for the *Nekuia* as a "decreasing doublet," an oral compositional technique, see Kelly 2007b.

[97] See Chapter 3, s.v. 3.2.8 The *Nekuia*: 11.380–466.

[98] de Jong (2001:568) finds this "breach of [chronological] realism" in the *Odyssey* comparable to the *Teichoskopia* of the *Iliad*, and we might also add to such "breaches" the duel between Paris and Menelaos in *Iliad* 3.

lot!" (ἦ τ' ἄρα καὶ σοὶ πρωῗ παραστήσεσθαι ἔμελλε / μοῖρ' ὀλοή). The surprise in Achilles' voice is captured by the poet through his use of "Yet in fact" (ἦ τ' ἄρα καί). Denniston notes the effect of ἄρα with a past tense: "The reality of a past event is presented as apprehended … at the moment of speaking" (Denniston 1950:36, II. [2]; so also de Jong 2001:568). It makes what follows "neu und interessant" (Denniston 1950:32 [agreeing with Hartung]). Further, it is not solely ἄρα that suggests this, but rather, its use here in a formulaic system that includes ἦ, which together more greatly emphasize irony and surprise. The poet's choice of this expression to fill the first colon serves well to cue what ensues.

The irony and surprise in Achilles' voice is followed by a vain wish (24.30: ὡς ὄφελες), but also a potential history of events of what would have happened if Agamemnon had actually died at Troy (32–33): "In that land for you, a monument, all-Achaians would have made, / and for your son, great fame you would have won afterward" (τῷ κέν τοι τύμβον μὲν ἐποίησαν Παναχιοί[99] / ἠδέ κε καὶ ᾧ παιδὶ μέγα κλέος ἦρατ' ὀπίσσω). No doubt the audience is also thinking about the real, rather than the potential history of Agamemnon's son, Orestes, who acts as a foil for Telemachos.[100] Further, the irony and surprise that met us in the midst of Achilles' speech ("Yet in fact!" [ἦ τ' ἄρα καί]) are now completed with a temporal contrariety:[101] "But in reality, by contrast, it had been doomed for you, by a most pitiable death, to be taken" (νῦν δ' ἄρα σ' οἰκτίστῳ, θανάτῳ εἵμαρτο[102] ἀλῶναι, 24.34). The poet's choice of "had been doomed" (εἵμαρτο), as Dietrich (1965:282) points out, references an unpleasant mode of death in Homer. The poet wants us to see the deep *pathos* of Agamemnon's situation.

Agamemnon's response to Achilles incorporates a description of the ritual surrounding Achilles' funeral, including the visit by Thetis and her divine attendants. Of note is the sudden threatened rout to the ships (50), which Agamemnon says would have transpired (51–52), "except a man restrained [them], knowing many and ancient things— / Nestor, whose counsel even earlier appeared best" (εἰ μὴ ἀνὴρ κατέρυκε παλαιά τε πολλά τε εἰδώς, / Νέστωρ, οὗ καὶ πρόσθεν ἀρίστη φαίνετο βουλή). The traditional phrase "knowing many and ancient things" (παλαιά τε πολλά τε εἰδώς) occurs three times in the *Odyssey*.[103] In all its occurrences, including its use as a description of Nestor by Agamemnon, it

---

[99] This traditional language is also employed in the *Odyssey* by Eumaios (24.32) to describe what could have been done for Agamemnon; and by Telemachos (1.239), to describe what could have been done for Odysseus.

[100] Cf. my comments in this chapter, s.v. 3.2.1 Agamemnon's *Nostos* and the *Oresteia*: 1.30–43.

[101] That is, it provides the contrast for the whole μέν clause.

[102] On εἵμαρτο (the root perhaps also responsible for μοῖρα and αἶσα), see Dietrich (1965:184, 207, 263–264, 278, 282).

[103] The adjective παλαιά, here used substantively, only occurs in Homer within this traditional phrase. The phrase does not occur in the *Iliad*.

is associated with an aged traditional figure characterized by an ability to give sound advice. The counsel is not necessarily accepted and followed by everyone within a particular narrative setting, however. In *Odyssey* 2.188, it is used to describe Halitherses, an aged warrior and prophet. It is embedded within a threat by Eurymachos, following Halitherses' warning and advisement to him and the other suitors. Eurymachos does not listen. Eurymachos should have listened and acted, however, as the plot of the *Odyssey* makes clear! In *Odyssey* 7.157, the poet himself employs the idiom to describe the aged hero Echeneos as he gives counsel to Alkinoos, who does listen (and act). In the present story, Agamemnon indicates that Nestor's advice was timely, and in giving it to the trembling Achaians (*Odyssey* 24.49), he notes, it stayed their fear (57) and changed the outcome of events through changed action.

We do wonder at this moment, and will continue to wonder in future chapters, why Agamemnon himself was not in charge at critical moments, or at least capable of thoughtful planning. Nonetheless, the void left by Agamemnon was more than adequately filled in this case by the restraining speech of Nestor. After all, as the ensuing traditional line—"Nestor, of whom even earlier, [his] counsel appeared best" [Νέστωρ, οὗ καὶ πρόσθεν ἀρίστη φαίνετο βουλή]—makes clear, here as elsewhere in Homer, Nestor has always been known in this way.[104] The formula also suggests thoughtful planning and immediate action. Agamemnon's speech outlines the enviable ceremony and *kleos* attached to Achilles' death at Troy. Its primary purpose in the poet's plan, however, is to provide a foil for Agamemnon's own *kakos nostos*, a point that Homer has Agamemnon himself make (24.93–97):

> Thus you yourself certainly did not, dying, destroy your name, but
>> for you always
> among all men, [your] fame will be noble, Achilles.
> Yet for me in fact, what delight [is there], after I have carried
>> through the war?
> For on [my] return, for me Zeus devised lamentable destruction
> by the hand of Aigisthos and [my] destructive wife.

---

[104] See Nestor in Chapter 2, s.v. 2.2.3 Nestor: 4.293–326. Cf. *Iliad* 7.325, 9.94. In contrast with this formulaic line as a whole, which references only Nestor, a segment of this traditional collocation, "[his] counsel appeared best" (ἀρίστη φαίνετο βουλή), exists outside of this formula in a larger idiom, where it is used only of figures other than Nestor. It suggests thought that leads to action: of Zeus pondering how he will bring Achilles honor (*Iliad* 2.5); of Agamemnon who is thinking during the night and considering what he should do (10.17); of Hera who wants to beguile Zeus (14.161); of Odysseus, who is ruminating about how to defeat the Cyclops (*Odysseus.* 9.318); of Odysseus, who considers how to leave the Cyclops' cave (9.424); and of Odysseus, as he decides how best to question *pseuchai* in the underworld (11:230).

ὡς σὺ μὲν οὐδὲ θανὼν ὄνομ' ὤλεσας, ἀλλά τοι αἰεὶ
πάντας ἐπ' ἀνθρώπους κλέος ἔσσεται ἐσθλόν, Ἀχιλλεῦ·
αὐτὰρ ἐμοὶ τί τόδ' ἧδος, ἐπεὶ πόλεμον τολύπευσα;
ἐν νόστῳ γάρ μοι Ζεὺς μήσατο λυγρὸν ὄλεθρον
Αἰγίσθου ὑπὸ χερσὶ καὶ οὐλομένης ἀλόχοιο.

The placement of "certainly" (μέν) after "you" (σύ, 93) is meant to emphasize the pronoun that precedes it (Denniston 1950:360, s.v. 2). Taken together with the following strongly adversative expression, "Yet for me in fact" (αὐτὰρ ἐμοὶ, 95)—"Yet in fact" (αὐτάρ) taking the place of "but" (δέ)—the ensuing contrast between Achilles and Agamemnon is given a greater level of focus for Homer's hearers (Denniston 1950:55). Further, Agamemnon blames Zeus for his destruction. This is caused in part by the character's limited narrative perspective, but it may also point to Agamemnon's traditional character that includes a habitual unwillingness to face his own errors.[105]

What is new in the foregoing description by Agamemnon of his own demise is the association of Clytemnestra with the physical killing of Agamemnon, a feature not until this time so openly foregrounded by the *Odyssey* poet. It seems clear here that Agamemnon wants us to consider that he is not only the victim of his wife's machinations, but also her harmful actions. She was also physically involved in the homicide itself. This becomes apparent when we consider the traditional idiom, "by the hand of" (ὑπὸ χερσί), used in the phrase "by the hand of Aigisthos and a destructive wife" (Αἰγίσθου ὑπὸ χερσὶ καὶ οὐλομένης ἀλόχοιο), unless "hands" (χερσί) is to be taken metaphorically in this passage. Standing against a metaphorical view is the fact that all the other occurrences of the collocation "by the hand of" (ὑπὸ χερσί) in the *Iliad* (sixteen times) and *Odyssey* (one other time) refer to a physical act (usually death, but always minimally of subduing another in some way, physically): of Chromis and Nastes, subdued by Achilles (*Iliad* 2.860, 874); in a prayer by Menelaos to strike down Paris (3.352); by Hector of his own possible death (6.368); of the Achaians struck down by the Trojans (8.344); by Diomedes about to kill Dolon (10.452); of Agamemnon killing Trojans (11.189); and of the killing of Trojans by Greeks (15.2). It describes the potential death of Sarpedon in Zeus' choice (16.438) and the action of Patroklos to take the gates of Troy (16.699). It is used of the Achaians who "bit the dust" during Achilles' absence from the war (19.62) and by Aeneas who relates how he was once nearly subdued by Achilles (20.94). It is spoken by Poseidon, who

---

[105] Blaming Zeus, as we will see in the next chapter, is a character trait strongly attached to Agamemnon in Homer's tradition.

threatens the subjugation of any god who does not leave the battlefield (20.143); by Priam, of the portending destiny for Troy—destruction and the dragging away of his daughters-in-law (22.65); by Epeios the boxer who threatens to beat down any opponent with great violence and lay him flat (23.675); by Priam of his son Hector, subdued by Achilles (24.638). Beyond our present example, the expression is also used by the *Odyssey* poet himself as narrator of the portending subjugation of Antinoos "by the hand and spear" (ὑπὸ χερσὶ καὶ ἔγχεϊ, *Odyssey* 18.156) of Telemachos. Agamemnon's death as narrated in *Odyssey* 24 suddenly looms all the more sinister and grisly, then, since the tradition appears from this perspective to include the physical act of being killed by his own wife. This is something not directly mentioned by Homer before this moment. It is a reality, too, filled with shame.

The traditional audience is aware of this aspect and needs no excessive elaboration of what was clearly a distasteful matter. Clytemnestra's killing of her husband may be represented on a seal from around 700 BC. Knoepfler (1993:21) feels that this interpretation is more likely than an erotic reading, which "semble bien moins vraisemblable." The extra-Homeric iconographical correlatives to the killing of Agamemnon are otherwise sparse. The reluctance to show the slaughter of Agamemnon in iconography, as Prag (1985:5) suggests in his detailed study, is due to its unsettling nature for societal norms, something that I suggest is the case too for the Homeric *aoidos* singing to his audience.[106] Thus we note that social mores have conditioned the nature of the representations that are acceptable in the creation of iconography (or perhaps more accurately, that would have been supported by patrons), just as they have affected the tenor of the presentation of the Homeric *aoidoi* who do not play up the killing of Agamemnon by his wife. The Homeric performance was conditioned by audience taste. Agamemnon's death at his wife's hand was a shameful thing, yet part of his character's history, and so could not be wholly kept "off stage."[107]

---

[106] As a control for this contention concerning social norms, we may compare the death of Aigisthos in the collected plates in Prag's study. He is justifiably killed by a male agent of vengeance, and this act is represented in manifold ways and makes up the greater number of plates in Prag's study. Further, while iconography exists portraying Aigisthos and Clytemnestra being led to their death, there are virtually no images showing the actual matricide, another socially distasteful aspect of the *Oresteia*. Prag (1986:35–43) appropriately rejects earlier, more questionable attempts to read scenes of the killing of Clytemnestra into extant iconography. Actually, even with the clear indication of Clytemnestra's killing of Agamemnon found in Aeschylus, there is only very limited (extant) iconography picturing the event after the play's production. Instead, the more palatable killing of Aigisthos remains front and center. For conjecture about societal conditions for Homeric epic, see Latacz 1996:32–59.

[107] Cf. the wish of Abimelech in Judges 9.54 to avoid being killed by a woman. Even though he had just had a millstone dropped on his head, his concern was first with a loss of honor that being killed by a woman would bring.

The pitiable return of Agamemnon, his demise at the hands of both Aigisthos and his wife, ends the recorded conversation between Agamemnon and Achilles. The final verbal exchange of Agamemnon in *Odyssey* 24 takes place when a suitor, Amphimedon, is newly come to Hades. Agamemnon addresses him in a moment of emphatic apostrophe (*Odyssey* 24.192–202) directed at the more blessed outcome for Odysseus: "Blessed child of Laertes, much-devising Odysseus, to be sure you acquired a wife with great virtue!" (ὄλβιε Λαέρταο πάϊ, πολυμήχαν' Ὀδυσσεῦ, / ἦ ἄρα σὺν μεγάλῃ ἀρετῇ ἐκτήσω ἄκοιτιν, 192–193). The narrative moment serves to highlight a theme from Homer's tradition that we have heard before, that of the *kakos nostos* of Agamemnon versus the *olbios nostos* (24.192) of Odysseus. Homer names the consequences of the two opposed homecomings as a "favorable song" (ἀοιδήν ... χαρίεσσαν, 197–198) for Penelope, but a "loathsome song" (στυγερή ... ἀοιδή, 200) for Clytemnestra. It is fitting that our consideration of the *Odyssey*'s text should end here, since the whole poem has as its principal foil such antitheses. Such thematic contrasts, however, have at their core not only Penelope versus Clytemnestra,[108] with all that could describe these two polarities in character, but also Odysseus versus Agamemnon.[109] As de Jong (2001:567)points out, moreover, Agamemnon lies on the very bottom of an ascending scale of outcomes among leading Greek heroes woven into the fabric of the *Odyssey*.

[108] On the contrasting dual of Penelope vs. Clytemnestra in Homer, see D'Arms and Hulley 1946:211–212, Suzuki 1989:74, Marquardt 1992:244, van Duzer 1996:309–313, and de Jong 2001:287–289.

[109] On the use of Agamemnon's story as a [negative] "Exemplum-Charakter" for Odysseus, see Danek 1998:97; and Heubeck in Heubeck et al. 1988. Such antithesis or "doublets" (cf. Fenik 1974:172–207) are not simple binaries, however. More than one contrast can exist. Penelope is a case in point, since she also acts as a contrast for Helen, as Blondell (2013:88–95) has observed.

4

The Characterization of Agamemnon in the *Iliad*

4.1 Introduction

A vivid picture of what Agamemnon's character was like for the *Odyssey* poet and his core audience emerged from our discussion in the last chapter, and it joins the portrait we began to see develop already in Chapter 2. We have noted that Agamemnon is known within Homer's tradition as a character who dies a shameful and pitiful death at his wife's hands. Further, as we began to see in Chapter 2, Agamemnon's traditional personality in *Iliad* 4 is shown to be one given to thoughtless, foolish, and rash words and actions. These traits will continue to resonate strongly with the picture the *Iliad* poet paints in the rest of his epic. Other traits less pronounced in the *Odyssey* also emerge from a close reading of the rest of the *Iliad*, where Agamemnon is still the living leader of the war against Troy. In the *Iliad*, we will encounter Agamemnon in many scenes as a leader with a penchant for arrogance, imperiousness, irreverence, and insult.[1] He also appears as inept and unconvincing in his relations with others, certainly in his dealings with the *basileis* who have accompanied him on an expedition to regain Menelaos' wife and honor.

This chapter is written, as was the previous, in the format of a commentary. Further, as we have seen already, characterization for the ancient audience was not abstracted and separated from events, but rather attached inextricably to "word and deed" housed within the tradition already known to singer and audience. Consequently, both of these elements will continue to provide us with an opportunity to see what Agamemnon was like for the poet and his ancient audience.

---

[1] A chronological consideration of Agamemnon in the *Iliad* will necessarily focus on his most significant appearances: 1.6–344, 2.16–440, 477–483, 3.267–302, 4.231–418, 9, 10.3–127, 11.91–283, 14.41–134, and 19.76–144. We will, nevertheless, through discussion and notes, refer to most every instance where Agamemnon is mentioned, even when Agamemnon is not himself present.

4.2 Commentary

4.2.1 Agamemnon's Dishonoring and Hubristic Actions: 1.6–344

Immediately following the *prooimion*, the *Iliad* begins with strife between Achilles and Agamemnon (1.9). The priest Chryses had come supplicating the Atreidai and the "other well-greaved Achaians" for his daughter (1.12–21). Despite the army's supporting assent "to reverence the priest and to receive the splendid ransom" (αἰδεῖσθαί θ' ἱερῆα καὶ ἀγλαὰ δέχθαι ἄποινα, 22), he is irreverently rebuffed (24–32). Agamemnon will not be swayed, but rather gives way to his anger. The language introducing Agamemnon's reply to Chryses is no less telling than the response itself (24–25): "But not to Atreus' son Agamemnon was it pleasing in [his] spirit, / badly instead he sent [the priest] away, and a strong command he laid upon [him]" (ἀλλ' οὐκ Ἀτρεΐδῃ Ἀγαμέμνονι ἥνδανε θυμῷ, / ἀλλὰ κακῶς ἀφίει, κρατερὸν δ' ἐπὶ μῦθον ἔτελλε). Agamemnon lays a "strong command" (κρατερὸν ... μῦθον) upon the priest. As Martin (1989:22) has demonstrated, the *muth-* stem marks "proposals and commands or threats and boasts." It implies authority and implicit power for the speaker. The priest, "a low-status person with special powers" (Redfield 1975:94), is no match for Agamemnon, whose authoritative speech act includes a firm warning (1.26–32):

> Let me not come upon you, old man, by the hollow ships,
> either now lingering or afterward again coming,
> lest for you a scepter not be of help, nor the fillet of a god.
> I will certainly not ransom her! Earlier upon her, in fact, old age will
>   come
> in our house, in Argos, far from [her] fatherland,
> working over the loom and sharing my bed.
> But come! Do not provoke me, so that more safely you may go.

> μή σε γέρον κοίλῃσιν ἐγὼ παρὰ νηυσὶ κιχείω
> ἢ νῦν δηθύνοντ' ἢ ὕστερον αὖτις ἰόντα,
> μή νύ τοι οὐ χραίσμῃ σκῆπτρον καὶ στέμμα θεοῖο·
> τὴν δ' ἐγὼ οὐ λύσω· πρίν μιν καὶ γῆρας ἔπεισιν
> ἡμετέρῳ ἐνὶ οἴκῳ ἐν Ἄργεϊ τηλόθι πάτρης
> ἱστὸν ἐποιχομένην καὶ ἐμὸν λέχος ἀντιόωσαν·
> ἀλλ' ἴθι μή μ' ἐρέθιζε σαώτερος ὥς κε νέηαι.

The vehemence of Agamemnon's defiant reply is a "brutal rejoinder" (Rabel 1997:40) that forces Chryses to leave immediately and leads to Apollo's plague. The force of Agamemnon's threatening reply is seen in the strength and number of negations he employs (1.26, 28, 29, 32). Further, the use of "I" (ἐγώ, 26) is the result not just of metrical filling, but of the active oral delivery of the poet who searches for emphasis in the rhythm of the hexameter. Agamemnon means what he says. Yet, Agamemnon's arrogant response stands in stark contrast to Chryses' own powerless supplication and the army's earlier call to support the priest's request. The staff of office (*skēptron*, 28) sets Chryses apart as a priest of Apollo, just as Agamemnon's staff sets him apart as the leading *basileus* (Naiden 2006:56–57). The *stemmata* ("wool ribbons" of the priest's garb, 14) indicate Chryses' position as a suppliant (Griffin 1980:26).[2] The sanctity of the priest wearing *stemmata* is as powerful as that of an altar's sanctity, showing that the suppliant "is both unthreatening and favored by the gods" (Naiden 2006:56). The priest comes as a suppliant (nb. λίσσετο πάντας Ἀχαιούς, 15), whose role, as Létoublon (1980:334) has shown, predates our epic tradition.[3] Further, suppliants, since they are helpless and receive divine *charis*, are "more deserving of respect" (*aidoioteroi*) and when wronged become "incarnate curses" (*araioi*).[4] The priest Chryses is also old, making Agamemnon's response all the more irreverent. Yet, can we conclude that Agamemnon was understood by Homer's audience to be acting irreverently by dishonoring the suppliant?[5] After all, no request for battlefield ransom in the actual time frame of the *Iliad*'s action is ever successful in saving a suppliant.[6] Perhaps the audience thought that Agamemnon was acting just as anyone else would have.

---

[2] Alden (2001:207) disagrees, but I think Griffin is correct. For a consideration of suppliants and supplication, see Giordano 1999 and Naiden 2006; for the language of supplication, see Létoublon 1980 and Patera 2012:65–71.

[3] Létoublon also notes that the basic meaning of the *lit-* root, that of touching, is still active in modern Lithuanian cognates.

[4] On the relation of the traditional audience expectation of divine *charis* and supplication, see Patera (2012:68): "Ces prières qui promettent ou qui rappellent, joignent en fait à la demande la raison pour laquelle la divinité doit y répondre. ... Il s'agit de la réaction à une faveur qui peut être considérée comme un remerciement, qui implique la notion de la reconnaissance pour le don reçu." On incarnate curses, see Murray 1934:88.

[5] For a view that such action was condemned, see Gould 1973:90–101. Gagarin (1987) enlarges upon the traditional list of those most vulnerable: (usually "guests, beggars, and suppliants") to include also "larger groups, such as the Achaian army as a whole." For other early examples of Greek attitudes towards the helpless, see Hesiod's *Erga* (327–344), where Zeus is shown as imposing a "harsh recompense" (χαλεπήν ... ἀμοιβήν) upon all who commit evil acts against a "suppliant" (ἱκέτης) or "stranger" (ξεῖνος); and cf. Euripides' *Bacchae*, where Cadmos is spared being shackled for his Bacchic behavior because of "grey old age" (γῆρας πολίον, 258).

[6] Fenik (1968:82) speaks of battle supplication, but Wilson (2002:31) perhaps too restrictively. See her reaction to Robbins (1990:12–13, 192n86), against whom she argues that: "ransom is not [to be] conflated with supplication." I am not so sure that this division is sharply maintained in

In the *Iliad*, there is at least one instance of successful supplication off the battlefield in real time. It proves a contrast to Agamemnon's own refusal. In *Iliad* 24, Priam, an elder like Chryses in *Iliad* 1, comes to Achilles as a suppliant outside of the arena of battle and is successful, albeit he comes for a corpse rather than to ransom a living son. Achilles, however, does respect his plea.[7] Outside of the actual time frame of the *Iliad*'s action, moreover, one recalls that Achilles himself had, more than once, shown mercy for living prisoners of war before Patroklos' death (*Iliad* 6.425–427, 11.104–106; cf. Naiden 2006, n. 99).

Chryses, however, is not a warrior pleading for his life. Neither is he a father pleading for his captured warrior son. Rather, he is a priest of Apollo asking to redeem his daughter for appropriate ransom during a struggle in which he is not personally involved. Surely there are more appropriate comparisons for Agamemnon's relation to suppliants than warriors begging for their lives on the battlefield or even a warrior-king coming for the corpse of his son. If one assumes resonance not just between the *Iliad* and *Odyssey*, but also between the *Odyssey* and *Iliad* as argued in Chapter 1, a better comparison may be that of the *aoidos* Phemios supplicating Odysseus for sanctuary after a *tisis* perpetrated upon the suitors (*Odyssey* 22.365–380). There, as in the case of the priest (*arētēr*) Chryses in *Iliad* 1, the singer was not personally involved, but instead a victim of circumstances. Yet, quite unlike the reception of Chryses by Agamemnon, when Phemios entreated Telemachos as a suppliant, he was immediately spared by Odysseus' consent. In Homer's cultural outlook, priests and singers are a special group worthy of respect. While an *arētēr* is unsurprisingly not mentioned in the Odyssey's list of traveling professionals (17:383–386), priests' importance equally places them with the *mantis* in a professional religious class deserving of special status and respect. [8] As we saw with Chryses' supplication, even the army recognized that releasing the captive Chryseïs to her priest-father was

---

Homer. See also Naiden (2006:120) on the difference between what Homer places in the foreground and background in cases of supplication.

[7] The parallel between the supplication of Chryses and Priam has been noted by Rabel 1990:429–440 and Goldhill 1990b:373–376. We will return to Priam's supplication in *Iliad* 24 later in this chapter.

[8] Hernández (2002:323–324) contrasts Agamemnon's mistreatment of Chryses with another priest (a *hiereus*) of Apollos in the *Odyssey*, Maron (*Odyssey* 9.200), whom Odysseus saves during an Achaian attack on Ismaros. We have fewer specifics about why Odysseus acted as he did in the case of Maron, but the participle ἀζόμενοι as Hernández suggests, serves to contrast the responses of Odysseus and Agamemnon. One reader suggested that the figure of Leiodes (*Odyssey* 22.310–329), a suitor with some prophetic abilities, may be a contrasting instance that suggests Odysseus' mercilessness. Yet, the singer's inclusion of the "looking darkly" (ὑπόδρα ἰδών) formula (see Chapter 2) suggests instead that we should not see the poet-narrator as looking favorably upon Leiodes' request. While Leodes is certainly a sympathetic character, he is part of the class of suitors who have invaded Odysseus' *oikos* and gets what he deserves (see Chapter 2), even if he has prophetic ability. His death is placed before Phemios just to show that it is merited.

the right thing to do (and shouted their support). Yet, Agamemnon persisted in his denial, and so already at the beginning of Homer's song, he showed his true colors.

Latacz notes that Agamemnon's is "eine Unverhältnismäßigkeit der Reaktion" (Latacz 2000a:37). This evaluation catches something of the significance of Homer's creative emphasis. It shows that the story is part of the poet's tradition and provides a glimpse of a character known for his disproportionate reactions. Yet, the scene's emphatic placement here at the commencement of the epic, at the outset of the singer's creation, is equally significant. Its placement is a function of the singer's choice, when he considered where to begin, the phrase "from which point" (ἐξ οὗ, 1.6) of the *prooimion*.[9] The singer is in competition with his peers in producing the most impressive story, so the way he begins his rendition sets a mood that strikes the audience.[10] And where he begins, which is intertwined somehow with the cosmic will of Zeus, suggests that he has an interest in displaying aspects of Agamemnon's character.

Agamemnon is also excessively harsh here, if we read the implications of one idiom. It is not good enough for Agamemnon to send the priest away with a stern warning, but there is also a threatening boast in his tone. The priest's daughter is to be taken "far from [her] fatherland" (τηλόθι πάτρης, 1.30), an idiom used a total of five times in Homer.[11] The expression is always associated with the misery of permanent separation experienced by an individual because of the loss of one's fatherland, but also the effect that this loss has on another. A couple of examples will show the idiom's meaning. The next use, chronologically, of "far from fatherland" (τηλόθι πάτρης) expresses the distance of Sarpedon from his own country in *Iliad* 16.461, when he is about to die under Patroklos' spear in Troy. Sarpedon will lose his homeland, with all that meant to the ancient audience.[12] Yet, the expression's meaning does not stop there. It is further associated with Zeus through his corresponding title as *patēr*, which

---

As Hernández (2002:320n5) suggests, Odysseus (quite unlike Agamemnon when he is killed) "is the executioner who reestablishes justice and the due order of things."

[9]   While the meaning of ἐξ οὗ is ultimately ambiguous and likely is connected with the *Dios boulē* (Marks 2002, Allan 2008), I cannot rule out its connection also (so Redfield 1979:96, Lenz 1980:42n1) as a temporal marker with ἄειδε in *Iliad* 1.1. Latacz (2000a:21) notes that the temporal conjunction functions to emphasize the irreversibility of the moment. On the meaning of the proem in relation to the cosmic *Dios boulē*, see especially Allan 2008. For a consideration of the generic quality of epic proems, see Petropoulos 2012.

[10]   Cf. the competition noted in Chapter 1, n. 32, in pre-Parry and Lord South Slavic epic performance.

[11]   *Iliad* 1.30: Chryseïs; 16.461: Sarpedon; 18.99: Patroklos; 24.86: Achilles; and *Odyssey* 2.365: Odysseus.

[12]   On Greek experiences and attitudes over loss of homeland, see Garland 2014. On loss of homeland and women's songs of lament, see Dué 2006. Cf. the later *apolis* theme in Euripides (*Hypsipyle* 1.4.18, 12.107, *Medea* 255, 646, *Hippolytus* 1029, *Hecuba* 669, 811, etc.).

was just mentioned by the poet three lines earlier ("father of men and of gods," πατὴρ ἀνδρῶν τε θεῶν τε, 558). Not only will Sarpedon lose his fatherland, then, but Zeus will also lose a son. The loss is experienced by the "father of men and of gods" sweating, literally "pouring down [from above] drops of blood" (αἱματοέσσας δὲ ψιάδας κατέχευεν, 459), over what was about to take place. So, Homer, through this local clustering of *patrēs* and *pāter*, wants his audience to hear about the loss of a homeland experienced by Sarpedon, but as emphatically, the personal loss felt by Zeus. Similarly, this double sense of loss is exemplified by Achilles' grief over Patroklos' loss of his homeland, but also Achilles' own grievous loss of his *hetairos* Patroklos in *Iliad* 18.98.[13]

The loss threatened by the idiom "far from [her] fatherland" (τηλόθι πάτρης) in *Iliad* 1 likewise includes this double traditional reference. It assumes Chryseïs' loss of a homeland, but also a significant disruption of the *oikos* and its normal function for Chryses.[14] The priest's daughter would not be married off, but taken as booty, and Chryses would be left at a loss. Yet, none of this loss appears to concern Agamemnon. He instead taunts Chryses with the future repeated rape of his daughter (ἐμὸν λέχος ἀντιόωσαν, *Iliad* 1.31). Agamemnon's brash and irreverent response will have unfortunate consequences, however, in the ensuing narrative, not just for himself but also for the whole Greek expedition. They too will experience loss.

Apollo's plague follows immediately, resulting in the burning of pyres on a continual basis (αἰεὶ δὲ πυραὶ νεκύων καίοντο θαμειαί, 52), a penalty prayed for by the priest (1.42). The magnitude of the reprisal of Apollo in his wrath is comparable to the excesses of Agamemnon's own earlier reaction to the priest's initial "höfliche Bitte" in supplication for his captive daughter (Latacz 2000a:36). The military losses lead Achilles, rather than Agamemnon, to call the Achaians to assembly (1.53–54) on the tenth day. The payback has begun, and Achilles, in light of Agamemnon's silence, asks that the Achaians engage a prophetic figure of some type to declare why Apollo is angry. Kalchas steps forward hesitantly to use his craft as seer (72, 92). He is worried about Agamemnon's anger (78) and voices his concern. Kalchas, like Apollo's priest Chryses (80), occupies a vulnerable position. His role demands he say things that may place him in harm's way. He is reassured, however, by Achilles, who deflects Agamemnon's anger from the prophet to himself (Louden 2006:160). Kalchas, now under Achilles' protection, responds with a priamel that has as its "cardinal point" (Race 1982:14) the singling out of Agamemnon's dishonorable act (1.93–95):

---

[13] Achilles says to Thetis that he, too, will not return to his fatherland (πατρίδα γαῖαν, 18.101), and so Thetis also will experience loss.

[14] One might compare this with the war's disruption of family life evoked by the meeting of Hector with his wife Andromache and son Astyanax (*Iliad* 6.390–493).

For neither indeed with prayer does he find fault nor with hecatomb,
but on account of the priest whom Agamemnon dishonored,
and neither released [his] daughter nor received the ransom,

οὔ ταρ ὅ γ᾽ εὐχωλῆς ἐπιμέμφεται οὐδ᾽ ἑκατόμβης,
ἀλλ᾽ ἕνεκ᾽ ἀρητῆρος ὃν ἠτίμησ᾽ Ἀγαμέμνων,
οὐδ᾽ ἀπέλυσε θύγατρα καὶ οὐκ ἀπεδέξατ᾽ ἄποινα,

The seer's priamel, further enlarged by the addition of details of what Agamemnon did not do and receive (1.95), is accompanied by a threat. There will be continued reprisal by Apollo unless there follows the restoration of the unwed maiden (κούρη) to her father (96–98).

Not insignificantly, in Kalchas' prophecy[15] Agamemnon is no longer promised any ransom (1.99) as a consequence of his earlier rejection of the priest's offer.[16] Yet in his reply (106–120), Agamemnon insists upon his preference for Chryseïs over his own wife (113–116):

For in fact I prefer [her] to Clytemnestra
my wedded wife, since [Chryseïs] is not worse than she,
neither in body nor in character, neither in judgment nor in works.

καὶ γάρ ῥα Κλυταιμνήστρης προβέβουλα
κουριδίης ἀλόχου, ἐπεὶ οὔ ἑθέν ἐστι χερείων,
οὐ δέμας οὐδὲ φυήν, οὔτ᾽ ἂρ φρένας οὔτέ τι ἔργα.

Agamemnon makes it clear that he wants to take Chryseïs home with him (112–113). Felson and Slatkin note that the competition among males is conducted through a woman, and that the "confluence of desire, strife and gender … recapitulates the etiology of the Trojan War."[17] The struggle over Chryseïs is like the struggle over Helen, who, as Blondell articulates it, represents

---

[15] I use "prophecy" here in one of its functions, in its verbal form, to "speak forth" the truth of the situation with special, privileged, divinely inspired knowledge not accessible to humans without this prophetic art. A prophet knows all three temporal frames: the present, future, and past (ὅς ἤδη τά τ᾽ ἐόντα τά τ᾽ ἐσσόμεθα πρό τ᾽ ἐόντα, *Iliad* 1.70). For further discussion, see Flower 2008:22–103.

[16] οὐδ᾽ ὅ γε πρὶν Δαναοῖσιν ἀεικέα λοιγὸν ἀπώσει /πρίν γ᾽ ἀπὸ πατρὶ φίλῳ δόμεναι ἑλικώπιδα κούρην /ἀπριάτην ἀνάποινον, ἄγειν θ᾽ ἱερὴν ἑκατόμβην / ἐς Χρύσην· τότε κέν μιν ἱλασσάμενοι πεπίθοιμεν (1.97–100).

[17] Felson and Slatkin 2004:95. Cf. Dué (2002:40), who argues that Briseïs is a substitute for Helen in the "micronarrative" of *Iliad* 1; cf. also Suzuki 1989:21–29.

"the conundrum of female beauty," which is "intrinsically desirable" yet also connected with destruction.[18] Agamemnon's association of Chryseïs with Clytemnestra, moreover, may resonate for Homer's audience with implications for more than just its connection in the oral tradition with Helen and the centrality of a woman in the commencement and dilemma of the Trojan War. It may also implicate Agamemnon's future, his "dismal homecoming" (*kakos nostos*). We will ponder this point more fully in a moment. It is necessary first to consider the implications of Agamemnon's comments about his concubine Chryseïs.[19] This is best accomplished by a brief overview of the practice of concubinage in Homer and other early Greek literature.[20]

While the keeping of a "slave-concubine" (παλλακίς) was common practice in Homeric society (at least for the lord of a household) and certainly not considered unacceptable, it could cause conflict. The question of sexual relations with one's concubine emphatically announced by Agamemnon in *Iliad* 1.31 was a subject of potential concern. It reflected real tension not to be too quickly dismissed, as evidence from Homer and early Greek literature suggests. Potential problems were related to questions of inheritance and primacy of place among the women (and their children) of the household.[21] The narrative of Phoinix's autobiography (*Iliad* 9.450-452), as well as Laertes' arrangement with Eurykleia (*Odyssey* 1.433), both point to the possibility of household angst. In each case, the sexual relationship between the male and his concubine in the home is portrayed as vexatious, actually or potentially. In the first instance, with Phoinix, the very act of sleeping with one's concubine can cause strife.[22] Phoinix's father Amyntor slept with his concubine, and, so, Phoinix tells

---

[18] Blondell 2013:22; see also 1-95, on Helen's role in the *Iliad*; cf. Blondell 2010.

[19] Latacz (2000a:38) notes that it is an open question whether Agamemnon meant Chryseïs "als Konkubine ... oder Nebenfrau," but I think the former is likely.

[20] Certainly slave-concubinage (though not bigamy) was a practice that continued into the Classical Period (see *Lysias* 1.12-14; cf. the comments of Scheidel 2010:111). The vagaries and hope of Andromache in Euripides' play bearing her name well match the picture we have in Homer of concubinage. Especially pertinent is Andromache's scornful remarks to Hermione about the practice of Thessalian *tyrannoi* (*Andromache* 215-218): εἰ δ' ἀμφὶ φρήκην τὴν χιόνι κατάρρυτον/τύραννον ἔσχες ἄνδρ', ἵν' ἐν μέρει λέχος/δίδωσι πολλαῖς εἷς ἀνὴρ κοινούμενος,/ ἔκτεινας ἂν τάσδ'; For a study of terminology for female courtesans and related practices, see McClure 2003:1-25. On the changing practices from Homer to Classical Athens, see Ogden 1996:72-75.

[21] Herodotus' (7.2) comments that the children of Darius are apt. The sons were rivals "because they were not from the same mother" (Ἐόντες δὲ μητρὸς οὐ τῆς αὐτῆς).

[22] The ongoing jealousy over a sustained sexual relationship between the husband and his concubine is made clear by the iterative imperfects of *Iliad* 9.450-451. They refer to the husband's dilatory activities, but also the wife's attempts to persuade her son Phoinix to take action. Phoinix did comply. On the pattern of the father-son hostility, see Sourvinou-Inwood 1991:252; on the centrality of father-son relationships in Homer, see Wöhrle 1999:32-48. Alden (2012:123-125) argues that Peleus does not completely replace Amyntor as a father, since he sees the

us, dishonored (ἀτιμάζεσκε) his wife. Second, in the case of Laertes, the possibility of stirring up anger in his wife kept him from sleeping with Eurykleia.[23] Furthermore, Odysseus' lying tale to Eumaios (*Odyssey* 14.200–215) shows some of the potential problems for a bastard son. In a contrived autobiography, Odysseus narrates that he is the son of a concubine and experienced a great deal of competition from his arrogant half-brothers upon the death of their father.[24]

Aeschylus' *Agamemnon* offers further relevant cultural information in Clytemnestra's response to Agamemnon. There we find a litany of references to Cassandra's and Agamemnon's sexual relations with each other, and by innuendo, Cassandra's with other Achaians (e.g. *Agamemnon* 1438–1447). Nor is the theme of women's jealousy in the household in Euripides' plays, such as that experienced with almost unparalleled intensity by Medea over Jason's marriage to the princess in the *Medea*, simply all the fabrication or emphasis of the playwright himself.[25] Rather, such dramatic dilemmas join the other examples we have discussed in showing the very real tension that could adhere to the practice of concubinage (and polygyny) in early Greece (as it could in other Mediterranean cultures).[26] All of these instances, however anecdotal, indicate that there could be conflict and tension from multiple female partners sharing one household in ancient Greek society as pictured in the Homeric epics.

I am suggesting that cultural tensions dovetail with traditional implications in the poet's presentation. Agamemnon's open and defiant declaration in the Achaian assembly, where he forcefully admits his preference for Chryseïs, creates tension and would have sounded rather thoughtless and foreboding. Homer's core audience was well aware of Clytemnestra's infidelity, so patently

---

relationship more in terms of a *metanast*. He allows that his relationship is "quasi-filial," but I think that Phoinix's role goes beyond that of a *metanast*. See especially *Iliad* 9.485–491.

[23] Eurykleia did, however, become a wetnurse to Odysseus, so must have had a baby at some point (Pomeroy 2011:26–27). On the complex nature of the position of slaves and concubines in the Homeric *oikos*, see Thalmann 1998:74–83.

[24] The son (but perhaps also a daughter, cf. *Iliad* 13.171–176) of a concubine could, however, enjoy equality in the household with legitimate sons (as could an "adopted" son, *Iliad* 18.18), at least while the father was alive according to Homer's account (as Odysseus' lying tale also makes clear). The best of situations could always change at death, something evident in Classical Athens, as poor old blind Arignotos found out after his brother died (see Aeschines *Against Timarchus* 103–104).

[25] Ogden (1996:194–211) notes that this is a Euripidean proclivity. The comment of the female chorus in Euripides *Hippolytus* (151, 153–154) directed toward Phaedra presents what appears to be a normal concern: ἦ πόσιν ... / ποιμαίνει τις ἐν οἴκοις / κρυπτᾶι κοίται λεχέων σῶν;

[26] Cf. the comments of Hubbard 2011:790. A competitive tension existed in other ancient Mediterranean societies, even where polygamy was regularly practiced. See e.g. Genesis 16.1–6, 28.28–29.24, for Rachel and Leah; and Plutarch *Life of Alexander* 9.5, for Olympias in Macedon.

a theme in the *Odyssey* (which may be instanced in her very name).[27] For them, Agamemnon's admission must have resounded loudly with irony and created a sardonic reaction. Not only is Agamemnon upsetting the stability of his warrior culture through his insulting reaction to the priest and his requests, he is also potentially upsetting the stability of his own *oikos*. His present attitude and actions parallel his wife's by displaying a lack of concern for the *oikos*. While Agamemnon is dallying in Troy, his wife is dallying in Argos.

There are also potential references in this scene to Agamemnon's *kakos nostos* and the *Oresteia* in Homer's tradition. The singer may have been intending a link between Agamemnon's callousness here and the seer's earlier activity at Aulis (including his prophecy), an event included in the epic cycle's *Cypria* as outlined in Proclus' epitome (*Chrestomathy* 138–141):

> But after Kalchas had told them of the wrath of the goddess and had bid them sacrifice Iphigeneia[28] to Artemis on the pretense that she would marry Achilles, having sent for her, they set about sacrificing her.

> Κάλχαντος δὲ εἰπόντος τὴν τῆς θεοῦ μῆνιν καὶ Ἰφιγένειαν κελεύσαντος θύειν τῇ Ἀρτέμιδι, ὡς ἐπὶ γάμον αὐτὴν Ἀχιλλεῖ μεταπεμψάμενοι θύειν ἐπιχειροῦσιν.

Agamemnon had sacrificed his daughter at the urging of the prophet. The presence of this backstory in the minds of Homer's audience seems plausible enough, especially if we accept the proposition that the Cyclic epics belong to the same mythological tradition as the Homeric poems.[29] The allusion to Kalchas' past prophecies likely created a foreboding tone and impacted the way the scene was heard.[30] It summoned up for the traditional audience a memory of Agamemnon's past, when he put his daughter to death, but perhaps also his future, when he died at his wife's hands. His wife's murderous action upon his

---

[27] As suggested in Chapters 1 and 2, the *Odyssey* in some form was certainly known to the poet of the *Iliad* and his audience. On the possible implications from onomastics, see Marquardt 1992:245–252.

[28] The sacrifice of Iphigenia, probably the same daughter as the Homeric Iphianassa (*Iliad* 9.145), is never overtly mentioned in Homer, however.

[29] Burgess (2001:31–33) argues that earlier (oral) forms of the Cyclic epics are ultimately from the same tradition that gave us the Homeric epics. Kullman (2015) thinks that at least the *Faktenkanon* of Cyclic motifs originated orally before Homer.

[30] Scodel (2002:106) accepts this background (cf. Kirk 1985:65), but is less sure that the audience is actually aware of it: "The poet probably had the sacrifice in mind as he generated angry words for Agamemnon, but the audience need not follow the allusion. The poet, then, does not rely on prior knowledge of Chalcas."

return home is an event also linked in later tragedy to Agamemnon's earlier sacrificing of their daughter at Aulis.[31]

It may be that Homer's audience heard Agamemnon's critique of Kalchas himself with this tradition in mind. Agamemnon is certainly actively thinking of the past when Kalchas steps forward as *mantis* during his heated dispute with Achilles (*Iliad* 1.106–108):

> Seer of evil, not ever for me have you spoken what is good!
> Always for you what is evil is dear to your heart to prophesy,
> but a noble word not in any way have you ever spoken or
>   accomplished!

> μάντι κακῶν οὐ πώ ποτέ μοι τὸ κρήγυον εἶπας·
> αἰεί τοι τὰ κάκ' ἐστὶ φίλα φρεσὶ μαντεύεσθαι,
> ἐσθλὸν δ' οὔτέ τί πω εἶπας ἔπος οὔτ' ἐτέλεσσας·

With Aulis as the historical backdrop for Agamemnon's stern reply, then the "not ever" (οὐ πώ ποτέ) and "always" (αἰεί) of his prophecies join the events at Troy to Aulis. Thus, there are at least two potential examples of metonymic allusion here. First, the comparison between Clytemnestra and Chryseïs and second the characterization of Kalchas at Aulis and Troy. Together, these make Agamemnon's response all the more ironic and portentous. As we have seen in our consideration of the *Odyssey* in the last chapter, and now note for the *Iliad*, past and future are always impinging on the narrative present.

Kalchas' traditional character as a prophet who speaks the truth (however little Agamemnon likes it!) will cause Agamemnon to accept the necessity of returning Chryseïs. Yet, while grudgingly agreeing to return the concubine to save his Achaian warrior host (1.116–117), Agamemnon demands that he receive a compensatory "war prize" (γέρας): "But for me, prepare a war prize at once!" (αὐτὰρ ἐμοὶ γέρας αὐτίχ' ἑτοιμάσατ', 118). The force of Agamemnon's words are brought out by the joining of "But for me" (αὐτὰρ ἐμοί) with other markers of his authoritarian voice.[32] "But for me" indicates strong emotional involvement by the speaker. Agamemnon is intent on getting what he considers his due and won't settle for less. He demands his *geras*, even though, as Achilles immediately

---

[31] Aeschylus *Agamemnon* 1521–1529, 1555–1559, *Choephoroe* 918, *Persae* 1054–1065. On its part in ritual, see Alexiou 2002:6.

[32] On the "strongly adversative" sense of the αὐτάρ, see Denniston 1950:55. αὐτὰρ ἐμοί, already a traditional collocation with force in Homer (cf. *Iliad* 21.157, *Odyssey* 3.351, 4.481, 538, 548, 7.151, etc.) is joined by the poet with αὐτίχ' and an imperative.

observes, the distribution of the spoils by the army has already been made (162).[33] Agamemnon's retort to the priest's declaration and his demand for compensation "fatally" disturb "a fragile economy of reciprocal battlefield honors and benefits" (Felson and Slatkin 2004:94) within the warrior community.[34] Indeed, the immediate effect of Agamemnon's response is strife between himself and Achilles (the "best of the Achaians").[35] This contention forms the backdrop of books 1 through 9 in particular, although it is ultimately the backstory, too, for action and plot development in the rest of the *Iliad*.

Considering Agamemnon's imperious and arrogant rejoinder, it is little wonder that Achilles replies acerbically by calling him "[the] greatest lover of things of all men" (φιλοκτεανώτατε πάντων, 1.122). In response—as though affirming Achilles' charge—Agamemnon returns to the question of a war prize. He includes a threat made all the more emphatic by the use of the future perfect. He describes what is to be the angry emotional state (κεχολώσεται, 1.139) of the one whom he will visit to take his compensatory prize. As Chantraine expresses it, the future perfect tense has an immediately tangible quality about the certainty of the consequences.[36] The poet next has Agamemnon move from argument to action with the imperative rejoinder, "But now come!" (νῦν δ' ἄγε, 141), a "rhetorical fulcrum" that divides Agamemnon's speech and "initiates a call for action" (Foley 1999:224–225).[37] Agamemnon urges that they immediately act to appease the archer god. Yet, he speaks as though his abusive behavior could suddenly be forgotten in the wake of his imperious command.

Achilles, however, is not prepared simply to overlook Agamemnon's menacing threat, and the tenor of his reaction is carried in a traditional phrase: "*At him darkly looking,* spoke swift-footed Achilles" (τὸν δ' ἄρ' ὑπόδρα ἰδὼν

---

[33] As Taplin (1990:81) notes, if it is so improper that he go without a *geras* in such a situation, it is "strange" that no one does anything to correct the situation. The demand for immediate compensation is certainly not something Achilles feels Agamemnon should require (*contra* Wilson 2002:56). Achilles only concedes that a replacement *geras* is appropriate at some future time (*Iliad* 1.127–129).

[34] Cf. Crotty (1994:34), "by exercising that power without regard to the dictates of shame, Agamemnon brings about a violent rupture in the warrior society..." Wilson (2002:50) suggests that Kalchas and Achilles' argument "is also the narrator's argument," suggesting that it is the authoritative point meant to be taken away by the audience. Cf. Lloyd-Jones (1971:12–13), who characterizes Achilles as "undoubtedly in the right" since Agamemnon is violating justice and the *timē* of Achilles. Adkins (1982:287, 303–306) rejects this argument in favor of an argument for pure self-interest. See Gagarin (1987) for an attempted *via media*.

[35] Nagy (1979:26–41) argues that the *Iliad* attempts to present Achilles as the best of the Achaians. Four other Achaians, including Agamemnon, vie for this title, but in the poet's plan only Achilles is *aristos/phertatos*.

[36] Chantraine 1963:200, "sensible."

[37] I see the singular νῦν δ' ἄγε (cf. *Iliad* 22.391 and *Odyssey* 12.213's νῦν δ' ἄγεθ') as a variant way of expressing ἀλλ' ἄγε[τε], the actual formula that Foley considers in his study.

προσέφη πόδας ὠκὺς Ἀχιλλεύς, 148; emphasis mine). As we saw in Chapter 2, Holoka has demonstrated that this formula (τὸν δ' ἄρ' ὑπόδρα ἰδών) functions to highlight disrespectful breaches in social conventions, and he suggests its utility as part of a response to encourage propriety.[38] Achilles' scowl, given him by the poet as narrator, is one that here sums up the state of affairs and means to check the hubristic behavior of the Achaians' paramount *basileus*. Achilles' objurgating response (1.149–171) centers upon Agamemnon's "lack of shame" and is brought home through local repetition of words centering upon Agamemnon's "shamelessness" (ἀναιδείην, 149; ἀναιδές, 158). The diachronic meaning of "shamelessness" includes a lack of constraint.[39] Examined in close detail in Homer, however, one finds "shamelessness" used in desperate circumstances that entail the idea of destruction threatened or carried out upon others (especially in the case of instruments like stones) or eventually upon the self (particularly in the case of humans as agents). The word describes stones that smash a warrior's leg (*Iliad* 4.521), that are carried by a forceful current (*Iliad* 13.140), or are pushed to the crest of an underworld peak (*Odyssey* 11.598, by Sisyphos). The epithet also embodies the tumult of war (*Iliad* 5.593). It is very often employed to describe the suitors whom Athena, Odysseus, Telemachos, and Penelope want to see destroyed (*Odyssey* 1.254, 13.376, 20.29, 39, 386, 23.37); but also the unfaithful serving women (*Odyssey* 22.424) or beggars (*Odyssey* 17.449) who end up as slaves in foreign lands. The thoughtlessness of human perpetrators of shamelessness is apparent. Of course, stones cannot consider their actions, but many humans seem as deaf or as unresponsive as inanimate objects to warnings about their own self-destruction that portends in each case. Agamemnon's shameless attitude, then, suggests his unresponsive disregard for self-harm and its inevitable consequences.

Agamemnon's shamelessness is also given characteristics in *Iliad* 1. It seeks personal gain (κερδαλεόφρον, 149) and wealth (πλοῦτον, 171). Achilles' earlier speech had characterized Agamemnon through his address as "[the] greatest lover of things of all men" (φιλοκτεανώτατε πάντων, 1.122). Now he says that Agamemnon gets the greatest portion of any spoil, while he receives but "a precious small" allotment (ὀλίγον τε φίλον τε, 167).[40] There is, consequently, resonance with Achilles' previous speech (but also with a later moment in the *Iliad*, as we will see) since Achilles continues to portray Agamemnon

---

[38] See Chapter 2, s.v. 2.2.4 Menestheus and Odysseus: 4.327–364.

[39] For a diachronic consideration of *aoidos*, see Cairns 1993 (for criticism of Cairn's methodology, see Belfiore 1994). Taking Cairns's findings as a whole, however, ἀναιδείη/ἀναιδής suggest a marked lack of inhibition by internal or external constraint (so, guilt or shame).

[40] Should Troy ever be taken, Agamemnon would receive a far superior portion of the spoils (163–166). This is a traditional refrain in Homer, as we saw in Chapter 2, n. 38.

as oblivious, not only to the need of the Achaians, but also to what is best for himself. Agamemnon is demonstrating a complete dearth of leadership qualities expected of the paramount *basileus*. He is acting most thoughtlessly in his selfishness. As a contrast, Achilles reminds Agamemnon that it was not for personal revenge that he came to Troy, nor because any Trojan had done him wrong. It was instead for the honor of Menelaos (157), "and," Achilles adds most pointedly, "for you, dog-face" (σοί τε κυνῶπα, 158).[41]

Of course, in some contexts, references to canines or canine qualities can have positive or neutral qualities in actuality or in metaphor.[42] Dogs both inside and outside of similes can act as hunting and guard (or attack) dogs or even be kept more as pets for show by noblemen.[43] Yet, dogs are otherwise most strongly characterized as animals (usually with birds, including vultures) that act to scavenge the corpses of fallen heroes.[44] It is likely this last traditional association that makes "dog" (κύων) an apt term to characterize a human enemy with connotations that suggest the basest of qualities. Homer's traditional lexicon, in fact, carries a wide range of canine words, that, when applied to humans, create a very negative stigma. These include not only "dog" (κύων), but also "dog-like" (= "shameless," κύνεος), "more like a dog, more shameless" (κύντερος), "most dog-like, most shameful" (κύντατος), "dog-fly" (κυνάμυια), and "dog-face" (κυνώπης/κυνῶπις).

The Trojans call their Achaians enemies "doomed dogs" (κύνας κηρεσσιφορήτους, *Iliad* 8.527), and Menelaos calls the Trojans "bad *bitches*" (κακαὶ κύνες, *Iliad* 13.623), a taunt that is clearly meant not only to suggest their shamelessness but also their absolute weakness as warriors. The Trojans swooping in on Ajax, Menelaos, and Meriones, as they attempt to retrieve and protect the body of Patroklos, are freely compared to dogs (κύνεσσιν ἐοικότες, *Iliad* 17.725). Penelope uses the term "heedless bitches" (κύνας οὐκ ἀλεγούσας, *Odyssey* 19.154) for her maidservants who discover her secret and compel her

---

[41] Achilles employs "you" thrice for emphasis: ἀλλὰ σοί ... ὄφρα σὺ χαίρῃς ... σοί, 158–159.

[42] On the positive qualities of Argus, see Scodel 2005; for a consideration of dogs in similes see Kelly 2007a:300–302. As Kelly shows, however, even in similes, when dogs do not act in coordination with humans, they are "uniformly unsuccessful." Interestingly, Agamemnon in *Iliad* 1 is acting out of step with his own human warrior community.

[43] For dogs as companions in the hunt, see *Iliad* 3.26, 5.476, 9.545, 10.360, 11.292, 414, 549, 12.41, 147, 13.198, 475, 15.272, 17.65, 110, 282, 658, 725, 18.578, 581, 584, 22.29; *Odyssey* 2.11, 17.62, 19.429, 436, 438, 444, and 20.145; as guard dogs, see *Iliad* 10.183, 186, 15.187; *Odyssey* 7.91, 11.623, 14.21, 29, 35, 37, 531, 16.4, 6, 9, 162, and 17.200; as attack dogs, see *Odyssey* 21.340 and 363; as show dogs, see *Odyssey* 17.309; nor did Argos (17.300) any longer serve a useful role outside of his position as Odysseus' (now neglected) hunting dog. On the role of dogs in ancient society as symbols of the health of a household, see especially Beck 1991.

[44] See *Iliad* 1.4, 2.393, 8.379, 13.831, 15.351, 17.153, 241, 558, 18.271, 283, 22.42, 66, 75, 89, 335, 339, 348, 354, 509, 23.183, 184, 185, 24.211, 411, *Odyssey* 3.259, 14.133, and 18.105 (but of beggars).

to complete the shroud for Laertes. The serving-women who tease the beggar Odysseus are also called "bitches" (κύνες *Odyssey* 19.372) for their abusive attitude toward a beggar. Odysseus uses the vocative "dogs" (ὦ κύνες, *Odyssey* 22.35) to address the suitors in his first public *anagnorismos* after arriving home on Ithaca. Even Helen, in moments of derogatory self-degradation, refers to herself as a "bitch" (ἐμεῖο κυνὸς, *Iliad* 6.344, 356).[45]

The comparative κύντερος is used by Zeus of Hera, whose resentment he finds "more bitch-like" (*Iliad* 8.483) than anything else. Odysseus finds his belly to be likewise "more dog-like" as a driving force that controls him (*Odyssey* 7.215). Agamemnon describes his own wife in her scheming to murder him in the same terms (*Odyssey* 11.427), as does Odysseus when narrating the outrage of the Cyclops in eating his companions (*Odyssey* 20.18). The singular use of the superlative "most dog-like" (κύντατος) expresses anticipated devastation (*Iliad* 10.503). The dog compound "dog-fly" (κυνάμυια) is used twice in a derogatory manner by the *Iliad* poet in book 21, the first occurrence clustered in close proximity to the next (394, 421). First, Ares uses it as a derogatory name for Athena (394), calling attention to her earlier assistance of Diomedes that resulted in his wounding by a spear in the stomach (cf. *Iliad* 5.855–857). Then Hera uses it with equal disgust to name Aphrodite (421), when she sees her leading Ares back into the melee of battle.

The instances of the compound "dog-face" (κυνώπης/κυνῶπις), beyond *Iliad* 1, are also telling. In *Iliad* 18, Hephaistos uses it loathingly of his own mother, when describing how she threw him off Olympos onto Lemnos (*Iliad* 18.396); then again of his wife Aphrodite who has just cheated on him (*Odyssey* 8.319). Helen turns the expression on herself as the cause for the Achaians stirring up the Trojan War (*Odyssey* 4.145). Helen's half-sister, on the other hand, is pictured by Homer as less than contrite. Even after butchering her husband, Clytemnestra refuses to act decently and close Agamemnon's eyes and mouth. She earns the name "bitch-faced" (*Odyssey* 11.424) from her husband in Hades as he narrates his sorry tale to Odysseus.

The full metonym "dog-face" (κυνῶπα) is especially suggestive of Agamemnon's hubristic actions and attitude. What is more, the traditional term "dog-face" (κυνῶπα) used in book 1 appears to have affected the poet's choice of words in book 9. There, the poet has Achilles say of Agamemnon: "He would not certainly / dare, *dog* though he is, to look upon my *face*" (οὐδ' ἂν ἔμοιγε /

---

[45]   See Monsacré (1984:159) for the uniqueness of Helen's sense of remorse among female characters in *Iliad*. For Helen's gendered role in self-blame, see Blondell 2010. Blondell also discusses Helen's use of this self-designation on two other occasions (*Iliad* 3.180 to Priam; *Odyssey* 4.145 at home before members of her *oikos* and visitors) and finds that Helen affirms responsibility (and so agency), while males excuse her for reasons of gender.

τετλαίη κύνεός περ ἐὼν εἰς ὦπα ἰδέσθαι, 9.372–373).[46] The rare use of the perfect optative (τετλαίη) makes the charge of Agamemnon's "dog-likeness" (κύνεος) stand out all the more for Homer's audience. Agamemnon's "dog-likeness" is not the only point of resonance with book 1, however. Rather, within two lines, Achilles describes Agamemnon's character as one of "constant shamelessness" (αἰὲν ἀναιδείην, 9.372), uttering the same charge he used eight books earlier (ἀναιδείην, 1.149; ἀναιδές, 1.158). It is no coincidence that the poet has Achilles yell "dog-face" and "shameless" in almost the same breath on two separate occasions. The association of these two terms, rare in Homer, but really quite apposite, suggests that the poet is attached to the sort of referential qualities these words bring forward for Agamemnon.[47] Agamemnon's association with "dog" as voiced by Achilles creates a depth of metonymic meaning that places Agamemnon in the adversary's camp; he is one who is working against the Achaians' best interests and is the object of disgust. Achilles closes his rebuttal with a stark declaration—he is heading back to Phthia!

Agamemnon replies that he will not entreat Achilles to stay (he may as well flee, 1.173), since he has others who honor him. The response of Agamemnon to his leading Greek warrior-*basileus* is arrogant and thoughtless. In his heated reply he uses two equivalent idioms to drive his point home (1.180–181): "But about you I do not care, / Nor do I have regard for you in your anger!" (σέθεν δ' ἐγὼ οὐκ ἀλεγίζω, / οὐδ' ὄθομαι κοτέοντος). Agamemnon's response brings together words that voice a complete rejection of any need for Achilles. "I do not care" (οὐκ ἀλεγίζω) "is characteristic of both mortal and divine figures who suffer the consequences for failing to take due consideration before acting" (Kelly 2007a:346–348). In fact, the joining of "I do not care" (οὐκ ἀλεγίζω) with a second statement, "I do not have regard" (οὐδ' ὄθομαι), creates, I suggest, an even more emphatic response by Agamemnon, since the poet could have chosen to use just one negative remark as he does elsewhere.[48] The same two negated components used in *Iliad* 1 in the form of personal statements, "I care" (ἀλεγίζω) and "I regard" (ὄθομαι), are used in *Iliad* 15.106–107 by a "perturbed" (νεμεσσηθεῖσα, 15.103) Hera to describe Zeus in a negative and malicious way: "but he sitting apart does not care / nor have regard [for us]!" (ὃ δ' ἀφήμενος οὐκ ἀλεγίζει/οὐδ'

---

[46] εἰς ὦπα + verb, at *Iliad* 3.158, 15.147, *Odyssey* 1.411, and 22.405, shows different possibilities. The significance here is not that the "face" has changed from Agamemnon's to Achilles', but rather the echo of the original κυνῶπα in the formation by the poet of the present narrative moment. Cf. κυνὸς ὄμματ' ἔχων, *Iliad* 1.225.

[47] This is one of many resonances between *Iliad* 1 and 9, as we will see when we consider book 9 later in this chapter.

[48] Unlike ἀλεγίζω, ὄθομαι appears in the *Iliad* only in negative statements. Both words are equally employed in Homer, occurring in various forms eleven times in total (six in the *Iliad* and five in the *Odyssey*).

ὄθεται).⁴⁹ In the case of Agamemnon as a mere mortal, however, the response carries with it an irony in the larger tradition for Homer's informed audience. They know that Agamemnon will in fact very soon need Achilles whose absence will bring near-devastation to the Achaian forces at Troy.

Agamemnon is, however, not content to leave things at a rhetorical level. Instead, he presses Achilles with a vexatious threat. As Chryseïs is taken from him by Phoibos Apollo, so he will lead away Briseïs, Achilles' prize (a threat he soon carries out: *Iliad* 1.321–325, 387–388). He wishes Achilles to know "how much superior" (ὅσσον φέρτερος, 186) he is, so that no one will again presume "to speak on equal terms" (ἶσον ... φάσθαι, 187) with him (cf. Willcock 1978:191), or even to suggest a verisimilitude! These polemically acerbic words about personal superiority, which deserve to be punctuated with several exclamation points in any English translation, close Agamemnon's reply to Achilles. The question is not, of course, whether Agamemnon is superior or not. He is. The question is how and why he [mis-]uses his power. As we will see, Agamemnon's unsuccessful desire to force a public recognition of his own superiority will form a theme that recurs in book 9.

The ensuing scene in *Iliad* 1 has Athena appear to Achilles alone (198). The conversation between goddess and hero highlights Achilles' anger but also his decision (214) to show restraint in the face of Agamemnon's hubris (203). The particulars of the scene need not detain us in their every detail. A few overall observations help in our quest for Agamemnon's characterization. First, it is important to note that Achilles will show restraint. He will moderate his actions when wronged, and his response will stand out in marked contrast to Agamemnon's own quick, thoughtless, and despotic decision to seize what he sees as his royal due. Moreover, Athena's promise of future recompense for present correct and responsive action, something suggested by Kalchas earlier but ignored cavalierly by Agamemnon (cf. 213–214 and 218–219), is implicitly accepted by Achilles.⁵⁰ This is another point of contrasting characterization. The poet wishes to amplify the arrogant disposition of Agamemnon at this crucial moment in his song. Second, the proverbial comment of Achilles, that it is better for humans to obey the gods since this brings their active attention and response (note especially ἔκλυον, 218), will stand in direct opposition to Agamemnon's irreverent reaction to the priest of Apollo.⁵¹ Achilles has in fact

---

⁴⁹ This is an instance of the emphatic use of formulae of the sort noted by Di Benedetto (1994:131).

⁵⁰ On the traditional nature of this form of appeal, see my comments in Chapter 2, n. 38.

⁵¹ Achilles comments that ὅς κε θεοῖς ἐπιπείθηται μάλα τ' ἔκλυον αὐτοῦ. This response acts as an immediate foil for Agamemnon, but perhaps also metonymically for Achilles himself, who does not accept the offered amelioration of the assembly in *Iliad* 9. As a result, Zeus continues (part of the *Dios boulē*) to bring about the slaughter of the Achaians, including Achilles' *philtatos*, Patroklos. The verb κλύειν, used of the gods' relationship with mortals (cf. *Iliad* 1.457 [479]; 5.121

responded to Athena's prompting. He has shown restraint and is first speaking to his own situation when he voices a general truth.[52] Yet, at the same time, Achilles is also here stating the "selbstverständliche kollektive Überzeugungen" (Latacz 2000a:95) of all the Achaians.

Athena quits the scene, and Achilles revisits his impassioned exchange with Agamemnon (1.225–244), but now without the physical violence he had been tempted to employ earlier. The renewed verbal scourge, encouraged as an appropriate alternative by Athena, exceeds the intensity of his last speech (225–231). He charges Agamemnon with taking a war prize the easy way, by snatching it from anyone who speaks in opposition. This is an obvious reference to Achilles' own predicament. Achilles' harangue terminates with an oath and a prophetic warning. There will come a future "yearning" (ποθή, 240) for the rebuffed Achilles. The oath is sworn upon a scepter, and the poet creates emphasis by slowing the narrative moment through expansion. He proffers an extended description of the scepter's emergence from its origins as a tree (234–36). The tree-turned-scepter is now equated with civic justice tended by those who administer justice "from Zeus" (πρὸς Διός, 239).[53] Achilles then makes his case against Agamemnon vivid through action, by flinging the scepter to the ground before sitting down. In hurling to the ground the very object in the assembly connected with the justice of Zeus, Achilles is stating unequivocally that he has received no justice from Agamemnon and that the paramount *basileus* has even cast down the justice of Zeus himself. He is at this point, as Hammer has argued, quitting the public sphere.[54]

Not surprisingly at this impasse, the poet has Nestor step in. As we saw in Chapter 2, Nestor is a well-respected and positively represented sagacious hero. His counsel is highly valued, and he is known within Homer's tradition for his heroic feats from a former generation.[55] He advises Agamemnon to let Achilles keep the prize bestowed by the army and Achilles to concede place to the scepter-bearing *basileus*. Nestor closes by counseling Agamemnon to put aside his "anger" (μένος/χόλος, 282–283) against Achilles. His advice is not taken, however, despite his intentions of reuniting the Achaians behind their

---

[23.771], 24.314), is inclusive here both of the act of hearing and the state of agreement with (or act of positive response to) the petitioner. This aspect is missed by Chantraine 1968:541, s.v. κλέος (s.v. κλύω), but noted by *LfgrE* 14.1458, s.v. κλυεῖν, κλύω B. (G. Markwald), "oft erhören."

[52] Lardinois 2000:645 notes that Achilles references are more generally to himself.

[53] *Iliad* 1.238–239 ἐν παλάμης φορέουσι δικασπόλοι, οἵ τε θέμιστας / πρὸς Διὸς εἰρύαται·

[54] Hammer (1997:12) describes Achilles' throwing of the scepter as a symbolic withdrawal from the political sphere and argues that through this act Achilles is envisioning "an eventual return to his [own] household."

[55] See Chapter 2, s.v. 2.2.3 Nestor: 4.293–326, on the traditional implications of Nestor's history in Homer's tradition.

leader. This spells doom in the minds of Homer's core audience who know that such a rejection is full of foreboding. It will lead to a serious division.

Audience foreboding is likely too if we consider the resonance of this moment with the prior warning in the prologue. There the very first word of Homer's song was *mēnis*, a "wrath" that is described as "destructive" (οὐλομένην, 1.2), and only found in Achilles among mortals.[56] It is a wrath, too, that the audience knows is connected with strife (ἐρίσαντε, 1.6), when two individuals were staunchly separated (διαστήτην, 1.6), "the ruler of men, son of Atreus, and noble Achilles" (Ἀτρεΐδης τε ἄναξ ἀνδρῶν καὶ δῖος Ἀχιλλεύς, 1.7). Strife was to be the beginning of great losses that hurled Achaian warriors into Hades (1.4–5). It was now, so the audience doubtless recognized, that the Achaian's sorry losses were set to begin. The likelihood is that the audience of *Iliad* 1 shared with the poet other prior knowledge of what was about to unfold. The necessity of certain background knowledge is in fact keyed by one assumption the *aoidos* makes in uttering the prologue. I refer to his use of the epithet "son of Atreus" (Ἀτρεΐδης). It is employed by Homer of Agamemnon and Menelaos as individuals, of both as a pair, and even of Orestes as a grandson of Atreus.[57] So to whom is the poet referring? Clearly Homer believes the audience knows. But do they? The epithet "ruler" (ἄναξ) would be less helpful in determining which brother is meant, since it is used of both Agamemnon and Menelaos (and many others) in Homer's tradition.[58] Only when the fuller title, "ruler of men" (ἄναξ ἀνδρῶν), is considered, do we find that Menelaos is excluded as a possibility in the proem. The title is nowhere else used of Menelaos. It is, however, used of other heroes, and so the poet clearly assumes referential knowledge in his core audience.[59] Otherwise, the epithet is obfuscating to say the least. The audience, who knew enough of the story to recognize exactly whom the poet was talking about, is waiting for the "anger" (μένος/χόλος) of Agamemnon to cue the greater "wrath" (μῆνις) of Achilles.

Nestor's advice is not heeded, since Agamemnon rejects any mediation. The assembly is broken up by the two still in contention (1.304–305). Achilles has kept himself from violence, but that will not stop Agamemnon from taking what

---

[56] The scholiasts understood it as "einen chronischen Erzürntheitszustand," as Latacz (2000a:13) glosses ἐπίμονος ὀργή (schol. D) and κότος πολυχρόνιος (Aristotle); and similarly Chantraine (1968:696, s.v. μῆνις) suggests a *colère durable*. On the *mēnis* theme see especially Redfield 1979, Slatkin 1991:86, *LfgrE* 15.187, s.v. μῆνις (Beck), Di Benedetto 1994:111, and Muellner 1996:94–132.

[57] For example, of Agamemnon here and in *Iliad* 2.6, 3.193, 11.158; *Odyssey* 1.35, 3.156; of Menelaos: *Iliad* 3.347, 5.55, 13.646; of both: *Iliad* 1.16–17, 2.249; and of Orestes: *Odyssey* 1.40.

[58] Hermes (*Iliad* 2.104), Apollo (5.105), and others in the nominative, although it is used of Menelaos only in the vocative: ἄναξ Μενέλαε (*Iliad* 23.588).

[59] The epithet ἄναξ ἀνδρῶν is employed of Anchises: *Iliad* 5.268; of Aineias: 5.311; of Augeias: 11.701; and of Euphetes: 15.532.

he wants. Agamemnon will misuse his power and position. He is swift to fulfill his threat against Achilles (318–325), although his own messengers display an immediate revulsion toward carrying out his orders (327).[60]

We need not consider at length all the particulars of the embassy. One comment of Achilles is particularly pertinent, however. In his hospitable address and conversation with Agamemnon's emissaries, he absolves them of blame for their thankless task. Yet, he remonstrates that Agamemnon chose a thoughtless course of action that would spell destruction for the army.[61] Achilles characterizes Agamemnon's thoughtlessness (343–334): "And not in any way does he know how to consider at the same time before and after, / so that by the ships safely the Achaians might fight" (οὐδέ τι οἶδε νοῆσαι ἅμα πρόσσω καὶ ὀπίσσω, / ὅππως οἱ παρὰ νηυσὶ σόοι μαχέοιντο Ἀχαιοί). This despairing comment of Achilles carries ironic import. It portends the eventual, desperate fighting of the *Iliad*'s action, when in book 12 the walls about the ships—yet to be built in the story's actual linear chronology—will be breached, and the Achaians will in fact be fighting by their own ships in grave danger. Consequently, it seems fair to suggest that the poet would have us take Achilles' words as accurate metonymic markers of the larger myth, rather than merely representing the isolated and insignificant mumbling of a disgruntled warrior. They resound within the larger context of the *Iliad*'s story known to the poet's audience. Agamemnon's inability here and elsewhere will form part of a negative refrain by those around him, as we will see.

Achilles' remark about Agamemnon's deficiency, that he is incapable of discerning "before and after" (πρόσσω καὶ ὀπίσσω), says quite a bit. This traditional element is employed three other times in Homer. It is uttered by Menelaos (*Iliad* 3.109). He contrasts the sagacity of old age with the impetuousness of youth (a familiar motif in Homer) in his bid to solicit the participation of the elderly Priam in the sacrifice and oath ceremony before the duel between himself and Paris.[62] He remarks that an elder man [e.g. Priam] discerns "before and after" (πρόσσω καὶ ὀπίσσω). His comments bring unity of opinion from the Greeks and Trojans (111). The traditional idiom is also employed by the poet-narrator in *Iliad* 18.250 to describe Hector's *hetairos* Polydamas, who in the Trojan general assembly (ἀγορή) addresses the troops after Achilles' return to war. The mood is one of fear. He advises the Trojans to return to the protection of Troy's walls, since they are, he argues, too far from it in the plain (256). Hector censures and

---

[60] Nb. ἀέκοντες.

[61] Latacz (2000a:123) notes that Achilles' speech here (and in 335–338) "hat den Charakter einer … 'Verlautberung' die an den 'Eid' in 233–244 erinnert."

[62] Nestor is himself, unsurprisingly, a standard sagacious contrast for less thoughtful youthful impetuousness. On Nestor's wisdom opposed to rash action, see *Iliad* 1.254–284; as a contrast to panic, see *Odyssey* 24.54. For Nestor as a contrast to his own son's recklessness, see Kahane 2005:114.

rebukes Polydamas, however, and argues instead for pressing on (285–309). The *Iliad* poet offers his perspective at this point in the narrative for the external audience attending his epic performance. He comments that Hector and the clamoring Trojans are "thoughtless children" (νήπιοι), with all the foreboding undercurrents this traditional term carries. It has the tradition-based effect of highlighting a character's misapprehension of a situation, while implying unenviable and foreboding consequences, as we saw in Chapter 3.[63] The term carries ironic disdain directed towards the person it references and his choice in a particular situation. Athena, moreover, is described as taking away the Trojan warriors' wits. The poet further overtly characterizes Hector's counsel as evil (310–311) in contrast to that offered by Polydamas, who, as Reinhardt noted, is added by Homer as Hector's "warner" (Reinhardt 1961:272–277). The audience was very much aware that Hector could not see "before and after" and that his own death would consequently follow.

The final occurrence of this formula is found in the *Odyssey*. There the poet uses it positively to describe favorably the Ithacan warrior-prophet Halitherses (24.452). He advises the disgruntled fathers of the slain suitors not to pursue Odysseus (454–462). Against him stands Eupeithes, father of Antinoos, who urges a "punishment" (τίσις). Not surprisingly, considering the etymology of his name, Eupeithes' speech wins over a majority, but the poet comments (469–471):

> But to these Eupeithes spoke in their thoughtless childishness;
> And he said that indeed he would avenge the murder of his child, but
> > not in reality was he about
> to return again, but there he was to encounter his fate.

> τοῖσιν δ' Εὐπείθης ἡγήσατο νηπιέῃσι·
> φῆ δ' ὅ γε τείσεσθαι παιδὸς φόνον, οὐδ' ἄρ' ἔμελλεν
> ἂψ ἀπονοστήσειν, ἀλλ' αὐτοῦ πότμον ἐφέψειν.

Ironically, in the perspective presented once again to the poet's external audience, the suitors ignore the wise counsel of Halitherses.[64]

Consideration of the formula "before and after" (πρόσσω καὶ ὀπίσσω), and the sort of meaning adhering to its usage, makes it immediately apparent that Achilles' characterization of Agamemnon is much more damning than it first appears. Read in the traditional register, it portrays Agamemnon as without the requisite thoughtfulness of the sort that can find a wise path. Agamemnon is

---

[63] See Chapter 3, s.v. 3.2.3 Nestor's Stories of Quarrel, *Nostoi*, and *Oresteia*: 3.136–310.
[64] On irony and the ironic use of traditional language cues, see Chapter 2.

not a Polydamas or Halitherses character. He is not being portrayed as the sort of person we realize instantaneously will end up right when everyone else is wrong. Instead, Agamemnon is being pictured as an individual sure to err in his hardheaded response to the best of the Achaians, because he is incapable of considering "at the same time before and after" (ἄμα πρόσσω καὶ ὀπίσσω). The poet, familiar with the connotations of the formula he employs, is forecasting the coming disaster originating from the strife of *Iliad* 1. He intentionally places this formula in the mouth of Achilles so that his audience hears the inherent nature of Agamemnon as a character within the larger epic story, as well as to create narrative momentum for the story plot.

Agamemnon's guilt is proverbial for the poet's epic tradition (e.g. 13.111–114). His hubristic seizure of Achilles' war prize (*geras*) will form a refrain for the singer in the mouth of various characters: Achilles (1.355–356), Thetis (1.506–507), and Thersites (2.239–240). The act will also unsurprisingly form an ongoing complaint for Achilles himself: "he dishonored [me], for he seized and holds the war prize he himself took away!" (ἠτίμησεν; ἑλὼν γὰρ ἔχει γέρας αὐτὸς ἀπούρας).[65] The local clustering of this refrain, as Di Benedetto (1994:115) remarks, suggests "che nel suo cervello è rimasta depositata una certa memoria e lui riproduce una certa cadenza, anche senza rendersene conto." The local clustering of this idiom, and the larger influence of this idiom on *Iliad* 9, suggest its depth within the singer's traditional register.[66]

4.2.2 Agamemnon's Dream and the Testing of the Troops: 2.16–440

Agamemnon is tricked by a "destructive dream" (οὖλον ὄνειρον, 2.6). The poet's choice of idiom here may in fact suggest at the outset that Agamemnon is headed on a course of action destined for failure.[67] Agamemnon now thinks that he can take Priam's city. As a result, the poet addresses Agamemnon as a "thoughtless

---

[65] Teffeteller (1990) notes that the expression αὐτὸς ἀπούρας signals the autocratic character of Agamemnon's rule. That Agamemnon did not come in person is suggested by Taplin (1992:72, "it is beneath his dignity"), but the larger meaning of Achilles' words are effectively brought out by Scodel (2003). She suggests that Agamemnon is not, in any case, demonstrating insincerity or offering an inappropriate number of gifts.

[66] ἠτίμησας, ἑλὼν γὰρ ἔχεις γέρας, *Iliad* 9.11; cf. 9.107. Clustering, as Beye (2006:82) notes, is a proclivity of Homeric poetry.

[67] So also οὖλε ὄνειρε (*Iliad* 2.8). By way of contrast, the other Homeric use of ὄνειρον filling the same metrical space, αἰνόν ὄνειρον (*Odyssey* 19.568), ends in a better outcome for the dreamer (Penelope). West (1997:185–190, 356) suggests comparisons with a few Near Eastern examples to show that dreams also came to kings in those traditions to stir them into battle. My concern here, however, is with the unique cues in the Homeric tradition that allowed the audience to interpret both the nature of the dream and the character of Agamemnon, something not a part of West's study.

child" (νήπιος, 2.38), a traditional term significant for what it implies negatively about him, as we saw in Chapter 3.[68] It suggests that Agamemnon misapprehends what the best course of action to take is; the idiom is full of foreboding. Indeed, the very propensity of Agamemnon to act thoughtlessly seems traditional, since, as we have seen, "thoughtless child" (νήπιος) is used to describe him in both epics.

The subsequent actions of Agamemnon in testing (πειρήσομαι, *Iliad* 2.73; πειρᾶται, *Iliad* 2.193) the troops are problematic too. They include no straightforward mustering of the forces for an assault on Troy, but rather a convoluted and all too enticing form of testing that ends up in disarray. First, Agamemnon calls a council of his leading *basileis* (2.53-55) where he outlines the imperative of the dream that has come to him in the night, including the taking of Troy. Agamemnon determines that he will make trial of (πειρήσομαι, 73) the troops. He claims that the act of testing he will propose, which is to include his own encouragement for the troops to retreat and engage in a *nostos* (74), is itself a conventional prerogative (ἢ θέμις ἐστί 73).[69] Agamemnon next announces to his *basileis* that, after he has ordered the troops to flee, they are to stop the troops' retreat from every direction (ὑμεῖς δ' ἄλλοθεν ἄλλος ἐρητύειν ἐπέεσσιν, 75). Significant here is the use of the plural "you" (ὑμεῖς) in his order to all the *basileis*. They are all to carry out his orders as a group. Clearly Agamemnon feels that the *basileis* will respond by restraining the men's urges after he has advised them to give up and go home.

Immediately after Agamemnon sits down, Nestor rises to speak. His reply (2.80–83) is ironic for the poet's audience who share the narrator's omniscient point of view:

> If, then, any other Achaian spoke the dream,
> we would say [it was] a lie and turn away in disdain all the more;
> But now he saw [it], who strongly boasts that he is the best of the
>   Achaians;
> But come, if somehow we can arm the sons of the Achaians!

> εἰ μέν τις τὸν ὄνειρον Ἀχαιῶν ἄλλος ἔνισπε
> ψεῦδός κεν φαῖμεν καὶ νοσφιζοίμεθα μᾶλλον·

---

[68] See Chapter 3, s.v. 3.2.3 Nestor's Stories of Quarrel, *Nostoi*, and *Oresteia*: 3.136–310.

[69] Schmidt (2002) saw no clear motive for Agamemnon's test (cf. Heiden 1991:4). Certainly, as Christensen (2015; cf. Heiden 1991:6) argues, the *diapeira* does function to draw in the audience, a vital feature for oral performance. Cf. my comments and Murko's experience of intense South Slavic oral performance in Chapter 1, n. 32.

νῦν δ' ἴδεν ὃς μέγ' ἄριστος Ἀχαιῶν εὔχεται εἶναι·
ἀλλ' ἄγετ' αἴ κέν πως θωρήξομεν υἷας Ἀχαιῶν.

Nestor says that he would be inclined to disdain such a message as false had it originated from anyone other than the one who boasts that he is the best of the Achaians. The traditional phrase, "boasts that he is the best of the Achaians" (ἄριστος Ἀχαιῶν εὔχεται εἶναι), introducing a reported claim, is an idiom without the speaker's active validation.[70] Further, I do not think that the bleak reality of the present situation, ironically noted by Nestor's comment centered on doubt (2.80–81), is meant to be limited to the dream that Agamemnon has just experienced. After all, Agamemnon's idea to test the troops by a call for a *nostos* with the possibility of mass pandemonium was also perhaps in Nestor's mind as he hesitatingly accepted Agamemnon's plan for the Achaians.[71] Further, it is likely that Nestor's retort is meant to suggest for the audience the irony of both aspects of Agamemnon's undertaking: his false belief that the Achaians will take Troy and also the potentially disastrous means he suggests to bring about troop preparedness, an appeal to retreat and *nostos*. Agamemnon may be making two mistakes, then. First, he believes the dream, and, second, he chooses to test the troops as he does.

Analysts early excised the scene, viewing it as a later addition, and noted that Agamemnon, Odysseus, and Nestor never actually made reference to the dream.[72] But this *argumentum ex silentio* is a less persuasive reason for denying its place in Homer's song. More convincingly, Morrison (1992a:42, 132n18) discusses the unusual nature of Agamemnon's test. He notes that exhortation to battle can include "advice, criticism, or warning (cf. 2.381–393, 4.223–421, 19.408–417)." He follows Schadewaldt (1966:29–40), who notes nine elements in a prelude to battle anticipatory sequence: 1. divine incitement to battle; 2. mortal decision to fight; 3. sacrifice; 4. meal; 5. gathering of the army; 6. arming (the whole army or an individual); 7. marching to battle; 8. review of troops; and 9. exhortation. The action of Agamemnon is certainly novel within exhortations to battle or in other type scenes that form the battle preparatory sequence.

---

[70] Di Benedetto (1994:120) sees it as suggesting "vanto" / "orgoglio" as a basic meaning.

[71] On confusion, see Kirk 1985:140; Heiden (1991:4) and Schmidt (2002) see no clear motive for Agamemnon's test.

[72] Leaf (1902a:66–69) earlier suggested excising the scene, noting that nothing is lost if it is removed, leaving Agamemnon in utter despondency proposing that the siege be abandoned. Von der Mühll (1946) and Mazon (1948:146–151) emphasized a lack of reference to it by Agamemnon, Odysseus, and Nestor, thus giving further support from an analyst perspective.

The Trojans, moreover, know nothing of the sort of testing that Agamemnon introduces.[73] Nor, for instance, does such testing form a part of Achilles' exhortation to battle for his Myrmidons in *Iliad* 16.198–211, except in one negative way. As Elmer (2013:89) points out, Achilles makes a brief reference to his own troops' desire to return home (205–206) only to "consign that desire rhetorically to the past," before charging his soldiers to enter the fray with courage. Achilles as a leader would have none of the sorts of tactics employed by Agamemnon. Further, when the gods appear in human guise to stir the troops, they also act directly without such complications. To take one example, when the gods perceive that the Achaians are perishing in book 5, Hera initiates divine action (711–718). A rally of the troops is done with a forthright appeal to "shame" (αἰδῶς, 787) and is very effective: "Thus having spoken, she stirred the courage and spirit of each man" (ὣς εἰποῦσ' ὄτρυνε μένος καὶ θυμὸν ἑκάστου, 792).

Further, appeals to what is traditional (*themis*) do not always represent established custom, as much as the speaker's own desire (Griffin 1986:38–39). This point should not be missed. The act of testing and the type of test used are two different matters. Nor, as McGlew (1989:288–289) has suggested, can we take *Iliad* 9.9–78 or 14.27–146 to be equivalent testing scenes *in potentia*, despite the similarity in vocabulary.[74] As we will see when we survey these other scenes, at each of these narrative junctures Agamemnon really does want to leave.

On the other hand, scholars from various perspectives have tried to justify Agamemnon's actions. McGlew (1989) argues that Agamemnon was attempting to shame the troops into fighting, and that, since he was without goods to distribute, he maintained his status as *wanax* by this very act. He suggests that Agamemnon's plan worked. While his argument is consistently made, I disagree with the conclusion that Agamemnon actually devised the outcome that followed, since it didn't really go according to plan.[75] Dentice Di Accadia (2010:229) goes further and argues that the test is "assolutamente necessaria" when it is considered through the eyes of the ancient critics (Hermogones, Dionysus of Halicarnasos, etc.). The Ancient critics, however, imbue Agamemnon with a deep capacity for understanding the sentiments of others.[76] As will be apparent from my discussion here and elsewhere, such arguments do not take

---

[73] Cf. *Iliad* 2.786–808 and McGlew 1989:286 (although he posits a different political reality for the Trojans as the possible cause for this discrepancy, rather than its novelty).

[74] Cf. the conclusions of Hainsworth 1993:62 and Elmer 2013:91.

[75] *Iliad* 2.75, moreover, seems to envisage a group effort at halting any retreat. It was instead Odysseus, stirred on by Athena, who actually stopped the flight at the last moment by upbraiding the *basileis* (*Iliad* 2.185–205), a point we will return to.

[76] Dentice Di Accadia 2010, e.g. 242, "Agamennone non può fare altro che invitare i soldati a tornare in patria, mostrando di comprendere e condividere la loro stanchezza." Ancient critics, including the scholiasts, however, have a great ability in reading into an action every sort of motivation,

into account the full character of Agamemnon in Homer's oral tradition nor its influence on any particular moment of narrative creation. We must consider Agamemnon not within one narrative moment only, but against the backdrop of many other epic moments. Agamemnon is not really that thoughtful or sympathetic a person within Homer's tradition, as we have already seen in our consideration of him to this point (and will note further). So, the explanation of ancient critics is not convincing.

Kelly's recent argument for another Homeric theme within an exhortation to battle sequence in Homer's oral template suggests that part of the test was not entirely odd. Kelly demonstrates that our present scene includes a "uniquely long example of the 'suggestion of retreat'" theme.[77] Kelly (2014:37n26) outlines the existence of this theme, both here and in other passages in Homer.[78] Interestingly, however, I note that only Agamemnon (of all the Iliadic examples) ever suggests that the Achaians both retreat and also engage in a *nostos*. Consequently, even assuming a "suggestion of retreat" theme, Agamemnon's decision is still unparalleled in Homer. As a unique addition to the traditional battle anticipatory sequence, then, Agamemnon's test of the troops may have thus been employed ironically by the poet to show the foolishness of both Agamemnon's perception and his qualities as a leader, including his inability to inspire his followers to action.[79] As a traditional "suggestion of retreat" theme, the choice of Agamemnon to include a call for a *nostos* displays his pathetic character as paramount *basileus*. As will be the case here and in other moments, whenever he suggests a retreat, no one will follow his lead. The whole *diapeira* highlights the inept attempt of Agamemnon to stir the passion of his troops. It provides "an important index of Agamemnon's rather troubled authority within the camp" (Kelly 2014:39). The test is "ill suited" and shows an "indifference toward the principles that undergird political stability" (Elmer 2013:89, 90), much the same as occurred in the opening scenes of *Iliad* 1.

After the initial meeting with his *basileis*, Agamemnon and his council (βουλή) gather together with the assembly (ἀγορή) of the entire Achaian

---

but they are often less concerned with the sorts of oral traditional questions I ask throughout my argument. Cf. the comments of Anne Amory Parry 1973:7.

[77] The theme may also be expanded by more than one rejection or amplification, for instance.

[78] The other Iliadic examples of Agamemnon's use of this theme (cf. 9.16–77, 14.64–132) and its use by others include Polydamas (12.208–229; 18.249–309), Diomedes (8.138–144), Thoas (15.281–300), and Meriones (17.621–623). We can also add to Kelly's list Achilles' own dismissal of such an idea (theme).

[79] Morrison (1992a:39–41, 131n9) discusses Agamemnon's interrupting the movement to battle with his testing of the troops. He points out (40) that "In calling Agamemnon a fool (νήπιος), the narrator reminds the audience that Agamemnon's expectations are ill-founded. Defeat, not victory, awaits him, as the predictions from Book 1 have clearly indicated." See my discussion of νήπιος earlier in this chapter, but also Homer's use of irony in Chapter 2.

force, where Agamemnon delivers his deceptive exhortation to leave Troy. His words to the troops vacillate between several elements: blaming Zeus for falsely misleading him (2.114);[80] an attempt to inculcate shame (119–122);[81] and tempting his homesick men to achieve a *nostos* and so reunite with their absent spouses and children who "sit in [our] houses waiting; But for us [there is] work / as ever without completion for which we arrived here" (ἥατ᾽ ἐνὶ μεγάροις ποτιδέγμεναι· ἄμμι δὲ ἔργον / αὔτως ἀκράαντον οὗ εἵνεκα δεῦρ᾽ ἱκόμεσθα, 137–138).[82] The irony of Agamemnon's words would have been immediately apparent to the singer's audience who share his omniscient point of view. While Agamemnon says that Zeus has engaged in an evil deception (κακὴν ἀπάτην, 2.114), really it is Agamemnon himself who is devising the present lying propositions. The audience is viewing Agamemnon both as deceiver and deceived; as a cognizant perpetrator and an incognizant recipient of "deception" (ἀπάτη).[83] Only Homer's audience, rather than any of the story characters (the internal audience), shares in the full knowledge and implications of the scene's action. As we will see when we consider his later admission of error against Achilles in *Iliad* 19, Agamemnon seems incapable of recognizing his true state of delusion and is punished. Agamemnon is a complex figure, one whose ability to recognize his own errors is effectively problematized by the poet here and elsewhere.[84]

Further, if Agamemnon's speech does include a tradition-based "suggestion of retreat," one should, I suggest, also compare *Iliad* 2 with a scene from the *Odyssey* and suggest resonance. In presenting Agamemnon's testing of the troops, the *Iliad* poet may also have had in mind the "suggestion of retreat" found in the Odyssean episode of Helen and the wooden horse. Agamemnon seems to play the sort of role Helen does when she attempts to destroy the morale of the warriors in the wooden horse (also set during the Trojan War). Of course, the surreal scene cannot have Helen actively aware of the presence of the men within, and her role seems to be as temptress. The scene is meant to be heard by Homer's audience as a struggle to resist her alluring song.[85] She, like Agamemnon, reminds the men of their families back home (*Odyssey* 4.277–279)

---

[80] νῦν δὲ κακὴν ἀπάτην βουλεύσατο.

[81] αἰσχρὸν γὰρ τόδε γ᾽ ἐστὶ καὶ ἐσσομένοισι πυθέσθαι / μὰψ οὕτω τοιόνδε τοσόνδε τε λαὸν Ἀχαιῶν / ἄπρηκτον πόλεμον πολεμίζειν ἠδὲ μάχεσθαι / ἀνδράσι παυροτέροισι, τέλος δ᾽ οὔ πώ τι πέφανται·

[82] On the negative use of *nostos* in the *Iliad*, see Maronitis 2004:63–76.

[83] The ironies of the situation are only partly known then to ὅσσοι οὐ βουλῆς ἐπάκουσαν, 2.143; but see 1.194, where the actions of some *basileis* do not appear to match their knowledge, as Odysseus' question seems to indicate (unless his query is to be taken simply as a means of castigation).

[84] Cf. Christensen (2015) on Agamemnon's ambiguous nature in *Iliad* 2.

[85] On Helen's allure, see Blondell 2013:1–95.

and suggests a *nostos*.[86] As in the *Iliad*, it is Odysseus who comes to the rescue, providing leadership for the troops (*Odyssey* 4.284-289). Odysseus is credited with restraining the *basileis*, as we will see was also his role in *Iliad* 2. In both cases, moreover, Odysseus makes his voice heard through physical force (*Iliad* 2.198-199, 265-269; *Odyssey* 4.284, 287-289). The wooden horse story, as Danek (1998:110) notes, "war zweifellos in unzähligen Versionen ausgemalt worden," and so was well known. Danek also shows similar motivation with another moment in the *Iliad*, although he misses the comparison I make here between *Iliad* 2 and *Odyssey* 4. Such resonance makes Agamemnon's actions problematic.

It is difficult to escape the conclusion that Agamemnon thoughtlessly miscalculated the reactions of his troops and overplayed his role. He is portrayed as a weak character.[87] Agamemnon chose a defective form of testing, and, further, was unable to provide the necessary leadership to carry out his plans. His speech nearly cost the Achaian army the *telos* of its mission as ensuing events illustrate. There follows a flight to the ships, which is barely checked by Odysseus, who hears the voice of Athena urging that he stop the rout (2.173-181). Odysseus takes and puts to use Agamemnon's "hereditary scepter" (σκῆπτρον πατρωϊον, 186). The action of Odysseus is at best an increase in, and at worst a departure from, the role that Agamemnon seemed to have envisioned any one *basileus* having to play when he first addressed the council. There he was contemplating a united effort by all *basileis* (ὑμεῖς, 2.75), each exerting his influence over his own warrior contingent (2.73-75), "one from one place, one from another":

> But first, with words I will test [them], which is custom,
> and to flee on their benched ships will be the orders I will give;
> But you—one from one place, one from another[88]—restrain them
> with words.

> πρῶτα δ' ἐγὼν ἔπεσιν πειρήσομαι, ἣ θέμις ἐστί,
> καὶ φεύγειν σὺν νηυσὶ πολυκλήϊσι κελεύσω·
> ὑμεῖς δ' ἄλλοθεν ἄλλος ἐρητύειν ἐπέεσσιν.

Odysseus, in reality, takes the place of Agamemnon when the actual consequences of Agamemnon's troublesome order occur, as Bergold (1977:13-14)

---

[86] Further, both Helen and Agamemnon make strong appeals to *atē*. We will note Agamemnon's connection to this enigmatic term later in this chapter.

[87] Reinhardt (1961:101): "der Charakterschwäche des Agamemnon."

[88] *LfgrE* 4.543, s.v. ἄλλοθεν (Radt), notes its use with a lot of people "die alle die gleiche Handlung ausüben."

notes. The other *basileis* to a man have apparently ignored his instructions. Odysseus attempts to restrain the fleeing mass of troops by urging the *basileis* to restrain their own contingents. The "gentle words" he speaks "standing beside" each leader (τὸν δ' ἀγανοῖς ἐπέεσσιν ἐρητύσασκε παραστάς, 189) include the refrain, "In the council did we not all hear what he spoke?" (ἐν βουλῇ δ' οὐ πάντες ἀκουσάμην οἷον ἔειπε; 2.194).[89] I take this to be a question.[90] The cause of the inactivity and outright retreat of the *basileis* and their troops is given in Odysseus' interjection (2.190): "*Daimonie*, it is not fitting that you be fearful like a coward!" (δαιμόνι', οὔ δε ἔοικε κακὸν ὥς δειδίσσεσθαι).[91] It is fear, but a fear that is met by Odysseus' persuasive appeal to fear (2.195–198):

> Let not [Agamemnon] do evil to the sons of the Achaians
> But the spirit is great in Zeus-nourished *basileis*,
> but [his] honor springs from Zeus, and he is loved by counselor Zeus.

> μή τι χολωσάμενος ῥέξῃ κακὸν υἷας Ἀχαιῶν·
> θυμὸς δὲ μέγας ἐστὶ διοτρεφέων βασιλήων,
> τιμὴ δ' ἐκ Διός ἐστι, φιλεῖ δέ ἑ μητίετα Ζεύς.

Odysseus has taken charge on the field. Further, in the ensuing assembly, Odysseus, not Agamemnon, speaks to the gathered troops as friends (2.299, φίλοι), encouraging them to endure (2.299, τλῆτε).[92]

Odysseus' speech is followed immediately by that of Nestor, who, as we saw in Chapter 2, has a consistent characterization in Homer's tradition. He is not only an excellent speaker (as he shows himself to be here) but also a wise strategist. Nestor's traditional characterization is highlighted by the poet through

---

[89] Odysseus treats the lower ranks attempting to achieve a retreat and *nostos* severely, however (*Iliad* 2.198–199).

[90] The verse can still be read as a less direct, albeit gentler rebuke when taken as a reported statement. A scholion of the T codex (Erbse 1969–1988:1.223) notes the quandary of a question: εἰς ὑπόνοιάν τε αὐτοὺς ἄγει καὶ οὐ δοκεῖ ἐκφαίνειν τὰ τοῦ βασιλέως ἀπόρρητα, ἀλλὰ συγκαλύπτει τὸν τοῦ λόγου νοῦν. The scholion suggests that this is a statement (and in the first person plural), ἵνα μὴ καταισχύνῃ τοὺς ἄλλους. Accepting this punctuation would soften Odysseus' rebuke, but not lessen his appeal to fear.

[91] Kirk (1985:135) may be correct in translating δειδίσσεσθαι transitively, as is the case in its other occurrences: "it is not fitting to try and terrify you as though you were a coward." This translation would be more conciliatory, it is true, but it in no way lessens the truth that the *basileis* are here very much afraid and not doing their job. The surrounding verses make it plain that they are fearful and are barely being restrained by Odysseus.

[92] Scodel (2008:66) suggests that the benefits of Odysseus' intervention outweigh the negative impact of his taking charge on Agamemnon's concerns to save face.

the use of the aristocratic and likely martial epithet ἱππότα, used exclusively of Nestor in the *Odyssey* and nearly exclusively of him in the *Iliad*.[93] Nestor's directive to Agamemnon, "But, ruler, you yourself plan well and heed another" (ἀλλὰ, ἄναξ, αὐτός τ' εὖ μήδεο πείθεό τ' ἄλλῳ, 360), includes two character-istic elements found within the tradition connected with Nestor.[94] Nestor urges that Agamemnon plan carefully and be guided by another, and he gives specific tactical advice. The action and speech of Odysseus and the speech of Nestor save the day, indeed the whole expedition to Troy, for Agamemnon.

Agamemnon responds with his own speech (*Iliad* 2.381–393), the content of which displays his ability to direct the army as the paramount warrior-*basileus*. The disclaimer that precedes this sound call for action, however, is also part of the poet's presentation of Agamemnon. Here we find the Achaian leader begin-ning with a divinely directed castigation (2.375–376): "But for me, the aegis-bearing son of Kronos, Zeus, has given grief, / who casts me toward fruitless strife and quarrels" (ἀλλά μοι αἰγίοχος Κρονίδης Ζεὺς ἄλγε' ἔδωκεν, / ὅς με μετ' ἀπρήκτους ἔριδας καὶ νείκεα βάλλει). Agamemnon admits that he was the first to become angry in his contention with Achilles. He insists, however, that it was Zeus who drove him to it, a remark that may point to a traditional element of Agamemnon's character. The motif of blaming the gods is clearly significant throughout the *Odyssey*, commencing with the *prooimion* (*Odyssey* 1.7) and the complaint of Zeus to the divine council (*Odyssey* 1.32–33).[95] It seems inherent, too, in the *Iliad*, though it does not receive as direct and programmatic a place in that poet's presentation.[96] The complaint is simply registered by the poet in

---

[93] The epithet is found in the second hemistich, as part of an attributive epithet: Γερήνιος ἱππότα Νέστωρ in *Odyssey* 3.68, 102, 210, 253, 386, 397, 405, 417, 474; 4. 161; *Iliad* 2.336, 433, 601; 4.317; 7.170, 181; 8.112, 151; 9.52, 162, 179; 10.102, 128, 138, 143, 157, 168, 203, 543; 11.516, 655; 14.52. In only four instances is the epithet used of other heroes (perhaps influenced by the Nestor tradi-tion): of Phyleus (*Iliad* 2.628), Tydeus (*Iliad* 5.126), Oineus (*Iliad* 14.117), and Peleus (*Iliad* 16.33, 23.19). The Dark Age origin of this epithet may be suggested by the emphasis on horses apart from chariots, which in the Mycenaean Age acted as a platform for archers (Drews 1995:119–120). Lang (1906:296) reminds us of the presence of clearly Dark Age warfare in Homer; see Donlan (1997:656–657) for the raising of horses as a sign of social status in the Dark Age. Kristiansen and Larsson (2005:170) prefer an origin in the Mycenaean Period, when the "breeding of horses was a major elite activity at the palaces."

[94] See Chapter 2, s.v. 2.2.3 Nestor: 4.293–326.

[95] The *Odyssey* is concerned to show divine justice in the face of humans blaming the gods, on which see Schadewaldt 1958:31, Rütern 1969:70, Andersen 1973:12–14, Fenik 1974:209–227, Clay 1983:34–38, Schein 1984:62–64, and Segal 1994:200n12, 219–220. The whole of the *Odyssey* is inviting the audience to ponder whether human recklessness is "such a powerful force that it can bring on suffering that both gods and fate have not initiated" (Newton 2005:143n9).

[96] But cf. *Iliad* 4.409, 22.104, and Taplin 1992:208; O'Brian 1993:77, 81, 93 on Iliadic theodicy, sees Hera as a "viper," and a "source for demonic power" and rage (81–94). I find Deneen's (2003:58–81) skepticism about theodicic elements in Homer and his view of divine involvement in both epics to be too limiting. A more balanced account can be found in Allan 2006.

Agamemnon's response. Yet, the audience is here aware (as it will be when they hear Agamemnon's words in *Iliad* 19) that it is the chief *basileus* who has acted improperly.

As we will discover in our consideration of *Iliad* 19, however, blaming the gods makes an individual no less responsible for his or her actions. Nor is it the case here of theodicic questions, as it is elsewhere in Homer. The gap between divine action and human awareness is pervasive as a motif (and forms a significant type of irony in Homer), but here no such gap seems intended.[97] It is rather Agamemnon's unbridled *thumos* that has caused his difficulty, which we saw was also the case earlier in this chapter. Agamemnon appears to Homer's audience as niggling, and his thoughtless actions make him an unconvincing leader.

Perhaps the capping moment in the poet's portrayal of the *diapeira* scene of *Iliad* 2 is Agamemnon's prayer, which is full of aspirations that Zeus was not to accomplish. It is a moment in the narrative sharpened through ironic antithesis: "Rather, he [Zeus] in fact received the offerings, but [Agamemnon's/ the army's] undesired toil he increased" (ἀλλ' ὅ γε δέκτο μὲν ἱρά, πόνον δ' ἀμέγαρτον ὄφελλεν, 420). The poet has juxtaposed and contrasted the sacrifice of Agamemnon with the increased labor for himself and the Achaians. Moreover, after the sacrifice and communal meal, Nestor quickly suggests they talk no more about the events that have just transpired but look instead to future military operations (434–440). Perhaps some things are best forgotten! Blame is placed squarely on Agamemnon's shoulders, however unwilling he is to bear it (cf. Haubold 2000:56).

Two further observations also deserve comment, especially since they affect our understanding of Agamemnon as a traditional character in the poet's presentation and the audience's reception of this scene. One observation touches on Agamemnon's connection to the House of Atreus, while a second deals with the interjection of Thersites in the assembly. At the beginning, we saw that Agamemnon's address to the troops was exceptional in its lack of thoughtful consideration and was nearly disastrous in its outcome. One wonders also, if the poet, in his representation of Agamemnon's words and actions, did not also have in mind at least one other disaster from Agamemnon's own past. I refer to the House of Atreus, a story I have already shown to be reflected in the *Odyssey*.[98] The point cannot be made in absolute terms here, yet there are verbal cues that indicate it might well have been in the poet's mental purview when he sang his *Iliad*.

---

[97] On irony in the *Iliad* and *Odyssey*, see Chapter 2; on the gap between divine action and human awareness (in the *Odyssey*), see Dekker 1965.

[98] See Chapter 3, s.v. 3.2.5 Proteus' Account of Agamemnon's Death: 4.512–537. Haubold (2000:45, 56) suggests the destructive Theban war (*Iliad* 6.223) as another possible backstory.

The feud between Atreus and his brother Thyestes is not actively spoken of in the *Iliad*. In the lengthy pedigree attached to Agamemnon's scepter of office, however, we do hear of Thyestes. The passage reviews the history of the scepter of Agamemnon given by Zeus himself (*Iliad* 2.100–109):[99]

> But up lord Agamemnon
> stood, holding the scepter, which Hephaistos toiled contriving.
> Hephaistos gave [it] to ruler Zeus, son of Kronos,
> yet it seems Zeus gave [it] to the runner Argeiphontes;
> But Hermes the ruler gave [it] to Pelops smiter of horses,
> yet in turn Pelops gave [it] to Atreus shepherd of the people,
> but Atreus dying left [it] to Thyestes rich in sheep,
> yet in turn Thyestes for Agamemnon was leaving [it] to carry,
> to rule over many islands and all Argos to rule.
> Leaning upon this, in fact, [these] words to the Argives he spoke:

> ἀνὰ δὲ κρείων Ἀγαμέμνων
> ἔστη σκῆπτρον ἔχων τὸ μὲν Ἥφαιστος κάμε τεύχων.
> Ἥφαιστος μὲν δῶκε Διὶ Κρονίωνι ἄνακτι,
> αὐτὰρ ἄρα Ζεὺς δῶκε διακτόρῳ ἀργεϊφόντῃ·
> Ἑρμείας δὲ ἄναξ δῶκεν Πέλοπι πληξίππῳ,
> αὐτὰρ ὃ αὖτε Πέλοψ δῶκ' Ἀτρέϊ ποιμένι λαῶν,
> Ἀτρεὺς δὲ θνῄσκων ἔλιπεν πολύαρνι Θυέστῃ,
> αὐτὰρ ὃ αὖτε Θυέστ' Ἀγαμέμνονι λεῖπε φορῆναι,
> πολλῇσιν νήσοισι καὶ Ἄργεϊ παντὶ ἀνάσσειν.
> τῷ ὅ γ' ἐρεισάμενος ἔπε' Ἀργείοισι μετηύδα·

Kirk (1985:127) noted no direct indication of a family feud or curse in these lines. He felt, however, that this omission was meant to avoid distracting detail, since the principal point of the passage is kingship passing from Zeus to Agamemnon. It was not overtly emphasized, in order to keep the focus from being drawn away too far from the present narrative emphasis (Cf. Scodel 2002:15). If the feud was well known, however, then the violence that erupted could not be wholly ignored in a passage that names Thyestes, since the very naming of a character would bring to mind stories related to him.

Further, Kirk also suggested that the use of the verb "left" for "gave" (ἔλιπεν for δῶκεν) in line 106 provides an acknowledgment of this tradition by the poet.

---

[99] For an outline of the House of Atreus myth, see Gantz 1993:489, 540, 544–556.

Analysis of line 106 seems to make Kirk's suggestion feasible. The verb "left" (ἔλιπεν) occupies the third colon and could as easily be δῶκεν. Perhaps "left" is used here for its ambivalence—the choice of this verb in performance allows for the singer's (and his core audience's) knowledge of this latent discord within the tradition.[100] The use of "left" (ἔλιπεν) perhaps influenced the ensuing employ- ment of "was leaving" (λεῖπε) in 107 (a verbal form very common in Homer), with the choice of the imperfect resulting from the need for a spondee.[101] Yet, unless a change in tense was meaningful, why not return to the aorist "gave" (δῶκε)? What are we to make of this change in verb and tense? Does it suggest the ongoing conflict that existed between Atreus' sons over the right to rule?[102] The line, moreover, ends with the epithet "rich in sheep" (πολύαρνι, a hapax). Unless this is a generic epithet, it may reach into the tradition about the golden ram, first mentioned (securely) in Euripides' *Orestes*.[103] The golden ram was at the center of a dispute between Atreus and Thyestes, since its owner was marked as the rightful king. Thyestes seduced Atreus' wife to get it, and this act led to the tragic events we discussed in Chapter 3, the bane of the House of Atreus.[104] Latacz allows that the story, if known to the *Ilias-Dichter*, may have been suppressed in all its gruesome details.[105] He notes that the story of Thyestes' son Aigisthos was known to the *Odyssey* poet, although he misses the possible allu- sion to the golden ram here. Since, as I have argued in Chapter 1, the *Iliad* poet did indeed know some story like the *Odyssey*, it is likely that he was aware, not only of the later acts of Aigisthos, but also of the earlier family feud. The poet's choice of language here raises a number of possibilities, then, beyond those we considered in Chapter 3.[106]

A second observation is in order before we leave this section of the *Iliad*, having to do with Thersites' negative characterization of Agamemnon. For his speech he received the scepter as physical punishment, as we saw in Chapter 2.[107] I also noted there (*Iliad* 2.225–242) that Thersites, a socially inferior figure,

---

[100] ἔλιπε(ν) occurs thrice otherwise.

[101] After the C2 break (see Appendix A), i.e. for the fifth foot.

[102] This conflict is not directly related before Aeschylus, although his (and the Cyclic epic *Alkmaionis*') references to it may show that it was well known.

[103] Euripides *Orestes* 996–1000: ὅθεν δόμοισι τοῖς ἐμοῖς / ἦλθ' ἀρὰ πολύστονος, / λόχευμα ποιμνίοισι Μαιάδος τόκου, / τὸ χρυσόμαλλον ἀρνὸς ὁπότε / γένετο τέρας ὀλοὸν / Ἀτρέως ἱπποβότα·

[104] See Chapter 3, s.v. 3.2.5 Proteus' Account of Agamemnon's Death: 4.512–537.

[105] Latacz 2000b:39: "Falls der Ilias-Dichter den Mythos in dieser Form kannte, zog er es offensich- tlich vor, alle grausigen Züge zu unterdrücken."

[106] See Chapter 3, s.v. 3.2.5 Proteus' Account of Agamemnon's Death: 4.512–537. We saw there that Homer referenced the *nostos* of Agamemnon, a journey that connected him through traditional language cues to other heroes (Menelaos, Odysseus) who experienced difficulty, but also to Thyestes.

[107] See Chapter 2, s.v. 2.2.5 Diomedes and Sthenelos: 4.365–418.

addressed and chastised Agamemnon, but that what he said was ostensibly true and appropriate. Thersites' harangue in essence contained much argumentation in common with Achilles' complaint, as many scholars have noted.[108] Yet Thersites suffered a rebuke by a superior in rank (Odysseus) who acted to maintain the social gradation, and, more importantly, social order (Elmer 2013:94–97).[109] In short, the poet even used socially inferior figures to advance his audience's understanding of Agamemnon's character. The man, not the argument, was rejected. Thersites' words highlighted a character trait involved in Agamemnon's conflict with Achilles once again: his inept arrogance as paramount *basileus*. So, while Agamemnon leads by the command of Zeus, as Seibel notes, any ability to plan or act according to a balanced assessment of the emotions of the masses is absent.[110] Proper leadership is lost on him in the poet's character portrayal. Multiple utterances, even those of underlings, give voice to his dismal personality. These voices were echoing character traits for Homer's early auditors, from the singer's tradition.

4.2.3 Agamemnon, the Preeminent Leader in Battle: 2.477–483

The Achaians have reentered the war following Agamemnon's dream and his nearly disastrous call for a *nostos*. Now, however, under the encouragement of the *basileis* and Athena, the Achaians have gathered about Agamemnon. He will lead them into battle. At this point, the poet wishes to stress the sheer grandeur of Agamemnon and his role as the foremost leader of the Achaians. The description may be a bit strained at points, as noted in one scholion, but the poet has included a number of traditional themes. [111] Agamemnon is said to have eyes and head "comparable to Zeus, hurler of the thunderbolt" (ἴκελος Διὶ τερπικεραύνῳ, 478). The comparison with Zeus' head doubtless intends superiority in power. His waist is like Ares, and his chest like Poseidon's (478–479). Nowhere else in Homer are so many divine comparisons brought together in one place. The oral themes extend beyond artistic images known from real life. However significant the advances in theme found on the vases of the Dipylon Master of the Late Geometric Period, the sort of differentiation suggested here has not yet developed in the plastic arts.[112] The language is taken rather from

---

[108] See Chapter 2, n. 96.

[109] Cf. *Iliad* 4.405–409 when the inferior, Sthenelos, is rebuked by Diomedes.

[110] Seibel 1995:386: "die Eigenschaft des Planens, gleichsam des Moderierens im Sinne der rechten Einschätzung und Handhabung der Emotionen der Masse ist ihm verlorengegangen."

[111] The bT scholiast (Erbse 1969–1988:2.283) comments: καλλίων τῆς ἀληθινῆς καὶ μεγαλοπρεπεστέρα ἡ ὄψις ἀναπέπλασται. Individual themes, however, such as comparison with Ares, are traditional (Kelly 2007a:228–232), although comparison to Hermes by itself may have a negative sense.

[112] For an excellent discussion of the advances of the Dipylon Master and his predecessors, see Hurwitt 1993:31–36 and Coldstream 2003:110–119. For a Near Eastern comparison, see West 1997:243.

the traditional imagination of what real warriors of divine stature must surely look like, and the artistry is seen in the metonyms.

As a whole, the description appears to reference the foremost character of Agamemnon as a mighty warrior and hegemon in battle (Cf. Latacz 2000b:139). The ensuing rural simile drives the point home still further, as Agamemnon is compared to a bull, preeminent in the herd. "Bull" (ταῦρος, 481) is made more prominent through its position (i.e. added *enjambement*).[113] Homer uses rare emphatic terms in the comparison, such as "remarkable" (μεταπρέπει, 481) and "conspicuous" (ἐκπρεπέα, 483). These descriptions draw attention to what was already made clear in the preceding comparison of Agamemnon to various gods: his preeminence as the paramount *basileus* leading his troops into battle. "Conspicuous" (ἐκπρεπέα) does not occur elsewhere in Homer.[114] It seems that the poet is influenced here by his choice of "remarkable" (μεταπρέπει), a term also used sparsely as a verb.

The poet's choice of "outstanding" (ἔξοχος 480, 483), however, is particularly notable when employed to suggest Agamemnon's prominence. A consideration of this more regularly occurring description suggests its meaning for Homer and his audience. Its nineteen occurrences cover a wide territory, yet all are meant to demonstrate a person's or thing's superiority in some way or other. The word may suggest a leading military rank, which is related to fighting prowess, strength, or even stature. Both Aeneas and Idomeneus are said to be "outstanding" warriors (*Iliad* 13.499). Ajax is described in identical terms when he forces other Achaeans to fight with him to guard the corpse of Patroklos, although they want to give ground in the bloody battle (*Iliad* 17.358). The term may be used to specify superiority in honor or some other virtue. It is employed to describe any soldier who has superior *aretē* (*Iliad* 14.118). It also describes animals (*Odyssey* 21.266) or land (*Iliad* 6.194) that is of the very best quality, such as that given to the hero Bellerophontes (*Iliad* 6.194) or said to be the object of Aeneas' hope (*Iliad* 20.184). It is even employed by Calypso, eager to retain Odysseus, to describe the driving strength of the gods' jealousy (*Odyssey* 5.118).[115]

The use of "outstanding" (ἔξοχος), then, and the employment of other words that support the martial ability of Agamemnon should not be missed. It is clear that, while Agamemnon lacks felicitous qualities of interpersonal skills and the ability to provide capable and thoughtful leadership in the council and assembly, he is nevertheless capable of prowess on the battlefield. Of course, the

---

[113] Zeus is named as the causal agent of his appearing so conspicuous. The action of a god increasing a hero in some way is itself conventional (e.g. *Odyssey* 6.229–237).

[114] *LfgrE* 11.506, s.v. ἐκπρεπής (M. Schmidt), suggests "Hervorragend."

[115] For other examples of these categories, see also *Iliad* 2.188, 3.227, 9.631, 641, 12.269, 18.56, 437; *Odyssey* 6.158, 18.205, and 19.247.

sorts of virtues that are needed to head a charge into battle are not the same as those required to plan or lead otherwise. There could even be something about Agamemnon's impulsive rush into battle that, while flattering, also parallels the sorts of thoughtlessness we noted in our consideration of Agamemnon's character in the *Odyssey*. After all, "Fools rush in where angels fear to tread" (Pope 1711:36).[116]

4.2.4 Agamemnon's Prayer, Oath, and Sacrifice: 3.267–302

Part of the ceremony that will precede the duel between Paris and Menelaos is one of oath-sacrifice, to assure that any "pledges" (ὅρκια) have the gods as witnesses and guardians (3.280). Agamemnon does his part in preparing for the sacrifice, an event meant to solemnize the oath between the Achaians and Trojans (271–274, 292–296). He moves center stage for the action, as we might expect from his rank. He is embodying the sentiment expressed by Priam in the *Teichoskopia* (clustered near this scene and just proceeding it), who described him as beyond anyone he had seen in his "dignified bearing" (γεραρός, 170), and one who "resembles a kingly man" (βασιλῆϊ ... ἀνδρὶ ἔοικε, 170), having many beneath his sway (183). In our present scene, Agamemnon shows that he is indeed in charge and acting his part, by sending Talthybios to fetch the sacrificial lambs (118–120). Hitch suggests that this is a positive role, although it is a role he usually leaves to others, even when the sacrifice is made at his own shelter (cf. *Iliad* 7.313–320 and Hitch 2009:85). Achilles also led in making sacrifice (*Iliad* 24.621–624), but only in slaughtering the animal. The butchering, carving, and spitting of the animal were all left to his men.

During the ceremony, Agamemnon offers a prayer as part of the oath. What is interesting about this prayer is that it not only fulfills the customary requirements of swearing to certain gods, but also includes the tenor of Agamemnon's personality in its lines. Specifically, the prayer's balance of customary and ancient consequences, should either side win, is tipped heavily in favor of the Achaians.[117] If Paris wins, so Agamemnon exhorts, let the Trojans keep Helen and the stolen goods she and Paris brought to Troy when they fled Greece. If Paris loses to Menelaos, the Trojans are to return not only Helen and her possessions,

---

[116] Interestingly, Pope's warning is leveled at those critics, who, when offering criticism, without thinking, entered into depths over their heads: "Be sure yourself and your reach to know / How far your genius, taste, and learning go," (6), the result of "pride, the never-failing vice of fools" (14). So, too, Agamemnon's impetuous and less thoughtful nature is often apparent, as we saw in Chapter 3. We will revisit this theme further for the *Iliad* (for Agamemnon, but also for Dolon), when we consider Agamemnon in *Iliad* 10.

[117] See *Iliad* 3.281–291. It is a compact that exceeds other proposals, such as that by Hector in *Iliad* 7.76–86.

"but let them make requital [τιμή] that is fitting, / which, among people yet to be, will come to be known."[118] The prayer is then sealed with Agamemnon's personal promise to stay and fight, almost as if solitary, should the ransom not be given at a level that he has stipulated to be fitting (3.288–291):

> But if to me the honor-price Priam and the children of Priam
> do not wish to pay after Alexandros has fallen,
> then I even in that case will fight on behalf of compensation,
> remaining here, until I find an end to the war.

> εἰ δ' ἂν ἐμοὶ τιμὴν Πρίαμος Πριάμοιό τε παῖδες
> τίνειν οὐκ ἐθέλωσιν Ἀλεξάνδροιο πεσόντος,
> αὐτὰρ ἐγὼ καὶ ἔπειτα μαχήσομαι εἵνεκα ποινῆς
> αὖθι μένων, ἧός κε τέλος πολέμοιο κιχείω.

Whether the *poinē* that is the object of Agamemnon's struggle is "compensation or vengeance," it is still more demanding than the metrically equivalent *timē*, in Homer's oral register (cf. Scodel 2008:90). Kirk's comments seem apt: "The king is in one of his imperious and impressive moods: *he* will stay and fight (although doubtless he will have to have the Achaians with him)" (Kirk 1985:306). Of course, Agamemnon may be thinking about the wrong done to Menelaos as a host in that sacred relationship. Yet, even here, the large sum suggested seems inordinate, or at least fanciful.[119] There is excess in this addition of Agamemnon in two ways: 1. the extent of what is "fitting"—the *timē* envisioned: "Which among people yet to be, will be known" (ἥ τε καὶ ἐσσομένοισι μετ' ἀνθρώποισι πέληται, 3.287); and 2. Agamemnon's promise, should he be wronged, personally to find an end to the war. We observe, then, that this narrative moment embodies the poet's comprehension of Agamemnon's traditional character. We found in the initial portrait the poet paints of Agamemnon that he can be thoughtlessly excessive in his demands,[120] and this seems to be the case here as well. His earlier threat to go personally to Achilles' hut if need be (*Iliad* 1.185) also parallels the veiled threat in his current prayer. Certainly

---

[118] τιμὴν δ' Ἀργείοις ἀποτινέμεν ἥν τιν' ἔοικεν, / ἥ τε καὶ ἐσσομένοισι μετ' ἀνθρώποισι πέληται (3.286–287). The verb πέλομαι emphasizes a continuing outcome (*se produire*, Chantraine 1968:877, s.v. πέλομαι). Cf. the note by Willcock 1978:220. Powell (2014) hits the meaning: "one such as men not yet born will speak of," if we understand the speaking as implying a future progressive sense, i.e. "will be speaking of."

[119] Wilson (2002:176, 178) disagrees, arguing instead that the added compensation simply replaces the plundering of Troy. This is less likely, and other indications I note for the episode seem instead to make it a clumsy elocutionary act by an overly imperious leader. On the large sum, see Kirk (1985:306), who notes that this seems beyond the normal double amount.

[120] See Chapter 4, s.v. 4.2.1 Agamemnon's Dishonoring and Hubristic Actions: 1.6–344.

Agamemnon will also add inordinate and infelicitous extras in his speech in *Iliad* 9, as we will see when we consider that narrative moment.

There may also be internal resonance, moreover, in Agamemnon's personal promise to find an end to the war, with a similar self-exaltation espoused by Achilles to Patroklos in book 16.[121] There, in a moment of intense emotion, Achilles verbalizes his wish for permanent isolation and so the absolute destruction of all that is meaningful in heroic life. Achilles says to Patroklos (16.97–100):

> For would that by Zeus father and Athena and Apollo
> not one then of the Trojans would escape death, as many as there
>   are,
> nor one of the Argives, but that we two would put off death,
> so that alone the sacred citadel of Troy we could destroy.

> αἲ γὰρ Ζεῦ τε πάτερ καὶ Ἀθηναίη καὶ Ἄπολλον
> μήτέ τις οὖν Τρώων θάνατον φύγοι ὅσσοι ἔασι,
> μήτέ τις Ἀργείων, νῶϊν δ' ἐκδῦμεν ὄλεθρον,
> ὄφρ' οἶοι Τροίης ἱερὰ κρήδεμνα λύωμεν.

What good would it do to perform such a heroic deed if there were no witnesses to honor the memory of its accomplishment? The community of warriors is not in Achilles' mind as he speaks. Even so, while Agamemnon does not go as far as Achilles, his sentiments have the same flavor. They sit on the same trajectory that dismisses completely the communal for the individual, the sort of pathway possible for any hero with an unbridled *thumos* or affected by "harmful delusion" (*atē*, about which we will say more, at the end of this chapter). It is a remarkable indifference.[122] In short, it does not seem too speculative to suggest that the poet molds Agamemnon's prayer beyond more typical elements, through expansion (3.288–291), to fit his traditional personality for this narrative moment.

After Paris is mysteriously whisked away by Aphrodite, Agamemnon's prayer will further metamorphose into a short and impassioned speech (3.456–460). The event causes Agamemnon (and Menelaos, 449) consternation and confusion to say the least. Agamemnon will stand forth to declare Menelaos the clear winner and ask once again for a recompense that will be known to future

---

[121] On internal resonance, see Di Benedetto 1994:115–120.

[122] Elmer (2013:118) offers a similar sentiment about Diomedes who, he suggests, shows a "remarkably bald indifference to the sentiments of the group as a whole" in *Iliad* 9.46–49. Diomedes "dismisses the importance of coordinated effort."

generations, only to be answered by the divinely appointed (4.70–72) arrow of the oath-breaking Pandaros (4.134–140).

4.2.5 Agamemnon's Address To the Troops: 4.231–418

We have already discussed at length the content and tenor of Agamemnon's address to his troops in Chapter 2. We need here only to highlight points that bear directly on his characterization. What we noted in Chapter 2 was the traditional nature of characterization surrounding Agamemnon's address (and the poet-narrator's description), but also, the less than adroit quality of his speeches to Odysseus[123] and Diomedes.[124] In Odysseus' case, we saw that, as insulting as it was, Agamemnon's address to him as one "with a heart set on gain" (κεκασμένε κερδαλεόφρον, 339) contained the same significant descriptive element that Athena used to address him in the *Odyssey*. In an admiring summary, her remarks highlighted "cunning" that attempts to get the best advantage (κέρδος). The comments of Athena were meant to affirm Odysseus' character, as we noted. Conversely, the remarks by Agamemnon were meant to be anything but flattering. They formed a disparaging censure.

We saw, too, that Agamemnon's initial impetuous and insulting remarks were soon retracted and replaced with a placating reply (357–363), a wish that the gods make all things "forgotten" (μεταμώνια, 363). No clear apology was forthcoming for Diomedes, however. For the moment the hero took the abuse of Agamemnon who claimed that Tydeus begot a son "worse than himself in fighting, but in the assembly better" (εἷο χέρεια μάχῃ, ἀγορῇ δέ τ' ἀμείνω, 400). While Diomedes (quite unlike Odysseus) accepted the calumny at this juncture as a respectful minion, Diomedes' favorable traditional characterization[125] rendered our estimation of Agamemnon's immediate comments problematic. They were high-handed and rash. As we further noted in Chapter 2, it would not be until later moments in the *Iliad* poet's story (9.34–36, 14.126) that we would hear vocalized Diomedes' repressed feelings and the community of warriors' judgment of Agamemnon's actions in *Iliad* 4. It is to the first of these two scenes that we now turn.

---

[123] 4.340–341: καὶ σὺ κακοῖσι δόλοισι κεκασμένε κερδαλεόφρον / τίπτε καταπτώσσοντες ἀφέστατε, μίμνετε δ' ἄλλους;

[124] 4.370–373: ὤ μοι Τυδέος υἱὲ δαΐφρονος ἱπποδάμοιο / τί πτώσσεις, τί δ' ὀπιπεύεις πολέμοιο γεφύρας; / οὐ μὲν Τυδέϊ γ' ὧδε φίλον πτωσκαζέμεν ἦεν, / ἀλλὰ πολὺ πρὸ φίλων ἑτάρων δηΐοισι μάχεσθαι.

[125] See the evidence gathered in Chapter 2, s.v. 2.2.5 Diomedes and Sthenelos: 4.365–418.

4.2.6 Grievances Against Agamemnon—Revisiting His Past Wrongs: Book 9

Book 9 acts as a complete scene, with the whole book encapsulated in a large ring structure.[126] It is central to the progression of the plot of the *Iliad*. When it is done, Achilles will have dug in his heels and resisted reasonable recompense, leaving the Achaians to feel fully the destructive impact of the Trojans' onslaught (beginning in book 11). Book 9, which has as its *telos* the embassy's visit to Achilles, opens with the various past wrongs committed by Agamemnon, who is portrayed as a rather peevish leader (cf. Sammons 2009:172–173). These wrongs, formerly submerged, now come to the fore at a moment of imminent crisis for the Achaians. Within the narrative of book 9, we twice become auditors of the resounding yet significant silence of the Achaians, as well as the complaints of Diomedes, the reprimand of Nestor, and the excessively angry response of Achilles.[127]

The book begins with Agamemnon's call for an assembly and a *nostos*. The situation is dire. The Achaians have been beaten back to the ships, held by "panic" (φύζα) and "fear" (φόβος, *Iliad* 9.2). All the foremost warriors have been struck "by an unbearable grief" (πένθεϊ δ᾽ ἀτλήτῳ, 9.3), a noun-epithet combination that joins other noun-epithets combinations to picture the plight of individuals suffering the effects of trauma.[128] The warriors are troubled and in doubt (9.8). The Trojans are now on the other side of the defensive ditches keeping watch till dawn (8.508; 9.1, 76–77, 232–235), when they will strike (8.529–538; 9.232–239). They have eaten their evening meal and the horses have been well cared for (8.503–508, 564–565). The watch fires have been set in great number (8. 507–511, 553–563), and all is in a state of preparedness for the morning assault on the Achaian defenses (9.351–352). The poet displays the intensity of the

---

[126] The book begins with an *agorē*, which includes the members of the *boulē* (cf. 54), and ends with a smaller meeting of what is essentially the embassy in a council session like the *boulē*. Although these are not strictly speaking, the same, they both include the principal leaders of the Achaians who meet for advisement and to plan action. The second council session serves to bring the action full circle—now the Achaians know where Achilles stands. On my use of "ring composition," see Chapter 2, n. 60.

[127] The cautionary words spoken by Idomeneus to Meriones in *Iliad* 13.292–293 may also allude, one final time in the *Iliad*, to the earlier rebuke of Agamemnon.

[128] Homer's idioms for grief depend on case, but all are meant to emphasize the deep effects on the sufferer(s) (real or feigned). In the dative, when in the adonean clausula, the poet uses πένθεϊ λυγρῷ (*Iliad* 22.242, *Odyssey* 2.70), but otherwise also στυγερῷ ... πένθεϊ. In the nominative or accusative, Homer has other traditional words for grief: μέγα πένθος (*Iliad* 1.254, 4.417, 7.124, 17.139, etc.), κρατερόν ... πένθος (*Iliad* 11.249), πένθος ἄλαστον (*Iliad* 24.105, *Odyssey* 1.342), ἀάσχετον ... πένθος (*Iliad* 24.708; or, πένθος ἄσχετον, *Iliad* 16.549), στυγερόν ... πένθος (*Odyssey* 10.376), and πένθος ἀμέτρητον (*Odyssey* 19.512).

moment by having not only the Trojan men but even their horses eagerly await the arrival of Dawn (*Iliad* 8.565).

It is at this moment that Agamemnon calls an assembly. In stark contrast to his earlier testing of the troops considered already (2.16–440), where Agamemnon uniquely feigns a desire to return home in order to test the warrior's mettle and encourage them to fight, here Agamemnon really does want to leave. It is no ruse.[129] This seems clear from the poet's representation of the paramount *basileus*. Agamemnon is described by the poet before his address as helping to gather the troops "with great grief struck in [his] heart" (ἄχεϊ μεγάλῳ βεβολημένος ἦτορ, 9.9). It is a line that includes the same verb used earlier to characterize the sorrowful Achaians.[130] Agamemnon is as distraught as the common soldier. The description of Agamemnon in such a high state of fearful grief finds resonance with a synonymous expression in book 10 of the *Odyssey*. There, a different metrical space necessitates some variation: "in [his] heart with great grief struck" (κῆρ ἄχεϊ μεγάλῳ βεβολημένος, 247). The expression registers the intense grief of Eurylochos who in tears could not speak after witnessing his companions being suddenly changed into swine by Kirke. He is crying in sorrow described by words connected with lamentation.[131] He fears the very worst. Yet, unlike Agamemnon with his troops, Odysseus will provide a resolute and proactive leadership response for his distraught second-in-command, Eurylochos (*Odyssey* 10.261–227).

As the fearful Achaians sat for assembly, Agamemnon "stood up, tears flowing as a spring from dark depths" (ἵστατο δάκρυ χέων ὥς τε κρήνη μελάνυδρος) and addressed the Achaians "deeply groaning" (βαρὺ στενάχων, 9.16).[132] The inclusion of this last formula, "deeply groaning" (βαρὺ στενάχων), spanning in every instance of its use the better part of the first hemistich of the line, is especially revealing.[133] In each instance of its use by the *Iliad* poet, the formula is adduced (once in a rhetorical apostrophe) to suggest a deep emotional crisis.[134] It is used by the poet to index the affective state of various characters who are to speak: of Achilles, before his tale of woe to his mother Thetis (*Iliad* 1.364); of

---

[129] Cf. McGlew 1989:288, Barker 2009:62–63, and Elmer 2013:91.

[130] πένθεϊ δ' ἀτλήτῳ βεβολήατος (9.3). Yet, ἀτλήτῳ does not otherwise occur with πένθεϊ.

[131] γόον δ' ὤΐετο θυμός. As Arnould (1990:147) notes, γόος "est spécialisé dans le deuil: Il désigne la lamentation traditionnelle," and he notes the motif in *Iliad* 21.123–124, 22.352–353 (cf. *Iliad* 14.502, 664); *Odyssey* 9.467, and 19.264. Arnould (22–24) also connects fear and tears as traditional motifs in various types of Homeric scenes.

[132] Kelly (2007a:164–165) places this idiom in the context of a group of suggestions for retreat preceded by divine intervention. Cf. Kelly (298) on βαρέα στενάχοντα in *Iliad* 8.334, 13.423, 538, 14.432.

[133] The half-line formulaic system varies only in what precedes it as a *longum* and *breve* (τὴν δέ, τοῖς δέ, ὥς ὁ, etc.).

[134] The formula does not occur in the *Odyssey*.

Agamemnon, about to give a fearful reply after Menelaos has been wounded by Pandaros (4.153); of Patroklos, before his response to Achilles, as he grieves over the present fate of the Achaians (16.20); and of Achilles, on the verge of replying to Thetis, as he laments the death of Patroklos (18.78). It introduces the lamentation of Achilles over the loss of Patroklos (18.323) and describes Achilles' mood in sleep (following the communal lamentation), setting the tone somewhat proleptically before his response to Patroklos' ghost (23.60).[135]

The formula "deeply groaning" (βαρὺ στενάχων) helps the traditionally informed audience realize that this call by Agamemnon for a *nostos* is unquestionably real. Agamemnon does not mean it as a test for the troops' faltering in spirit. His emotion is not feigned; he is in deep distress.[136] Agamemnon feels that Zeus "entangled [him] in a base deception" (ἄτη ἐνέδησε βαρείῃ, 9.18=2.111) and calls for a "return home" (*nostos*). Agamemnon says virtually the same thing for the first nine lines here in book 9 that he did in book 2 (9.17–25=2.110–118). He excludes, however, the emphasis on shame (seen in 2.119–138, before again using the same closing in his speech in 9.26–28 [=2.139–141]). Furthermore, the formula "deeply groaning" is conspicuously absent from the narrator's introductory description in book 2.[137]

The silence formula with which the troops respond to Agamemnon indicates their present state of discomfort. The poet may have wanted his audience to recall other debacles such as that recorded in *Iliad* 2, which recollection may well have been cued by the poet's use of recurring lines. Unlike the last time Agamemnon told them to leave in book 2, however, this time they sit still: "Thus he spoke, but they in fact all were stricken to silence" (ὣς ἔφαθ', οἱ δ' ἄρα πάντες ἀκὴν ἐγένοντο σιωπῇ, 9.29). This different response may stem from the troops' common experience and be meant to represent their collective grievance over the last enticement to flee, when, as we saw earlier, their response was met with stern rebuke. Yet, as I have shown elsewhere, the significance of the "stricken to silence" formula lies not principally in what precedes, but rather in what follows. The formula "Thus he spoke, but they in fact all were stricken to silence" (ὣς ἔφαθ', οἱ δ' ἄρα πάντες ἀκὴν ἐγένοντο σιωπῇ, 9.29) is used in both the *Iliad* and *Odyssey* in addressing a group and results in a (quite often delayed) response by one of the members of the group that sets out the

---

[135] This is the only instance where the formula is separated from the ensuing speech by the speech of another, here, Patroklos' ghost, so a most emotional scene.

[136] The characters within the epic are not aware of the narrator's language in a given scene. The formula is meant first for the external audience of the epic singer himself. Yet, while the internal audience does not hear the formula βαρὺ στενάχων, they could of course hear the groaning itself, and so could in such cases be aware of the implications. Cf. the discussion of the internal versus the external audience in Porter 2011:496–507.

[137] *Iliad* 2.109: τῷ ὅ γ' ἐρεισάμενος ἔπε' Ἀργείοισι μετηύδα.

subsequent narrative trajectory. The formula cues the audience that an "official" or "representative" reply will come, one that is in concert with the feelings of the group.[138] As we will see in a moment, it is just such a representative response that Diomedes steps forward to offer in book 9, when he expresses his "repressed" grievance.

First, however, it is necessary to note that the lower ranks cannot normally express their grievances openly. As I proposed in Chapter 2, and affirmed earlier in this chapter, frank criticism from below is not allowed in Homer's society where the poet constantly and consistently affirms the social mores of his constituency.[139] Aristocratic values would not likely abide the outburst of an importunate underling.[140] Yet even so, as I also argued, the actual complaint (whether from a lower member of the troops or higher leadership strata) could still further the poet's purpose and draw the listeners' attention and the scene's focus toward the salient moment of narrative action and character portrayal.

---

[138] While occasionally another person in the group speaks to add something, it is never to denounce the substance of the speech introduced by the formula, nor does it ever contradict or stand at odds with the main point of the representative speech. When another speech follows, it is generally meant to elucidate consequent issues related to what has been brought forth, or to outline some particular action. The most basic, discernable pattern of the "Stricken to Silence" formula is: initial speech—formula—authoritative response—group acceptance (Porter 2011:496).

[139] As we saw in Chapter 2 (s.v. 2.2.5 Diomedes and Sthenelos: 4.365–418), Sthenelos said what we might have expected Diomedes to say, yet was rebuked; likewise Thersites had said much the same thing as Achilles and was chastised by a superior in rank. Cf. the similar observations of Schadewaldt 1966:152, Whitman 1958:161, Kirk, 1985:142, Rose 1988:19, McGlew 1989:290–292, Patzek 1992:132, Lowenstam:1993:78, Barker 2009:60 (cf. 56–61 for a close consideration of Thersites and the management of dissent), and Elmer 2013:93.

[140] I do not share Dalby's (1995) revisionary view that places the lower classes at the focus of epic performance and situates the performance location outside of aristocratic homes, at least not as a *primary* venue for the copy of the epics we possess. I have no doubt that performances also took place outside of aristocratic venues, but, to use the South Slavic experience, "on distingue les chants destinés aux paysans de ceux qui sont destinés aux classes cultivées" (Murko 1928:340), and Homer's songs seem to reflect the interests of the latter. The powerful naturally affirmed the "proper" sphere, activity, and allegiance of the less powerful. It is also interesting that Murko found that "maints seigneurs entretenaient leur chanteurs particuliers" (1928:331; cf. 334). This seems the most reasonable picture of the *aoidos* presented to us in the *Odyssey*. Moreover, as Di Benedetto (1999:214) shows, the references to aristocratic values between the *Iliad* and *Odyssey* are also recognizable by comparison of common themes between *Iliad* 6.206–210 and *Odyssey* 24.505–519 (with the *Odyssey*'s narrative language, in Di Benedetto's view, assuming something of the *Iliad*'s). Both epic moments recall, among other cultural norms, "un valore fondamentale della cultura aristocratica, quello di non disonorare la propria famiglia." Cf. Strasburger (1982:493–494) on Homeric social classes; and Danek's (1998:137–138) comments about the necessity of Athena's spreading a mist over Odysseus so that every beggar does not think it is his right to approach a queen ("andernfalls könnte ja jeder Bettler auf diese Weise permanent seine Lage verbessern"). So, the question is not really whether there are representations of the "peasant viewpoint" (Russo et al. 1992:71) in Homer, but rather what view is predominant in Homer's perspective.

At this early moment in the assembly (*Iliad* 9.29), the silence of the troops, in this reading of the scene, speaks volumes. Any attentive audience member would not have soon forgotten the sort of contrasting bedlam that engulfed book 2. The larger story doubtless makes the current narrative moment more poignant,[141] in part through the recurrence of traditional language.[142] Here in book 9, the troops sit still, and Diomedes, on cue from the poetic "stricken to silence" formula, delivers the representative response after a moment of delay.[143] Following Diomedes' speech, they expectably shout in concert with the reply itself (9.50).

In his speech, Diomedes begins by revisiting the earlier rebuke from Agamemnon that remains a sore point.[144] He turns the tables on the paramount *basileus* (9.32–39), however, indicting him for his inability to help provide assistance and protection (*alkē*)[145] for his warrior community:

> Son of Atreus, with you first I will fight, in your thoughtlessness,
> which is custom, ruler, in the *agorē*; but may you not in any way
>> become angry.
> My vigor for helping others first, you reproached among the Danaäns
> saying that I was unwarlike and cowardly; But all these things
> the Argives know, both young and old.
> But to you, two divergent gifts were bestowed by the son of Kronos of
>> the crooked counsels;
> The scepter to you he gave to be honored above all,
> but the capacity to help, to you he did not give, which is the greatest
>> possession.

> Ἀτρεΐδη σοὶ πρῶτα μαχήσομαι ἀφραδέοντι,
> ἦ θέμις ἐστὶν ἄναξ <u>ἀγορῇ</u>· σὺ δὲ μή τι χολωθῇς.
> ἀλκὴν μέν μοι πρῶτον ὀνείδισας ἐν Δαναοῖσι
> φὰς ἔμεν ἀπτόλεμον καὶ ἀνάλκιδα· ταῦτα δὲ πάντα
> ἴσασ' Ἀργείων ἠμὲν νέοι ἠδὲ γέροντες.
> σοὶ δὲ διάνδιχα δῶκε Κρόνου πάϊς ἀγκυλομήτεω·

---

[141] The grievance by the troops is the most natural background too for reading *Iliad* 1.49–51 and 13.107–114.

[142] *Iliad* 9.17–25; 26–28=2.110–118; 139–141.

[143] On ὀψὲ δὲ δὴ μετέειπε, see Kelly 2007a:87 and Porter 2011:500.

[144] For Agamemnon's remarks, see Chapter 2, s.v. 2.2.5 Diomedes and Sthenelos: 4.365–418.

[145] *LfgrE* 3.494 s.v. ἀλκή (Geiß) notes a connection with ἀλέξω and ἀμύνω, which suggests assistance and protection.

σκήπτρῳ μέν τοι δῶκε τετιμῆσθαι περὶ πάντων,
ἀλκὴν δ' οὔ τοι δῶκεν, ὅ τε κράτος ἐστὶ μέγιστον.

Agamemnon is incapable of sustaining what Hammer has called "collegial space," the shared rights in the political sphere inhabited by the Achaian *basileis* (Hammer 2002:133; see also 114–143). The tenor of Diomedes' whole speech in the foregoing verses is indicated by the poet's repetition of "to you" (τοι, 38, 39), after the initial "to you" (σοί, 37) in Diomedes' intense address to Agamemnon.[146] Diomedes' whole rhetorical antithesis—note especially the "my" (μοι) and "I" (ἔμεν) of lines 34 and 35—is meant in part to counter Agamemnon's earlier castigation of him (32–35), revisited here in this relatively respectful complaint.[147] Agamemnon has said they should leave, but Diomedes says they should stay and fight until Troy is sacked (46). Traditionally, and on cue from the "Stricken to Silence" formula, the troops respond in agreement immediately upon the speech's closure: "Thus he spoke, but in fact all the sons of the Achaians shouted in approval, / marveling at the word of Diomedes tamer of horses" (ὣς ἔφαθ', οἳ δ' ἄρα πάντες ἐπίαχον υἷες Ἀχαιῶν / μῦθον ἀγασσάμενοι Διομήδεος ἱπποδάμοιο, 50–51).

The silence of the troops, which awaited the representative reply from higher up, turns to shouting. Diomedes has used Agamemnon's own earlier rebuke as a springboard against his commander's present dismal suggestion. Meanwhile, the troops have not begun to move. They are perhaps nursing, as I have suggested, their own dismal reflections of Agamemnon's past action. Nestor's reminder of the need for class-conscious and age-appropriate decorum follows. Yet, Nestor does not mean to contradict Diomedes' rebuke. After all, Nestor says to Diomedes, despite his age, "nevertheless you are speaking wisely / to the *basileis* of the Achaians, since you spoke sensibly" (ἀτὰρ πεπνυμένα βάζεις / Ἀργείων βασιλῆας, ἐπεὶ κατὰ μοῖραν ἔειπες, 58–59). Nestor uses the same diplomatic tone as Diomedes does with Agamemnon (cf. Hainsworth 1993:67). This mirroring tone in the supportive speech is in keeping with what we see in the other instances of Homer's use of the "stricken to silence" formula (Porter 2011:496–507). Nestor is more diplomatic, but he is also, like Diomedes, reacting against a past grievance.

In his remarks to Agamemnon, Nestor himself revisits earlier events (those of *Iliad* 1). His comments are meant to offer an alternative to Agamemnon's

---

[146] It should be noted concerning the use of the personal pronoun/particle τοι in Homer that it appears more than seventy times, but never as the very first word of a poetic line, either as an enclitic pronoun or an affirmative particle, except in the compound τοίγαρ. The emphasis of the poet, consequently, is no less emphatic in lines 38 and 39 than it was in 37 with σοί.

[147] Cf. Taplin 1992:149 and Wilson 2002:73. For Agamemnon's earlier remarks, see Chapter 2, s.v. 2.2.5 Diomedes and Sthenelos: 4.365–418.

proposed *nostos*, against which Diomedes was reacting on behalf of the group. Nestor suggests that they try to persuade Achilles to return (9.111–113). In suggesting this course of action, Nestor reprimands Agamemnon for not following his earlier authoritative *muthos*. He claims that he has had this on his mind for some time (105b–111),

> formerly and even now
> even from the time when, Zeus-bred, the virgin daughter of Briseïs
> from angry Achilles you led out, having taken [her] away from [his] hut,
> not in any way in accordance with our purpose; For very much to you I certainly
> had spoken a *muthos* many times in dissuasion; But you to your great-hearted spirit
> having given way, an exceptional man, whom the deathless ones in fact esteemed,
> you dishonored. For having seized his war prize, you presently possess it.

> ἠμὲν πάλαι ἠδ' ἔτι καὶ νῦν
> ἐξ ἔτι τοῦ ὅτε διογενὲς Βρισηΐδα κούρην
> χωομένου Ἀχιλῆος ἔβης κλισίηθεν ἀπούρας
> οὔ τι καθ' ἡμέτερόν γε νόον· μάλα γάρ τοι ἔγωγε
> πόλλ᾽ ἀπεμυθεόμην· σὺ δὲ σῷ μεγαλήτορι θυμῷ
> εἴξας ἄνδρα φέριστον, ὃν ἀθάνατοί περ ἔτισαν,
> ἠτίμησας, ἑλὼν γὰρ ἔχεις γέρας·

Nestor, I suggest, makes the third claimant (after Diomedes and the Achaians) of a grievance against Agamemnon. His criticism is based upon Agamemnon's continual unwillingness to be dissuaded from his ways by a wise *muthos* (πόλλ᾽ ἀπεμυθεόμην). The placement of antithetical terms in the last lines—the deathless gods "esteemed," but Agamemnon has "dishonored"—displays Nestor's character trait as the "clear-voiced speaker of the Pylians" (λιγὺν Πυλίων ἀγορητήν) in action, something that is a traditional character trait for Homer.[148] Nestor next revisits Agamemnon's crime against Achilles and suggests that he consider how to make good his wrong (9.111–113).

---

[148] See our discussion in Chapter 2, s.v. 2.2.3 Nestor: 4.293–326, for further discussion of this traditional idiom and Nestor, who had lived through three generations (*Iliad* 1.250–252).

Agamemnon's reply is bombastic, but also generous. He blames an indwelling "harmful delusion" (*atē*) (9.115, 116, 119).[149] Agamemnon offers generous compensation, including the return of Briseïs and an oath that he has not slept with her (131–134), along with the traditional pledge of future booty (135–140). Agamemnon ends this speech by insisting that he occupies a higher station in life than Achilles (160–161): "And let him submit to me as much kinglier I am, / and as much older in age I claim that I am" (καί μοι ὑποστήτω ὅσσον βασιλεύτερός εἰμι / ἠδ' ὅσσον γενεῇ προγενέστερος εὔχομαι εἶναι). Agamemnon's directive includes a traditional formulaic hemistich, "as much kinglier I am" (ὅσσον βασιλεύτερός εἰμι), that represents a speaker's statement of authority, in this case, "Agamemnon's greater age and authority" (Kelly 2007a:79).[150] The comment itself comes as no surprise. Agamemnon has shown himself more verbally abusive and reactive than thoughtful and responsive in many of the scenes we have considered so far. When the embassy does head off to Achilles, and its members deliver their diverse pleas for his return, it is very telling that Odysseus decides to relate Agamemnon's offer of recompense without this "invidious" (Elmer 2013:78) comment by the leading *basileus*.[151]

In the plot of the *Iliad*, however, Agamemnon's offer is to be refused by Achilles, who is unwilling to let go of his anger. Agamemnon's offer of compensation is real and fair, however.[152] Certainly Nestor and Phoinix think so (*Iliad* 9.163–164; 515–523). Achilles, however, is possessed by his grievance against Agamemnon (330–336). This grievance, already alluded to by Nestor as we have seen, is emphatically brought forth by Achilles as the cause of his resolute intransigence in response to the embassy.[153] Unfortunately for Achilles, however, his wish for a penalty (τίσις), for the Achaians to suffer loss as payback for Agamemnon's hubris, will find partial fulfillment in the death of Patroklos, a topic outside the scope of our present inquiry.

Agamemnon emerges from book 9 as a less than sympathetic character. His leadership skills cannot meet the crisis and he is overwhelmed. While the poet describes the dire situation of the Achaians in the vivid language of suffering, he is equally interested in characterizing Agamemnon's faltering spirit.

---

[149] This is a theme we will revisit in greater detail in the reconciliation of book 19.

[150] I agree with Kelly that Agamemnon meant for this statement to be delivered.

[151] Cf. the comments of Wilson 2002:85. Line 299 leaves off its repetition of Agamemnon's speech at 157, so excluding 158–161.

[152] This point has been made by Monro 1884:338–339, Bowra 1930:19, Hainsworth 1993:56, 143, Griffin 1995:21, and Cairns 2012:20. Other scholars regard Agamemnon's offer as sprung from his arrogance, or at least not in a positive light: Redfield 1975:15, Lynn-George 1988:86–92, 106–201, Scodel 1989:93, Taplin 1992:72–73, Yamagata 1994:7, and Wilson 2002:77–83. Their arguments seem less convincing.

[153] Nb. the repeating negatives in the anaphora of 385–391.

Agamemnon wants to "jump ship," as it were, or rather flee on the Achaean ships to achieve his desperately envisioned *nostos*. No one will go with him, but instead Agamemnon is reproached for his past leadership debacles. Themes from this scene resonate with past and (chronologically) future difficulties. Various ranks criticize their imperious leader for his lack of wisdom and suggest rapprochement with Achilles. After sufficient excuses, Agamemnon accepts the idea, yet not without an invidious little jab at Achilles that Odysseus' embassy wisely decides not to repeat. Ingrained habits are difficult to change.

4.2.7 Agamemnon in the *Doloneia*: 10.3–127

Book 10's place in the *Iliad* is questioned in the scholia and by many scholars.[154] I do not dispute the oddity of certain elements of the *Doloneia*,[155] although its word forms alone, as Janko (1982:201–220; cf. 2012:26) has observed, do not make its actual morphology later than the memorialization of the *Odyssey*.[156] Furthermore, an ambush story, including the slaying of Rhesos, was doubtless popular and made for favorable retelling.[157] At least some of book 10's oddities are the result of its concentration on the ambush theme, as Shewan, Fenik, and

---

[154] The T scholia—so also Eustathius. 785, 41—records (Erbse 1969–1988:1.1): φασὶ τὴν ῥαψῳδίαν ὑφ' Ὁμήρου ἰδίᾳ τετάχθαι καὶ μὴ εἶναι μέρος τῆς Ἰλιάδος, ὑπὸ δὲ Πεισιστράτου τετάχθαι εἰς τὴν ποίησιν. On the history of the controversy over book 10, see Hainsworth 1993:155 and Dué and Ebbott 2010:3–29. If the *Doloneia* was in fact a later addition to the *Iliad*, and I am not convinced it is, whether or not it was added sometime before Plato is difficult to assert with any level of confidence based upon so few references (*Iliad* 10.224: *Protagoras* 348 d, *Symposium* 174d; *Iliad* 10.482: *Symposium* 179b.). The scholia's idea that the *Doloneia* was necessarily appended earlier by Peisistratos cannot be proven either and may simply be a later conjecture. For an early suggestion of the book as an interpolation, see Ranke 1881.

[155] See Danek's (2012) discussion on the *Doloneia*'s breaches of Zielinski's (1899–1901) law, where he suggests that the *Doloneia* was added to the *Iliad* after it was written down by a poet whose style and narrative practices were different from those of the *Iliad* poet (but see a reconsideration of Zielinski's "law" by de Jong 2007:30–31, Scodel 2008b, and Graziosi and Haubold 2010:5). For other peculiarities, see Danek 1988:221–241; 2012:108–110 and Hainsworth 1993:151–210. Erbse (2005) argues, in one of several possibilities, that book 10 was added by the *Odyssey* poet to the *Iliad*, although it is not clear how this would have worked (see Chapter 1, and Ready [2015] for the complexity of the issue). For a Unitarian rejection of book 10, see Reinhardt 1961:243–250.

[156] Danek's (2012:107) own observations of connective particles yielded a similar result. These findings may not rule out an early, writing rhapsode, well-attuned to the traditional idiom. On the different classes of oral performers, the relationship between oral and written poetry, and the problem with simple divisions of oral versus written (the "Great Divide"), see Foley 2002:22–57. Cf. also the observations of Danek 2012:116–121. On the process of textualization, see especially Ready 2015.

[157] See Fenik (1964) and Dué and Ebbott (2010:90–106) on the traditional nature of the Rhesos story as well as possible backstories for Rhesos and his horses. See also the defense of book 10's style and placement by Thornton 1984:164–169. For other views that it is Homeric, see Shewan 1911, Schnapp-Gourbeillon 1982:53–74 (studied in relation to the characterization of Diomedes), and Cirio 2003. For a traditional Unitarian defense of the *Doloneia*'s appropriateness, see Deichgräber 1972.

more recently, Dué and Ebbott have cogently argued.[158] The *Doloneia* was perhaps included at this point in the *Iliad* to give grounds for the Achaians' subsequent, if only short-lived, renewal of spirits, which led them to drive the Trojans back toward their city.[159] The *Doloneia* heightens the seriousness of the situation that will confront Patroklos and cause him to take to the field in *Iliad* 16. It is imprudent, then, to excise it.[160]

We meet Agamemnon first in book 10 when, as the poet tells us, he cannot sleep while most others can (1–3). A break in a traditional idiom immediately alerts us to the importance of what is to come, since the conventional use of the formula "they seized the gift of sleep" (ὕπνου δῶρον ἕλοντο) that ended book 9 usually refers to a straight transition from night to morning without nighttime activity.[161] Nighttime activity is usually the preserve of other idioms.[162] The activity that occurs despite the presence of this traditional idiom may be an ironic cue. It is a cue that suggests that something will transpire on this restless night as, only a stone's throw away, the menacing Trojans await the break of dawn. The poet is perhaps creating suspense, preparing his audience for the approaching night foray.[163]

Agamemnon's sleeplessness, moreover, is indicated by language that is focused on internal unrest (10.4, 9–10) and a simile, which compares his sleepless state to a storm sent by Zeus (5–10). While the simile's comparison and

---

[158] Shewan 1911:55, Fenik 1964:12–13; the idea is more fully developed by Dué and Ebbott 2010, and Dué 2012. Further, the "inconsistencies" of oral style noted in *The Wedding of Smailagić Meho* (Wender 1977:333–334) should act as a warning against quick assumptions of interpolation or multiple authorship in Homer.

[159] The *Doloneia* can be seen as preparatory for what follows (cf. Wilcock 1976:114; Powell 2007:124) or as encouraging the transition from books 9 to 11 (Thornton 1984:165). Its problem as a standalone book with no real connection in the rest of the *Iliad* (that is, it needs and references other parts of the *Iliad*, but the *Iliad* does not really need or reference it) has long been recognized (Hainsworth 1993:151–155). It does, however, contain overall parallels with other parts of the *Iliad* (Van Duzer 1996:319–322). Bierl (2012) outlines shared themes and patterns such as the *rite de passage* and *katabasis*, among others. Cf. the shared themes highlighted by Dué 2012.

[160] West (1998) has bracketed book 10 in his edition, but, as Bierl (2012:134) rightly points out, there is no manuscript authority for this.

[161] Instead, here we must await book 11, which begins with the second formulaic element Ἠὼς δ᾽ ἐκ λεχέων παρ᾽ ἀγαυοῦ Τιθωνοῖο/ὄρνυθ᾽. Contrast *Iliad* 7.482, *Odyssey* 16.481, 19.427. Since, however, the number of times ὕπνου δῶρον ἕλοντο appears is small, any conclusions must remain tentative.

[162] As a contrast to ὕπνου δῶρον ἕλοντο (/ Ἠὼς δ᾽ ἐκ λεχέων παρ᾽ ἀγαυοῦ Τιθωνοῖο / ὄρνυθ᾽), we need but consider the implications of other traditional (and more numerous) signs for sleep, such as "sweet sleep" (γλυκὺς ὕπνος: *Iliad* 1.610, 2.71, 23.232; *Odyssey* 7.289, 9.333, 10.31, 13.282, 18.199, 19.49; cf. Foley 1999:230–232) and formulae clustered around the phrase "upon the eyelids" (ἐπὶ βλεφάροισι: *Iliad* 14.165; *Odyssey* 1.364, 2.398, 12.338, 13.79, 16.451, 19.604, 20.54, 21.358), which do not usually precede an immediate sunrise but allow instead for extended activity during the sleeper's rest (so act oppositely to our present formula's regular usage).

[163] On the metonymic irony in this scene, see Chapter 2.

structure may not be Homer's best,[164] the comparison does enhance audience comprehension of Agamemnon's tempestuous state. The moment is made more vivid with mention of Zeus' causing "a great storm of rain" (πολὺν ὄμβρον, 6), "or a terrifying hailstorm" (ἀθέσφατον ἠὲ χάλαζαν), "or a snow cloud" (ἢ νιφετόν), the last of which the poet perhaps wants us to see as comparable to a cloud of soldiers (10.8; cf. Dué and Ebbott 2010:238–245). The metaphor's change to soldiers works well as a transition to what follows. We are next given a portrait of Agamemnon when he "caught a glimpse" (ἀθρήσειε, 11) of the Trojan plain, marveling (θαυμάζε) at the "many fires" (12; cf. 8.553–563) and the voice emanating from the throng of people and "from their double-reed pipes[165] and panpipes" (αὐλῶν συρίγγων τ', 13). While the "double-reed pipe" (αὐλός) could be played at both festivals and funerals, the panpipe (σῦριγξ) could not (West 1994:81–107, 109–112). Rather, it was part of extemporaneous musicmaking for Trojan victories during the day just passed. It functions as a sure indicator that the poet is painting a picture of celebration, merriment, and confident leisure in the Trojan camp as a foil for the Achaian's dismal and defeatist paralysis. After all, the Achaians are quiet by contrast (14), and the only ones stirring are Agamemnon and his worried *basileis*.[166]

Agamemnon is struck as he lies there by the contrast in what he sees. His reaction is sorrowful lamentation. The quality and intensity of Agamemnon's sorrow, which we saw in book 9 was also very much present, is again cast before Homer's audience (cf. the comments of Dué and Ebbott 2010:239–244). Agamemnon even pulls out his hair in helpless distress, an intensely emotional response. It is paralleled, among other places in Homer, by Priam in his desperation to keep Hector from facing Achilles but also death (*Iliad* 22.77–78). This background referent for Priam's and Agamemnon's disquiet is suggested by a ritual parallel. The cutting of the hair for the dead, after all, was something practiced for animals (e.g. *Iliad* 3.273, 19.254, *Odyssey* 3.446), when sacrificed, and for humans (*Iliad* 23.46, *Odyssey* 4.198, 24.46), when their remains were honored.[167] The traditional resonance and ritual parallel suggest that the present moment

---

[164] Among other things, the simile's change from storm to war has been criticized scornfully by Leaf (1902a:426–427) but less so by Hainsworth (1993:157). For suggestions of possible links with other themes in *Iliad* 10, see Dué and Ebbott 2010:237–246.

[165] That is, an oboe. Homer means something like an oboe, then, rather than a flute (which has no reed) or clarinet (whose reed is single), as West (1994:82–85) notes.

[166] Menelaos is already awake (*Iliad* 10.25–28), as perhaps is Nestor (10.80–85), despite Agamemnon's intention to rouse him (10.54–55); but contrast Odysseus (10:137–139).

[167] On the ritual aspect, cf. Aeschylus *Choephoroe* 423–443. See further Van Wees 1999; Dué and Ebbott (2010) compare the Achaians (*Iliad* 23.211) and other mourners. One difference in ritual, however, is that it is the sacrificed animal's hair that is burnt up, while it is the hair of a mourner, in the case of humans.

reeks of imminent death for Agamemnon. Agamemnon fears utter destruction. The poet follows up this portrayal of the royal *aporia* with Agamemnon's decision to go to Nestor to seek someone who could assist him with a "plan" (μῆτις, 19), one that would ward off evil for the Danaäns in their present dilemma.

Agamemnon seems at a loss, yet he is not alone for long. Menelaos has also lain awake and has already put on his leopard's hide.[168] Menelaos makes it to his brother's side not long after Agamemnon has left his hut. When Menelaos arrives, Agamemnon orders him to run quickly along the ships and call on Ajax and Idomeneus (10.53–54). He will go to Nestor. Agamemnon even advises his inquisitive sibling to give due honor when calling upon each man, and to avoid haughtiness.[169] It is advice that in many ways sounds curiously thoughtful for Agamemnon given his rash advice and leadership we have witnessed freely displayed in the *Odyssey* and the *Iliad* (and for which he was just rebuked in book 9).[170] Yet, while the advice seems a bit odd, and the logic of what is said may be lacking (Stanley 1993:122), Agamemnon's attitude toward the human objects of his injunction, Ajax and Idomeneus, mimics his own earlier attitude toward these two excellent warriors.[171]

Agamemnon heads off to Nestor, in whose presence he describes himself as sleepless and weighed down by war and the cares of the Achaians. His heightened concern for the Danaäns[172] is leading him to wander utterly distraught.[173] His whole being is "thus shaken by fear" (σαλευόμενος οὕτως ὑπὸ τοῦ φόβου), as ancient commentators noted.[174] His heart is metaphorically jumping out of his chest (ἔξω/στηθέων ἐκθρῴσκει, 95), and his knees are knocking (τρομέει δ' ὑπὸ φαίδιμα γυῖα, 95). Hainsworth (1993:165) notes a parallelism in Agamemnon's reaction to that of Andromache (*Iliad* 22.453–455) when she fears Achilles may have killed her husband (which indeed he had). Yet a nearer parallel in actual

---

[168] This is the first of numerous breaches of Zielinski's law according to Danek 2012:111–116.

[169] μηδὲ μεγαλίζετο θυμῷ, 69.

[170] For the *Odyssey*, see Chapter 3. For the *Iliad*, see our discussion on book 9 in this chapter. Indeed, a similar question arises over Agamemnon's use of a traditional salutation to Diomedes in *Iliad* 10.243: Τυδεΐδη Διόμηδες ἐμῷ κεχαρισμένε θυμῷ. Perhaps Agamemnon, once rebuked openly, has reformed his ways, at least for a moment, and become ready to preach to his brother. Of course, as we have seen in our discussion of *Iliad* 2, Agamemnon is certainly always ready to give out advice.

[171] As we saw in Chapter 2 (see Agamemnon's address and comments, s.v. 2.2 Typical and Specific Appeals), Agamemnon recognized both warriors' traditional heroic status and treated them with appropriate dignity.

[172] αἰνῶς γὰρ Δαναῶν περιδείδια, 10.93. The heightened concern found in the adverb αἰνῶς with the compound verb περιδείδια is not drastically mitigated by the textual variant from Herodianus (see West's 1998 edition) Δαναῶν πέρι δείδια. Herodianus' is an unlikely reading, given Homer's avoidance otherwise of such an ambivalent placement of this preposition.

[173] οὐδέ μοι ἦτορ/ἔμπεδον, ἀλλ' ἀλύκτημαι, 10.93–94.

[174] Posidonius fr. 409, line 69; Galen *On the Doctrines of Hippocrates and Plato* 4.5.40.

language is Patroklos (*Iliad* 16.805), when he was made vulnerable by Apollo and Delusion;[175] or Hera and Athena (*Iliad* 8.452), in Zeus' threatening description (albeit imagined) of their fearful response should he serve them up a thunderbolt as a consequence for their scheming interference.[176] Agamemnon is completely distraught.

Agamemnon urges Nestor, who is equally sleepless (10.96), to go with him to check the sentries and make sure they are attentive to any possible attack at night. Nestor's response is to try to reassure Agamemnon that Hector will face difficulties should Achilles ever return (105–107).[177] Moreover, sensing Agamemnon's fear, he rises to the occasion with support: "For I will myself certainly accompany you!" (σοι δὲ μάλ᾽ ἕψομ᾽ ἐγώ, 108). He urges that other Achaian leaders be called on as well. Yet, Agamemnon is not heard from for the rest of the book, even after the return of Odysseus and Diomedes who have perpetrated a stunning night raid on the Trojan lines and have returned to celebrate. It seems as though his leadership is not really needed for the night raid. It is little wonder, considering the picture of fearful and distraught incapacity we have received of him at a critical moment in the war. Schnapp-Gourbeillon is more generous in describing Agamemnon's actions, but only by passing over the scene's details and focusing on Nestor as "maître de la *mētis*" (Schnapp-Gourbeillon 1982:54). Of course, this is part of Nestor's characterization in Homer, as we saw in Chapter 2, but Nestor's wisdom does not make Agamemnon's incapacity any less striking. The royal *aporia* the poet has brought to our attention was fortunately filled by others, and Agamemnon's paralysis did not get in the way of heroic efforts to strike under the cover of night.

4.2.8 Agamemnon's *Aristeia*: 11.91–283

Book 11 begins with a description of Agamemnon's arming, the Achaian advance against the Trojans, and Agamemnon's *aristeia*. It is the army's common wish to engage the Trojans in battle rather than leave Troy.[178] In this scene, much appears to emerge that would endorse our viewing Agamemnon as a staunch warrior. Yet, there is a lightly fatalistic tenor in the poet-narrator's comments and his

---

[175] τὸν δ᾽ ἄτη φρένας εἷλε, λύθεν δ᾽ ὑπὸ φαίδιμα γυῖα.

[176] τρόμος ἔλλαβε φαίδιμα γυῖα. On the possible Olympiomachia backstory behind Zeus' present threats, see Porter 2014:510–511; 520–526.

[177] The mention of Achilles has caused consternation for some commentators (Leaf 1902b:423, Hainsworth 1993:166), yet the possibility for his reentry was also voiced at the end of book 9 by Diomedes (9.702–703). Moreover, Achilles is himself part of the narrative indirectly—his horses and chariot are the object of Dolon's vain desire (10.321–323). Taking Achilles' horses may also presuppose his being killed as Dué and Ebbott (2010:266) argue.

[178] 11.13–14: τοῖσι δ᾽ ἄφαρ πόλεμος γλυκίων γένετ᾽ ἠὲ νέεσθαι / ἐν νηυσὶ γλαφυρῇσι φίλην ἐς πατρίδα γαῖαν.

use of this scene within the greater plot structure. In the end, Agamemnon's actions seem resolute but somewhat hollow and mundanely and minimally presented by the poet to his audience.[179]

The action begins quickly at dawn with the goddess's cry, the first of the conventional elements in a battle anticipatory sequence.[180] The action then immediately moves to an arming scene centered upon Agamemnon (11.15–16): "But Atreus' son cried out and to gird up for action was his order / to the Argives; But he himself got into the gleaming bronze" (Ἀτρεΐδης δ' ἐβόησεν ἰδὲ ζώννυσθαι ἄνωγεν / Ἀργείους· ἐν δ' αὐτὸς ἐδύσετο νώροπα χαλκόν). The entire ensuing scene is itself highly traditional.[181] It incorporates a metaphor that makes the glint from Agamemnon's bronze armor into a lightning bolt (note the use of "flashed," λάμπ', in 11.45) met by a divine response of thunder sent from Hera and Athena. The effect is to focus our attention on Agamemnon fully armed (44–46):

> ... but far off his bronze armor from the very spot into heaven
> flashed; But in response thundered Athena and Hera
> to honor the king of rich-in-gold Mycenae.

> ... τῆλε δὲ χαλκὸς ἀπ' αὐτόφιν οὐρανὸν εἴσω
> λάμπ'· ἐπὶ δ' ἐγδούπησαν Ἀθηναίη τε καὶ Ἥρη
> τιμῶσαι βασιλῆα πολυχρύσοιο Μυκήνης.

Our attention is drawn in this poetic description to the warrior fully armed and ready for battle. This arming of Agamemnon and his ardent *aristeia* initially move him "from victory to victory," and yet, Agamemnon's victory ironically assists one of two Achaian advances ultimately "doomed to failure" (Scott 2009:81; cf. Hainsworth 1993:211). This failure brings about first Patroklos', then Achilles' own reentry into battle in the *Iliad*'s plot. The *aristeia*'s doomed nature is part of the larger poetic purpose, to give, as Zeus planned (and as some of the other Olympians opined), "renown" (κῦδος, 11.79) to the Trojans. Zeus is keeping the promise he made to Thetis to bring honor to her son (*Iliad* 1.528–530).

Agamemnon's *aristeia* itself displays typical elements, including repeated stylized killings and a traditional lion simile. Before refusing the supplications of Peisandros and Hippolochos (characterized elsewhere as villains by the poet[182]), Agamemnon "rose like a lion" (ὦρτο λέων ὥς, 11.129). The formulaic

---

[179] Cf. the comments of Moulton 1977:96–99 and Postlethwaite 2000:154.

[180] See Schadewaldt 1966:29–40 and Morrison 1992a:42, 132.

[181] Arend 1933:92–97, Armstrong 1958, Fenik 1968:78–114, and West 2011:135, 248–249, 315.

[182] Their loyalty was bought off by Paris: *Iliad* 11.122–125. Here, Peisandros is killed for a second time.

simile highlights his heroic posture and actions (cf. 11.173–178), and his power in battle, as Scott (2009:83–84) has shown through consideration of traditional referents. This same sort of referential emphasis is given to other heroes or heroic groups, such as Achilles and the Trojans.[183] Clarke (1995:151–152), however, sees a less favorable connotation in the lion simile itself, arguing that it suggests a warrior's "self-destructive recklessness."[184] Yet, surely the reckless- ness that, as Clarke notes, "goes beyond the bounds of mortal self-restraint" is instead just the sort of psychological approach a warrior must take in order to engage in an *aristeia* in the first place. It is not a matter of the poet's (or tradi- tion's) disdain.

Agamemnon, who is said to cause the Trojans to flee in terror (178), takes his place in the fighting. Then, "he rushed forward, but he wished to fight very much ahead of all [the others]" (πρῶτος ὄρουσ', ἔθελεν δὲ πολὺ προμάχεσθαι ἀπάντων, 217). Even Agamemnon's hands are given a typically heroic epithet, "redoubtable" (ἀάπτους, 11.169),[185] when he is "eagerly" (σφεδανόν, 165) chasing the Trojans who are running, desiring to reach the safety of the city. The epithet "redoubtable" is regularly employed in battle scenes. The *Iliad* poet uses it to describe Ajax's hands (7.309); the Trojan Asios invokes it of his own and other Trojan warriors' hands (12.166); Poseidon (*déguisé*) applies it to the Trojans' hands (13.49); and Idomeneus adduces it for the whole Achaian force that will resist Hector and the other Trojans' onslaught (13.318). Ajax employs it of Hector's hands (17.638); the *Odyssey* poet has Achilles use it of his own hands in the *Nekuia* (11.502); and the suitors instance it to depict Odysseus' hands (22.70, 248). As Kelly remarks, "χεῖρες ["hands"] are only ἄαπτοι ["redoubtable"] when they belong to ascendant figures" (Kelly 2007a:338).

We need not, moreover, make Agamemnon out to be uniquely "brutal"[186] when we consider the poet's full description (11.168–169): "but he, crying out, was following always / Atreus' son, but with gore he was bespattering his redoubtable hands" (ὃ δὲ κεκλήγων ἔπετ' αἰεὶ / Ἀτρεΐδης, λύθρῳ δὲ παλάσσετο χεῖρας ἀάπτους). The formulaic phrase "but with gore he was bespattering [his] redoubtable hands" (λύθρῳ δὲ παλάσσετο χεῖρας ἀάπτους) is just the stuff of a proper *aristeia* and needs to be read as part of any heroic "snapshot" of a warrior at the peak of his glory.[187] The same or similar formulaic collocation is used

---

[183] For Achilles see *Iliad* 20.164; for the Trojans see *Iliad* 11.173–178; for other examples see Ready 2011:62n124. On the implications of the lion simile for the victims, see Moulton 1977:96–99.

[184] We will consider similarly misguided charges of "brutality" in a moment.

[185] Chantraine 1968:2, s.v. ἄαπτος.

[186] So Fenik 1968:15, 84; Hainsworth 1993:213, and Clarke 1995:151: "unusually extreme violence."

[187] This is quite different, of course, from suggesting that Homer glorifies war, *per se*. Indeed, Homer's very description of war has been seen as negative in its mirroring of contemporary wartime activity (Eck 2012:131–210).

to describe the valorous accomplishments of other central heroes in Homer: Hector of himself (*Iliad* 6.268); the *Iliad* poet of Achilles (20.503); the *Odyssey* poet of Odysseus (22.402); and Eurykleia describing Odysseus to Penelope (*Odyssey* 23.48).[188] "Gore" is a good thing for a foremost hero absorbed in his rush for glory through continual slaughter, especially gore on "redoubtable hands."

Further, Agamemnon has been characterized as especially brutal in what he says when advising his brother Menelaos, in *Iliad* 6. Menelaos is about to spare a suppliant (51–53), Adrestos, when Agamemnon gives him a timely reminder of the Trojans' (i.e. Paris') disgracing of his home. The word is enough to change Menelaos' mind, and Agamemnon then himself pushes Adrestos back from his brother and kills him. This could be seen as a case of brutality, since he urges the utter destruction of every Trojan male "down to the baby in the womb," and all this "lest someone should escape" (μή τις ὑπεκφύγοι, 57). Crucially, however, the poet himself does not take it this way, commenting instead that Agamemnon's advice was "fair" (αἴσιμα). The poet's use of "fair" (αἴσιμα, 62) says it all, really. The "fair" (αἴσιμ-) root occurs twenty-two times in Homer, helping to create a number of formulae.[189] The present formula applied to Agamemnon, "urged what was fitting" (αἴσιμα παρειπών, 62), is also used in *Iliad* 7.121. There Agamemnon offers caring words to his brother, who is ready to make up for the lack of spirit in the other Achaians by personally facing Hector in battle. A similar phrase (αἴσιμα εἶπες) occurs in *Odyssey* 22.46, where Eurymachos speaks in agreement with the "fairness" of Odysseus' overview of the atrocities committed against his household while he was away. Another expression, "thinking fair thoughts" (αἴσιμα εἰδώς), but this one dealing with thoughts that lead to action, shows a similar concern. Of particular note is its use in *Odyssey* 2.231, where Mentor voices one favorable characteristic of a good king before the haughty suitors. He employs the idiom "knowing fairness" (αἴσιμα εἰδώς), which forms a natural antithesis to "he would act unfairly" (αἴσυλα ῥέζοι).[190]

It would be strange if Agamemnon as hegemon of the Greek forces at Troy was not at times brutal, since war is by nature gruesome.[191] No one gets

---

[188] For further examples, see Kelly 2007a:338.

[189] Beyond the idioms I mention here, Homer has αἴσιμα πάντα (*Odyssey* 7.310, 8.348, 15.71), αἴσιμον ἦμαρ (*Iliad* 8.72, 21.100, 22.212, *Odyssey* 16.80) αἴσιμα ἔργ'[α] (*Odyssey* 14.84), as well as αἴσιμα as a simple predicate (e.g. *Iliad* 9.245) or singular instances as an adverb, such as the thoughtless Centaur Eurytion not drinking αἴσιμα (*Odyssey* 21.294). Although used less frequently, the compound base ἐναίσιμ- carries an essentially equivalent meaning but covers a different metrical space when used within formulae (e.g. *Odyssey* 2.122, 7.299) or otherwise.

[190] Homer also has αἴσιμα εἰδῇ and αἴσιμα ᾔδη (*Iliad* 15.207, *Odyssey* 14.433), expressions equivalent to αἴσιμα εἰδώς.

[191] Compare the brutal prayer for consequences for anyone on either side who breaks a sworn oath in the *Iliad*, that ὧδέ σφ' ἐγκέφαλος χαμάδις ῥέοι ὡς ὅδε οἶνος / αὐτῶν καὶ τεκέων, ἄλοχοι δ' ἄλλοισι δαμεῖεν (3.300–301). Lateiner (2004:20) is of course right that Nestor is "gentler," at least

ransomed alive in the actual time frame of the *Iliad*'s battles; every suppliant is slain, as Fenik (1968:83) notes.[192] When a man is in a fight for his life, as Friedrich (1956:57) remarked, we should not be astonished that "hin und wieder ein Krieger den andern durch Abschlagen des Kopfes tötet." Even the foremost Trojan warrior was not given to clemency during "baleful war" (δαῖ λυγρῇ, *Iliad* 24.739), as Andromache herself says when describing her deceased husband to their son Astyanax. What else does a warrior enter battle to do?[193]

This reading does not deny that Agamemnon can be brutal in his leadership role, a character trait we discussed earlier in this chapter (but not because of hands sullied by war).[194] *Iliad* 24, however, has been said to harken back to earlier books' brutality.[195] Yet, there is little to be labeled as physical brutality in these earlier books, as we have noted. So, how should we read Agamemnon's role in *Iliad* 24? And what can be taken from that scene to help us understand the sort of person he was for Homer? In *Iliad* 24, Priam has made his way to Achilles' "lofty shelter" (κλισίην ... ὑψηλήν, 448–449). It is not a coincidence that of the nearly ninety occurrences of "shelter" (κλισίη) in all of its cases, this is the only one that is characterized as "lofty" (ὑψηλή).[196] Remarkably distinctive in the *Iliad*, here we have a glimpse into the inner workings of a camp dwelling, and this has affected poetic diction. There must be room for the singer to present the scene: for Achilles to sit with a couple of his friends (472–474), for others to sit apart, and for Priam to slide in unnoticed (477–479) to entreat Achilles and kiss his "manslaughtering" (ἀνδροφόνους) hands.[197] Achilles accepts the *apoina*,

---

in his handling of conflict, but I am not convinced that Homer's representation of Agamemnon would have "alienated" ancient audience sympathies. One might compare the use of the "stéréotypé" lion simile, which assumes the lion "bondissant au milieux des tropeaux" (Schnapp-Gourbeillon 1982:57). There is no shortage of action-packed violent images in Homer that seem intended, at least in part, to make the performance of poetry more vividly interesting for the audience.

[192] But see my earlier comments at the start of this chapter about ransom occurring off the battlefield.

[193] Battle is a premier place to win heroic *kudos*, as traditional idioms suggest: μάχη ἔνι κυδιανείρῃ (*Iliad* 6.124, 7.113, 8.448, 24.391); or μάχην ἐς κυδιάνειραν (*Iliad* 4.225, 12.325, 13.270, 14.155).

[194] See Chapter 4, s.v. 4.2.1 Agamemnon's Dishonoring and Hubristic Actions: 1.6–344.

[195] Richardson (1993:345) suggests that the last mention of Agamemnon in the *Iliad* (24.653–655) may "remind us of his brutality in the early parts of the poem."

[196] κλισίη (19 times), κλισίην (31), κλισίης (14), κλισίης (3), κλισίῃσι (8), κλισίῃσιν (12), κλισίηφι (1). It is a noun that has few epithets, in fact. On the other hand, "lofty" (ὑψηλ-) is a well-used adjective in Homer, but is only found with "shelter" (κλισίη) in our present passage. But various areas of Priam's and Odysseus' palaces are given the epithet (*Iliad* 22.440, *Odyssey* 1.126, 3.402, etc.).

[197] As with the earlier discussion of brutality, the epithet ἀνδροφόνος is what marks a true war hero. Such is the case with the formula applied almost exclusively to Achilles' hands (*Iliad* 18.317, 23.18) and to Hector's person (Ἕκτορος ἀνδροφόνοιο, eleven times). For Priam as a suppliant, see Naiden 2006:108. For the presence of the *metanast* theme, see Alden 2012:128–129.

and Priam is told that he is to depart on the morrow. Priam is to return to Troy under Achilles' protective aegis to grieve and hold a funeral.

Achilles urges Priam to sleep in a secluded spot lest his visit be discovered. His concern is that someone of the upper echelon (βουληφόρος, *Iliad* 24.651) may find out and tell Agamemnon.[198] There would then be a delay in Priam's leaving and in the ransoming of Hector's body (656). Hermes comes to Priam with similar concerns as he sleeps in the portico of Achilles' shelter (683–688). He enlarges upon the reason Priam could be delayed in setting out. Agamemnon may in fact learn of Priam's stay and hold him for three times as much *apoina* as he was bringing for Hector (686–688). Yet, the only brutality threatened in the whole scene is a moment when Achilles himself seems on the verge of losing self-control and letting his own grief for Patroklos cause him to harm his suppliant-guest (559–570).[199]

It seems, consequently, that the poet is not so much concerned with showing Agamemnon's brutality in this scene as he is in suggesting that Agamemnon may claim a suppliant as war booty. This connection to war booty may be further suggested by the participle "taunting" (ἐπικερτομέων, 24.649), used to introduce Achilles' warning to Priam (650–655). The rare word has caused problems of interpretation for some, but the form is strongly connected with the heroic taunt, including adversarial tones in and off the battlefield.[200] The whole scene may be understood, at least in part, to revisit themes from book 1: Agamemnon's taking advantage of an aged suppliant, but also in taking what he wants regardless of Achilles' rights, here as host to a suppliant. In book 1, Agamemnon snatched Briseïs from Achilles, part of Achilles' *geras* awarded by the army. Here, he may, further, steal away Priam who came with *apoina*, to increase his own *apoina* (24), jeering as he does so. There are, then, in *Iliad* 24, tradition-based connotations of Agamemnon's proclivity for distasteful despotism. He takes what he wants from his *basileis*. The poet's intention is to bring into question Agamemnon's thoughtless and despotic leadership style. To summarize, the

---

[198] The meaning of βουληφόρος is the upper echelon (whether in the *boulē* or in the *ekklēsia*). Cf. *Iliad* 1.144–147, 2.24, 61, 5.180, 633, 7.126, etc.; Cf. Apion *Grammaticus* (Latte 1965:305), who suggests βασιλεύς ἤ ἡγεμών. There seems little concern about Achilles' own troops saying anything in *Iliad* 24.

[199] Cf. Alden 2012:129, who says that Achilles' aggression is similar to Agamemnon's in book 1, but that Achilles, unlike Agamemnon, "receives Priam with pity and kind words."

[200] See especially Hooker 1986. For variations in interpretation, see Leaf 1902b:584, Heubeck 1981:79, Jones 1989, Richardson 1993:344–345, and Clay 1999. While Clay sees a problem with Hooker's attributing "taunting" to Achilles in our present passage, I hope that my present analysis shows that it is quite possible to see it as such. Further, while Homer seldom uses the composite form elsewhere (*Iliad* 16.744, *Odyssey* 22.194), as Hooker has shown, he regularly uses the simple form in a similar fashion. Cf. *LfgrE* 14.1390–1391, s.v. κερτομέω (Führer) "(ver)spotten" and ἐπικερτομέω "dabei spotten."

brutality of book 11 is not really odd within the context of the Trojan War,[201] but book 24 does assume an Agamemnon who is selfishly despotic. [202]

In due course in *Iliad* 11, Agamemnon is wounded in the arm by the Trojan Koön (11.251–253). Yet he fights on, hurling the traditional large stones (265) that so amazed the poet as he described events of the epic past.[203] Eventually, however, pain overcomes him. He shouts an order to his commanders to carry on the fight and returns in his chariot to the ships. Agamemnon's withdrawal from battle will be the signal for Hector to advance in the first great push of the Trojans toward the Achaian ships. Zeus makes this narrative direction plain in his speech to Iris, aimed at spurring on Trojan Hector (191–194):

> Yet when he [Agamemnon] either having been struck with a
> spear or hit with an arrow
> towards [his] horses springs, then for him [Hector], strength
> I will grant
> to kill until that point when he should arrive on the well-
> benched ships
> and the sun set and divine dusk descend.

> αὐτὰρ ἐπεί κ’ ἢ δουρὶ τυπεὶς ἢ βλήμενος ἰῷ
> εἰς ἵππους ἄλεται, τότε οἱ κράτος ἐγγυαλίξω
> κτείνειν εἰς ὅ κε νῆας ἐϋσσέλμους ἀφίκηται
> δύῃ τ’ ἠέλιος καὶ ἐπὶ κνέφας ἱερὸν ἔλθῃ.

We suddenly recognize as attentive auditors that the poet has placed the *aristeia* of the paramount *basileus* in a location that is sure to make his effort

---

[201] For an opposing interpretation about war and the *Iliad* (with a corresponding negative reading of Agamemnon's martial brutality in this and other places in the *Iliad*), see King 1987 and Taplin 1990:72. I think that Wilson's (1952) point is also perceptive, that the *Iliad* has many other more important emphases than depicting war, as he demonstrates through an analysis of Iliadic battle scenes. Concerning war in the *Odyssey*, Di Benedetto's (1999:216) remarks that there is an "animus antibellicista" (e.g. 8.521–532) towards "la guerra esterna," but not "la guerra all' interno della polis." In this reading, the poet accepts the need for violence, but is only interested in its use to bring about a stable peace at home.

[202] The "normal" sort of wartime brutality of *Iliad* 11.58-60 does serve another larger poetic goal. It is one that, like Hector's funeral that closes the *Iliad*, points ahead in time. It points within the tradition, as Graziosi and Haubold (2010:91) suggest, to the fall of Troy, which "now seems imminent and is countenanced in all its horror." Agamemnon's actions, then, point thematically back to the beginning of the *Iliad*'s strife, but also outside of the *Iliad*, to the impending renewed strife after the funeral rites promised by Achilles to Priam (24.660–670). The brutality of the fall of Troy and other cities is also portrayed by Homer in a simile in *Odyssey* 8.524–531, as we noted in the last chapter (s.v. 3.2.6 Agamemnon's Joy: 8.75–82).

[203] Cf. *Iliad* 5.302–304, 11.541, 12.378–386, 445–449, 13.323, 16.774, and 20.285–287.

less significant, since it is destined to end in retreat following Agamemnon's departure (a point the poet chooses especially to emphasize by these words of Zeus to Iris). As quickly as the Achaian advance has begun, it will know reversal, "ignomy and defeat" (Hainsworth 1993:212).[204] Further, the whole assault by the Achaians, led without preamble by Agamemnon, lacks many traditional elements of an anticipatory battle sequence, such as the sacrifice, the meal, the gathering of the army, the review of the troops, and the exhortation to battle.[205] All the troops ever get is a quick yell (11.15). There exists, then, a suggestive peculiarity in the brevity of the whole scene, in the dearth of traditional cues or expected elements for Homer's core audience—hardly what we might expect from the poet in a scene involving such a central character. It seems ironic that the longest of the four full-scale arming scenes in the *Iliad* should be accompanied by so little else, other than a *basileus* fervently rushing into battle ahead of his forces.

What are the implications of all this? The syncopation may just be meant to accentuate the urgent nature of the situation, which it certainly does. Yet, the fact that the poet places Agamemnon's *aristeia* here could suggest rather that he wished to show, not Agamemnon's lack of fighting prowess, but rather, his impetuous leadership style.[206] It is a theme very much familiar to us by this time. The short duration of this *aristeia*, as Taplin (1990:72) points out, keeps us from being "mesmerized," especially when compared to those of Achilles, Paris, Patroklos, and Hector. Mueller (2009:93) describes Agamemnon's *aristeia* as "the shortest and the simplest."[207] The scene's terseness (and the lesser status of Agamemnon's actual victims) may even suggest that Homer knew no particular *aristeia* story connected to Agamemnon and had to make one up on the spot from traditional elements, as Fenik (1968:85–89) proposed.[208]

Yet it is important to note that although the poet's presentation may be showing us an Agamemnon who is given to impetuous, less thoughtful

---

[204] Further, Hector's advance will bring Patroklos, most immediately, but then, additionally, Achilles himself into battle.

[205] Mueller (2009:93) feels that elaboration would obscure the narrative, which has as its focus the successive wounding of Achaian soldiers. Yet, this assumes that the poet is simply narrating a fixed tradition, something I doubt. If this were the case, then surely the *aristeia* could have been narrated elsewhere to avoid such syncopation.

[206] After all, one could hardly credit the tradition with the minute ordering of *aristeia* within the Trojan Saga as a whole. Cf. my analogy in Chapter 1 of Odysseus' wanderings in Euripides *Trojan Women*.

[207] Note as well the other, fuller arming scenes in the *Iliad*, including those of Achilles (19.369–391), Paris (3.330–338), Patroklos (16.131–133), and Hector (17.192–212).

[208] Fenik also discusses traditional scene patterns and themes that influenced the poet's mental template. Cf. West 2011:248–249 on the scene's terseness, invention, and the insignificance of the victims.

decisions, Agamemnon's fighting prowess is seldom disparaged or presented by the poet as second rate. Many short references in the *Iliad*, besides the episodes we have looked at in detail already, support this conclusion. In the catalogue of ships, Agamemnon is described as leading the largest contingent to Troy. A small ring composition (2.577, 580) opens and closes the description of Agamemnon's forces from various places (569–575).[209] In the middle of this ring structure, our attention is centered upon Agamemnon himself, who is dressed in gleaming bronze (νώροπα χαλκόν, 578) as he bears himself proudly (κυδιόων, 579). He is distinguished among all the heroes (πᾶσιν δὲ μετέπρεπεν ἡρώεσσιν, 579). Agamemnon is said to be "best" (ἄριστος, 580), in a passage that troubled Zenodotus, who wanted to restrict the use of this description.[210] Despite the concern of Zenodotus, it need not be rigidly circumscribed as an exclusive epithet within any particular part of the *Iliad*. Rather, its traditional use for Achilles, Agamemnon, Ajax, and Diomedes (5.103) simply supports the foremost martial quality adhering to the traditional recollection of each warrior.[211] The use of ἄριστος carries an emphasis on martial prowess as an identifying quality of Agamemnon's character, just as it carries an emphasis on other occasions for countless other "best" qualities.[212]

We might compare *Iliad* 4, for another instance of Agamemnon's fighting prowess. After Menelaos has been hit and wounded by the arrow of the oath-breaking and fame-seeking Pandaros, the Achaians are assaulted by the ranks of "shield-bearing Trojans" (4.221). At this point in the narrative, through negation (including litotes), the poet's descriptive narrative creates a positive characterization of Agamemnon as a warrior (223–225):

> Not then dozing would you have seen divine Agamemnon
> nor cowering in fear nor unwilling to fight,
> but very much hastening into the renown-bringing fight.

---

[209] Visser (1997:476–478) notes that the general geographical ordering of verses 569–572 describes northern Argos and verses 573–575 western Argos. For a discussion of the mythological and historical contexts of the catalogue's geography, see Simpson and Lazenby 1970:65–73, Kirk 1985:212, and Visser 1997:151–213.

[210] A scholion (Erbse 1969–1988:1.307) comments that Zenodotus athetized this line because ἄριστος is also used of Ajax in book 2, but in fact it does go on to suggest that each is "best" in his respective spheres: ὁ μὲν [Αἴας] πλούτῳ καὶ εὐγενείᾳ, ὁ δὲ [Ἀγαμέμνων] τῇ κατὰ πόλεμον ἀρετῇ.

[211] Rather than referring, as the scholia would suggest, to possessions and lineage for Ajax and war prowess for Agamemnon.

[212] The various Homeric uses of *aristos* and its cognates can be gleaned by a representative sampling of their many occurrences, and include augury (Κάλχας Θεστορίδης οἰωνοπόλων ὄχ' ἄριστος *Iliad* 1.69; Πριαμίδης Ἕλενος οἰωνοπόλων ὄχ' ἄριστος 6.76), counsel (ἥδε δέ οἱ κατὰ θυμὸν ἀρίστη φαίνετο βουλή, 2.5), the female figure (Ἄλκηστις Πελίαο θυγατρῶν εἶδος ἀρίστη 2.715), horses (τίς τ' ἄρ τῶν ὄχ' ἄριστος ἔην σύ μοι ἔννεπε Μοῦσα αὐτῶν ἠδ' ἵππων, οἳ ἄμ' Ἀτρεΐδῃσιν ἕποντο. 2.761–762), etc.

Ἔνθ' οὐκ ἂν βρίζοντα ἴδοις Ἀγαμέμνονα δῖον
οὐδὲ καταπτώσσοντ' οὐδ' οὐκ ἐθέλοντα μάχεσθαι,
ἀλλὰ μάλα σπεύδοντα μάχην ἐς κυδιάνειραν.

Agamemnon is alert: "Not then dozing would you have seen divine Agamemnon" (Ἔνθ' οὐκ ἂν βρίζοντα ἴδοις Ἀγαμέμνονα δῖον). He is likewise brave: "Nor cowering in fear nor at all unwilling to fight" (οὐδὲ καταπτώσσοντ' οὐδ' οὐκ ἐθέλοντα μάχεσθαι). He hastens eagerly into the "renown-bringing fight" (μάχην … κυδιάνειραν). Even the panting of Agamemnon's freshly driven horses helps to suggest the fervid effort of their lord.[213] As we saw in our earlier consideration of the ensuing scene, Agamemnon's leadership qualities are portrayed less admirably in what follows, and the scene's force is greatly diminished by the poet's decision to locate Agamemnon's *aristeia* here in his song.[214] Yet this reality doesn't deter the poet from presenting us with Agamemnon as a capable fighter.[215]

4.2.9 Agamemnon's Third Call For A *Nostos*: 14.41–134

This section of the *Iliad* includes a third call for a *nostos* by a dejected Agamemnon. Many of the same themes in his call for a *nostos* in book 9 recur here. Within this narrative moment, we also glimpse explicit references and possible allusions to earlier grievances, something persistently adhering to the poet's presentation of Agamemnon and the Troy story he has received and sings with his own emphases.[216] In the poet's cameo at the end of *Iliad* 13, the Trojans are being held at the walls they have breached while the leading figure from each side—Hector and Ajax, respectively—makes a speech (13.810–832). When book 14 opens, many of the Achaian *basileis* are injured and out of action, while the Trojans press the battle to the very ships (14.55–57).

The poet now brings Nestor back into view. He is still drinking the Pramnian wine he began in book 11, a rather long time to be doing so, but quite in keeping with Homer's storytelling technique (and Zielinski's law [Zielinski 1899–1901, Janko 1994:150]). All the while he hears the clamor that reaches the aether (13.837–14.1) and considers what he should do. Should he enter the fray, or,

---

[213] 226–227: ἵππους μὲν γὰρ ἔασε καὶ ἄρματα ποικίλα χαλκῷ/καὶ τοὺς μὲν θεράπων ἀπάνευθ' ἔχε φυσιόωντας.

[214] See Chapter 2 and the present chapter, s.v. 4.2.5 Agamemnon's Address to the Troops: 4.231–418.

[215] Of note, too, are other passing references to Agamemnon's martial valor. In *Iliad* 5.38–39, for example, Homer gives his audience a two-line snapshot of Agamemnon in action against "Great Odios": πρῶτος δὲ ἄναξ ἀνδρῶν Ἀγαμέμνων / ἀρχὸν Ἁλιζώνων Ὀδίον μέγαν ἔκβαλε δίφρου·

[216] Homer's account also picks up, in many cases, on action from earlier books, before he took us to the battlefield in books 12 and 13. This is a part of a large ring structure as noted by Scodel and Whitman 1981.

alternatively, find Atreus' son? He decides upon the latter course of action and discovers Agamemnon among the wounded leaders gathered in a safer location by the ships.[217] When Agamemnon sees Nestor, he addresses him, querying why he has left the battle. Agamemnon expresses his fears that mighty Hector's (ὄβριμος Ἕκτωρ)[218] "word" (ἔπος) may come to pass (14.44). He and other Achaians have had many opportunities to hear Hector, including his exhortations for his troops to engage the Achaians in battle or his direct threats to the Achaians themselves.[219] The fear is that the warrior Hector may be successful in his bid to set fire to the ships.

The present danger is magnified in Agamemnon's mind because of the possibility for lingering grievances from the troops (a worry that possessed Agamemnon earlier during his emotional crisis in book 9).[220] Agamemnon opines (14.49–51):

> O my, my, in fact even the other well-greaved Achaians
> are, in their spirits, casting anger against me, as in fact Achilles [is],
> and they do not wish to fight at the sterns of the ships.

> ὦ πόποι ἦ ῥα καὶ ἄλλοι ἐϋκνήμιδες Ἀχαιοὶ
> ἐν θυμῷ βάλλονται ἐμοὶ χόλον ὥς περ Ἀχιλλεὺς
> οὐδ' ἐθέλουσι μάχεσθαι ἐπὶ πρυμνῇσι νέεσσι.

The poet has Agamemnon use the formula "O my, my" (ὦ πόποι), an exclamation we have seen already in a larger traditional hemistich.[221] As we saw earlier, the formula keys in its onomatopoeic consonance, as well as in its metonymic meaning, the level of personal anxiety and concern that Agamemnon is experiencing. He considers the possibility that the troops will not obey him out of anger for his past actions towards Achilles, and it worries him.[222] Nestor's reply strongly emphasizes the confusion of the Achaians in the face of the Trojan

---

[217] They are farthest away from the battle and closer to the sea (*Iliad* 14.31–36), but see Janko (1994:154) for this grammatically problematic passage.

[218] The epithet used to describe Hector, "mighty" (ὄβριμος), may have the connotation of "mighty *in battle*," since it is only otherwise used of Ares (and once of Achilles) as a character. Other regular choices for an epithet to modify Ἕκτωρ (φαίδιμος, κορυθαίολος) are not possible here.

[219] E.g. *Iliad* 11.286–290, 12.231–250, 440–441, 13.149–154, 824–832.

[220] See 4.2.6, s.v. Grievances against Agamemnon—Revisiting His Past Wrongs: Book 9.

[221] See my discussion in Chapter 3, s.v. 3.2.9 Avoiding Agamemnon's *Nostos*: 13.383–385. There are fifty-one occurrences of ὦ πόποι in Homer. In the present verse, ὦ πόποι (to A1) is followed by sufficient 'filler' (A1–B2) to meet the upcoming hemistich (B2–line end) that ends with the traditional noun-epithet formula, ἐϋκνήμιδες Ἀχαιοί. See Appendix A for metrical terms.

[222] Agamemnon's fear may even include the thought of Nestor's hesitation according to Kelly 2007a:179. A range of intense emotions are outlined by Papadogiannaki 2009:123.

onslaught, both generally (58–59), and thrice emphatically through closely packed vocabulary in 59–60: "being thrown into confusion" (ὀρινόμενοι), "thrown about" (κλονέονται),[223] and "mixed indiscriminately" (ἐπιμίξ). The defense in which they put their confidence has failed. Nestor advises a plan, but one that does not necessitate that the injured *basileis* reenter the fighting (61–63).

Agamemnon's response is meant to accentuate the dire situation facing the Achaians. For the most part, he takes up each of Nestor's points (14.65=57, 66=55, 68=56, 69=53). He also adds his own expanded commentary on the activity and intention of Zeus,[224] a commentary that includes a fatalistic and somewhat ironic emphasis on Agamemnon's personal knowledge of just what he himself thinks Zeus is up to (14.71–73):

> For I knew [it] when eagerly he defended the Danaäns,
> but I know [it] now when upon these, equal to the blessed gods
> he bestows renown, but our courage and hands he binds.

> ἤδεα μὲν γὰρ ὅτε πρόφρων Δαναοῖσιν ἄμυνεν,
> οἶδα δὲ νῦν ὅτε τοὺς μὲν ὁμῶς μακάρεσσι θεοῖσι
> κυδάνει, ἡμέτερον δὲ μένος καὶ χεῖρας ἔδησεν.

Agamemnon is certain that Zeus is portending destruction and consequently urges for the third time that they flee on their ships. On this occasion, like the last, he means it. After all, so he says, Zeus "honors" (κυδάνει) the Trojans "equally with the blessed gods" (ὁμῶς μακάρεσσι θεοῖσι). Such a comparison to the "blessed gods" is found nowhere else in Homer.[225] The almost exclusive use of "blessed" (μακάρεσσι) with the gods is certainly a traditional component, however. Through this idiom, the Olympian gods are recognized to be in a world apart from humans.[226] It is in fact the very distance the referential aspect of

---

[223] Chantraine 1968:544, s.v. κλόνος, suggests "bousculer," a sort of knocking into one another in a confused state.

[224] Agamemnon's speech evolves so that, in verse 70, it is Zeus' wish νωνύμνους ἀπολέσθαι ἀπ' Ἄργεος ἐνθάδ' Ἀχαιούς (cf. *Iliad* 12.70, 13.227). This line also serves to accentuate Agamemnon's worry through emphasis and hyperbaton: νωνύμνους ... Ἀχαιούς.

[225] Another idiom, ἐχθρὸς γάρ μοι κεῖνος ὁμῶς Ἀΐδαο πύλῃσι, is comparable in its negative intensity with the subterranean Hades. We find it employed for one's hatred of liars by both Achilles (*Iliad* 9.312) and Odysseus (*Odyssey* 14.156).

[226] The noun-epithet combination, μακάρεσσι θεοῖσι, is fairly widespread: *Iliad* 1.599, in relation to divine laughter; 5.340, to divine ichor; 15.38, to divine oaths sworn on Styx; *Odyssey* 1.82, in relation to divine designs to rescue Odysseus; and 5.186, to oaths. Equivalent forms of this noun-epithet formula occur: in *Odyssey* 5.819 (μακάρεσσι θεοῖς) in relation to Athena's order to Diomedes not to fight against the gods, except Aphrodite; and in 6.141, where Diomedes will not fight against the gods; in *Odyssey* 4.755 (θεοῖς μακάρεσσι), with Eurykleia's comforting words that Odysseus' family

the noun-epithet combination creates for the Trojan advantage that makes Agamemnon's statement all the more hyperbolic. Well, at least from the audience's point of view. Agamemnon hardly sees it as overstatement, however, as his subsequent response shows. Agamemnon answers Nestor's call for a plan of action for the troops in battle (62) with a plan of action for the troops to leave the fighting (75–80), adding the proverb: "Better off is he who fleeing escapes evil than he who is captured [by it]" (βέλτερον ὃς φεύγων προφύγῃ κακὸν ἠὲ ἁλώῃ, 81). The ships closest to the shore, he directs, should be dragged down during the day, and the rest during the night.

Odysseus' retort begins with the idiom "looking darkly" (ὑπόδρα ἰδών), a formula that, as we noted in Chapter 2, highlights a significant breach in social convention,[227] and this traditional cue is followed by another Homeric formula that reinforces this sentiment: "what sort of word has escaped the barrier of your teeth!" (ποῖόν σε ἔπος φύγεν ἕρκος ὀδόντων, 14.83).[228] This traditional, idiomatic expression, as Foley (1999:226–227) discovered, and as we saw in Chapter 2, means more than the sum of its parts in what it implicates. The idiom, as we saw, is employed in circumstances that mean, to employ another English expression, "I expected better things from you!" Indeed, Agamemnon should know better, and both Odysseus and the troops had expected better things from their paramount *basileus*.

The direct address that follows shows the increased agitation of Odysseus at Agamemnon's leadership (14.84–85): "Cursed[229] man! Would that you, of another shabby army / were leader, but not a ruler over us!" (οὐλόμεν' αἴθ' ὤφελλες ἀεικελίου στρατοῦ ἄλλου / σημαίνειν, μὴ δ' ἄμμιν ἀνασσέμεν). Odysseus, however, is not yet finished. He continues his confrontational assault by sarcastically asking Agamemnon if he really intends to leave (88–89). In the very next breath, however, he tells him to keep quiet, so that none of the other Achaians will hear any "order" (μῦθος, 91) for going home. This is the sort of order, Odysseus berates, that neither man nor king should utter. In Janko's summary of Odysseus' argument, we note immediately that Odysseus deftly

---

line will not perish, since it is "not hateful" to the blessed gods; and in *Odyssey* 13.55 and 18.426 (θεοῖσιν … μακάρεσσι), in relation to libations poured out to the gods. The epithet μάκαρες θεοί or θεοὶ μάκαρες is also employed in the nom. pl. 16 times and θεῶν μακάρων four times (once even without a noun in *Odyssey* 10.299, since the association is so strong). The genitive plural is often used to contrast θνητῶν ἀνθρώπων. There are other idioms that allow for comparison between mortals and immortals, although this is mainly to highlight heroic stature: *Iliad* 1.265, 4.394, 11.60; *Odyssey* 3.468, 7.209, 8.14, 8.174; 16.187, 21.14, 37, 23.163, and 24.371.

227 See Chapter 2, s.v. 2.2.4 Menestheus and Odysseus: 4.327–364.

228 Cf. *Iliad* 4.350, 14.83, *Odyssey* 1.64, 3.230, 5.22, 19.492, 21.168, and 23.70.

229 Janko (1994:160) comments, "οὐλόμενε means 'accursed,' someone to whom one would say ὄλοιο, since he causes ὄλεθρος."

uses the device of climax in an ascending scale of significance, beginning at line 91 and ending at line 94:[230]

> Such a thing should not be voiced by a *man* (ἀνήρ is pointed), let alone one of sense, let alone a king, let alone one with an obedient people, let alone one with a people as numerous as Agamemnon's!

Haubold's (2000:67) comments are apt: "Agamemnon's counseling as a 'leader of the people' ... is so directly detrimental that he had better not counsel at all."[231]

Agamemnon's reply suggests that he is affected by Odysseus' rebuke, and his response is both revisionist and apologetic (14.104–106):

> O Odysseus, very much, in some way you have affected me in my
> spirit with [your]
> harsh rebuke; But I certainly did not order the unwilling
> to drag to the sea [their] well-benched ships—the sons of the
> Achaians.

> ὦ Ὀδυσεῦ μάλα πώς με καθίκεο θυμὸν ἐνιπῇ·
> ἀργαλέῃ· ἀτὰρ οὐ μὲν ἐγὼν ἀέκοντας ἄνωγα
> νῆας ἐϋσσέλμους ἅλα δ᾽ ἑλκέμεν υἷας Ἀχαιῶν.

The μέν of line 105 belongs to "μέν the bachelor," rather than "μέν the widower" (Denniston 1950:359). It is patently an emphatic μέν meaning "certainly," and it makes the preceding "but not" (ἀτὰρ οὐ) that much stronger (Denniston 1950:362, 55). This collocation makes Agamemnon's personal denial all the more resounding. On the one hand, if Agamemnon is not trying to redeem himself here and did actually think that some heroes would stay and others leave (something that I doubt and his fellow warriors missed), then we have a thematic corollary with similar stories of dissension in the Epic Cycle. An example is the contention between Agamemnon and Menelaos, as told in the *Nostoi* tales:

> Athena brings Agamemnon and Menelaos into contention about
> the departure voyage. Agamemnon then, to appease Athena's
> wrath, remains behind.

---

[230] Janko (1994:160–161) is following Eustathius 968.13–18.
[231] Hammer (2002:156) categorizes Agamemnon as "endanger[ing] the stability of the public space."

Ἀθηνᾶ Ἀγαμέμνονα καὶ Μενέλαον εἰς ἔριν καθίστησι περὶ τοῦ
ἔκπλου. Ἀγαμέμνων μὲν οὖν τὸν τῆς Ἀθηνᾶς ἐξιλασόμενος
χόλον ἐπιμένει.

Proclus *Chrestomathy* 279–282

In Proclus' story, it is Agamemnon who stays. In *Iliad* 14, by contrast, it is Agamemnon who wants to leave, despite his plea and assurance that he did not in fact issue an authoritative command (14.91, 105), but just an invitation (105–106). Agamemnon is backtracking. He wishes to revise the past with a new interpretation. It occurs, because "Heroes fear and detest any threat to their positive face" (Scodel 2008:14). If the reactions of others are relevant in our evaluation of Agamemnon, they imply that Agamemnon has acted impetuously and miscalculated the response of his fellow warriors. I suggest that he now feels regret for what he has proposed. In the *Iliad* poet's story, this will be the last time we hear him recommend a *nostos*. Any *nostos* must remain hypothetical in any case, since it resides "outside ... the will of the gods and established Trojan myth." To allow a *nostos* at this point would be to transgress "the dictates of the epic tradition."[232]

Agamemnon emerges from *Iliad* 14 as an inept leader once again. Nestor came to him for advice and got none, but instead was treated to yet another call for a *nostos*. Odysseus and the troops expected superior things from their leader, yet all anyone seemed to get was a peevish attempt to revise the past or retract patently thoughtless plans. Agamemnon's personal crisis of book 9 was mirrored here also, since personal anxiety and self-doubt hindered any effective decision. In Agamemnon's speech, his fear of the Trojans is nearly apotheosized, and he not only miscalculates the response of his fellow warriors, but also acts impetuously enough to lose any face he may have been trying to save.

4.2.10 Agamemnon and *Atē*: 19.76–144

An assembly has been called (apparently by Achilles, 19.34, 41), and the Achaians gather. Achilles there "unsays" his anger (35, 67–68, 74–75), prompting a joyous response by the Achaian warriors. Agamemnon, to whom Achilles' speech is addressed, is the first to respond. His rejoinder (78–144) follows an ambiguous, uneasy, if not self-deprecating, introduction. He will offer restitution to Achilles; yet, by sitting rather than standing, fashions himself overtly as a victim.[233] He shows limited signs of personal regret for the disastrous consequences his

---

[232] Maronitis 2004:66; cf. 63–76 for the significance of the *nostos* theme in the *Iliad*.

[233] *Iliad* 19.77: αὐτόθεν ἐξ ἕδρης, οὐδ' ἐν μέσσοισιν ἀναστάς. Erbse (1952:243–247) feels Agamemnon was standing, but I don't think this is the case. Thornton (1984:128) argues that Agamemnon takes a seated position as a suppliant; Edwards (1991:244) adds that Agamemnon is speaking while sitting down because Homer is employing a "'wounded men sit down' motif." The motif is

actions have caused, however, even though he is held accountable by others and must pay the indemnity. The introductory lines of Agamemnon's speech seem meant to suggest his hesitation at speaking (78–82):

> O friends, Danaän warriors, servants of Ares,
> it is good for one standing to listen well, and it is not fitting
> to break in; For [this would be] difficult, even for one being skilled.
> But among men in a great uproar, how would any man listen
> or speak? But he is affected even though being a clear speaker.

> ὦ φίλοι ἥρωες Δαναοὶ θεράποντες Ἄρηος
> ἑσταότος μὲν καλὸν ἀκούειν, οὐδὲ ἔοικεν
> ὑββάλλειν· χαλεπὸν γὰρ ἐπισταμένῳ περ ἐόντι.
> ἀνδρῶν δ' ἐν πολλῷ ὁμάδῳ πῶς κέν τις ἀκοῦσαι
> ἢ εἴποι; βλάβεται δὲ λιγύς περ ἐὼν ἀγορητής.

Not surprisingly, considering the results of Agamemnon's words and actions narrated in *Iliad* 1, Agamemnon is uneasy about the subject he raises. On the whole, Agamemnon's immediate opening to his speech suggests his incapacity and hesitation in the present situation (the "tentative" nature of his introduction), rather than his audacity as a speaker.[234] Agamemnon's remarks are preparing his audience for the upcoming explanation of his quarrel with Achilles (a natural part of a *prooimion*).[235] "How would any man listen or speak?" (πῶς κέν τις ἀκοῦσαι ἢ εἴποι;) he asks. This may be Agamemnon's attempt to ingratiate himself with a hostile crowd. Agamemnon's words appear, at first glance, to have a kernel of what Dentice Di Accadia (2012:225) classifies as a gnomic *captatio benevolentiae*. The first part of Agamemnon's saying, however, would not really have sounded especially endearing to either Homer's internal or external audience. A speaker earns no credit with his audience by saying that they make so much of a "racket"

---

meant, Edwards argues, to enhance Agamemnon's wound in contrast with Achilles' health (the consequence of the latter's inactive state), and his suggestion seems reasonable.

[234] On the tentative nature of Agamemnon's introduction, see Willcock 1984:273. Edwards's (1991:244) reading of Agamemnon's speech to Achilles—he sees him as "ungracious and jealous, not humble or apologetic"—while striking me as a bit strong in the present context, nevertheless is certainly not out of keeping with Agamemnon's traditional character *in toto*.

[235] This is one of numerous examples of the presence of *taxis* in Homeric speeches (cf. the structure of Phoinix's speech in *Odyssey* 9.429–595) that support the argument for the natural evolution of speech divisions instanced in later rhetorical handbooks, something suggested in passing by de Brauw 2010:189.

(ὅμαδος) that he can hardly speak.[236] Agamemnon is a little tongue tied here, to say the least. This is to be expected. Agamemnon's attitudes and actions towards Achilles and many other *basileis* have been the target of strong criticism by the Achaians throughout the *Iliad*'s narrative. This background now causes renewed discomfort for the paramount *basileus*. If Agamemnon's hesitation here is real, as I suggest, rather than rhetorical, it may be caused in part by the "instability of the crowd" (Hammer 2002:156). Yet, it is an instability created by Agamemnon's own past actions now returning to haunt him.

The poet elucidates overtly this ineluctable history, not only by what Agamemnon says, but also by how he has him say it (19.83–85):

> To the son of Peleus I will declare myself; yet you other
> Argives listen up, and let [my] word be well recognized by each.
> Many a time before [now] to me this word the Achaians spoke
> and also me they would chastise; but I am not blameworthy,

> Πηλεΐδη μὲν ἐγὼν ἐνδείξομαι· αὐτὰρ οἱ ἄλλοι
> σύνθεσθ' Ἀργεῖοι, μῦθόν τ' εὖ γνῶτε ἕκαστος.
> πολλάκι δή μοι τοῦτον Ἀχαιοὶ μῦθον ἔειπον
> καί τέ με νεικείεσκον· ἐγὼ δ' οὐκ αἴτιός εἰμι,

Agamemnon has been over these things before, though Achilles has not been present. He well knows the sentiments of his troops and is fully aware that any conversation with Achilles will bring forward in the men's minds their own aggrieved feelings. These are feelings they have expressed again and again (πολλάκι ... ἔειπον, 84), and on more than one occasion.[237] What the men have said seems indicated in Agamemnon's present denial, which reaches over the past conversations in one broad sweep. They had, on the one hand, been consistently blaming him; yet now Agamemnon emphatically asserts, he (was and) is not the blameworthy "cause" (αἴτιος, 85) of the quarrel and Achilles' subsequent refusal to fight. As Dentice Di Accadia (2012:227) argues, at this point Agamemnon is less concerned with convincing Achilles than he is in convincing the rest of the troops.

What or whom then does Agamemnon blame, if it was not in fact his "unbridled greed" (Teffeteller 2003:19) that caused his unacceptable behavior?

---

[236] ἀνδρῶν δ' ἐν πολλῷ ὁμάδῳ. ὅμαδος fits better the clash and confusion of battle. Cf. *Iliad* 13.797, 15.689, 16.295, etc., and *LfgrE* 17:673, s.v. ὅμαδος (Schmidt) offers "Lärm."

[237] Nb. Agamemnon's use of iterative νεικείεσκον in verse 85.

Agamemnon diligently places blame on the gods: "Zeus and Moira, and the mist-walking Erinys" (Ζεὺς καὶ Μοῖρα καὶ ἠεροφοῖτις Ἐρινύς, 19.87). They are at fault, Agamemnon says, because on "that day" (ἤματι τῷ, 89) when the Achaians came together under siege from Apollo, "they in the assembly cast into my mind wild *atē*" (οἵ τέ μοι εἰν ἀγορῃ φρεσὶν ἔμβαλον ἄγριον ἄτην, 88). He asks, seeking the sympathy of those who hear: "But what could I have done?" (ἀλλὰ τι κεν ῥέξαιμι; 90). As we see from his subsequent explanation, the ellipsis in thought, when expanded, can be understood as part of a past contrary-to-fact conditional question that ran something like, "Even if I had tried, what could I have done?"[238] At face value, when we read Agamemnon's response in isolation, it seems that he is the helpless victim of *atē*, "[harmful] delusion" (Cairns 2012, Porter 2017). An appeal to *atē* comprises, in fact, the better part of Agamemnon's speech.

Agamemnon's speech following his claim to *atē* pursues the well-known story of Hera's deception of Zeus, in which she takes advantage of the leading god's public declaration. Zeus had announced (19.103–105):

> Today Eileithyia of the Labor Pains will bring to light
> a man who will rule over those around him,
> of the generation of men who are born of my blood.

> σήμερον ἄνδρα φόως δὲ μογοστόκος Εἰλείθυια
> ἐκφανεῖ, ὃς πάντεσσι περικτιόνεσσιν ἀνάξει,
> τῶν ἀνδρῶν γενεῆς οἵ θ' αἵματος ἐξ ἐμεῦ εἰσί.

Hera's subsequent conniving, described in a virtual *figura etymologica* as a ruse contriver contriving ruses,[239] sees her next coaxing out an oath from her unsuspecting husband, one that would guarantee he keep his word. The gist of Hera's covert plan is to replace Zeus' chosen ruler over the Argives, Herakles, with her own choice, Eurystheus (19.101–124), by slowing up the birth of the former and speeding up the delivery of the latter.[240] While *atē*-words are not present in the

---

[238] In line 90, Agamemnon is referring to past incidences, rather than present potential (so the aorist optative of past possibility in conditional sentences). On the use of the optative here, see Wakker 1994:154, s.v. 435; on the past potential, see pp. 176–179; cf. Smyth 1920:2662, 408 s.v. 1829; 520 s.v. 2311b. Wilmott (2007:116–124) explores other meanings for the use of the optative in conditional sentences, with the intent of calling into question the default idea of "remote possibility" for every Homeric unreal condition. His corrective study is needed, but I doubt that his objections in other constructions using the optative cast serious doubt on the idea of "remote possibility" meant here by Agamemnon in this past contrary-to-fact apodosis. Agamemnon intentionally presents himself as helpless; he could have done nothing, so he says.

[239] δολοφρονέουσα ... δολοφροσύνην extends over a number of lines (*Iliad* 19.106 and 112).

[240] Both Herakles (*Iliad* 5.396, 14.323–324) and Eurystheus (through Perseus, *Iliad* 19.122–124, 14.319–320) are noted as being the offspring of Zeus in Homer's tradition, making Hera's ruse effective and intelligible for the traditional audience.

story proper, Agamemnon does interject into the middle of his tale the comment that Zeus "was deceived" (ἀάσθη, 113), in this case by swearing a "great oath." In contrast, the introduction to the tale and the actions of Zeus following Hera's intrigues (as interpreted by Agamemnon) are full of *atē*-words, both nouns and verbal forms.[241] The poet's presentation is made all the more striking by his extremely rare inclusion of a personified *Atē* herself.[242] Following this etiological story, we hear Agamemnon declare what he feels naturally follows from his personal entanglement with *atē*: he should pay restitution (137–138):[243] "Yet, *since* I was deluded and Zeus snatched away my wits, / I am willing to make things right again and to offer considerable compensation" (ἀλλ᾽ ἐπεὶ ἀασάμην καί μευ φρένας ἐξέλετο Ζεύς, / ἂψ ἐθέλω ἀρέσαι, δόμεναί τ᾽ ἀπερείσι᾽ ἄποινα).

Modern audiences are unsurprisingly struck by the force of causal "since" (ἐπεί). What Agamemnon assumes as his personal responsibility seems not to follow from his *atē*-based plea. Certain earlier scholarly explanations for this apparent logical discrepancy sought to address the assumed contradiction in Agamemnon's speech.[244] The consensus that developed, and the one that seems most representative of Homer, is a dual model of causality: internal and external, human and divine, or "double motivation" (see Porter 2017:3). Further, as I have shown elsewhere, human cause (paralleling divine impetus) for the onset of *atē* is discernable in each instance of *atē*'s onset, when the full story around each scene is considered (Porter 2017). What becomes clear is that Homer's core audience assumed, in each case, a human cause for the onset of *atē*. No matter what Agamemnon may claim, then, those accustomed to the poetic rendition were quite used to hearing about individuals being at least partly the cause of their own *atē*. This would not change, no matter what Agamemnon claimed. Moreover,

---

[241] *Iliad* 19.91, 95, 97, 129, 136, 137.

[242] In Homer, this is an exceptional switch from the more usual use of *atē* impersonally or abstractly. Cf. Phoinix's parable of the *Litai* in *Iliad* 9.502–512.

[243] We saw a parallel explanation earlier in this chapter, s.v. 4.2.6 Grievances against Agamemnon—Revisiting His Past Wrongs: Book 9.

[244] It was suggested that there must be, in the outlook of "Homeric man," an external agency completely responsible for such a strange action and *atē* is it (i.e. Dodds 1951:2–8 and Willcock 1978:216–217). Such a diagnosis was made possible thanks to Snell's earlier psychosomatic description of Homeric man. Cf. *thumos*, *noos*, and *psychē* in the schema of Snell 1953:14. Snell (see 1953, n8) was influenced by Boehme (1929). Snell claimed that there was no word for a living body in Homer and so no sense of the self as a whole. For Snell's position, see Snell 1930:141; 1953:1–22. Reaction followed to show that Snell had overstated his case, from Lesky 1961:1–52, Lloyd-Jones 1971:10, Sullivan 1988:4–6, Gill 1990, Teffeteller 2003, Scodel 2008:112, and Blondell 2013:7, 37, *et passim*. Further, as Gill 1990 and Teffeteller 2003 suggest, the individual is a complex of voices and processes (internal dialogue), which reminds us that, while Snell was incorrect in his extreme views, the concept of self in Homer or modern day research is a complex subject. The important role of the internal self, however, has replaced the wholly external view of motivation suggested by Snell and Dodds.

as Cairns and others have shown,[245] Homer's listeners were also used to recognizing that each individual was accountable (and suffered consequences) for his or her actions, except when prayer warded off a negative outcome (*Iliad* 9.502–512); and also, understandably, in the case of Zeus. Who, after all, can hold Zeus accountable?[246] In short, there are usually human causes and harmful consequences for anyone infected by *atē*.

Consequently, Agamemnon's idiom of expression, his appeal to *atē*, is in no way unique to himself; nor is it negated by the causal use of "since" (ἐπεί), when his response is heard within the tradition. Agamemnon's expression is not declaring that he is unaccountable and is free from any consequences. His traditional appeal to *atē* does not mean in the eyes of either the internal or external core audience that he is not the "subject" or "agent" of his own actions, to borrow Blondell's (2010) terminology for Helen. In Agamemnon's case, however, with the unique story of the deception of Zeus and very rare use of a personified *Atē* as a comparison for his own actions, he certainly attempts to appeal to his internal audience's pity. It is a rhetorical *conclusio a maiore ad minus*, as he seeks to hide behind the harmful delusion of Zeus to shelter his own faltering ego.[247]

But what about responsibility? The need for Agamemnon to recognize that he is accountable, I would further suggest, includes the presumption that he is also responsible. This is so, not only because Agamemnon, like all others affected by *atē*, suffers negative consequences, but also because he can take action to avoid a similar outcome in the future. It seems that the internal audience of Homer's narrative, as well as the poet himself, assumes that action can be changed through advice. This is something Odysseus makes clear to a rather thick-skulled Agamemnon in *Iliad* 19.181–183:

> But you, son of Atreus, hereafter, more just toward another
> will surely be, for not in any way should a *basileus* be vexed
> to appease a man when a certain one was first to rage.

> Ἀτρεΐδη σὺ δ' ἔπειτα δικαιότερος καὶ ἐπ' ἄλλῳ
> ἔσσεαι. οὐ μὲν γάρ τι νεμεσσητὸν <u>βασιλῆα</u>
> ἄνδρ' ἀπαρέσσασθαι ὅτε τις πρότερος χαλεπήνῃ.

---

[245] My 2007 (210–221) dissertation provided an overview and discussion of the presence of accountability and consequences surrounding *atē*, but Cairns's (2012) article has since made the point in greater depth.

[246] Homer has made it quite clear that Zeus is able to thwart, albeit with help if needed, any Olympian attempt to usurp his sole control: *Iliad* 1.396–407, 8.5–27 (see Porter 2014:510–511, 20–26).

[247] On the *conclusio a maiore ad minus*, see the discussion of Dentice Di Accadia 2012:228.

There is a note of emphatic indignation in Odysseus' voice. He suggests that Agamemnon has learned his lesson and will no doubt improve by acting more responsibly next time round.[248] Such counsel to act responsibly mirrors a familiar choice formula first used by Athena to Achilles (*Iliad* 1.207). She urges him to stop his anger from ending in a physical assault on the leading *wanax*; that is, she prods in her address to him, "if you will obey" (αἴ κε πίθηαι). This traditional saying indicates that an important decision is at hand. It does not, despite certain scholarly opinion (e.g. Kirk 1985:75), assume that Achilles will agree and relent. It is in no way a *fait accompli*. After all, the same formula on another occasion (*Iliad* 11.791) references a decision of Achilles, and whether he will be willing to relent, when approached by Patroklos. When the moment comes, Achilles will not in fact agree to help his comrades, but only gives in a bit by allowing Patroklos to enter the battle in his armor. The expression "if you will obey" (αἴ κε πίθηαι), then, is not deterministic, but rather, as Schadewaldt (1966:140) observes, typical of "Ungenauigkeit." Odysseus' words seem to be a real call for more responsible action the next time round. It is up to Agamemnon to react appropriately and to embody a clear response in the future.

It is with the foregoing understanding of Agamemnon's appeal to *atē* that we are to hear Agamemnon's claim, "but I am not blameworthy" (ἐγὼ δ' οὐκ αἴτιός εἰμι, 19.86), a conclusion that naturally precedes his appeal. Agamemnon, after all, in accordance with oral style, followed his conclusion by the evidence of his assertions.[249] The evidence, as we have seen, helps us to recognize that Agamemnon's appeal does not deny his responsibility in the matter, at least not for Homer's audience used to hearing about *atē*. Further, Agamemnon is called to change by Odysseus.

But would Agamemnon act differently on a future occasion? His character, as we have seen it unfold from this and earlier chapters, seems consistent enough for his audience to doubt that possibility. Even Agamemnon's claim of blamelessness (ἐγὼ δ' οὐκ αἴτιός εἰμι), moreover, depends upon how the core (external) audience, who know the fuller stories Homer sings, viewed his character.[250] This is especially important since a survey of this traditional idiom shows that it can be either true or false, sincere or otherwise. For instance, in *Iliad* 3, we are given a picture of Priam and other senior Trojan leaders with Helen on the

---

[248] Cf. the comments of Cairns (2001:18n54) that "there is no point in warning someone to behave well in the future if it is not in his power to do so."

[249] Cf. discussion in Chapter 3, s.v. 3.2.6 Agamemnon's Joy: 8.75–82, where we noted that premises regularly follow conclusions in orally composed arguments.

[250] Cf. Teffeteller (2003:23), who appropriately notes that the objective reality of any claim to blamelessness is known only to Homer's privileged audience members. She raises important (sometimes unanswerable) questions about what is and what is not objective reality for the epic audience.

citadel walls overlooking the battlefield and troops. There, we become privy to Priam acting as perhaps any male would, to borrow Blondell's assessment, when he says that Helen is not to blame (οὔ τί μοι αἰτίη ἐστί, 3.164) for the Trojan War. He does so despite the likelihood of Helen's agency, demonstrated by her own self-blame.[251] Whether, as Teffeteller (2003:23) asks, Priam is blinded by Helen's charms as are the other elders (3.156–160, which seems likely from the poetic portrait) or just demonstrates the affection of a father-in law (or both), we cannot know for sure. Priam's use of the traditional address, "dear child" (φίλον τέκος, 162),[252] does suggest that Priam takes his role as a caring father-in-law figure seriously. So, Priam's words are kind, but are not likely meant to represent objective truth.[253]

In another example of Homer's use of blame language, we find Odysseus in the underworld exclaiming to Ajax that Zeus, rather than himself, is to blame (αἴτιος, *Odyssey* 11.553–560).[254] He makes this claim despite the probable backstory that he beguiled the Achaians into giving him the arms of Achilles.[255] The backstory of Odysseus gaining Achilles' arms instead of Ajax clearly affects Homer's presentation. Odysseus adopts an assuming approach (οὐκ ἄρ' ἔμελλες ... λήσεσθαι, 553–554) that is markedly rebuffed, even though Odysseus reminds Ajax that he "is indeed dead" (οὐδὲ θανών, 554). Ajax will not let go of his anger against Odysseus, however, "stemming from the accursed arms" (εἵνεκα τευχέων οὐλομένων). There follows a possible reference to Ajax's suicide in lines 556–558.

At other times, however, when for example Achilles' talking horse Xanthos says that he and Balios are not to blame (οὐδέ τοι ἡμεῖς / αἴτιοι, *Iliad* 19.409–410) for his master's imminent doom, but rather "a great god and powerful Moira," the objective reality seems probable enough.[256] A talking horse is divinely appointed to speak the truth. Why else would he be given articulate speech?

---

[251] Blondell (2010:15): "Such blame is, in its way, an acknowledgement of her power."

[252] See our earlier discussion of φίλον τέκος, its synonyms and antonyms, in Chapter 3, s.v. 3.2.3 Nestor's Stories of Quarrel, *Nostoi*, and *Oresteia*: 3.136–310; also Chapter 3, n. 18.

[253] Teffeteller (2003:23) wonders if Priam's words reflect "the actual view of the matter." Surely this is not a pertinent question. Her suggestion of civility (but it was not feigned, as such), is closer to the mark, but of course it is civility toward his daughter-in-law and the most beautiful woman in the world.

[254] I agree with Teffeteller (2003:19), who calls Odysseus' words "a veiled reference to himself." This proposition assumes the audience's knowledge of the larger backstory.

[255] The dispute over the arms of Achilles and Ajax's subsequent madness and suicide were topics for Lesches of Lesbos (in his *Little Iliad* according to Proclus frg. 1, Bernabé 1987:74–75), Pindar (*Nemean* 7.25–27, 8.23–27), and Sophocles (*Ajax*).

[256] Xanthos is part of a group who receive special, divine knowledge, such as that given to seers, or to those who receive sudden, divine illumination while dying: e.g. Patroklos, before dying, tells Hector that his life is about to end in *Iliad* 16.844–854; cf. Danek's (1998:222) note on Elpenor's "übermenschliche Wissen" of the future in *Odyssey* 11.69–70.

And, we can probably take Zeus' word for it when he complains that he is tired of listening to mortals blaming the gods for their own "recklessness" (*atasthalia*) in the *Odyssey*'s opening speech (*Odyssey* 1.32–34).[257]

The informed external audience knows the fuller stories, even when unknown to the poem's internal audience. They could hear past the surface influence of gender (Helen and Priam), narrative silence (Odysseus and Ajax), and questions of narrative perspective and power (Xanthos and Zeus), when listening to the characters speak. Homer's core audience could consider the narrative moments against (diachronically) past, present, and future stories. They remembered the sort of traits that made characters who they were from their words and actions at other times. Helen's character resonated for Homer's audience with implications from her connection in the oral tradition with the commencement and dilemma of the Trojan War. As we saw earlier, she represents "the conundrum of female beauty," which is "intrinsically desirable" yet also connected with destruction.[258] Her ability to entice males, even her own husband after Troy fell (cf. Euripides *Troades* 1036–1059), is always just under the surface. Priam is not exempt from her influence. Odysseus' role, as we saw in Chapters 1 and 2, is also known to the Iliadic audience from the *Odyssey* story. As we saw in Chapter 2, he is a hero marked by "cunning, stratagems, and endurance," whom Plato thought was an even stronger speaker than Nestor. While Odysseus' claim on Achilles' arms raises a number of questions that cannot detain us here, his ability as a "ruse-strategist" would come as no surprise to the singer's audience.[259] Can Odysseus help it if his abilities are not matched by those of Ajax who, as we saw, was known as a hero whose martial prowess was equaled by a corresponding terseness of speech?[260] Xanthos was, presumably, regarded as a faithful and almost magical horse of Achilles. He was known to the audience in any case, since he was apparently famous enough to be sought out by Dolon (*Iliad* 10.321–323) in that traditional story, as we saw earlier in this chapter.[261] Of course, as noted, Xanthos' utterance is tied to his receiving privileged, revealed knowledge, a traditional pattern related to special moments in

---

[257] A connection between *atasthalia* and *atē* seems likely enough, if not in reality (so Seiler 1954:15 and Wyatt 1982:268), then as a folk etymology of the sort that was often authoritative to an ancient audience and which seems to have influenced Hesychius, on which see Chantraine 1968:132, s.v. ἀτάσθαλος, and Cairns 2012:35–49. For other examples of blame, see Teffeteller 2003:23–26.

[258] In this chapter, see, for example, s.v. 4.2.1 Agamemnon's Dishonoring and Hubristic Actions: 1.6–344; and 4.2.4 Agamemnon's Prayer, Oath, and Sacrifice: 3.267–302.

[259] On Odysseus' communitarian-based *dolos*, see Chapter 2, s.v. 2.2.4 Menestheus and Odysseus: 4.327–364.

[260] See Chapter 2, s.v. 2.2.2 Aiantes: 4.273–292.

[261] See s.v. 4.2.7 Agamemnon in the *Doloneia*: 10:3–127.

epic narrative. Further, Zeus' claims are related to his own traditional character and the theme of justice in human affairs, admittedly a controversial but character-based question, nonetheless.[262]

In Agamemnon's case, too, the audience is well aware of his larger character traits.[263] Agamemnon's response is itself to be read against this backdrop. We saw earlier in this chapter that Agamemnon would not deny that he was the problem to his leading *basileis* (although there too he had blamed *atē*: 9.115, 116, 119).[264] Yet, despite this awareness, we observed that he nevertheless added on something extra to his offer of recompense to be brought by the embassy to the estranged Achilles; something less than conciliatory to his offer of compensation—an insistence that his higher station in life be recognized. It is consequently unsurprising, when Agamemnon comes face to face with Achilles in book 19, that he adds not merely a conventional comment about *atē*, but also an extra-long "explanation" about why he himself is not to blame. In the end, the difficulty seems to be that the troops have to force Agamemnon's hand to make him see that he has acted inappropriately. It is not like him to come to this realization himself.

For the core audience who had heard the whole of the *Iliad* and *Odyssey* in some form before, and for the singer who works within a deep performance tradition, Agamemnon is not a suddenly invented character. Rather, he is traditionally recognizable to the poet and to the external audience (and, in a more limited way, to the internal audience also). What they know of him moreover, is that he is, in short, a pathetic despot, with few redeeming qualities. While a full summary of Agamemnon's personal qualities must await the next chapter, suffice it to say here that he is just the sort of character who could all too easily make a claim to no blame. In the end, as in many other moments of Agamemnon's innate ineptness in Homer's songs, no one is really convinced. To adapt what Seneca says about people trying to cure a malady of the soul by going on vacation, Agamemnon's problem is simply this: *secum fugit*.[265] He is stuck with himself, a self well known to both singer and audience. Perhaps Agamemnon's less-than-admirable character also provides answers to other questions not dealt with here: Why is it that some individuals are affected by

---

[262] On Zeus' traditional character, see Chapter 2, n. 28.

[263] Taplin's (1992:209) explanation and his proposal, picked up and developed by Scodel (2008), that Agamemnon wished rather to save face, catches one nuance of Agamemnon's character. Scodel (2008) develops the thesis that face saving by different heroes is a response to a need to preserve *timē*.

[264] Nb. οὐδ' αὐτὸς ἀναίνομαι, 9.115. Cf. 4.2.6, s.v. Grievances against Agamemnon—Revisiting His Past Wrongs: Book 9.

[265] *Epistulae Morales* 28.10 "Quaeris quare te fuga ista non adiuvet? tecum fugis."

atē, while others are not? Why was Agamemnon likely both a recipient and at least a partial cause of *atē* in others?[266]

Agamemnon seems a marked contrast to certain other characters affected by *atē* who take more responsibility for their actions. We might instance Helen. She affirms her own agency in the actions that led to the Trojan War despite the gendered silence of males around her. Or, we might contrast Achilles' different attitude toward his own excessive anger, an anger that led to Patroklos' death.[267] At least Achilles is shown by the poet mourning Patroklos by self-deprecatingly describing himself as "a useless burden upon the earth" (ἐτώσιον ἄχθος ἀρούρης, 18.105) who was no "light" (φάος) for his friends (102–104).[268] Achilles, like Agamemnon, is really at fault, as he himself admits. Yet, there is no quibbling when Achilles realizes where his aloofness from battle has led, and no plea that he is not to blame for the death of his friend or the losses of his fellow warriors. Rather, just the opposite. There is a personal realization of the consequences of his prolonged anger and a resolute plan of action to honor his fallen companion.

The poet and audience knew the sort of character Agamemnon was. It is in this context, the context of character traits known within the performance tradition, that we must read Agamemnon's claim regarding *atē* and statement that he is not "blameworthy." Agamemnon's plea that he is not *aitios*, then, is really no excuse at all. The words of Poseidon from book 13 offer an objective "control" for my assertions. The narrative perspective of a divinity, after all, is certainly a step up from the more limited human vista. Poseidon addresses the Achaian troops (*Iliad* 13.111–114):

> But if indeed altogether truly *blameworthy* is
> the heroic son of Atreus, wide ruling Agamemnon,
> because he dishonored swift footed Achilles,
> then we really should not slack off in battle.

> ἀλλ' εἰ δὴ καὶ πάμπαν ἐτήτυμον <u>αἴτιός</u> ἐστιν
> ἥρως Ἀτρεΐδης εὐρὺ κρείων Ἀγαμέμνων
> οὕνεκ' ἀπητίμησε ποδώκεα Πηλεΐωνα,
> ἡμέας γ' οὔ πως ἔστι μεθιέμεναι πολέμοιο.

---

[266] See Porter (2017:6), where I suggest that Agamemnon's *atē* is partly the cause for Achilles'.

[267] There is little reason not to accept that Achilles was in a state of *atē*, at least when he rejects the embassy in *Iliad* 9. As Cairns (2012:8) observes, "the mistake which Achilles would be making if he rejected the Embassy would be as disastrous in its consequences as the original offence." Cf. Porter 2017:5-7.

[268] οὐδέ τι Πατρόκλῳ γενόμην φάος οὐδ' ἑτάροισι / τοῖς ἄλλοις, οἳ δὴ πολέες δάμεν Ἕκτορι δίῳ, / ἀλλ' ἧμαι παρὰ νηυσὶν ἐτώσιον ἄχθος ἀρούρης.

Poseidon's "if" is met by an instantaneous and unified reaction from the Achaians, who eagerly rally behind their leaders in tight battle ranks. If action is a reply, it is a resounding confirmation that Agamemnon is to blame. This is the last we really hear from Agamemnon. As Taplin notes, Agamemnon is "out of sight" for the rest of the *Iliad*, except for a minor appearance in the funeral games for Patroklos.[269]

As we have seen throughout this chapter, Agamemnon appears to be impetuous—he acts first and thinks afterwards—but he is also given to unusually insulting and even irreverent comments. His actions are often chastised by his inferiors and end up in apology and retraction; he blames divinity, yet is still responsible and suffers the consequences. As we noted in the preceding chapter, the *Odyssey* is one with the *Iliad* in presenting us with an Agamemnon who is impetuous, thoughtless, rash, and foolish. As we saw for the *Odyssey* in Chapter 3, Agamemnon is on the bottom of an ascending scale of outcomes among leading Greek heroes, a scale woven into the very fabric of the Odyssean tradition. Agamemnon's disappointing character seems as much a part of the Iliadic tradition. The *Iliad*, however, since its setting is the battle for Troy, foregrounds other traits not as immediately apparent in the context of the *Odyssey*'s narrative. We are presented with an Agamemnon who is also inept and unconvincing as a leader, plagued with a personality displaying problems of arrogance, imperiousness, irreverence, and insult.

What is the background of Homer's picture of Agamemnon? Why is Agamemnon such a pathetic leader? Is there an impinging influence within the underlying oral tradition that has affected his characterization? These questions inform our consideration of Agamemnon's character in the next chapter.

---

[269] Taplin (1990:77–78) notes that Agamemnon has nothing to say at the games, while others "go out in a blaze of attention."

5

The Traditional Characterization of Agamemnon

What has emerged from a consideration of Agamemnon's appearances in person, name, or through retrospective narrative, is the tenor of his characterization in the *Iliad* and *Odyssey*. As I have noted throughout the foregoing chapters, Agamemnon's involvement in other story patterns, such as that contained in the *Odyssey*, provides helpful background for understanding Agamemnon's characterization in the *Iliad*. In this chapter, after a review of Agamemnon's character traits, I will further argue that particular story patterns such as Agamemnon's *kakos nostos*, but also the *miasma* and cursed family history of the House of Atreus (potentially alluded to in both epics), are influencing the presentation (and reception) of Agamemnon in the *Iliad* (and *Odyssey*).

The picture of Agamemnon embedded within the Homeric epics, is, on the whole, quite unfavorable. Certain descriptive traits have recurred in the foregoing chapters. As a leader and character, there appears a rather consistent portrayal of Agamemnon as: 1. impetuous, thoughtless, foolish, and rash; 2. arrogant, imperious, irreverent, and insulting; and 3. inept and unconvincing. A better character trait, albeit still somewhat ambivalent, is Agamemnon's "stalwart" nature when a warrior in battle, an attribute we will deal with fourth, if only to conclude our summary on a better note. While some of my English word choices to describe Agamemnon are influenced by Greek, a taxonomy based solely upon individual Greek words would prove insufficient.[1] There is, necessarily, also overlap in taxonomy. Yet the foregoing terms, their division and arrangement, allow us to look over our findings from various story contexts as threads woven back together to display a tapestry of Agamemnon's characterization. Further, as we have seen, the poet often portrays Agamemnon with only

---

[1] The ancients did not always have a single term for everything, as for example the phenomenon of the "priamel" (Race 1982:10), nor is it usual in any case to find complete correspondence between any one Homeric term and an English "equivalent." Further, in Homer's lexicon, traditional elements are often greater than any singular adjective in Greek or English.

limited direct comment by himself or another character. Instead, the audience is left to draw conclusions based upon its traditional knowledge and the tenor of the words or actions of a particular character in a local narrative moment as it transpires.

5.1 Impetuous, Thoughtless, Foolish, and Rash

A consistent portrayal of Agamemnon as a leader and character is embedded in both the *Odyssey* and *Iliad*. He is impetuous, thoughtless, foolish, and rash. In our overview of *Odyssey* 3 we saw that Nestor's narrative began with a quarrel between the sons of Atreus that effectively resulted in two separate departures and Agamemnon's arrival home alone.[2] Significantly, the language of Nestor's retrospective implied that Agamemnon's stance in this quarrel with his brother was the plan of a "thoughtless child" (νήπιος), "for he did not know what he was about to suffer" (οὐδὲ τὸ ἤδη, ὃ οὐ πείσθαι ἔμελλεν). The many appearances of the vocative νήπιος used of an adult, support "thoughtlessness" as part of its traditional meaning. The traditional cue, "thoughtless child," insinuated, through ironic disdain, an element of thoughtless miscalculation, often by a character involved in a foolhardy action. The limited perspective of Agamemnon then was not the sole reason for the use of this descriptive word by Nestor of Agamemnon in a dispute between him and Menelaos. By using "thoughtless child," Nestor became the spokesman for the tradition as a whole. The implications for Agamemnon were portentous, since it would be a lack of thoughtfulness that would bring about his own death.

A second example of thoughtlessness came in *Odyssey* 4. In reply to Telemachos' admiration over his home's apparent affinity to that of Olympian Zeus, Menelaos countered that his absence from Argos came at a cost: his brother's death.[3] Agamemnon was portrayed in this section of the *Odyssey* as being killed "by stealth," in circumstances where, outlining his thoughtlessness, he was not personally expecting—"unexpectedly" (ἀνωϊστί)—what came. At the base of this rare descriptive word, as we saw, is "expect" (οἴομαι), a verb that stresses a more personal and thoughtful reflection, which in Agamemnon's case was clearly absent. Within the ongoing narrative of Menelaos, we heard too from Proteus details of Aigisthos' ambush of Agamemnon. Agamemnon's death was here represented by a traditional simile from Proteus' mouth: he was killed like an ox slaughtered at feeding time. Agamemnon's ignorance of the trap set for him is emphasized, a lack of awareness or reflective forethought that led to

---

[2] See Chapter 3, s.v. 3.2.3 Nestor's Stories of Quarrel, *Nostoi*, and *Oresteia*: 3.136–310.
[3] See Chapter 3, s.v. 3.2.4 Menelaos' Delay and Agamemnon's Death: 4.90–92.

the success of the plot to take his life.[4] It was the sort of inattentiveness that had cost other characters dearly, including the youthful Lykaon, whom Achilles had captured while the lad was out cutting fig branches.

The rash impetuousness of Agamemnon seemed to be invoked by the poet within his tale in *Odyssey* 8.[5] We saw that the poet made reference to an earlier episode in the Trojan War story, when Agamemnon visited the oracle in Delphi and rejoiced in his spirit over the oracle's response. Yet, what seemed a boon to Agamemnon (he rejoiced at what he believed to be the commencement of an oracle's fulfillment), turned to grief and misery as the poet immediately told us. Agamemnon's rejoicing, set immediately against such metonymic realities as a long war and sad homecoming, was full of irony for Homer's core audience. Agamemnon was both naive and thoughtless in his comprehension of, and impetuous in his reaction to, the quarrel.

In our consideration of *Odyssey* 11, we noted a string of interrogatives that ensued, employing the rhetorical device of the "erroneous question," which would have struck the audience, who knew how Agamemnon died, with the full force of metonymic irony.[6] No less an emphasis was discernible in the priamel with its twist (cardinal point) and expanded narrative that formed Agamemnon's sorry reply. The tension created for the poet's audience (not to mention Agamemnon himself) underscored Agamemnon's utter thoughtlessness in regard to the potential danger for himself and his men. They all experienced complete surprise at the bloody turn of events upon their homecoming. The focus of this scene was on Odysseus taking Agamemnon as an example to avoid and to do this by careful forethought. Further, the traditional idiom used by Agamemnon to introduce this second advisement to Odysseus, "But this other matter to you I speak, but you cast [this] in your heart" (ἄλλο δέ τοι ἐρέω, σὺ δ' ἐνὶ φρεσὶ βάλλεο σῇσιν), was, as we saw, a formula that yielded important implications in context. In its other occurrences the formula was used by a character to suggest the presence of extremely fervent emotion and personal participation in the information being shared. It also provided some form of imminent consequences (almost always menacing). The formula was most often followed by a very strong warning or plea. I suggested that the strong emotion of Agamemnon coupled with an injunction to Odysseus to act prudently formed a metonymic caution. Through the idiomatic cue of an emotional warning then, we saw the poet's portrayal of Agamemnon as an example to be avoided.

---

4   It is also possible also to see Agamemnon's thoughtlessness in the act of his being taken by a "ruse strategist" (something we considered under this heading in Chapter 3, in our discussion of *Odyssey* 1.299–300).

5   See Chapter 3, s.v. 3.2.6 Agamemnon's Joy: 8.75–82.

6   See Chapter 3, s.v. 3.2.8 The *Nekuia*: 11.380–466.

The same paradigmatic portrayal of Agamemnon was noted, moreover, in our discussion of *Odyssey* 3.[7] There, Odysseus' retort sought to reinforce Agamemnon as a paradigm that portended imminent danger to be avoided at all costs by thoughtful planning.

The *Iliad*, too, provided numerous instances of Agamemnon's impetuously thoughtless or foolish words and deeds. The *Iliad* opens with our first example.[8] Athena had come to Achilles and urged him not to draw his sword and kill Agamemnon, but to employ a verbal scourge instead. Agamemnon, however, was not content to leave things at a rhetorical level. Instead, he pressed Achilles with a vexatious threat: as Chryseïs was taken from him by Phoibos Apollo, so he would lead away Briseïs, Achilles' *geras*. It was a threat he soon carried out. He wanted Achilles to recognize "how much superior" (ὅσσον φέρτατος) he was so that no one would again presume to speak on equal terms with him. At that moment, Achilles' restraint and refusal to take action to avenge his being wronged stood out in marked contrast to Agamemnon's own quick, thoughtless, and despotic decision to take what he saw as his royal due.

We saw in *Iliad* 2 that Agamemnon was tricked by a destructive dream into thinking he could take Priam's city.[9] As in the *Odyssey*, so here he was characterized by the poet as a "thoughtless child" (νήπιος). How so? First, Agamemnon believed the dream, and, second—and this was the greater mistake—he chose to test the troops as he did. Only Agamemnon, of all the Iliadic examples, ever suggests that the Achaians both retreat and also engage in a *nostos*. The choice of Agamemnon to include a call for a *nostos* displays the pathetic character of Agamemnon as paramount *basileus*. We observed that Agamemnon's address to the troops was exceptional in its lack of thoughtful consideration and nearly disastrous in its outcome. The core audience was not surprised by such action, however. It highlighted the foolishness of both Agamemnon's comprehension of reality and his plan of action. It displayed the ambivalent character of Agamemnon as a paramount *basileus*: Agamemnon was both deceiver and deceived; both a knowing perpetrator and an unaware recipient of "evil deception" (ἀπάτη). His actions undercut the Achaians' political stability. Only the intervention and speech of Odysseus and the voice of Nestor saved the day, indeed the whole military enterprise at Troy, for Agamemnon.

In *Iliad* 4, we observed an Agamemnon who was impetuous and rash toward Odysseus and Diomedes.[10] In Odysseus' case, however, we saw that Agamemnon's

---

[7]   See Chapter 3, s.v. 3.2.9 Avoiding Agamemnon's *Nostos*: 13.383–385.

[8]   See Chapter 4, s.v. 4.2.1 Agamemnon's Dishonoring and Hubristic Actions: 1.6–344.

[9]   See Chapter 4, s.v. 4.2.2 Agamemnon's Dream and the Testing of the Troops: 2.16–440.

[10] See Chapter 2, s.v. Impetuous Agamemnon; and Chapter 4, s.v. 4.2.5 Agamemnon's Address to the Troops: 4.231–418.

comments, when heard against the larger tradition surrounding *dolos* and *kerdos*, demonstrate a significant misrepresentation of this intelligent and communitarian hero. This is especially so, considering the positive use of these terms in Homer's traditional register.[11] Agamemnon's misapprehension and caustic vilification of Odysseus would have struck Homer's audience as unfair, to say the least. In *Iliad* 9, moreover, Agamemnon was made painfully aware of his earlier castigation of Diomedes, a character who we saw was known by Homer's audience for his "inexorable courage."[12] We noted that the formula "Thus he spoke, but they in fact all were stricken to silence" (ὣς ἔφαθ', οἱ δ' ἄρα πάντες ἀκὴν ἐγένοντο σιωπῇ) cued for the audience that a "representative" reply would come, one that was in concert with the feelings of the group.[13] Diomedes stepped forward to offer such a response when he expressed his "repressed" grievance in *Iliad* 9, one of minimally five indictments of Agamemnon's character brought about by Agamemnon's past words and deeds.[14]

Next, in *Iliad* 11, even the otherwise stalwart nature of Agamemnon as a warrior in that book's action is tainted somewhat with a rash impetuousness.[15] I remarked that the whole assault by the Achaians, led without preamble by Agamemnon, lacked many traditional elements of an anticipatory battle sequence: the sacrifice, the meal, the gathering of the army, the review of the troops, and the exhortation to battle. All that the troops ever got was a quick yell. There appeared a suggestive peculiarity in the brevity of the whole scene, in the dearth of traditional cues or expectable elements—hardly what we might expect from the poet in a scene involving such a central character. It is ironic that the longest of the arming scenes in the *Iliad* should be accompanied by so little else, other than the Achaian leader fervently rushing ahead of his forces. Ironic too, was the placement of this scene in the *Iliad* poet's song. After all, as I suggested, one could hardly credit the tradition with the minute ordering of *aristeia* within the poet's story as a whole. The poet perhaps meant to show, not Agamemnon's lack of fighting prowess (which is never really in doubt), but rather, his impetuous leadership style. The rash leadership style of Agamemnon comes to the fore again in book 14, when Agamemnon, however much he wished to deny the import of his authoritarian call for a *nostos*, does a poor job in his attempt to revise the past.[16] Despite Agamemnon's plea and assurance that he had not in fact issued an authoritative command for a general *nostos* but just an

---

[11] See especially 2.2.4 Menestheus and Odysseus: 4.327–364.
[12] See Chapter 2, s.v. Impetuous Agamemnon, for Diomedes' "inexorable courage."
[13] See Chapter 4, s.v. 4.2.6 Grievances against Agamemnon—Revisiting His Past Wrongs: Book 9.
[14] See Chapter 4, s.v. 4.2.6 Grievances against Agamemnon—Revisiting His Past Wrongs: Book 9.
[15] See Chapter 4, s.v. 4.2.8 Agamemnon's *Aristeia*: 11.91–283.
[16] See Chapter 4, s.v. 4.2.9 Agamemnon's Third Call for a *Nostos*: 14.41–134.

open-ended offer and non-coercive invitation, he was plainly backtracking. He had acted rashly, and from a leadership perspective, foolishly and thoughtlessly. He miscalculated the reaction of his *philoi*, and he was doing all he could afterwards simply to save face.

5.2 Arrogant, Imperious, Irreverent, and Insulting

References to the arrogant, imperious, irreverent, and insulting attributes of Agamemnon's character do not usually appear as aspects of the *Odyssey* poet's portrait of Agamemnon's words and deeds. This is no surprise, since Agamemnon is no longer alive and hegemon of the Achaians. These traits have informed the *Iliad* poet's portrait in a number of passages, however. All of these aspects of Agamemnon's character are already present and assumed by the poet in the opening quarrel of *Iliad* 1. Agamemnon would not be swayed by the priest Chryses or his own troops, but rather gave way to anger.[17] As we observed, the vehemence of Agamemnon's reply was a brutal rejoinder that made Chryses immediately leave and pray to Apollo who responded by sending a plague. The priest was also old, making Agamemnon's response all the more irreverent and callous. Yet in his rejoinder, Agamemnon insisted arrogantly upon his preference for Chryses' daughter Chryseïs over his own wife. He wanted to take her home, a response that possibly cued another story for Homer's core audience.

Further, we noted that Agamemnon was also excessively harsh as the implications of one idiom suggested. It was not good enough for Agamemnon to send the priest away with a stern warning, but there was also a threatening boast in his tone. The priest's daughter was to be taken "far from [her] fatherland" (τηλόθι πάτρης). We saw that this expression is always associated with the misery of permanent separation experienced by an individual because of the loss of one's fatherland, but also the effect that this loss has on another. It assumes Chryseïs' loss of a homeland, but also a significant disruption of the *oikos* and its normal function for Chryses himself. The priest's daughter would not be married off, but taken as booty, and Chryses would be left at a loss. Yet, none of this concerned Agamemnon. He instead taunted Chryses with the future repeated rape of his daughter (ἐμὸν λέχος ἀντιόωσαν). His brash and irreverent response had unfortunate consequences, however, in the ensuing narrative, not just for himself but also for the whole Greek expedition. They too would experience loss. Apollo's plague ensued, resulting in the burning of continual pyres (αἰεὶ δὲ πυραὶ νεκύων καίοντο θαμειαί), a penalty prayed for by the priest.

---

[17] See Chapter 4, s.v. 4.2.1 Agamemnon's Dishonoring and Hubristic Actions: 1.6–344.

Further, while grudgingly agreeing to return his concubine Chryseïs to her father to save the warrior host, Agamemnon imperiously demanded that he receive a compensatory *geras*, even though as Achilles immediately observed, the distribution of the spoils had already been made. Agamemnon simply ignored Achilles' response. The immediate effect of Agamemnon's imperiousness was intense *eris* between the two that formed the backdrop for much of the *Iliad*. We noted that Agamemnon's rejection of Achilles' response (that it was not just for Agamemnon to take his *geras*) brought together words that denoted a complete rejection of any need for Achilles at all. The joining of "I do not care" (οὐκ ἀλεγίζω) and "I do not have regard" (οὐδ' ὄθομαι) created an emphatic response by Agamemnon. Agamemnon's arrogant imperiousness was resolute. Second, the proverbial comment of Achilles, that it is better for humans to obey the gods since this brings their active attention and response, stood in direct opposition to Agamemnon's irreverent reaction to the priest of Apollo. Agamemnon's irreverence also stands in opposition to the voices of his own army, which he ignored.[18] We need also to think, as I noted in Chapter 4, of the placement of this scene at the outset of the singer's rendition.[19] Its placement is a function of the singer's choice where to begin ("from which point" in the *prooimion*). The singer is in competition with his peers in producing the most impressive story, and where he begins suggests that he has an interest in displaying aspects of Agamemnon's character.

While uttered in the heat of argument, nevertheless we considered how Achilles' use of "dog-face" (κυνῶπα) in *Iliad* 1 was especially suggestive of Agamemnon's hubristic actions and attitude. We saw that dogs are most strongly characterized as animals that act to scavenge the corpses of fallen heroes. The use of this term for humans carried connotations that suggested the basest of qualities and a very negative stigma. It placed Agamemnon in the adversary's camp as one who was working against the Achaians' best interests and was the object of disgust. Further, the traditional term "dog-face" (κυνῶπα) used in book 1 appeared to have affected the poet's choice of words in book 9. There, the poet had Achilles say of Agamemnon: "He would not certainly / dare, *dog* though he is, to look upon my *face*" (οὐδ' ἂν ἔμοιγε / τετλαίη <u>κύνεός</u> περ ἐὼν εἰς <u>ὦπα</u> ἰδέσθαι). Agamemnon's "dog-likeness" was not the only point of resonance with book 1 that I noted. Rather, within two lines, Achilles described Agamemnon's character as one of "constant shamelessness" (αἰὲν ἀναιδείην, 9.372), uttering the same charge he used eight books earlier (ἀναιδείην, 1.149; ἀναιδές, 1.158). It was no coincidence that the poet had Achilles yell "dog-face"

---

[18] See Chapter 4, s.v. 4.2.1 Agamemnon's Dishonoring and Hubristic Actions: 1.6–344.
[19] See Chapter 4, s.v. 4.2.1 Agamemnon's Dishonoring and Hubristic Actions: 1.6–344.

and "shameless" in almost the same breath on two separate occasions. The association of these two terms, rare in Homer, but really quite apposite, suggests that the poet was attached to the sort of referential qualities these words bring forward for Agamemnon.

Agamemnon's prayer in *Iliad* 3, moreover, which formed part of the ritual of oath taking preceding the duel between Menelaos and Paris, displayed an overly imperious quality.[20] What was interesting about Agamemnon's prayer is that it seemed not only to fulfill the customary requirements of swearing to certain gods, but also excessively tipped the demands from any Achaian win far beyond what a Trojan victory would procure. What appeared to suggest excess was twofold: 1. the extent of what was "fitting"—the "honor" (τιμή) envisioned: "Which among people yet to be, will be known" (ἥ τε καὶ ἐσσομένοισι μετ' ἀνθρώποισι πέληται); and 2. Agamemnon's promise, should he be wronged, personally to find an end to the war. His earlier threat in book 1 to go personally to Achilles' hut if need be paralleled the veiled threat in his prayer in book 3.[21] A notable arrogance imbued Agamemnon's claim, perhaps comparable in kind, I suggested, to the arrogance of Achilles in his wish for only himself and Patroklos to take Troy. Such resonance indicates a pattern of behavior.

Two examples of Agamemnon's overly imperious nature came also from *Iliad* 4 and 9.[22] In the case of book 4, I emphasized what has been alluded to already in this chapter, Agamemnon's high-handed and arrogant abuse of Diomedes and his depiction of this stalwart warrior's character in a way completely incongruent with the traditional portrayal.[23] In book 9, the embassy delivered Agamemnon's offer to Achilles. As I noted there, however, Odysseus left off an offensive and arrogant bit about Agamemnon's superior station that he had been told to deliver. He could not change what Agamemnon was like as a leader, his ingrained habits, but he could chose not to include remarks that would further offend Achilles. In *Iliad* 24, as a final example, we heard Achilles urge Priam to sleep in a secluded spot.[24] We saw there that, while Agamemnon is not really unusually brutal, he does have a proclivity for selfishly despotic action. At least this was the fear, should Priam be found out. After all, Agamemnon had earlier snatched Briseïs away from Achilles. In book 24, there is the possibility of his snatching away Priam who came with *apoina*, to increase his own *apoina*, jeering

---

[20] See Chapter 4, s.v. 4.2.4. Agamemnon's Prayer, Oath, and Sacrifice: 3.267–302.

[21] Cf. the related discussion earlier in Chapter 4, s.v. 4.2.1 Agamemnon's Dishonoring and Hubristic Actions: 1.6–344.

[22] See Chapter 4, s.v. 4.2.5 Agamemnon's Address to the Troops: 4.231–418 and 4.2.6 Grievances against Agamemnon—Revisiting His Past Wrongs: Book 9, respectively.

[23] This is a comment that festers and reemerges as we observed, in Diomedes' grievance in book 9.

[24] See Chapter 4, s.v. 4.2.8 Agamemnon's *Aristeia*: 11.91–283.

(ἐπικερτομέων) as he does so. The parallel of dishonoring aged suppliants and dispossessing his *basileis* should not be missed. Despotism breeds such abuses.

5.3 Inept and Unconvincing

Agamemnon is in Hades whenever he speaks in the *Odyssey*, so it is little wonder that virtually no examples of Agamemnon's inept and unconvincing leadership style can be found there. The singular instance of these character traits may be indirect.[25] When Odysseus responds to the menacing Cyclops, he emphasizes his and his crew's connection to "Atreus' son Agamemnon," "of whom indeed now greatest under heaven is his fame (*kleos*)." He emphatically informs the ogre, through synonymous parallelism no less, that Agamemnon even "destroyed a people," and through *enjambement* adds "[so] numerous." The metonym "under heaven is his fame" (ὑπουράνιον κλέος ἐστί), we saw, was known from a heroic context in the Trojan War story and so made reference to the heroic world of the Trojan War and Agamemnon as the paramount leader of that military expedition. Yet, such introductions have no effect on the gluttonous monster. The whole scene makes a boast using Agamemnon's name sound rather impotent. There may also be something sardonic about the whole scene and the *kleos* referred to there may in fact include Agamemnon's pathetic *telos*. It did, at least, for Homer's core audience, even if the brute beast himself was not in touch with the singer's traditional language.

The first sure indication of Agamemnon's inept and unconvincing leadership style came in the first book of the *Iliad*.[26] Within the quarrel Agamemnon intends to move from argument to action with the "rhetorical fulcrum" "But now come!" (νῦν δ' ἄγε, 141). His order will not be followed by Achilles or his army immediately as he envisions, and his directive fails to convince. He talks of appeasing the archer god, but he speaks as though his abusive behavior could suddenly be forgotten in the wake of his despotic command. Consequent upon this moment of Agamemnon's imperious order and following the eventual breakdown of the assembly, Achilles was visited by Agamemnon's embassy. In the hospitable address and conversation with Agamemnon's emissaries, Achilles absolved them of blame, but complains that Agamemnon had chosen a thoughtless course of action that would spell destruction for the army. Achilles portrayed Agamemnon's *modus operandi* as inept, since he seemed incapable of discerning "before and after" (πρόσσω καὶ ὀπίσσω). As we saw, this traditional language cue pointed not just to Agamemnon's thoughtlessness (though it did

---

[25] See Chapter 3, s.v. 3.2.7 The People of Agamemnon of the Greatest Fame: 9.263–266.
[26] See Chapter 4, s.v. 4.2.1 Agamemnon's Dishonoring and Hubristic Actions: 1.6–344.

do this), but also to an innate inability for carrying out his duties as hegemon over the Greek forces at Troy. The poet, familiar with the formula's connotations and intent on foreshadowing the coming disaster originating from the *eris* of *Iliad* 1, placed it in the mouth of Achilles. It reminded the poet's audience of the inherent nature of Agamemnon as a personality within the larger tradition.

Another instance of Agamemnon's ineptness came from a character that, as we noted, was from a lower class, yet, nevertheless, was used by the poet to emphasize a particular theme. Thersites' remarks in book 2 were, in essence, very much in accord with Achilles' complaint.[27] The man, I argued, not his argument, was rejected (something I showed to be the case elsewhere in the *Iliad* with Sthenelos). Rather, Thersites' words brought forth issues from Agamemnon's conflict with Achilles once again, with all the ineptness that the remarks evoked for Agamemnon as paramount *basileus*.

In book 9, moreover, in the midst of the Achaian host's "panic" (φύζα) and "fear" (φόβος), Agamemnon encouraged flight and a *nostos*. Unlike in *Iliad* 2, however, this time it was not a test, but the response of a commander incapable of controlling his own fear. Agamemnon is overwhelmed by the immediate crisis. The poet commented that Agamemnon was struck with a great grief in his heart (ἄχεϊ μεγάλῳ βεβολημένος ἦτορ) and painted a vivid picture of a hegemon who was as terrified as the common soldier. Agamemnon's grief was accompanied by tears and a formulaic description "deeply groaning" (βαρὺ στενάχων) indicating deep distress. The response of the troops was the thematic silence that we saw represents both their collective grievance over the last enticement to flee (when their acceptance was met with stern rebuke) and the fact that a representative reply would follow. In this case, the spokesperson for the common angst was Diomedes, who gave voice to his own repressed grievance. We saw that he turned the tables on the paramount *basileus*, indicting him for his inability to help provide assistance and protection (*alkē*) for his warrior community. Diomedes was immediately followed by Nestor who reprimanded Agamemnon for not following his earlier authoritative *muthos*.

Agamemnon's portrait is further painted for us as later readers by the opening lines of book 10. Agamemnon, sleepless, was struck as he lay there by what he saw. The Trojans were making merry while the Achaians waited in virtual paralysis. His response was sorrowful lamentation. He pulled out his hair in distress, an act that clearly signified his helplessness. It was an action that had both a mythic and possibly a cultic parallel, as I noted. It suggested a fear of imminent death. The poet followed up this vignette portraying the royal *aporia* with Agamemnon's decision to go to Nestor to seek someone to assist him with

---

27 See Chapter 4, s.v. 4.2.2 Agamemnon's Dream and the Testing of the Troops: 2.16–440.

a "plan" (μῆτις), one that would ward off evil for the Danaäns in their dilemma. Agamemnon headed off to Nestor, utterly distraught. His whole being was "thus shaken by fear" (σαλευόμενος οὕτως ὑπὸ τοῦ φόβου), as ancient commentators noted. His heart was jumping out of his chest and his knees were knocking. His was in a condition comparable to that of Andromache who feared Achilles had killed her husband, or better yet, Patroklos who had been placed in a vulnerable position by Apollo and Delusion; or even to Hera and Athena in Zeus' menacing description (albeit imagined) of their fearful response should he serve them up a thunderbolt. While one accepts that going to Nestor for a conference with the senior warrior is a wise decision, Agamemnon's condition upon arriving suggested incompetence. He was wholly distraught. Fortunately, sensing his fear, the aged hero rose to the occasion, and after this, we heard no more from Agamemnon in book 10 despite the significant events that ensued (the night raid). His leadership added little that was productive to the action that followed. Yet, as I noted, at least he didn't ruin things, something we have seen to be quite within his capacity as a leader.

The next picture of Agamemnon's ineptness was uttered in strained tones in book 14. Nestor came to Agamemnon for advice and leadership and got none.[28] Rather, Agamemnon urged a *nostos*. Within our consideration of this narrative moment we saw the implications of the idiom "O my, my" (ὤ πόποι). As an exclamation it certainly highlighted the level of personal anxiety and concern that Agamemnon was experiencing. He was considering the possibility that the troops would not obey him out of anger for his past actions towards Achilles. Agamemnon was certain that Zeus was portending destruction and consequently urged for the third time that they flee on their ships. Odysseus' retort began with "looking darkly" (ὑπόδρα ἰδών), a formula that highlighted a significant breach in social convention as we noted in Chapter 2.[29] This traditional cue was followed by another Homeric formula that reinforced this sentiment: "what sort of word has escaped the barrier of your teeth!" (ποῖόν σε ἔπος φύγεν ἕρκος ὀδόντων). As I noted at this juncture, Odysseus (and the troops) clearly expected superior things from Agamemnon, whom they felt should know better. While Agamemnon's response was arguably his peevish attempt to revise the past, the foundation of the need for such a revision was his own ineptness in word and deed. It was he who had brought about this problematic impasse in the first place.

The last instance of Agamemnon's inept and unconvincing leadership style appeared in *Iliad* 19, where Achilles had just ended his isolation and publicly

---

[28] See Chapter 4, s.v. 4.2.9 Agamemnon's Third Call for a *Nostos*: 14.41–134.
[29] See Chapter 2, s.v. 2.2.4 Menestheus and Odysseus: 4.327–364.

revoked his anger.[30] In his response, Agamemnon blamed *atē*. In considering this term, however, we noted that the audience was used to hearing of human causes for *atē* that paralleled divine agency. Further, an individual was held accountable for his state of *atē* and suffered consequences. Additionally, I argued that however much such an appeal may have been a traditional response in Homer, the need for Agamemnon to recognize that he was accountable and I also suggested in this case responsible (the poet's narrative assumed that action can be changed through advisement), was something Odysseus made clear to him. Agamemnon stood in contrast to other heroes who took more responsibility for their actions. Further, when Agamemnon came face to face with Achilles in book 19, it was unsurprising that he added, not merely a conventional comment about *atē*, but also an extra-long "explanation" about why he himself was not to blame. While usual, Agamemnon's plea that he was not to blame, I concluded, was really not heard by the audience as exculpatory, when heard traditionally. The appeal was instead symptomatic of the general ineptness of an unconvincing leader. Agamemnon sought to hide behind the harmful delusion of Zeus to shelter his own faltering ego. The claim was characteristic of his personality.

5.4 Stalwart

After the tenor of the preceding characterization of Agamemnon, it seems necessary to mention Agamemnon's singularly more excellent quality, his stalwart nature as a warrior. In short, he was "a good fighter" (Griffin 1980:70). We saw this character trait first in *Iliad* 2,[31] albeit following a large personal fiasco.[32] Under the encouragement of the *basileis* and Athena, the Achaians had compacted about Agamemnon who led them into battle. At this point, the poet wished to stress the sheer grandeur of Agamemnon and his role as foremost leader of the Achaians. We noted key terms in the comparison, such as "standing out" (ἔξοχος), "conspicuous" (μεταπρέπει), and "remarkable" (ἐκπρεπέα). These qualities drew attention to what had already become clear in the preceding comparison of Agamemnon to various gods, his preeminence as the paramount *basileus* heading into battle. On the battlefield, he was no coward (Cf. Collins 1988:97).

Much more was noted about the quality of Agamemnon as a warrior in his *aristeia* in *Iliad* 11.91–283. We observed there that Agamemnon's hands were given the heroic epithet "redoubtable" (ἀάπτους), when he was "eagerly" (σφεδανόν) chasing the Trojans who were running, desiring to reach the safety

---

[30] See Chapter 4, s.v. 4.2.10 Agamemnon and Atē: 19.76–144.
[31] See Chapter 4, s.v. 4.2.3 Agamemnon, the Preeminent Leader in Battle: 2.477–483.
[32] See Chapter 4, s.v. 4.2.2 Agamemnon's Dream and the Testing of the Troops: 2.16–440.

of their city. The formulaic phrase used to portray Agamemnon in action—"but with gore he was bespattering [his] redoubtable hands" (λύθρῳ δὲ παλάσσετο χεῖρας ἀάπτους)—I remarked, was just the stuff of a proper *aristeia* and needs to be read as part of any heroic "snapshot" of a warrior at the peak of his glory. The same or similar formulaic collocations were used to describe the heroic moments of other central heroes in Homer. We saw that "gore" was a good thing for a foremost hero absorbed in his rush for glory through continual slaughter (even in the case of metonymic references to the brutality surrounding the fall of Troy). Further, in due course, the Trojan Koön wounded Agamemnon in the arm, yet still he fought on, hurling the traditional large stones that so amazed the poet as he described events of the epic past. All action points to Agamemnon as a stalwart warrior. Yet the placement of this scene, like the former, is problematic. His *aristeia*, consequently, is rendered less impressive, as we saw, especially considering its relative brevity.

The predicament of highlighting Agamemnon's excellence actually exists at most every turn, as we have seen in Chapters 2 to 4, even in the matter of his otherwise stalwart qualities as a warrior. Of course, even in the case of his acting as any good field commander might, the sorts of virtues that are needed to head a charge into battle are not otherwise the same as those required to plan or lead. One finds, beyond the occasional positive comment (e.g. *Iliad* 7.321–322), difficulty in highlighting any consistently favorable attributes for Agamemnon as paramount *basileus* that are not offset in the same or immediately surrounding scenes by the overwhelming presence of negative, or at best, ambivalent character traits. Some narrative moments are neutral, but more often than not, Agamemnon seems to fall precipitously into a great many scenes and come out rather scathed, at least as regards his characterization. The picture we have of Agamemnon through word and deed, even from his few good moments, does not, for the most part, impel Homer's audience to cheer. We are left asking why this is the case, a question we address in what follows.

5.5 The Pathetic Despot

The purpose of this section is to suggest further implications from our study of Agamemnon's character for how we are to read Agamemnon's character and characterization in the Homeric epics generally. As we have seen, the presentation of Agamemnon's character in the *Iliad* is affected by the impinging tradition from his past and future, and the *Iliad* poet's narrative (like the tradition behind his poetic rendition) has been molded by this awareness. Just as we saw in Chapters 1 and 2 that Odysseus could not leave behind his known, but chronologically later, "Odyssey" adventures when involved in the *Iliad* story, so

Agamemnon could not leave behind his larger epic legacy. The poet of the *Iliad* is aware of much else and presents us with an Agamemnon after the development (rather than the commencement) of a mature and deep performance tradition. Imbedded references to this tradition, while difficult for us to tease out as later readers, inform the early audience's experience as they hear the *aoidos*. This has implications for how Homer's core audience heard epic poetry and how we should read the *Iliad* (and *Odyssey*). It may provide one answer for the query of why Agamemnon is presented with so many ignoble character attributes.

What is the background of the *Iliad* poet's characterization of Agamemnon? Why is he such a pathetic leader who displays the sorts of negative character traits he does? The foundation for Agamemnon's characterization may lie partly in character type, as Hainsworth argues. He proposes that we see Agamemnon's actions (and so character) as a necessary product of the poet's belief that "the brave vassal is a better protector of society's values than his weak and ungrateful lord" (Hainsworth 1993:64; cf. 46–47). Agamemnon is, however, more than a character type, and the actual tradition connected with him, as I have been suggesting, is directly influencing the poet's artistry.[33] Moreover, why is one king good and another bad? To use Minchin's cognitive category, why doesn't the poet have Agamemnon live up to his "role theme"?[34] What factors in the tradition are guiding the poetic presentation?

Haubold argues convincingly that the view of the shepherd's role taken by Xenophon, Socrates, and Aristotle, that "the group is not there for the shepherd, but the shepherd for the group," is also the expected norm for leadership within Homeric, Hesiodic, and other early epics. The role of the shepherd is synonymous with the role of the good king who, as Haubold remarks, "must act as to avoid blame (νεικεῖν)" (Haubold 2000:26).[35] He observes that:

> As we would expect in a genre which has such clear ideas about the task of the shepherd but is relatively uninterested in his privileges, the leader's obligation is viewed as being primary.
>
> Haubold 2000:24

---

[33] Agamemnon is also portrayed as a *basileus*-type, but his family history makes him a specific *basileus* with a particular story. For the *basileus* typology, see e.g. *Iliad* 1.80, 165, 231, 2.196–197, 204–206, etc., but also the discussion of typical versus specific characterization in Chapter 2.

[34] Minchin 2011a.

[35] Haubold (2000:28) comments: "Throughout the surviving texts of early Greek hexameter, single agents are assigned the task of guaranteeing the well-being of the people." His list of examples includes (see 28n59): *Iliad* 1.117, 4.184 (negative), 5.643 (negative), 8.246, 9.98–99, 424, 681, 10.14–16, 13.47, *Odyssey* 11.136–137, 22.54, 23.283–284, Hesiod *Theogony* 84–87, Panyassis fr. 12.7–8 (Davies 1988), Callinus fr. 1.18 (West), Tyrtaeus fr. 11.13 (West 1989–1992).

Agamemnon, it appears from what we have seen of him, fails in his task as a shepherd to his people. He fails as the premier leader,[36] and his failure stems in part from his unwillingness to be guided by the collective will, especially of his fellow *basileis* (cf. Elmer 2013:66). Whether or not Agamemnon had a right to act so imperiously, it is not really, as Allan and Cairns have shown, how, *de facto*, leaders were to lead (Allan and Cairns 2011).

Odysseus, as a contrast to Agamemnon and other "divine" kings, is portrayed as a benevolent and good *basileus* in need of no vassal as protector of his people, who are well treated. The good that the *basileus* is to be doing is even voiced by Odysseus in the guise of a beggar. He says to shameless Antinoos (who ought to offer him, like the others, a bit of bread and meat): "Give, friend! Certainly you do not look like the basest of Achaians / but the very best, since you have the look of a *basileus*" (δός, φίλος· οὐ μέν μοι δοκέεις ὁ κάκιστος Ἀχαιῶν / ἔμμεναι, ἀλλ' ὥριστος, ἐπεὶ βασιλῆϊ ἔοικας, *Odyssey* 17.415–416).[37] Antinoos foolishly offers an insult and a hurled stool as his angry contribution (17.445–465).[38] By contrast, Odysseus is portrayed as a benevolent leader not given to outrage (e.g. *Odyssey* 4.691–695). Odysseus demonstrates in his role as king "del principio della regalità e di un retto esercizio del potere, del retto esercizio della sovranit, la formazione del consenso, and un principio etico che legittimasse l'intervento punitivo del detentore del potere," among other things, which form the social contract that regularly escapes Agamemnon's view (Di Benedetto 1999:220–221). Why does Agamemnon stand out as so soiled a despot who embodies a "political irrelevancy during the archaic period" (Stanley 1993:295)?

I propose that the character of Agamemnon in the *Iliad* exudes the consequences known to the audience of the effects of both past bloodguilt and a future demise at his wife's hand. The past bloodguilt is most clearly narrated in later poetry as a curse on the House of Atreus.[39] Homer was, I am arguing, aware

---

[36] I disagree with Taplin (1990) that Agamemnon is not the supreme leader of the expedition against Troy. There does, against Taplin's view, appear to be a hierarchy in the *Iliad*, although I agree that there are mutual obligations that are expected in his relationship with the *basileis* who are following him (cf. the role envisioned by Elmer 2013:63–85). Each *basileus* is of course supreme in his own "communauté politique," as Carlier (1984:145) notes (although I do hold to the overly authoritarian position proposed for Agamemnon in Carlier 2006:106). The problem is not the hierarchy in any case, but rather, Agamemnon's abuse of his position and inability to be an effective leader. Van Wees's (1988:19) position, essentially that Agamemnon inherited the leading position but did not prove "deserving" of it, is more likely. For further discussion, see Schadewaldt 1966:37–39, Carlier 1984:135–230 (esp. 136–139), and Morris 1986:98–99.

[37] Patera (2012:79) notes this verse in the specific context of the greater expectation for *basileis* offering sacrifice, but also in other contexts, such as the present one, when *Basileis* are to be "plus généreux que les autres," something Patera notes Nestor had to remind Agamemnon about in *Iliad* 9.69–70.

[38] Nb. the hemistich χολώσατο κηρόθι μᾶλλον at *Odyssey* 17.457.

[39] For a general overview of the House of Atreus myth, see Gantz 1993:489, 540, 544–556.

of the violent and cursed history of the House of Atreus (noted in Chapters 3 and 4), although he does not explicitly refer to it and call it a "curse." The first clear reference to a "curse" (ἀρά=Ionic ἀρή) infecting the House of Atreus comes in Aeschylus' *Agamemnon* and is most fully explicated by Aigisthos. Seeing his role as avenger of past wrongs (*Agamemnon* 1577–1582), he relates, in the vividness of historical presents, the former imprecation of Thyestes who had just been fed his own children by Atreus (1600–1602):

> Then he imprecates an intolerable doom upon the descendants of
> Pelops,
> kicking away the dinner with a curse,
> "Thus may the whole race of Pleisthenes perish!"[40]

> μόρον δ' ἄφερτον Πελοπίδαις ἐπεύχεται,
> λάκτισμα δείπνου ξυνδίκως τιθεὶς ἀρᾷ,
> οὕτως ὀλέσθαι πᾶν τὸ Πλεισθένους γένος.

This "intolerable doom" (μόρος ἄφερτος) upon Pelops' race, which embraces through dramatic irony Thyestes' own house by Aigisthos' eventual death as Aeschylus' *theatai* know, includes a curse that is played out in the subsequent *Oresteia*.[41]

The Homeric epic tradition, I suggest, knew something of this family history and Homer seems to touch on it, however subtly, at key points. While it is not necessary to review all points, some of the more important metonyms deserve emphasis. In Chapter 4, I suggested the possibility of the House of Atreus story affecting the poetic choice of language in *Iliad* 2.[42] The feud between Atreus and his brother Thyestes is not actively spoken of in the *Iliad*, yet, in the rather lengthy pedigree attached to Agamemnon's scepter of office, which speaks of the history of the scepter of Agamemnon given by Zeus himself, we hear of Thyestes. The choice of language may indicate knowledge of their discord.

---

[40] The actual place of Pleisthenes in the family tree of Pelops is in dispute. What is not in dispute is that his descendants (his "race") represent here for Thyestes the object of his cursing, whether, depending on the tradition, that is as the father to Atreus, or as a son of Atreus whom Thyestes raised as his own and sends to seek revenge (in this version of the story, Pleisthenes is unaware of just who his real father is). Thyestes, like Achilles (who gains honor at the cost of Patroklos' death), does not realize that his curse will include the death of his own son through Orestes.

[41] It is not necessary to state that the curse of Thyestes was the only curse on the House of Atreus, since Atreus' ancestry includes a grandfather, Pelops, served up by his father Tantalos in order to test the gods. On this see Pindar *Olympian* 1, Pausanias 5.13.1–17, Apollodorus *Epitome* 2.2–9, and Burkert 1983:99. This earlier curse, however, is not mentioned in Homer even indirectly, as far as I can discover.

[42] See Chapter 4, s.v. 4.2.2 Agamemnon's Dream and the Testing of the Troops: 2.16–440.

Further, the line ends with the noun-epithet formula "to Thyestes rich in sheep" (πολύαρνι Θυέστῃ) in the fourth colon, an epithet that may reach into the tradition about the golden ram that was at the center of a dispute between Atreus and Thyestes. Its owner was marked as the rightful king of Mycenae.

The curse of the House of Atreus is not actively spoken of in the *Odyssey* either, yet it is possibly alluded to there as well, as I argued in Chapter 3.[43] We considered that although the order, textual history, and geographical particularities of the passages in *Odyssey* 4 are problematic, yet, if not rearranged, they contain a very important narrative element. The poet seems to want us to see Aigisthos as living near Agamemnon within the kingdom of the son of Atreus. This heightens the portended danger that awaited Agamemnon through a "historic" vignette. I argued that the impending danger is further cued by formulae related to geographical locations and adverse winds and the poet's use of the rhetorical device of *correctio*. Agamemnon was facing a dilemma, and the traditional language supported the intensity of what followed in *Odyssey* 4, his demise.

One instance of *correctio* proves particularly interesting. We saw that the *Odyssey* poet, within Proteus' account of Agamemnon's death, has Proteus say that Agamemnon had arrived "at the outskirts of the country" where Thyestes had been living; but then he noted, "before, but then Aigisthos son of Thyestes lived [there]" (τὸ πρίν, ἀτὰρ τότ' ἔναιε Θυεστιάδης Αἴγισθος). I suggested that the poet was acknowledging the dismal story of the House of Atreus well known in fuller form from later Greek sources. The allusion to Thyestes may have been the poet's way of adducing a known, portentous story, which would likely have been distasteful to retell overtly and in full.[44] It served the poet's needs by building suspense around Agamemnon's arrival and portending his imminent death brought about by his wife, and, momentously, the very son of Thyestes himself.

The latter end of Agamemnon's life (his *kakos nostos*), but also the events following his death, so the other events of the *Oresteia*, are recorded in some detail in the *Odyssey* text. As we saw in Chapter 3, Agamemnon's death is said to have been "most pitiable" and "doomed," indicating a terrible end.[45] It was presumably apprehended beforehand by the traditional audience of the *Iliad* from earlier poetic performances of the *Odyssey* song. As we noted in detail in Chapter 3, Agamemnon's role in the *Odyssey* is that of an example to be avoided. Yet, there may even be a reference to the *kakos nostos* of Agamemnon in the

---

[43] See Chapter 3, s.v. 3.2.5 Proteus' Account of Agamemnon's Death: 4.512–537.

[44] The name "Thyestes" (cf. θύος) also suggests a link between myth and ritual, although in contrast to Pelops and the Olympic games, there is no clear historical evidence of such a connection (Burkert 1983:93–109).

[45] See Chapter 3, s.v. 3.2.8 The *Nekuia*: 11.380–466.

Iliad. In Chapter 4, in the opening scene of the *Iliad*, we observed Agamemnon in a state of hubris.[46] He insisted upon his preference for Chryseïs over his own wife and was intending to take her home. This association of Chryseïs with Clytemnestra may have resonated with implications for Homer's core audience well aware of Clytemnestra's infidelity (so patently a theme in the *Odyssey*). For them, the admission must have resounded with metonymic irony and created a sardonic reaction. Not only was Agamemnon upsetting the stability of his (Iliadic) warrior culture through his insulting reaction to the priest and army's requests, but he was also potentially upsetting the stability of his own *oikos*. Agamemnon's attitude and actions were in some symbolic sense parallel to that of his wife. The significance of traditional background may be further inferred if we recall the observation that the singer may have been intending a link between Agamemnon's callousness here and the seer's earlier activity at Aulis, including his prophecy (an event of the epic cycle's *Cypria* briefly outlined in Proclus' epitome). Homer may be pointing to the sacrifice of Iphigenia (or as he would say, Iphianassa). The impact of the theme of the *kakos nostos* on the *Odyssey* outlined in detail in Chapter 3 needs no further amplification here.

A few additional comments are in order, however, about the influence of backstories from Agamemnon's past and future on the *Iliad*, and how we should go about "reading" his character. I have already suggested that the thoughtless impetuousness of Agamemnon in the *Iliad* may be the consequence of his characterization in the larger tradition, now frozen in the *Odyssey*, where his lack of foresight ends up getting him killed at the end of his *nostos*.[47] If Agamemnon is not what we might expect in the *Iliad*, then perhaps it is because we expect a thoughtful, rather than a pathetic king. Would, however, a circumspect *basileus* come to such an end? The character of Agamemnon in the *Iliad* cannot be understood in isolation from the tradition of his *nostos* any more than we would read the picture or epithets of Odysseus in the *Iliad* without referencing the larger *nostos* tradition adhering to his character.[48]

Agamemnon in the *Iliad* is just the sort of character an audience, who knew of his ultimate shameful demise, would expect. And the shameful reversal of Agamemnon's fortunes is emphasized by the poet when Odysseus addresses Agamemnon with an erroneous question in *Odyssey* 11. As we heard from Agamemnon in a pointed priamel, the normal sort of male heroic activities—stealing livestock, sacking cities, battling men and seizing women as

---

[46] See Chapter 4, s.v. 4.2.1 Agamemnon's Dishonoring and Hubristic Actions: 1.6–344.

[47] See Chapter 3, but especially s.v. 3.2.8 The *Nekuia*: 11.380–466.

[48] This is something we considered in some detail in Chapters 1 (s.v. 1.4 The Relation of the *Iliad* and *Odyssey*) and 2 (s.v. 2.2 Typical and Specific Appeals—in particular 2.2.4 Menestheus and Odysseus: 4.327–364).

captives—were replaced after the end of war with a homecoming in which he was himself the victim. Further, rather than heroic death, he came to an unheroic end (now in a domestic setting), killed in stealth by Aigisthos, but also by the very hand of his own wife, as we saw in *Odyssey* 24.[49] This was all part of the tradition known to poet and audience. Thus the poet would compose and the core audience consider and experience Agamemnon's leadership style within a narrative context, metonymically. He was a character cursed in his family history, pathetic in his words and leadership during the Trojan War, and headed toward a shamefully pathetic end.

There are also, consequently, implications in what we have been arguing for an accurate way to read the oral-derived Homeric epics, although these implications are no doubt clear by now. Put simply, it is normal to approach the *Odyssey* with the *Iliad* as assumed tradition, something that is logical from a linear point of view that emphasizes the sequel tale to the Trojan War. Indeed, this is self-evident, since there can be no "return" (*nostos*) without a "journey" (*keleuthos*). We have seen in our consideration of Agamemnon, however, that we must also read the *Iliad* with the events of some earlier form of our *Odyssey* in mind. It is impossible of course to diagram the interplay and influence of one part of the tradition upon another or to show absolute cause and effect for the evolution of Agamemnon's character as it is presented in the Homeric epics as performed songs, memorialized after successive epic performances in written form. We cannot expect the *Iliad* poet to make overt temporal connections to the events of Agamemnon's *kakos nostos*, creating a temporal confound; nor do we usually expect epic characters within the story being told to have knowledge of particular activities beyond their purview. Any references of this sort must be made obliquely, as we noted first in Chapter 1.[50] Yet, as I have argued, those connections seemed to have existed in the poet's and audience's mind and to have affected character presentation and audience reception.

It is possible, then, to see the character of Agamemnon memorialized in the *Iliad* as a prequel to the story of Agamemnon in an oral *Odyssey*. He will soon be destroyed shamefully by his own wife, and his character in the *Iliad* confirms this eventuality. In this sense, Agamemnon is a *pathetic* despot, in that he experiences extreme *pathos* on his homecoming and it is a *pathos* that is seen everywhere in the history known to Homer and his core audience familiar with the *Odyssey*.[51] Agamemnon is destined, so the *Iliad* poet is well aware, to

---

[49] See Chapter 3, s.v. 3.2.11 *Nekuia Deutera: Odyssey* 24.19–97.

[50] See Chapter 1, s.v. 1.4 The Relation of the *Iliad* and *Odyssey*, where I made reference to the *Iliad* poet's mention of a *nostos* beyond what was fated, in *Iliad* 2.155.

[51] Cf. e.g. *inter alia*, from Chapter 3 on the *Odyssey*, the metonym of "death and baleful fate" (θάνατον καὶ κῆρα μέλαιναν), discussed s.v. 3.2.3 Nestor's Stories of Quarrel, *Nostoi*, and *Oresteia*:

experience suffering.[52] Far from merely being a typical king, then, Agamemnon was a doomed king in a bad homecoming. The *Iliad* gives us a character appropriate for meeting such a dismal end. In good Greek fashion, the *Iliad* shows that the seeds of Agamemnon's own destruction lie partially in events beyond his control (his family history and the scheme of Aigisthos and Clytemnestra), but, at least partly too, in his own errant actions and innate character. Agamemnon is a character who is pathetic as a leader in the *Iliad*: he causes *pathos* through his own words and deeds and experiences *pathos* in his role as hegemon of the Greek forces. As we noted in Chapter 4, for Homer, divine will or fate and human choice are usually inextricably linked in a co-terminus *telos*, a veritable "double motivation," no less.[53] The human causes for Agamemnon's bad end are embodied in Agamemnon's negative character attributes that have become part of Homer's tradition. This is, I propose, the reason we receive such a dismal picture of Agamemnon in the *Iliad*.

Foley's comments are apropos here:

> When we "read" any traditional performance or text with attention to the inherent meaning it necessarily summons, we are, in effect, recontextualizing that work, reaffirming contiguity with other performances or texts, or, better, with the ever-immanent ... immensely larger canvas of the tradition as a whole.[54]

> Foley 1991:9–10

That the larger canvas known to the traditional singer and audience of Homer's *Iliad* included other stories strategic to Agamemnon's character—the House of Atreus and the *kakos nostos* (the second of which is central to the story of the *Odyssey*) among them—is implied in the evidence we have presented in the foregoing chapters.

Our study, then, reinforces what we began saying in Chapters 1 and 2. Characters have a life outside of their present place in one epic rendition, a life known to the poet and too expansive to be contained in any singular epic

---

3.136–310; the pathetic simile of Proteus noted s.v. 3.2.5 Proteus' Account of Agamemnon's Death: 4.512–537; the pathetic priamel, s.v. 3.2.8 The *Nekuia*: 11.380–466; the *kakos nostos*, s.v. 3.2.9 Avoiding Agamemnon's *Nostos*: 13.383–385; and the *pathos* of Agamemnon, s.v. 3.2.11 *Nekuia Deutera*: 24.19–97.

[52] Cf. the insightful comments of Scodel (2002:24) about Telamonian Ajax and Locrian Ajax at the funeral games for Patroklos: "Telamonian Ajax, doomed to kill himself after Achilles' armor is awarded to Odysseus, is wounded, fighting against Diomedes; Locrian Ajax, who will die miserably at sea, falls into a pile of manure."

[53] See Chapter 4, s.v. 4.2.10 Agamemnon and *Atē*: 19.76–144 and Porter (2017).

[54] Cf. Chapter 1.

memorialization. As we have observed since Chapter 1, Homer's core audience had the advantage of knowing an intricate web of traditional stories, but also traditional characters. Audience members listened with their minds already predisposed to the sort of character they were hearing vividly presented at a particular narrative moment. A singer could take advantage of this by his choice of language, his use of rhetorical devices, his handling of type scenes, and his own creative presentation against the backdrop of traditional stories. Tradition-based components carried idiomatic meaning that provided cues for the audience's reception of character. We have seen that this is unquestionably the case for a great number of traditional characters in Homer, including Agamemnon.

Appendix
Colometry and Formulae

Oral-traditional tale-telling includes embedded cues to the larger back stories that begin at the level of cola and formulae. They are the first level of consideration in any search for characterization in Homer.[1] In colometry, "words," to borrow Foley's description, from particles to longer lexical (i.e. formulaic) components, are preserved whole.[2] What becomes clear from a survey of metrical studies of Homeric prosody since the initial work of Parry and Lord is "the intrinsically deep connection of many formulas and formulaic substitution systems to firm metrical structures (usually colometric units)" (Russo 1997:258). Cola and formulae are often coextensive, although formulae or formulaic systems can span multiple cola.

Cola are principal compositional units for an oral traditional composer.[3] It is to the individual and composite cola that we can often look for the building components of formulae and formulaic systems. In short, the colometrics of Homer's lines act as a guide for comprehending the poet's traditional idiom. The schema I adopt for the make-up of verse cola throughout this study is that of Peabody,[4] whose work is a variation of Fränkel.[5]

---

[1] On the colometry of the epic hexameter line, see Fränkel 1955:104, Halporn et al. 1963:11-12, Jones and Gray 1972, Nagy 1974, Peabody 1975:66-70, Edwards 1987:4-54, Foley 1990:80-82, Sale 1993, Nagy 2000, Edwards 2002, Garner 2011:3-17, and Porter 2011.

[2] I mean here by "words," both the Greek words of a traditional lexicon and, as Foley (1991:26n57) argues, composite words such as formulae, which should not be divided. The difference between cola and *metra* in this singular respect suggests the superior internal logic of colometrics for a consideration of the structuring of the Greek hexameter.

[3] Peabody 1975:68.

[4] 1975:66-70. See Foley (1990:73-80) for a favorable overview of Peabody and statistics on cola placement.

[5] 1955:104. The response of Kirk (1985:18-23; 1990: *passim*) to Fränkel and his predecessors was to question the developing principles of colometrics, including the four part line, essentially because of the number of bridges that occur and the location of the caesura in a certain percentage of Homeric lines. Kirk's stance is ameliorated somewhat by his own observation that Fränkel's (and other scholars') "analysis has been a productive one, since many Homeric verses do naturally fall into those [four] cola" (1985:20). While it is necessary to adopt a working principle for considering the cola of any line, it is unwise to speak in absolutes.

The Homeric line is made up of shorter cola, which can be divided under normal circumstances in any six places, as follows:[6]

$$-\overset{\smile\smile}{}\ |\ -\ |\overset{\smile\smile}{}\ -\ |\overset{\triangledown}{}\ |\overset{\triangledown}{}\ -\ |\overset{\smile\smile}{}\ |\overset{\smile\smile}{}\ -\ \times$$

A¹ A²   B¹ B² C¹ C²

Peabody's particular scheme, based upon his research of Hesiod's *Works and Days*, was praised by Albert Lord as representative of oral traditional composition in Greece (and of the Balkans).[7] Since Lord's observations reflect extensive field-work and a thorough knowledge of Homer, it seems reasonable to suggest, as a general rule of thumb, that colometric analysis is closely representative of the tectonic structure and compositional patterns of the original singers who gave us early Greek epic poetry.[8] Understanding Homer's language, then, involves the task of recognizing formulaic elements with the assistance of the natural cola of a line. While this approach is not always adequate, as Haslam (2003) has noted, and as anyone who works with the cola of the Homeric line can attest, it does very often indicate Homeric compositional units.

The preceding system of colometry can be illustrated by an example from the first book of the *Iliad*, where Achilles welcomes Agamemnon's heralds who come to take his girl, but adds damning aspersions on their despotic leader (1.333):

οὐδέ τι | οἶδε νοῆσαι | ἅμα | πρόσσω καὶ ὀπίσσω

A¹   B²   C¹

And not in any way | does he know how to consider |at the same
time | before and after

---

[6] The placement of the caesurae in no way negates the normal patterns suggested by Meyer's or Hermann's Bridge. In the case of Meyer's Bridge (affecting where the break occurs for the first cola), the rule is that if the second foot is a dactyl ($-\smile\smile$), then the two short syllables must be part of the same word-unit. This means for colometric analysis, which does not divide words in any case, that the break (unless bridged) would come at A1. In the case of Hermann's Bridge (affecting where the fourth cola begins, at C1 or C2), which observes that if the fourth foot is a dactyl, then the two short syllables must also be part of the same word-unit, the break would come at C2 (the adonean clausula), unless the second hemistich is bridged.

[7] Peabody 1975:xi-xiv. Cf. the comments of Austin 2009:95-96.

[8] It needs to be said that I have based most of my conclusions in Chapters 2-5 (even when I am considering the findings of others) on firsthand data gleaned from innumerable searches of Homer using the TLG database and incessant analysis of the poetic verse using the system of colometry I outline here. Consequently, any statistical mistakes are almost always my own.

As we saw in Chapter 4, the poet employed this final colon formula to suggest significant implications for Agamemnon's characterization for his core audience.[9] Cola commencement, bridging, and *termini*, often mark the beginning and completion of formulae (or formulaic systems).[10] In *Iliad* 1.148, we first noted the formulaic line:[11]

τὸν δ' ἄρ' ὑπόδρα ἰδὼν προσέφη πόδας ὠκὺς Ἀχιλλεύς

("At him darkly looking, spoke swift-footed Achilleus")

Here we saw the presence of a bridged A colon, with the formula τὸν δ' ἄρ' ὑπόδρα ἰδών ("At him darkly looking), ending at B1. As we noted there, the formula has implications as an idiom for Homer's audience.

Further, within and joining the cola of Homer's poetic lines are formulae or formulaic elements that are sometimes difficult to demarcate absolutely or exclusively, as Russo's review of studies since Parry's initial formulation suggests.[12] One cannot limit formulaic diction as a whole, moreover, to formulae that only fit Parry's early definition of "an expression regularly used, under the same metrical conditions, to express an essential idea,"[13] at least not for purposes of exploring what may in fact be the full extent of "formulaic" diction.[14] The more theoretical insights and developing approaches such as those of Nagler, Visser, and Bakker, however intangible, cannot be ignored.[15]

Yet, for practical purposes in seeing and comparing formulae, clear boundaries are necessary. I therefore limit my research to collocations of words that more obviously constitute formulae. I have employed the term formula to speak of recurring words or traditional idioms, employed, as Parry stated it, "under

---

[9] See 4.2.1 Agamemnon's Dishonoring and Hubristic Actions: 1.6–344.

[10] The most significant colon break is that of the mid line, followed by C2 respectively, but of course, formulae and formulaic systems can stretch to whole lines and beyond.

[11] 2.2.4 Menestheus and Odysseus: 4.327–364.

[12] Russo 1997: 2011.

[13] Parry 1971:13.

[14] Anyone who has spent time trying to find and analyze formulae has necessarily noted the flexibility of Homer's use of formulaic elements, including the substitutions, expansions, parallelisms, and differing degrees of fixity for particular parts of Homeric verse.

[15] Nagler 1967, Visser 1988, Bakker 1997. Russo's (1997, 2011) and Edward's (1997) overviews of these approaches are balanced. The sorts of observations that Hainsworth (1968) made about the greater flexibility of Homeric prosody are real and cannot be overlooked; cf. Higbie 1990:152-198. While I do not try to set rules as to the number of times a formula must occur to be named as such, I accept the idea of formula recurrence as one sign that an expression is formulaic. Sale (1993:101) calls a formula exactly repeating fewer than six times an "infrequent formula." I do not, as Peabody (1975:97) or Parry (1971:275n.), attempt to establish the minimum length for formulae.

the same metrical conditions, to express an essential idea."[16] Of course, what that "essential idea" is has been suggested by scholars working to comprehend the referentiality inherent in these units of meaning. The question of the "essential idea" has been the focus of my present study, as well. Formulae can also be part of formulaic systems, patterns of words with one or more important parts recurring as component(s), but with a varying amount of replacement of parts within the traditional idiom (and which can occasionally vary in length). Further, modifications and substitutions that affect metrical shape in a formulaic system have been noted throughout our present study.

Finally, since cola form the basic units that the Homeric poets employed for traditional language cues, my translations throughout the present work have been concerned first, not with the idiomatic rendering of Greek into English, but with maintaining, as far as possible, the cola of the original Greek line. A tendency toward formal equivalence, then, rather than dynamic equivalence, has been the goal in translation.[17] The style at times appear wooden, but also allows English readers to see many of Homer's sense units more clearly, as they hear Homeric characterization through traditional language cues.[18]

---

[16] Parry 1971:13; cf. 272: "a given essential idea."
[17] As a starting point for formal versus dynamic equivalence, see the bibliography listed in Pedro 2000:415.
[18] Kelly (2007) perhaps wisely eschews traditional terminology opting instead for a "unit" of meaning in his referential commentary.

Bibliography

Adkins, W. H. 1982. "Values, Goals, and Emotions in the *Iliad*." *Classical Philology* 77:292–326.

Alden, M. 2001. *Homer Beside Himself: Para-narratives in the Iliad*. Oxford.

———. 2012. "The Despised Migrant (*Il.* 9.648 = 16.59)." In *Homeric Contexts: Neoanalysis and the Interpretation of Oral Poetry*, ed. F. Montanari, A. Rengakos, and C. Tsagalis, 115–131. Berlin.

Alexiou, M. 1974. *The Ritual Lament in Greek Tradition*. 2nd ed. Lanham.

Alexiou, M., and V. Lambropoulos. 1985. *The Text and its Margins: Post-structuralist Approaches to Twentieth-Century Greek Literature*. New York.

Allan, W. 2006. "Divine Justice and Cosmic Order in Early Greek Epics." *Journal of Hellenic Studies* 126:1–35.

———. 2008. "Performing the Will of Zeus: The Διὸς Βουλή and the Scope of Early Epic Performance." In *Performance, Iconography, Reception: Studies in Honour of Oliver Taplin*, ed. M. Revermann and P. Wilson, 204–216. Oxford.

Allan, W., and D. Cairns. 2011. "Conflict and Community in the *Iliad*." In *Competition in the Ancient World*, ed. N. Fisher and H. van Wees, 113–146. Swanesa.

Allen, T. W., ed. 1917. *Homeri Opera*. Vols. 1–4. Oxford.

———, ed. 1930. *Homeri Ilias*. Vols. 1–3. Oxford.

Andersen, Ø. 1973. "Der Untergang der Gefährten in der *Odyssee*." *Symbolae Osloenses* 49:7–27.

Andersen, Ø, and D. T. Haug, eds. 2012. *Relative Chronology in Early Greek Poetry*. Cambridge.

Apthorp, M. J. 1980. *The Manuscript Evidence for Interpolation in Homer*. Heidelberg.

Arend, W. 1933. *Die Typischen Scenen bei Homer*. Berlin.

Arft, J. 2014. "Immanent Thebes: Traditional Resonance and Narrative Trajectory in the *Odyssey*." *Trends in Classics* 6:399–411.

Arieti, J. A. 1988. "Homer's *LITAI* and *ATE*." *Classical Journal* 84:1–12.

Armstrong, J. 1958. "The Arming Motif in the *Iliad*." *American Journal of Philology* 79:337–354.

Arnould, D. 1990. *Le rire et les larmes dans la littérature grecque d' Homère à Platon*. Paris.

Auffarth, C. 2002. "Agamemnon." In *New Pauly Encyclopedia of the Ancient World*, ed. H. Cancik and H. Schneider, 305–306. Leiden.

Austin, N. 1966. "The Function of Digressions in the *Iliad*." *Greek, Roman, and Byzantine Studies* 7:295–312.

———. 1972. "Name Magic in the *Odyssey*." *California Studies in Classical Antiquity* 5:1–19.

———. 2009. "Uncanny Homer." *Arion* 16:65–98.

Bader, F. 1998. "Le nom de Pénélope, tadorne à la πήνη." In *Quaestiones Homericae: Acta Colloquii Namurcensis habiti diebus 7-9 mensis Septembris anni 1995*, ed. L. Isebaert and R. Lebrun, 1–41. Louvain.

Bakker, E. J. 1995. "Noun-Epithet Formulas, Milman Parry, and the Grammar of Poetry." In *Homeric Questions*, ed. J. P. Crielarrd. Amsterdam.

———. 1997. *Poetry in Speech: Orality and Homeric Discourse*. Ithaca.

———. 2005. "Rhapsodes, Bards, and Bricoleurs: Homerizing Literary Theory." *Classics@* 3: https://chs.harvard.edu/CHS/article/display/1311.

Barcelona, A., R. Benczes, and J. Ibáñez. 2011. *Defining Metonymy in Cognitive Linguistics: Towards a Consensus View*. Philadelphia.

Barck, C. 1976. *Wort und Tat bei Homer*. Hildesheim.

Barker, E. 2009. *Entering the Agon: Dissent and Authority in Homer, Historiography and Tragedy*. Oxford.

Barker, E., and J. Christensen. 2006. "Flight Club: The New Archilochus Fragment and its Resonance with Homeric Epic." *Materiali e discussioni per l'analisi dei testi classici* 57:9–41.

Barker, E., and J. Christensen. 2014. "Even Herakles Had to Die: Homeric 'Heroism,' Mortality and the Epic Tradition." *Trends in Classics* 6:249–277.

Beck, F. A. G. 1964. *Greek Education: 450-350 B.C.* London.

Beck, W. 1986. "Choice and Context: Metrical Doublets for Hera." *American Journal of Philology* 107:480–488.

———. 1991. "Dogs, Dwellings, and Masters: Ensemble and Symbol in the *Odyssey*." *Hermes* 119:158–167.

———. 1993. "μῆνις." In *Lexikon des frühgriechischen Epos*, ed. Bruno Snell, 15.187–189. Göttingen.

Beekes, R. 2010. *Etymological Dictionary of Greek*. Vols. 1–2. Leiden.

Beneviste, E. 1969. *Le vocabulaire des Institutions indo-européens*, Vol. 2. Paris.

Bergold, W. 1977. *Der Zweikampf des Paris Und Menelaos*. Bonn.

Bernabé, A., ed. 1987. *Poetarum Epicorum Graecorum*. Part 1. Leipzig.

———. 1995. "Influences orientales dans la literature grecque. Quelques réflexions de méthode." *Kernos* 8:9–22.

Berndt, R., and C. Berndt. 1993. *The Speaking Land: Myth and Story in Aboriginal Australia*. Rochester, VT.

Beye, C. R. 1964. "Homeric Battle Narrative and Catalogues." *Harvard Studies in Classical Philology* 68: 345–373.

———. 2006. *Ancient Epic Poetry: Homer, Apollonius, Virgil: With a Chapter on the Gilgamesh Epic.* Wauconda, IL.

Bierl, A. 2012. "Orality, Fluid Textualization and Interweaving Themes: Some Remarks on the *Doloneia*; Magical Hourses from Night to Light and Death to Life." In *Homeric Contexts: Neoanalysis and the Interpretation of Oral Poetry,* ed. F. Montanari, A. Rengakos, and C. Tsagalis, 133–174. Berlin.

Bill, C. P. 1930. "The Location of the Palace of the Atridae in Greek Tragedy." *Transactions of the American Philological Association* 61:111–129.

Blondell, R. 2010. "'Bitch that I Am': Self-Blame and Self-Assertion in the *Iliad*." *Transactions of the American Philological Association* 1:1–32.

———. 2013. *Helen of Troy: Beauty, Myth, Devastation.* Oxford.

Boehme, J. 1929. *Die Seele und das Ich im Homerischen Epos.* Berlin.

Bolling, G. M. 1925. *The External Evidence for Interpolation in Homer.* Oxford.

Bonnéric, H. 1986. *La famille des Atrides dans la littérature Française.* Paris.

Bowra, M. 1930. *Tradition and Design in the Iliad.* Oxford.

———. 1962. "Composition." In *A Companion to Homer,* ed. A. B. Wace and F. H. Stubbings, 38–74. London.

Brauw, M. de. 2010. "The Parts of the Speech." In *A Companion to Greek Rhetoric,* ed. I. Worthington, 187–202. Malden, MA.

Broeniman, C. 1996. "Demodocus, Odysseus, and the Trojan War in the Odyssey 8." *Classical World* 90:3–13.

Brown, H. P. 2006. "Addressing Agamemnon: A Pilot Study of Politeness and Pragmatics in the *Iliad*." *Transactions of the American Philological Association* 136:1–46.

Burgess, J. 2001. *The Tradition of the Trojan War in Homer and the Epic Cycle.* Baltimore.

———. 2006. "Neoanalysis, Orality, and Intertextuality: An Examination of Homeric Motif Transference." In *Oral Tradition* 21:148–189.

———. 2012. "Belatedness in the Travels of Odysseus." In *Homeric Contexts: Neoanalysis and the Interpretation of Oral Poetry,* ed. F. Montanari, A. Rengakos, and C. Tsagalis, 269–190. Berlin.

———. 2015a. "Coming Adrift: The Limits of Reconstruction of the Cyclic Poems." In *The Greek Epic Cycle and Its Ancient Reception,* ed. M. Fantuzzi and C. Tsagalis, 43–58. Cambridge.

———. 2015b. *Homer.* London.

Burkert, W. 1983. *Homo Necans: The Anthropology of Ancient Greek Sacrificial Ritual and Myth.* Trans. P. Bing. Berkeley.

———. 1992. *The Orientalizing Revolution: Near Eastern Influence on Greek Culture in the Early Archaic Age.* Cambridge, MA.

Cairns, D. L. 1993. *Aidos: The Psychology and Ethics of Honor and Shame in Ancient Greek Literature*. Oxford.

―――. 2001. *Oxford Readings in Homer's Iliad*. Oxford.

―――. 2011. "Ransom and Revenge in the *Iliad*." In *Sociable Man: Essays on Ancient Greek Social Behavior in Honor of Nick Fisher*, ed. S. D. Lambert, 87–116. Swansea.

―――. 2012. "*Atē* in the Homeric Poems." *Papers of the Liverpool Latin Seminar* 15:1–52.

Cairns, D. L., and R. Scodel, eds. 2014. *Defining Greek Narrative*. Edinburgh.

Carlier, P. 1984. *La Royauté en Grèce avant Alexandre*. Strasbourg.

―――. 2006. "Ἄναξ and Βασιλεύς in the Homeric Poems." In *Ancient Greece: From the Mycenaean Palaces to the Age of Homer*, ed. Sigrid Deger-Jalkotzy and I. S. Lemos., 101–110. Edinburgh.

Camps, W. A. 1980. *An Introduction to Homer*. Oxford.

Cartledge, P. 2002. *Sparta and Lakonia: A Regional History 1300–362 BC*. London.

―――. 2003. *Spartan Reflections*. Berkeley.

Chantraine, P. 1952. "Le Divin et les dieux chez Homère." In *La Notion du divin depuis Homère jusqu' à Platon*, ed. H. J. Rose, 47–94. Geneva.

―――. 1958. *Grammaire Homérique*. Vol 1. Paris.

―――. 1963. *Grammaire Homérique*. Vol 2. Paris.

―――. 1968. *Dictionnaire étymologique de la langue grecque*. Paris. Repr. 1999.

Christensen, J. 2015. "Reconsidering 'Good' Speakers: Speech-Act Theory, Agamemnon, and the Diapeira of *Iliad*, II." *Gaia* 18:67–82.

Cirio, A. M. 2003. "Le Livre X de l'*Iliade*." *Gaia* 7:183–188.

Clarke, M. 1995. "Between Lions and Men: Images of the Hero in the *Iliad*." *Greek, Roman, and Byzantine Studies* 36:137–159.

Clark, M. 1997. *Out of Line: Homeric Composition Beyond the Hexameter*. Lanham.

―――. 2007. "Polydamas and Hektor." *College Literature* 34:85–106.

Classe, O., ed. 2000. *Encyclopedea of Literary Translation into English*. Vol. 1. Chicago.

Clay, J. 1983. *The Wrath of Athena*. Lanham.

―――. 1999. "*Iliad* 24.649 and the Semantics of ΚΕΡΤΟΜΕΩ." *Classical Quarterly* 42:618–648.

Codino, F. 1965. *Introduzione a Omero*. Rome.

Coldstream, J. N. 2003. *Geometric Greece*. New York.

Čolaković, Z. 2007. "Bosniac Epics—Problems of Collecting and Editing the Main Collections." *Forum Bosnae* 39:323–361.

Collins, L. 1988. *Studies in Characterization in the Iliad*. Frankfurt.

Combellack, F. M. 1965. "Some Formulary Illogicalities in Homer." *Transactions of the American Philological Association* 96:41–56.

Cook, E. 2003. "Agamemnon's Test of the Army in Book 2 and the Function of the Homeric *Akhos*." *American Journal of Philology* 124:165–198.

———. 2014. "Structure as Interpretation in the Homeric *Odyssey*." In *Defining Greek Narrative*, ed. D. L. Cairns and R. Scodel, 75–100. Edinburgh.

Crane, G. 1988. "Calypso: Background and Conventions of the *Odyssey*." Frankfurt.

Crielaard, J. P. 1995. "Homer, History, and Archeology." In *Homeric Questions: Essays in Philology, Ancient History and Archeology*, ed. J. P. Crielaard, 201–288. Amsterdam.

———. 2002. "Past or Present? Epic Poetry, Aristocratic Self-Representation and the Concept of Time in the Eighth and Seventh Centuries BC." In *Omero tremila anni dopo. Atti del congresso di Genova 6-8 luglio 2000*, ed. F. Montanari and P. Ascheri, 239–295. Rome.

Crotty, K. 1994. *The Poetics of Supplication*. Ithaca.

Cunliffe, R. J., and J. H. Dee. 2012. *A Lexicon of the Homeric Dialect*. Norman.

Dalby, A. 1995. "The *Iliad*, the *Odyssey* and their Audiences." *The Classical Quarterly* 45:269–279.

D'Arms, E. F., and K. Hulley. 1946. "The *Oresteia*—A Story in the *Odyssey*." *Transactions of the American Philological Association* 77: 207–213.

Danek, G. 1988. *Studien zur Dolonie*. Wien.

———. 1998. *Epos und Zitat: Studien zu den Quellen der Odyssee*. Wien.

Davies, J. K. 1984. "The Reliability of the Oral Tradition." In *The Trojan War: Its Historicity and Context*, ed. L. Foxhall and J. K. Davies, 87–100. Bristol.

Davies, J. K., and L. Foxhall, eds. *The Trojan War: Its Historicity and Context*. Bristol.

Davies, M. I. 1969. "Thoughts on the *Oresteia* before Aeschylus." *Bulletin de Correspondance Hellenique* 95:214–260.

———. 1988. *Epicorum Graecorum Fragmenta*. Göttingen.

Deichgräber, K. 1972. *Der letzte Gesang der Ilias*. Wiesbaden.

Dekker, A. F. 1965. *Ironie in de Odysee*. Leiden.

Deneen, P. J. 2003. *The Odyssey of Political Theory: The Politics of Departure*. Lanham.

Denniston, J. D. 1950. *Greek Particles*. Oxford.

Dentice Di Accadia, S. 2010. "La 'Prova' di Agamennone: Una Strategia Retorica Vincente." *RhM* 153:225–246.

———. 2012. *Omero e i suoi oratori: Tecniche eli persuasione nell' Iliade*. Berlin.

Di Benedetto, V. 1994. *Nel laboratorio di Omero*. Torino.

———. 1999. "Letteratura di secondo grado: l'*Odissea* fra riusi e ideologia del potere." *Prometheus* 25:193–225.

Dietrich, B.C. 1965. *Death, Fate, and the Gods*. London.

Dindorf, G. 1962. *Scholia Graeca in Homeri Odysseam*. Amsterdam.

Dodds, E. R. 1951. *The Greeks and the Irrational*. Berkeley.

Donlan, W. 1971. "Homer's Agamemnon." *Classical World* 65:109–115.

———. 1970. "Character Structure in Homer's *Iliad*." *The Journal of General Education* 21:259–269.

———. 1997. "The Homeric Economy." In *A New Companion to Homer*, ed. B. Powell and I. Morris, 649–667. Leiden.

Douglas, M. 2007. *Thinking in Circles: An Essay on Ring Composition*. New Haven.

Dowden, K. 2006. *Zeus*. New York.

Doyle, R. E. 1984. *'ATH: Its Use and Meaning*. New York.

Drews, R. 1995. *The End of the Bronze Age: Changes in Warfare and the Catastrophe ca. 1200 B.C.* Princeton.

Dué, C. 2001. "'Achilles' Goldern Amphora in Aeschines' 'Against Timarchus' and the Afterlife of Oral Tradition." *Classical Philology* 96:33–47.

———. 2002. *Homeric Variations on a Lament by Briseïs*. Lanham.

———. 2006. *The Captive Woman's Lament in Greek Tragedy*. Austin.

———. 2012. "Maneuvers in the Dark of Night: *Iliad* 10 in the Twenty-First Century." In *Homeric Contexts: Neoanalysis and the Interpretation of Oral Poetry*, ed. F. Montanari, A. Rengakos, and C. Tsagalis, 175–183. Berlin.

Dué, C., and M. Ebbott, eds. 2010. *Iliad 10 and the Poetics of Ambush*. Hellenic Studies 39. Washington, DC.

Dukat, Z. 1991. "Enjambement as a Criterion for Orality in Homeric and South Slavic Epic Poetry." *Oral Tradition* 6:303–315.

Dunkle, R. 1997. "Swift-Footed Achilles." *Classical World* 90:227–234.

Ebbott, M. 2003. *Imagining Illegitimacy in Classical Greek Literature*. Lanham, MD.

Eck, B. 2012. *La mort rouge: homicide, guerre et souillure en Grèce ancienne*. Paris.

Edmunds, L. 1997. "Myth in Homer." In *A New Companion to Homer*, ed. I. Morris and B. Powell, 415–441. Leiden.

Edwards, M. W. 1987. *Homer: Poet of the Iliad*. Baltimore.

———. 1988. "Homer and Oral Tradition: The Formula, Part II." *Oral Tradition* 3:11–60.

———. 1991. *The Iliad: A Commentary*. Vol. 5, *Books 17–20*. Cambridge.

———. 1992. "Homer and Oral Tradition: The Type-Scene." *Oral Tradition* 7:284–330.

———. 2005. "Homer's *Iliad*." In *A Companion to Ancient Epic*, ed. J. M. Foley, 302–314. Malden, MA.

Eisenberger, H. 1973. *Studien zur Odyssee*. Wiesbaden.

Elmer, D. 2013. *The Poetics of Consent: Collective Decision Making in the Iliad*. Baltimore.

Enos, R. 2002. "Literacy in Athens During the Archaic Period: A Prolegomenon to Rhetorical Invention." In *Perspectives on Rhetorical Invention*, ed. J. Atwill and J. Lauer, 176–191. Knoxville, TN.

Erbse, H. 1953. "Bemerkungen zu Homer und zu seinen Interpreten." *Glotta* 32:236–247.

———, ed. 1969–1988. *Scholia Graeca in Homeri Iliadem.* Vols. 1–7. Berlin.

———. 1972. *Beiträge zum Verständnis der Odyssee.* Berlin.

———. 2005. "Diomedes und Odysseus in Homers *Ilias.*" *Hermes* 133:3–8.

Felson, N., and L. Slatkin. 2004. "Gender and Homeric Epic." In Fowler 2004a: 91–114. Cambridge.

Fenik, B. 1964. *Iliad X and the Rhesos: The Myth.* Brussels.

———. 1968. *Typical Battle Scenes in the Iliad: Studies in the Narrative Techniques of Homeric Battle Description.* Wiesbaden.

———. 1974. *Studies in the Odyssey.* Wiesbaden.

Feydit, F. 1964. *David de Sassoun.* Paris.

Finkelberg, M. 1987. "The First Song of Demodocus." *Mnemosyne* 40:128–132.

———, ed. 2011. *The Homer Encyclopedia.* Vols 1–3. Malden, MA.

———. 2012. "Late Features of Speeches of the *Iliad.*" In *Relative Chronology in Early Greek Epic Poetry,* ed. D. T. Haug and Ø. Andersen, 80–95. Cambridge.

Finley, M. I. 1977. *The World of Odysseus.* London.

Finnegan, R. 2007. *The Oral and Beyond: Doing Things with Words in Africa.* Chicago.

Flower, M. 2008. *The Seer in Ancient Greece.* Berkeley.

Foley, H. P. 2001. *Female Acts in Greek Tragedy.* Princeton.

Foley, J. M. 1990. *Traditional Oral Epic.* Berkeley.

———. 1991. *Immanent Art: From Structure to Meaning in Traditional Oral Epic.* Bloomington, IN.

———. 1995. *The Singer of Tales in Performance.* Bloomington, IN.

———. 1999. *Homer's Traditional Art.* University Park, PA.

———. 2002. *How to Read an Oral Poem.* Chicago.

———, ed. and trans. 2004. *The Wedding of Mustajbey's Son Bećirbey.* Helsinki.

———. 2005a. "Fieldwork on Homer." In *Unbinding Proteus: New Directions in Oral Theory,* ed. M. C. Amodio, 15–42. Tempe

———, ed. 2005b. *A Companion to Ancient Epic.* Malden.

———. 2011. "Oral-Derived Texts." In *The Homer Encyclopedia,* ed. M. Finkelberg, 603. Malden, MA.

Fontenrose, J. 1978. *The Delphic Oracle: Its Responses and Operations with a Catalogue of Responses.* Berkeley.

Ford, A. 1992. *Homer: The Poetry of the Past.* Ithaca.

Fowler, R. 1983. Review of *Homer, Hesiod and the Hymns: Diachronic Development in Epic Diction,* by R. Janko. *Phoenix* 27:345–347.

———, ed. 2004a. *The Cambridge Companion to Homer.* Cambridge.

———. 2004b. "The Homeric Question." In *The Cambridge Companion to Homer,* ed. R. Fowler, 220–232. Cambridge.

Frame, D. 2009. *Hippota Nestor*. Hellenic Studies 37. Washington, DC.

Fränkel, H. 1955. *Wege und Formem*. Munich.

———. 1975. *Early Greek Poetry and Philosophy*. Oxford.

Fraser, J. 1898. *History of Lacedaemon*. New York.

Frazer, R. M. 1971. "Nestor's Generations, *Iliad* 1.250–52." *Glotta* 49:216–218.

Friedrich, R. 1987. "Heroic Man and Polymetis: Odysseus in the *Cyclopeia*." *Greek, Roman, and Byzantine Studies* 28:121–133.

———. 1991. "The Hubris of Odysseus." *The Journal of Hellenic Studies* 111:16–28.

———. 2007. *Formular Economy in Homer: The Poetics of the Breaches*. Stuttgart.

Friedrich, W. H. 1956. *Verwundung und Tod in der Ilias: Homerische Darstellungsweisen*. Göttingen.

Führer, R. 1991. "κερτομέω." In *Lexikon des frühgriechischen Epos*, ed. B. Snell, 14.1390–1391. Göttingen.

Gantz, T. 1993. *Early Greek Myth*. Baltimore.

Gagarin, M. 1987. "Morality in Homer." *Classical Philology* 82:285–306.

Garland, R. 2014. *Wandering Greeks: The Ancient Greek Diaspora from the Age of Homer to the Death of Alexander the Great*. Princeton.

Garner, R. Scott. 2011. *Traditional Elegy: The Interplay of Meter, Tradition, and Context in Early Greek Poetry*. Oxford.

Garvie, A. F. 1986. *Aeschylus Choephori*. Oxford.

Gasti, H. 1992. "Sophocles' 'Ajax': The Military 'Hubris'." *Quaderni Urbinati di Cultura Classica* 40:81–93.

Geiß, E. M. 1956. "ἀλκή." In *Lexikon des frühgriechischen Epos*, ed. H. Erbse et al., 3.494–499.

Genette, G. 1980. *Narrative Discourse: An Essay in Method*. Trans. J. E. Lewin. Ithaca.

Gill, C. 1990. "The Character-Personality Distinction." In *Characterization and Individuality in Greek Literature*, ed. C. Pelling, 1–31. Oxford.

Giordano, M. 1999. *La Supplica: Rituale, istituzione sociale e tema epico in Omero*. Naples.

Golden, M. 2003. "Childhood in Ancient Greece." In *Coming of Age in Ancient Greece: Images of Childhood from the Classical Past*, ed. J. Neils and J. H. Oakley, 13–30. New Haven.

Goldhill, S. 1990a. *The Poet's Voice*. Cambridge.

———. 1990b. "Supplication and Authorial Comment in the *Iliad*: *Iliad* Z 61–62." *Hermes* 118:373–376.

Goodwin, W. W. 1897. *Syntax of the Moods and Tenses of the Greek Verb*. Boston.

Gould, J. 1973. "Hiketeia." *The Journal of Hellenic Studies* 93:74–103.

———. 1990. "Dramatic Character and 'Human Intelligibility' in Greek Tragedy." *The Journal of Hellenic Studies* 77:247–254.

Graziosi, B. 2002. *Inventing Homer: The Early Reception of Epic*. Cambridge.

Graziosi, B., and J. Haubold. 2005. *The Resonance of Epic*. London.

———. 2010. *Homer: Iliad Book VI*. Cambridge.

Griffin, J. 1980. *Homer on Life and Death*. Oxford.

———. 1986. "Words and Speeches in Homer." *The Journal of Hellenic Studies* 56:36–57.

———. 1995. *Homer Iliad 9*. Oxford.

———. 2011. "Characterization." In *The Homer Encyclopedia*, ed. M. Finkelberg, 158–59. Malden.

Gulbekian, E. 1984. "The Attitude to War in 'The Epic of Sassoun.'" *Folklore* 95:105–112.

Hacikyan, A. J., et al., eds. *The Heritage of Armenian Literature*. Vol. 2. Detroit.

Hainsworth, B. 1993. *The Iliad: A Commentary*. Vol. 3, Books 9–12. Cambridge.

Hajnal, I. 2003. *Troia aus sprachwissenschaftlicher Sicht: Die Struktur einer Argumentation*. Innsbruck.

Halliwell, S. 1990. "Traditional Greek Conceptions of Character." In *Characterization and Individuality in Greek Literature,* ed. C. Pelling, 32–59. Oxford.

Halporn, J., M. Ostwald, and T. Rosenmeyer. 1963. *The Meters of Greek and Latin Verse*. 1st rev. ed. Norman, OK.

Hammer, D. 1997. "'Who Shall Really Obey?' Authority and Politics in the *Iliad*." *Phoenix* 51:1–24.

———. 2002. *The Iliad as Politics: The Performance of Political Thought*. Oklahoma.

Haslam, M. 1997. "Homeric Papyri and the Transmission of the Text." In *A New Companion to Homer*, ed. I. Morris and B. Powell, 55–100. Leiden.

Haubold, J. 2000. *Homer's People*. Cambridge.

Haug, D. T., and Ø Andersen, eds. 2012. *Relative Chronology in Early Greek Epic Poetry*. Cambridge.

Heath, J. 2001. "Telemachus ΠΕΠΝΥΜΕΝΟΣ: Growing into an Epithet." *Mnemosyne* 54:129–157.

Heiden B. 1991. "Shifting Contexts in the *Iliad*." *Eranos* 89:1–12.

Hernández, P. N. 2002. "Odysseus, Agamemnon and Apollo." *Classical Journal*, 319–334.

Herzfeld, M. 1985a. *The Poetics of Manhood*. Princeton.

———. 1985b. "Interpretation from Within: Metatext for a Cretan Quarrel." In *The Text and its Margins*, ed. M. Alexiou and V. Lambropoulos, 197–218. New York.

Heubeck, A. 1974. *Die homerische Frage: Erträge der Forschung*. Darmstadt.

———. 1981. "Zwei homerische πεῖραι." *Ziva Antika* 31:73–83.

Huebeck, A., and A. Hoekstra. 1989. *A Commentary on Homer's Odyssey*. Vol. 2, Books 9–16. Oxford.

Huebeck, A., A. Hoekstra, S. West, and J. B. Hainsworth. 1988. *A Commentary on Homer's Odyssey*. Vol. 1, *Books 1-8*. Oxford.

Higbie, C. 1990. *Measure and Music: Enjambement and Sentence Structure in the Iliad*. Oxford.

———. 1995. *Heroes Names, Homeric Identities*. New York.

Hinckley, L. 1986. "Patroclus' Funeral Games and Homer's Portrayal." *Classical Journal* 81:209–221.

Hitch, S. 2009. *King of Sacrifice: Ritual and Royal Authority in the Iliad*. Hellenic Studies 25. Washington, DC.

Holoka, J. 1983. "'Looking Darkly' ΥΠΟΔΡΑ ΙΔΩΝ: Reflections on Status and Decorum in Homer." *Transactions of the American Philological Association* 113:1–16.

Hölscher, U. 1967. "Die Atridensage in der *Odyssee*." In *Festschrift für Richard Alewyn*, ed. H. Singer and B. von Wiese, 392–412. Cologne.

———. 2000. *Die Odyssee: Epos zwischen Märchen und Roman*. Munich.

Honko, L. 1998. *Textualising the Siri Epic*. Helsinki.

Hooker, J. T. 1986. "A Residual Problem in *Iliad* 24." *Classical Quarterly* 36:32–37.

Hubbard, T. 2011. "Sexuality." In *The Homer Encyclopedia*, ed. M. Finkelberg, 789–790. Malden.

Hurwit, J. M. 1993. "Art, Poetry, and the *Polis* in the Age of Homer." In *From Pasture to Polis: Art in the Age of Homer*, ed. S. Langdon, 14–42. Columbia, MO.

Iser, W. 1974. *The Implied Reader: Patterns of Communication in Prose Fiction from Bunyan to Beckett*. Baltimore.

Janko, R. 1982. *Homer, Hesiod and the Hymns: Diachronic Development in Epic Diction*. Cambridge.

———. 1990. "The *Iliad* and its Editors: Dictation and Redaction." *Classical Antiquity* 9:326–334.

———. 1994. *The Iliad: A Commentary*. Vol. 4, *Books 13-16*. Cambridge.

———. 1998. "The Homeric Poems as Oral Dictated Texts." *The Classical Quarterly* 48:135–167.

———. 2012. "Πρῶτον τε καὶ Ὕστατον Αἰὲν Ἀείδειν: Relative Chronology and the Literary History of Early Greek Epos." In *Relative Chronology in Early Greek Poetry*, ed. Ø. Andersen and D. T. Haug, 20–43. Cambridge.

Jansen, W. H. 1967. Review of *David of Sassoun: The Armenian Folk Epic in Four Cycles*, ed. and trans. A. Shalian. *Journal of American Folklore* 80:94–96.

Jensen, M. S. 1980. *The Homeric Question and the Oral-Formulaic Theory*. Copenhagen.

———. 2011. *Writing Homer: A Study Based on Results from Modern Fieldwork*. Copenhagen.

Jones, B. N. 2010. "Relative Chronology within (an) Oral Tradition." *Classical Journal* 105:289–319.

Jones, A., and F. E. Gray. 1972. "Hexameter Patterns, Statistical Inference, and the Homeric Question: An Analysis of the LaRoche Data." *Transactions of the American Philological Association* 103: 187-209.

Jones, P.V. 1989. "*Iliad* 24.649: Another Solution." *The Classical Quarterly* 1989:247–250.

Jong, I. de. 1997. "Between Word and Deed: Hidden Thought in the *Odyssey*." In *Modern Critical Theory and Classical Literature*, ed. I. de Jong, 27–50. Leiden.

———. 1999. *Homer: Critical Assessments*. Vols. 1–4. New York.

———. 2001. *A Narratological Commentary on the Odyssey*. Cambridge.

———. 2005. "Convention versus Realism in the Homeric Epics." *Mnemosyne* 58:1–22.

———. 2007a. "Introduction: Narratological Theory on Time." In *Time in Ancient Greek Literature*, ed. I. de Jong and R. Nünlist. Leiden.

———. 2007b. "Homer." In *Time in Ancient Greek Literature*, ed. I. de Jong and R. Nünlist, 17–38. Leiden.

———, ed. 2012. *Homer: Iliad Book XXII*. Cambridge.

Kahane, A. 2005. *Diachronic Dialogues: Authority and Continuity in Homer and the Homeric Tradition*. Lanham.

Kajava, M. 2004. "Hestia Hearth, Goddess, and Cult." *Harvard Studies in Classical Philology* 102:1–20.

Kakridis, I. 1949. *Homeric Researches*. Lund.

———. 1971. *Homer Revisited*. Lund.

Kanavou, N. 2015. *The Names of Homeric Heroes: Problems and Interpretations*. Berlin.

Karanika, A. 2014. *Voice at Work: Women, Performance, and Labor in Ancient Greece*. Baltimore.

Kelly, A. 2006. "Neoanalysis and the Nestorbedrängnis: a Test Case." *Hermes* 134:1–25.

———. 2007a. *A Referential Commentary and Lexicon to Homer, Iliad VIII*. Oxford.

———. 2007b. "How to End an Orally-Derived Epic Poem." *Transactions of the American Philological Association* 137:371–402.

———. 2012. "The Mourning of Thetis: 'Allusion' and the Future in the *Iliad*." In *Homeric Contexts: Neoanalysis and the Interpretation of Oral Poetry*, ed. F. Montanari, A. Rengakos, and C. Tsagalis, 221–265. Berlin.

———. 2014. "Homeric Battle Narrative and the Ancient Near East." In *Defining Greek Narrative*, ed. D. L. Cairns and R. Scodel, 29–54. Edinburgh.

Kennedy, G. 1963. *The Art of Persuasion in Ancient Greece*. Princeton.

Kim, J. 2000. *The Pity of Achilles: Oral Style and the Unity of the Iliad*. Lanham.

King, K. 1987. *Achilles: The Paradigms of the War Hero from Homer to the Middle Ages*. Berkeley.

Kirk, G. S. 1985. *The Iliad: A Commentary*. Vol. 1, *Books 1-4*. Cambridge.

———. 1990. *The Iliad: A Commentary*. Vol. 2, *Books 5-8*. Cambridge.

Klinger, F., and Klaus B. 1964. *Studien zur griechischen und römischen Literatur*. Zürich.

Knoepfler, D. 1993. *Les imagiers de l'Orestie: mille ans d'art antique autour d'un mythe grec*. Zürich.

Kremmydas, C. 2013. "The Discourse of Deception and Characterization in Attic Oratory." *Greek, Roman, and Byzantine Studies* 53:51–89.

Kristiansen, K., and T. Larsson. 2005. *The Rise of Bronze Age Society*. Cambridge.

Kullman, W. 1960. *Die Quellen der Ilias*. Wiesbaden.

———. 1984. "Oral Poetry Theory and Neoanalysis in Homeric Research." *Greek, Roman, and Byzantine Studies* 25:307–324.

———. 2015. "Motif and Source Research: Neoanalysis, Homer, and Cyclic Epic." In *The Greek Epic Cycle and its Ancient Reception: A Companion*, ed. M. Fantuzzi and C. Tsagalis, 108–125. Cambridge.

Lada-Richards, I. 2002. "The Subjectivity of Greek Performance." In *Greek and Roman Actors: Aspects of an Ancient Profession*, ed. P. Easterling and E. Hall, 395–418. Cambridge.

Lamberton, R., and J. Kearney. 1992. *Homer's Ancient Readers: The Hermeneutics of Greek Epic's Earliest Exegetes*. Princeton.

Lang, A. 1906. *Homer and His Age*. New York.

Lang, M. 1983. "Reverberation and Mythology in the *Iliad*." In *Approaches to Homer*, ed. C. Rubino and C. Shelmerdine, 140-164. Austin.

Langdon, S. 1993. *From Pasture to Polis: Art in the Age of Homer*. Columbia, MO.

Lardinois, A. P. M. H. 2000. "Characterization through Ginomai in Homer's *Iliad*." *Mnemosyne* 53:641–661.

———, and L. McLure, eds. 2001. *Making Silence Speak: Women's Voices in Greek Literature and Society*. Princeton.

Latacz, J. 1996. *Homer: His Art and His World*. Trans. J. P. Holoka. Ann Arbor, MI.

———, ed. 2000a. *Homers Ilias: Gesamtkommentar*. Vol. 1, *Book 1*. Berlin.

———, ed. 2000b. *Homers Ilias: Gesamtkommentar*. Vol. 2, *Book 2*. Berlin.

Lateiner, D. 2004. "The *Iliad*: An Unpredictable Classic." In Fowler 2004a: ed. 11–30. Cambridge.

Leaf, W. 1902a. *A Companion to the Iliad*. Vol. 1, *Books 1-12*. New York.

———. 1902b. *A Companion to the Iliad*. Vol. 2, *Books 13-24*. New York.

Ledbetter, G. M. 1993. "Achilles' Self-Address: *Iliad* 16.7–19." *American Journal of Philology* 114:481–491.

Lentini, G. 2006. *Il "padre di Telemaco": Odisseo tra Iliade e Odissea*. Pisa.

Lesky, A. 1961. *Göttliche und menschliche Motivation im homerischen Epos*. Heidelberg.

————. 2001. "Divine and Human Causation in Homeric Epic." Trans. A. Holford-Strevans. In *Oxford Readings in Homer's Iliad*, ed. D. L. Cairns, 170–202. Oxford.

Létoublon, F. 1980. "Le Vocabulaire de la Supplication en Grec: Performatif et dérivation délocutive." *Lingua* 52:325–336.

Lloyd-Jones, H. 1971. *The Justice of Zeus*. Berkeley.

Lohmann, D. 1970. *Die Komposition der Reden in der Ilias*. Berlin.

Lord, A. B. 1953. "Homer's Originality: Oral Dictated Texts." *Oral Tradition* 16:222–239.

————. 1956. "Avdo Međedović, Guslar." *Journal of American Folklore* 69:320–330.

————. 1960. *The Singer of Tales*. Cambridge. 2nd ed. 2000, edited by S. Mitchell and G. Nagy.

————, trans. 1974. *Serbo-Croatian Heroic Songs Collected by Milman Parry: The Wedding of Smailagić Meho*. Vol. 3. Cambridge.

————. 1990. "Patterns of Lives of the Patriarchs from Abraham to Samson and Samuel." In *Text and Tradition*, ed. S. Niditch, 7–18. Atlanta.

————. 1991. *Epic Singers and Oral Tradition*. Ithaca.

————. 1993. *The Scepter and the Spear: Studies on Forms of Repetition in the Homeric Poems*. Lanham.

————. 1995. *The Singer Resumes the Tale*. Ithaca.

Louden, B. 1999. *The Odyssey: Structure, Narration, and Meaning*. Baltimore.

————. 2006. *The Iliad: Structure, Myth, and Meaning*. Baltimore.

Lowenstam, S. 1981. *The Death of Patroklos: A Study in Typology*. Hain.

————. 1993. *The Scepter and the Spear: Studies on Forms of Repetition in the Homeric Poems*. Lanham.

————. 1997. "Talking Vases: The Relationship between the Homeric Poems and Archaic Representations of Epic Myth." *Transactions of the American Philological Association* 127:21–76.

Mackie, H. 1996. *Talking Trojan: Speech and Community in the Iliad*. Lanham.

Malkin, I. 1998. *The Returns of Odysseus: Colonization and Ethnicity*. Berkeley.

————. 2001. *A Small Greek World: Networks in the Ancient Mediterranean*. Oxford.

Marg, W. 1956. "Das erste Leid des Demodokos." In *Navicula Chiloniensis: Festschrift für F. Jacoby*, ed. W. Marg, 16–29. Leiden.

Marks, J. 2002. "The Junction between the *Kypria* and the *Iliad*." *Phoenix* 56:1–24.

————. 2003. "Alternative Odysseys: The Case of Thoas and Odysseus." *Transactions of the Philological Association* 133:2–18.

————. 2005. "The Ongoing *Neikos*: Thersites, Odysseus, and Achilleus." *American Journal of Philology* 126:1–31.

————. 2008. *Zeus in the Odyssey*. Hellenic Studies 31. Washington, DC.

Markwald, G. 1991. "κλυεῖν, κλύω." In *Lexikon des frühgriechischen Epos*, ed. B. Snell, 14.1456–459. Göttingen.

Maronitis, D. N. 2004. *Homeric Megathemes*. Trans. D. Connolly. Lanham.

Marquardt, P. 1992. "Clytemnestra: A Felicitous Spelling in the *Odyssey*." *Arion* 25:241–254.

Martin, R. 1989. *The Language of Heroes: Speech and Performance in the Iliad*. Ithaca.

———. 1993. "Telemachus and the Last Hero Song." *Colby Quarterly* 29:1–19.

———. 2013. Review of *Homeric Contexts: Neoanalysis and the Interpretation of Oral Poetry*, ed. F. Montanari, A. Rengakos, and C. Tsagalis. *Bryn Mawr Classical Review* 09.21.2013.

———. 2015. "Festivals, Symposia, and the Performance of Greek Poetry." In *A Companion to Ancient Aesthetics*, ed. P. Destrée and P. Murray, 17–30. Hoboken, NJ.

May, J. M. 1988. *Trials of Character: The Eloquence of Ciceronian Ethos*. Chapel Hill, NC.

Mazon, P. 1948. *Introduction à l'Iliad*. Paris.

McClure, L. 2013. *Courtesans at Table: Gender and Greek Literary Culture in Athenaeus*. New York.

McGlew, J. F. 1989. "Royal Power and the Achaian Assembly at *Iliad* 2.84–393." *Classical Antiquity* 8:283–295.

Merkelbach, R. 1951. *Untersuchungen zur Odyssee*. Munich.

Minchin, E. 2005. "Homer on Biographical Memory: The Case of Nestor." In *Approaches to Homer: Ancient and Modern*, ed. R. J. Rabel, 55–72. Swansea.

———. 2007. *Homeric Voices*. Oxford.

———. 2011a. "'Themes' and 'Mental Moulds': Roger Schank, Malcolm Willcock and the Creation of Character in Homer." *Classical Quarterly* 61:323–343.

———. 2011b. "Ring Composition." In *The Homer Encyclopedia*, ed. M. Finkelberg, 751. Malden, MA.

Monro, D. B. 1884. *Homer: Iliad. Books 1–12*. Oxford.

———. 1891. *A Grammar of the Homeric Dialect*. Oxford.

Monsacré, H. 1984. *Les Larmes d'Achille: Le héros, la femme et la souffrance dans la poésie d'Homère*. Paris.

Montanari, F., and P. Ascheri. 2002. *Omero tremila anni dopo. Atti del congresso di Genova 6–8 luglio 2000*. Rome.

Montanari, F., A. Rengakos, and C. Tsagalis, eds. 2012. *Homeric Contexts: Neoanalysis and the Interpretation of Oral Poetry*. Berlin.

———. 2009. *Brill's Companion to Hesiod*. Leiden.

Montiglio, S. 2011. *From Villain to Hero: Odysseus in Ancient Thought*. Ann Arbor, MI.

Morris, I. 1986. "*The Use and Abuse of Homer*." *Classical Antiquity* 5:81–138.

————, and B. Powell. 1997. *A New Companion to Homer*. Leiden.

Morris, S. 1997. "Homer and the Near East." In *A New Companion to Homer*, ed. I. Morris and B. Powell, 599–623. Cambridge.

Morrison, J. V. 1992a. *Homeric Misdirection: False Predictions in the Iliad*. Ann Arbor, MI.

————. 1992b. "Alternatives to the Epic Tradition: Homer's Challenges in the *Iliad*." *Transactions of the American Philological Association* 122:61–71.

Moulton, C. 1974. "The End of the Odyssey." *Greek, Roman, and Byzantine Studies* 15:153–169.

————. 1977. *Similes in the Homeric Poems*. Göttingen.

Mueller, M. 2009. *The Iliad*. Bristol.

Muellner, L. C. 1976. *The Meaning of Homeric EYXOMAI through its Formulas*. Innsbruck.

————. 1996. *The Anger of Achilles: Menis in Greek Epic*. Ithaca.

————. 2012. "Grieving Achilles." In *Homeric Contexts: Neoanalysis and the Interpretation of Oral Poetry*, ed. F. Montanari, A. Rengakos, and C. Tsagalis, 197–212. Berlin.

Murko, M. 1928. "L'Etat actuel de la poésie populaire épique yougoslave." *Le Monde Slave* 5:321–351.

Murray, G. 1934. *The Rise of the Greek Epic*. Oxford.

Murray, O. 1978. *Early Greece*. London.

Murray, P. 1997. *Plato on Poetry*. Cambridge.

Nagler, M. 1967. "Towards a Generative View of Oral Formula." *Transactions of the American Philological Association* 98:296–311.

Nagy, G. 1979. *The Best of the Achaians*. Baltimore.

————. 1974. *Comparative Studies in Greek and Indic Meter*. Cambridge, MA.

————. 1990a. *Greek Mythology and Poetics*. Ithaca.

————. 1990b. *Pindar's Homer: The Lyric Possession of an Epic Past*. Baltimore.

————. 1992. *Greek Mythology and Poetics*. Ithaca.

————. 1996a. *Poetry as Performance*. Cambridge.

————. 1996b. *Homeric Questions*. Austin.

————. 2000. "Reading Greek Poetry Aloud: Evidence from the Bacchylides Papyri." *Quaderni Urbinati di Cultura Classica* 64:7–28.

————. 2002. *Plato's Rhapsody and Homer's Music: The Poetics of the Panathenaic Festival in Classical Athens*. Cambridge, MA.

————. 2004. *Homer's Text and Language*. Champaign, IL.

Naiden, F. 2006. *Ancient Supplication*. Oxford.

Neschke, A. 1986. "L'Orestie de Stésichore et la tradition littéraire du mythe des Atrides avant Eschyle." *L'Antiquité Classique* 55:283–301.

Neumann, G. 1991. "Die homerischen Personennamen: Ihre Position im Rahmen der Entwicklung des griechischen Namensschatzes." In *Zweihundert Jahre Homerforschung: Rückblick und Ausblick*, ed. J. Latacz, 311–328. Stuttgart.

Newton, R. M. 2005. "The Ciconians Revisited." In *Approaches to Homer: Ancient and Modern*, ed. R. J. Rabel, 135–146. Swansea.

Niditch, S. 2000. *A Prelude to Biblical Folklore*. Urbana.

Nilsson, M. P. 1940. *Greek Folk Religion*. Philadelphia.

Nordheider, H. W. 1989. "ἱστίη." In *Lexikon des frühgriechischen Epos*, ed. B. Snell, 13.1250.

———. 2008. "τηλύγετος." In *Lexikon des frühgriechischen Epos*, ed. B. Snell, 22.467–469.

Notopoulos, J. A. 1964a. "Studies in Early Greek Oral Poetry." *Harvard Studies in Classical Philology* 68:1–77.

———. 1964b. "Continuity and Interconnection in Homeric Oral Composition." *Transactions of the American Philological Association* 82:81–101.

Nünlist, R. 2009. *The Ancient Critics at Work*. Cambridge.

Ogden, D. 1996. *Greek Bastardy: In The Classical and Hellenistic Periods*. Oxford.

Olrik, A. 1909. "Epic Laws of Folk Narrative." In *The Study of Folklore*, ed. A. Dundas, trans. J. P. Steager, 129–141. Englewood Cliffs, NJ. Reprinted 1965.

Olson, S. D. 1990. "The Stories of Agamemnon in Homer's *Odyssey*." *Transactions of the American Philological Association* 120:57–71.

———. 1995. *Blood and Iron: Stories and Storytelling in Homer's Odyssey*. Leiden.

———. 2012. *The Homeric Hymn to Aphrodite and Related Texts: Text, Translation and Commentary*. Berlin.

O'Brian, J. V. 1993. *The Transformation of Hera: A Study of Ritual, Hero, and the Goddess in the Iliad*. Lanham.

Osborne, R. 2004. "Homer's Society." In Fowler 2004a: 206–219. Cambridge.

Palmer, L. R. 1963. *The Interpretation of Mycenaean Greek Texts*. Oxford.

Papadogiannaki, E. 2009. "Interjectional Phrases in the *Iliad* and in the *Odyssey*: Their Significance and Function." *Quaderni Urbinati di Cultura Classica* 93:121–135.

Paraskevaides, H. A. 1984. *The Use of Synonyms in Homeric Formulaic Diction*. Amsterdam.

Parker, R. 1983. *Miasma: Pollution and Purification in Early Greek Religion*. Oxford.

Parry, A. 1966. "Have We Homer's *Iliad*?" *Yale Classical Studies* 20:177–216.

———, ed. 1971. *The Making of Homeric Verse: The Collected Papers of Milman Parry*. Oxford.

———, ed. 1972. "Language and Characterization in Homer." *Harvard Studies in Classical Philology* 76:1–22.

———. 1973. *Blameless Aegisthus: A Study of* AMYMΩN *and Other Homeric Epithets.* Leiden.

Patera, I. 2012. *Offrir en Grèce ancienne: Gestes et Contextes.* Stuttgart.

Patzek, B. 1992. *Homer und Mykene: Mündliche Dichtung und Geschichtsschreibung.* Munich.

Peabody, B. 1975. *The Winged Word.* Albany, NY.

Pedro, R. de. 2000. "Equivalence: Formal and Dynamic." In *Encyclopedea of Literary Translation into English,* ed. O. Classe, 414-15.

Pelling, C. 1990. *Characterization and Individuality in Greek Literature.* Oxford.

Perrault, C. 1692–1697. *Parallèle des anciens et des modernes.* Vols. 1–4. Geneva.

Perrault, R. 1983. *Miasma: Pollution and Purification in Early Greek Religion.* Oxford.

Petropoulos, I. 2012. "The Telemachy and the Cyclic *Nostoi.*" In *Homeric Contexts: Neoanalysis and the Interpretation of Oral Poetry,* ed. F. Montanari, A. Rengakos, and C. Tsagalis, 291–308. Berlin.

Polinskaya, I. 2011. "Ajax the Lesser." In *The Homer Encyclopedia,* ed. M. Finkelberg, 26–27. Malden, MA.

Pomeroy, S. B. 2011. *Goddesses, Whores, Wives, and Slaves: Women in Classical Antiquity.* New York.

Pope, A. 1711. *An Essay on Criticism.* London.

Porter, A. E. 2011. "'Stricken to Silence': Authoritative Response, Homeric Irony, and the Peril of a Missed Language Cue." *Oral Tradition* 26:493–520.

———. 2014. "Laomedon's Reign: *Olympiomachia,* Poseidon's Wall, and the Earlier Trojan War in Homer's *Iliad.*" *Greek, Roman, and Byzantine Studies* 54:507–526.

———. 2017. "Human Fault and "[Harmful] Delusion" (ἄτη) in Homer." *Phoenix* 71:1-20.

Porter, J. I. 1992. "Hermeneutic Lines and Circles: Artistarchus and Crates on the Exegesis of Homer." In *Homer's Ancient Readers: The Hermeneutics of Greek Epic's Earliest Exegetes,* ed. R. Lamberton and J. J. Keaney, 67–114. Princeton.

Postlethwaite, N. 2000. *Homer's Iliad: A Commentary on the Translation of Richmond Lattimore.* Exeter.

Powell, B. 1970. "Narrative Patterns in the Homeric Tale of Menelaos." *Transactions of the American Philological Association* 101: 419–431.

———. 1997. "Homer and Writing." In *A New Companion to Homer,* ed. I. Morris and B. Powell, 3–32. Leiden.

———. 2000. "Text, Orality, Literacy, Tradition, Dictation, Education, and Other Paradigms of Explication in Greek Literary Studies." *Oral Tradition* 15:96–125.

———. 2007. *Homer.* Malden, MA.

———, trans. 2014. *The Iliad*. Oxford.

Prag, A. J. N. 1985. *The Oresteia: Iconographic and Narrative Tradition*. Chicago.

Raaflaub, K. 1997. "Homeric Society." In *A New Companion to Homer*, ed. I. Morris and B. Powell, 624–648. Leiden.

Rabel, R. J. 1990. "Apollo as a Model for Achilles in the *Iliad*." *American Journal of Philology* 111:429–440.

———. 1997. *Plot and Point of View in the Iliad*. Ann Arbor, MI.

Race, W. H. 1982. *The Classical Priamel from Homer to Boethius*. Leiden.

———. 1993. "First Appearances in the *Odyssey*." *Transactions of the American Philological Association* 123:79–107.

Radt, S. 1964. "ἄλλοθεν." *Lexikon des frühgriechischen Epos* 4.543–544.

Raeburn, D., and O. Thomas. 2011. *The Agamemnon of Aeschylus*. Oxford.

Ranke, F. 1881. *Die Doloneia*. Leipzig.

Rawson, B., ed. 2011. *A Companion to Families in the Greek and Roman Worlds*. Malden, MA.

Ready, J. L. 2011. *Character, Narrator, and Simile in the Iliad*. Cambridge.

———. 2015. "The Textualization of Homeric Epic by Means of Dictation." *Transactions of the American Philological Association* 145:1–75.

Redfield, J. 1975. *Nature and Culture in the Iliad*. Chicago.

———. 1979. "The Proem of the *Iliad*." *Classical Philology* 74:95–110.

Reece, S. 1993. *The Stranger's Welcome*. Ann Arbor, MI.

Reyes, G. M. 2002. "Sources of Persuasion in the *Iliad*." *Rhetoric Review* 21:22-39.

Reinhardt, K. 1948. *Von Werken und Formen: Vorträge und Aufsätze*. Göttingen.

———. 1961. *Die Ilias Und Ihr Dicthter*. Gottingen.

Richardson, N. 1993. *The Iliad: A Commentary*. Vol. 6, *Books 21–24*. Cambridge.

Richardson, S. D. 1990. *The Homeric Narrator*. Nashville, TN.

———. 2006. "The Devious Narrator of the *Odyssey*." *The Classical Journal* 101:337–359.

Rijksbaron, A. 2007. *Ion Or: On the Iliad*. Leiden.

Rinon, Y. 2006. "*Mise en abyme* and Tragic Signification in the *Odyssey*: The Three Songs of Demodocus." *Mnemosyne* 59:208–225.

Roisman, H. 2005. "Nestor the Good Counsellor." *Classical Quarterly* 55:17–38.

Rollinger, R. 2015. "Old Battles, New Horizons: The Ancient Near East and the Homeric Epics." In *Mesopotamia in the Ancient World: Impact, Continuities, Parallels*, ed. R. Rollinger and E. van Dongen, 5–32. Münster.

Roochnik, D. 1990. "Homeric Speech Acts: Words and Deeds in the Epics." *The Classical Journal* 85:289–299.

Rose, P. W. 1988. "Thersites and the Plural Voices of Homer." *Arethusa*. 21:5–25.

Russell, J. 2004. *Armenian and Iranian Studies*. Cambridge.

Russso, J. 1997. "The Formula." In *A New Companion to Homer*, ed. B. Powell and I. Morris, 238–260. Leiden.

———. 2011. "Formula." In *The Homer Encyclopedia*, ed. M. Finkelberg, 296–298. Malden, MA.

Russo, J., M. Fernandez-Galiano, and A. Heubeck. 1992. *A Commentary on Homer's Odyssey*. Vol. 3, *Books 17–24*. Oxford.

Rutherford, I. 2009. "Hesiod and the Literary Traditions of the Near East." In *Brill's Companion to Hesiod*, ed. F. Montanari, A. Rengakos, and C. Tsagalis, 9–35. Leiden.

Rüter, K. 1969. *Odysseeinterpretationen: Untersuchungen zum ersten Buch und zur Phaiakis*. Göttingen.

Ruzé, F. 1997. *Délibération et Pouvoir dans la cité grecque: De Nestor à Socrate*. Paris.

Sacks, R. 1987. *The Traditional Phrase in Homer*. Leiden.

Saïd, S. 2011. *Homer and the Odyssey*. Trans. R. Webb. Oxford.

Sale, W. M. 1993. "Homer and Roland: The Shared Formular Technique, Part I." *Oral Tradition* 8:87–142.

Sammons, B. 2009. "Agamemnon and His Audiences." *Greek, Roman, and Byzantine Studies* 49:159–185.

Schadewaldt, W. 1958. "Der Prolog der *Odyssee*." *Harvard Studies in Classical Philology* 63:15–32.

———. 1965. *Von Homers Welt und Werk: Ausätz und Auslegungen zur Homerischen Frage*. Stuttgart.

———. 1966. *Iliasstudien*. Darmstadt.

Scheidel, W. 2011. "Monogamy and Polygyny." In *A Companion to Families in the Greek and Roman Worlds*, B. Rawson, 108–115. Malden, MA.

Schein, S. 1984. *The Mortal Hero*. Berkeley.

———. 2016. *Homeric Epic and Its Reception: Interpretive Essays*. Oxford.

Schischwani, S. 1993. "Messenien und Sparta in der Odyssee." In *Σπονδές στον Όμηρο, Πρακτικά του σ' Συνεδρίου για την Οδύσσεια*, ed. I. Kakridis, 257–268. Ithaca.

Schmidt, J.-U. 2002. "Die 'Probe' des Achaierheeres als Spiegel der besonderen Intention des Iliasdichters." *Philologus* 146:3–21.

Schmidt, M. 1984. "ἐκπρεπής." In *Lexikon des frühgriechischen Epos*, ed. B. Snell, 11.506.

———. 1999. "ὅμαδος." In *Lexikon des frühgriechischen Epos*, ed. B. Snell, 17.673–674.

Schnapp-Gourbeillon, A. 1982. "Le Lion et le loup: Diomédie et Dolonie dans l'*Iliade*." *Quaderni di Storia* 8:45–77.

Schofield, M. 1986. "Eubolia in the *Iliad*." *Classical Quarterly* 36:6–31.

Schwinge, E. R. 1993. *Die Odyssee—nach den Odysseen: Betrachtungen zu ihrer individuellen Physiognomie*. Göttingen.

Scodel, R. 1989. "The Word of Achilles." *Phoinix* 30:314–327.

———. 1997. "Pseudo-Intimacy and the Prior Knowledge of Homeric Audience." *Aretheusa* 30:201–219.

———. 2002. *Listening to Homer: Tradition, Narrative, and Audience.* Ann Arbor, MI.

———. 2005. "Odysseus' Dog and the Productive Household." *Hermes* 133:401–408.

———. 2008. "Zielinski's Law Reconsidered." *Transactions of the American Philological Association* 138:107–125.

Scodel, R., and C. Whitman. 1981. "Sequence and Simultaneity in *Iliad* N, Ξ, and O." *Harvard Studies in Classical Philology* 85:1–15.

Scott, W. C. 2009. *The Artistry of the Homeric Simile.* Lebanon, NH.

Segal, C. 1983. "Kleos and its Ironies in the *Odyssey.*" *Antiquite Classique* 52:22–47.

———. 1992. "Bard and Audience in Homer." In *Homer's Ancient Readers: The Hermeneutics of Greek Epic's Earliest Exegetes,* ed. R. Lamberton and J. J. Keaney, 3–29. Princeton.

———. 1994. *Singers, Heroes, and Gods in the Odyssey.* Ithaca.

Seibel, A. 1995. "Widerstreit und Ergänzung: Thersites und Odysseus als Rivalisierende Demagogen in der *Ilias* (B 190–264)." *Hermes* 123:385–397.

Seiler, H. 1954. "Homerisch ἀάομαι und ἄτη." In *Sprachgeschichte und Wortbedeutung: Festschrift Albert Debrunner,* 409–417. Bern.

Shalian, A. K., ed. and trans. 1964. *David of Sassoun: The Armenian Folk Epic in Four Cycles.* Athens, Ohio.

Shewan, A. 1911. *The Lay of Dolon.* London.

Shipp, G. 1972. *Studies in the Language of Homer.* Cambridge.

Shive, D. M. 1987. *Naming Achilles.* Oxford.

Simpson, R. H., and J. F. Lazenby. 1970. *The Catologue of Ships in Homer's Iliad.* Oxford.

Slatkin, L. 1986. "The Wrath of Thetis." *Transactions of the American Philological Association* 116:1–24.

———. 1991. *The Power of Thetis.* Berkeley.

Smyth, H. W. 1920. *Greek Grammar.* Cambridge, MA.

Snell, B. 1930. "Das Bewusstsein von eigenen Entscheidungen in frühen Griechentum." *Philologus Supplement.* 85:142–158.

———. 1953. *The Discovery of the Mind.* New York.

Souza, P. de. 1999. *Piracy in the Ancient World.* Cambridge.

Stanford, W. B. 1952. "The Homeric Etymology of the Name of Odysseus." *Classical Philology* 47:209–213.

———. 1958. *The Odyssey of Homer.* Vol. 2, Books 13–24. New York.

———. 1963. *The Ulysses Theme.* Ann Arbor, MI.

Stanley, K. 1993. *The Shield of Homer: Narrative Structure in the Iliad.* Princeton.

Strasburger, H. 1982. *Studien zur alten Geschichte.* Hildersheim.

Stuurman, A. 2004. "The Voice of Thersites: Reflections on the Origins of the Idea of Equality." *Journal of the History of Ideas* 65:171–189.

Sullivan, S. 1988. *Psychological Activity in Homer: A Study of Phrēn.* Ottawa.

Surmellian, L. 1964. *Daredevils of Sassoun.* Denver.

Suzuki, M. 1974. *Metamorphoses of Helen: Authority, Difference, and Epic.* Ithaca.

Talbert, R. J. A. 1985. *Atlas of Classical History.* New York.

Taplin, O. 1990. "Constructing Agamemnon's Role in the *Iliad.*" In *Characterization and Individuality in Greek Literature,* ed. C. Pelling, 60–82. Oxford.

———. 1992. *Homeric Soundings: The Shaping of the Iliad.* Oxford.

Teffeteller, A. 1990. "Αὐτὸς ἀπούρας, *Il.* 1.356." *The Classical Quarterly* 40:16–20.

———. 2003. "Homeric Excuses." *The Classical Quarterly* 53:15–31.

Thalmann, W. G. 1998. *The Swineherd and the Bow: Representations of Class in the "Odyssey."* Ithaca.

Thomas, H., and F. H. Stubbings. 1962. "Lands and People in Homer." In *A Companion to Homer,* ed. A. J. Wace and F. H. Stubbings, 283–310. London.

Thornton, A. 1984. *Homer's Iliad: Its Composition and Motif of Supplication.* Göttingen.

Traill, D. A. 1990. "Unfair to Hector?" *Classical Philology* 85:299–303.

Tsagalis, C. 2004. *Epic Grief: Personal Laments in Homer's Iliad.* Berlin.

———. 2008a. *The Oral Palimpsest: Exploring Intertextuality in the Homeric Epics.* Cambridge, MA.

———. 2008b. Review of *A Referential Commentary and Lexicon to Homer, Iliad VIII,* by A. Kelly. *Bryn Mawr Classical Review* 2008.01.25.

Tsakirgis, B. 2007. "Fire and Smoke: Hearths, Braziers, and Chimneys in the Greek House." *British School at Athens Studies* 15:225–231.

Tsitsibakou-Vasalos, E. 2009. "Chance or Design? Language and Plot Management in the *Odyssey*: Klytemnestra ἄλοχος μνηστὴ ἐμήσατο." In *Narratology and Interpretation: The Content of Narrative Form in Ancient Literature,* ed. J. Grethlein and A. Rengakos, 177–212. Berlin.

Turkeltaub, D. 2005. "The Syntax and Semantics of Homeric Glowing Eyes: *Iliad* 1.200." *The American Journal of Philology* 126:157–186.

———. 2007. "Perceiving the Iliadic Gods." *Harvard Studies in Classical Philology* 103:51–81.

Uther, H.-J. 2004. *The Types of International Folk Tales.* Hellsinki.

Vergados, A. 2013. *The Homeric Hymn to Hermes: Introduction, Text and Commentary.* Berlin.

Visser, E. 1988. "Formulae or Single Words? Towards a New Theory on Homeric Verse Making." *Würzburger Jahrbücher für die Altertumswissenschaft* 14:21–37.

———. 1997. *Homers Katalog der Schiffe.* Stuttgart.

Vivante, P. 1982. *The Epithets in Homer.* New Haven.

Van Duzer, C. 1996. *Duality and Structure in the Iliad and Odyssey.* New York.

Van Nortwick, T. 2010. *The Unknown Odysseus: Alternate Worlds in Homer's Odyssey.* Ann Arbor, MI.

———. 2011. "Agamemnon." In *The Homer Encyclopedia,* ed. M. Finkelberg, 14–16. Malden, MA.

Van Wees, H. 1988. "Kings in Combat: Battles and Heroes in the *Iliad.*" *The Classical Quarterly* 38:1–24.

———. 1998. "A Brief History of Tears: Gender Differentiation in Archaic Greece." In *When Men Were Men: Masculinity, Power and Identity in Classical Antiquity,* ed. L. Foxhall and J. Salmon, 10–53. New York.

Von der Mühll, P. 1946. "Die Diapeira im B der *Ilias.*" *Museum Helveticum* 3:197–209.

Von Kamptz, H. 1982. *Homerische Personennamen: Sprachwissenschaftliche und historische Klassifikation.* Göttingen.

Wace, A. J. B., and F. H. Stubbings. 1962. *A Companion to Homer.* London.

Wakker, G. 1994. *Conditions and Conditionals.* Amsterdam.

Walcott, P. 1966. *Hesiod and the Near East.* Cardiff.

Wender, D. 1978. *The Last Scenes of the Odyssey.* Leiden.

West, M., ed. 1989–1992. *Iambi et elegi Graeci ante Alexandrum cantati.* Vols. 1–2. Oxford.

———. 1994. *Ancient Greek Music.* Oxford.

———. 1995. "The Date of the *Iliad.*" *Museum Helveticum* 52:203–219.

———. 1997. *The East Face of Helicon.* Oxford.

———. 1998. *Homeri Ilias.* Vols. 1–2. Stuttgart.

———. 2011. *The Making of the Iliad: Disquisition and Analytical Commentary.* Oxford.

Whallon, W. 1969. *Formula, Character, and Context: Studies in Homeric, Old English, and Old Testament Poetry.* Washington, DC.

Whitman, C. 1958. *Homer and the Heroic Tradition.* Cambridge, MA.

Willcock, M. M. 1978. *Homer: Iliad I-XII.* Bristol.

———. 1984. *Homer: Iliad XIII-XXIV.* Bristol.

Willets, J. 2007. *Matthew's Messianic Shepherd-King: In Search of "The Lost Sheep" of the House of Israel.* Berlin.

Wilmott, J. 2007. *The Moods of Homeric Greek.* Cambridge.

Wilson, D. 2002. *Ranson, Revenge, and Heroic Identity in the Iliad.* Cambridge.

Wilson, J. 2009. "Literacy." In *A Companion to Ancient Greece,* ed. K.A. Raaflaub and H. van Wees, 542–563. Malden, MA.

Wilson, P. C. 1952. "Battle Scenes in the *Iliad.*" *The Classical Journal* 47:269–274, 299–300.

Wöhrle, G. 1999. *Telemachs Reise: Väter und Söhne in Ilias und Odysee oder ein Beitrag zur Erforschung der Männlichkeitsideologie in der homerischen Welt.* Göttingen.

Worman, N. 1999. "Odysseus *Panourgos*: The Liar's Style in Tragedy and Oratory." *Helios* 26:35–58.

———. 2001. "This Voice is Not One: Helen's Verbal Guises in Homeric Epic." In *Making Silence Speak: Women's Voices in Greek Literature and Society*, ed. A. P. M. H. Lardinois and L. McLure, 19–37. Princeton.

Worthington, I. 2004. *Alexander the Great: Man and God*. Harlow, UK.

———. 2010. *A Companion to Greek Rhetoric*. Malden, MA.

———. 2013. *Demosthenes of Athens and the Fall of Classical Greece*. Oxford.

Wyatt, W. F., Jr. 1982. "Homeric *Atē*." *The American Journal of Philology* 103:247–276.

Wyatt, W. F. 2000. Review of *Homer's Traditional Art*, by J. Foley. *Bryn Mawr Classical Review* 2000.04.07.

Yamagata, N. 1994. "Phoinix's Speech—Is Achilles Punished?" *The Classical Quarterly* 41:1–15.

Zanker, G. 1994. *The Heart of Achilles: Characterization and Personal Ethics in the Iliad*. Ann Arbor, MI.

Zerba, M. 2009. "What Penelope Knew: Doubt and Scepticism in the *Odyssey*." *Classical Quarterly* 59:295–316.

Zielinski, T. 1899–1901. "Die Behandlung gleichzeitiger Ereignisse im antiken Epos." *Philologus Supplement* 8:405–449.

Index Locorum

Homeric Epics

Other Ancient Literature

Subject Index

Index of Greek Words and Phrases